Afghanistan

Afghanistan

Mullah, Marx, and Mujahid

Ralph H. Magnus
Eden Naby

Westview
PRESS

A Member of the Perseus Books Group

*To the Afghans who were and will be maimed and killed
by the ten million land mines strewn across their land
by the Soviet army during the jihad.*

The cover image includes details taken from a miniature at the Victoria and Albert Museum, London, United Kingdom. Called "Battle Scene," it illustrates the work *Akbarnameh*, a seventeenth-century biography of the Moghul Emperor Akbar (sixteenth century) flowing from the pen of Abu'l Fazl 'Allami. It was from the ashes of the Moghul Empire that the Pushtun state gradually arose.

Nations of the Modern World: Middle East

Copyright © 2002 by Westview Press, A Member of the Perseus Books Group

Westview Press books are available at special discounts for bulk purchases in the United States by corporations, institutions, and other organizations. For more information, please contact the Special Markets Department at the Perseus Books Group, 11 Cambridge Center, Cambridge MA 02142, or call (617) 252-5298.

Published in 2002 in the United States of America by Westview Press, 5500 Central Avenue, Boulder, Colorado 80301–2877, and in the United Kingdom by Westview Press, 12 Hid's Copse Road, Cumnor Hill, Oxford OX2 9JJ

Find us on the World Wide Web at www.westviewpress.com

A Cataloging-in-Publication data record for this book is available from the Library of Congress.

ISBN 0-8133-4019-5(Pbk.)
The paper used in this publication meets the requirements of the American National Standard for Permanence of Paper for Printed Library Materials Z39.48–1984.

10   9   8   7   6   5   4   3   2   1

Contents

Illustrations

Maps

Figures

Photos

Foreword
Dan Rather

Afghanistan is one of the most difficult places on earth to understand. Its history is long, its culture complex. Both are shrouded in mystery and myth.

The trouble with trying to tell the story of Afghanistan, now as ever, is that it is so difficult to get the story straight and to get it out. That is, not merely to distribute the story, but to get the story in the first place.

Reporters and scholars alike are thwarted. Facts are few, opinions are fierce. Fair and accurate reporting is at a premium. To understand Afghanistan properly, one must go there, stay awhile, absorb sights and sounds, then think—and keep on thinking.

Few outsiders do this, even many people who write about the place.

The trouble is ignorance, and it manifests itself variously. Despite Afghanistan's historic importance, I have met only a few people in any other country who are familiar with Afghanistan's history. In my own country I have met only a few people who know where Afghanistan is.

It has always been difficult to get in and out of Afghanistan, physically. Getting information in and out is also a challenge. The political and military crises of the past two decades suggest that the challenges will remain at least for the near term. In most of the world, people will remain ignorant of Afghanistan.

That's a shame and a waste, and not only because ignorance is always a shame and a waste. Americans in particular are already at jeopardy, because our ignorance of what happened, what really happened, in Afghanistan colors our interpretation of history. Some want to claim the end of the Cold War as the exclusive handiwork of Ronald Reagan and Mikhail Gorbachev, even to the point of ignoring nearly half a century of bipartisan American foreign policy and Western resolve. But many more of us tend to ignore the contributions of the Afghan mujahidin, who, by inflicting heavy losses over almost a decade, sent the Red Army into retreat and decline, helped to bankrupt the Soviet economy, and turned public sentiment against the Soviet Union throughout the Eastern Bloc and elsewhere.

Because so few outsiders have been to Afghanistan in recent years, because so few have been able to study firsthand and to report those stories to the rest of the world, it is also true that a great many persons have challenged the real story, in many cases without ever having gotten anywhere near Afghanistan's borders. They were political partisans, members of the intelligence and diplomatic establishments, academics and journalists, and in some cases members of religious organizations. Their purposes were many, but their means have generally been the same: They have favored propaganda or suppression to defy serious scholarship, firsthand accounts, and fair, eyewitness reporting. Propaganda and suppression are, of course, principal ingredients in a recipe for manipulation. So long as the inaccuracy and silence about Afghanistan endure, we are all vulnerable to manipulation.

That's a dangerous situation, and Eden Naby has been working without stopping for more than two decades to do her part to inform the world about the real situation in Afghanistan. This book, written with Ralph Magnus, is only one more effort among many she has made.

I first became acquainted with Ms. Naby in 1980, during a different attempt to tell the story of Afghanistan. The Soviet empire had just invaded the country. I was working at the CBS News magazine *60 Minutes*. Few people anywhere were paying much attention to the story at the time.

My instincts whispered that this might be more important than the world knew. At the very least, my hunch said, it was an interesting story in the making. And, yes, a yearning for adventure was part of the attraction—always a powerful pull for journalists of my generation, who grew up in the heyday of foreign correspondents.

Trouble was, what I knew about Afghanistan could be written on the stomach of a germ. I needed help, expert help. A few telephone calls turned up the information that, among Americans, a married couple at Harvard University knew as much or more about Afghanistan as anyone: Eden Naby and her husband, Richard Frye.

They were contacted, turned out to be as good or better than advertised, and soon agreed to help us decide two things: Was the story worth doing for *60 Minutes,* and, if so, how to get at it?

Eden Naby and Richard Frye went to northern Pakistan for us, to the pit that was Peshawar. It was a pit of international intrigue and betrayal directly connected to the new Afghanistan war.

We quickly determined that the story was, indeed, worth a *60 Minutes* effort. We also quickly learned that getting the story, and getting it out, would be extremely difficult—perhaps impossible. And that it would be dangerous.

If we had known how truly dangerous it would be, we might not have decided to go into Afghanistan and try. But we didn't know. We couldn't know until we were fully committed and already deeply inside the country.

Neither Eden nor Richard recommended that we go. They told us flat-out that, if we went in, we might not come out alive. But at the time even they did not know how great the danger was.

Once we decided to mount an expedition to see the war firsthand and record it for television, Eden was key. She, and only she among us, knew the language Dari/Farsi. Without her language skills, we had no chance.

We didn't know that, not yet. She did. Our view was that it certainly would be a plus, a big one, to have her with us. But we were foolish enough to believe that, well, even if she decided not to accompany us, we could somehow make it. Foolish indeed. And she knew it.

After long consultations with her husband, who was, wisely, opposed; and after much soul-searching, she finally agreed. Lucky for us. If she had not gone in with us, neither I nor other members of our CBS reporting team might be alive today.

She not only got us into Afghanistan—it is unlikely we could have done that without her—she also kept us alive once we were inside.

I chronicled the details of this trek in my own book, *The Camera Never Blinks Twice.* The step-by-dangerous-step heroics and wise counsel of Eden Naby are recounted there.

But one incident stands out and bears recollection here. We had followed a band of Afghan rebels for several days. One night we sought shelter in a cave, sitting down to one of the few cooked meals we would eat on our journey. Around the campfire, the Mujahidin, with the help of Eden's translation, told me of their intentions in this war. The Afghans would be delighted to receive American assistance, they said, although at the same time they cautioned that our assistance would buy us only a barrier to Soviet expansion and nothing more—not friendship, perhaps not even cooperation from the Afghans themselves.

But the Mujahidin insisted, with or without American assistance, the Afghans would rid their country of the Soviet invaders. No matter whether any other country came to their aid. No matter how many Afghans were killed in the struggle. No matter how long it took. They would fight, and keep on fighting.

I was impressed by their adamancy and by the fire in their eyes. I quickly learned that, of all the subjects in the world, there were only two on which the Afghans were united. One was the necessity of repelling the Soviet invasion. The other was the power of Allah. Beyond that, there was little agreement, even as to *how* the Soviets might be opposed, or *how* much Allah should be allowed to reclaim sovereignty over the lives of the people.

These were important lessons. Anyone who heard them and understood them would not have been surprised when the Mujahidin at last wore down the Soviet empire—anyone who heard and understood would not have been surprised a little later when the Afghan people fell into disagreement and civil war, unable to unite in strength following the years of Soviet domination.

Eden Naby translated those lessons for me, but, remarkable teacher that she is, she also made sure I got to the classroom, to Afghanistan itself.

This book is, among other things, Eden's story of Afghanistan. It tells you what you need to know about the Afghanistan of yesterday and today, and why you should care. Why the world should care.

It is the work of a superb teacher, whose great passion for this story is blended with knowledge and wisdom—and courage.

As Eden Naby and Ralph Magnus remind us, Afghanistan has been a vital link between Europe and Asia for thousands of years, of prime strategic importance since Alexander the Great's time. In the future, Afghanistan is liable to retain that strategic importance. Think of China, Russia, India, Pakistan, and Iran. Think of their hopes and fears. Think of our own. Then look on the map at Afghanistan. Then think again.

In the future, Afghanistan may perhaps acquire economic importance, too. Who knows? Political stability would bring a variety of economic opportunities to a country situated at the crossroads of so many of the world's great economic and political powers.

What is clear is that the need to understand Afghanistan isn't going away. Americans who hope to understand the world will need to understand Afghanistan. Toward that end, Eden Naby and Ralph Magnus have provided the reader with a thorough account of the background and context of Afghanistan's history, with a glimpse into its future. And I am here to tell you that you could not ask for better teachers.

Preface

When we began discussing writing this book, the Soviet Union, Afghanistan's fierce neighbor, had invaded over Christmas 1979. Spirits were flagging among Western researchers of the country, and Cold War–type observers on the right and left seemed to have a great deal to say about Afghans whom they did not know. Eden Naby, having just completed a few exciting weeks organizing access for the first television account of the Afghan resistance, Dan Rather's *Sixty Minutes* (1980), had become convinced not only of the injustice of the war but also of the amazing perseverance of the Afghan mujahidin. Ralph Magnus shared these views, and we compared memories of the Afghanistan we had known during the 1960s and 1970s and agreed to collaborate on a book.

The manuscript was completed in mid–1997 and published in 1998. At that time, the alliance of ethnic groups in northern Afghanistan, led by the Tajiks under the military leadership of Ahmad Shah Mas'ud, were losing ground before the steady push of the largely Pushtun Taliban. The ethnic mosaic, nurtured by chaos and severed from integrative national moorings, had already deteriorated, as predicted. The Taliban had brought general security to areas under their control at a great price to society in general and to women in particular. Encouraged by Muslim zealot political forces in Pakistan, and their rich friends among fanatical and dedicated Arabs, spearheaded by Osama bin Laden, the Taliban fell under obligation and financial debt to outsiders.

By the time of the first paperback printing of this book, the Taliban had all but complete control of Afghan territory, having driven Burhanuddin Rabbani to Dushanbe, Ahmad Shah Mas'ud to the caverns of the Panjshir, Abdul Rashid Dustam to Turkey, and Gulbuddin Hekmatyar to Iran. Despite their territorial gains, they could not persuade the world leader, the United States, that they ought to be recognized as the legitimate rulers of Afghanistan. And so they were prevented from entering into world bodies such as the United Nations and the Organization of the Islamic Conference. The Taliban ban on opium planting in 1998 did nothing to assuage a Washington whose policies on Afghanistan fell hostage to the red-button issue of Afghan women. The Taliban, in turn, continued to shelter bin Laden despite his involvement with the destruction of U.S. embassies. The poorer and more isolated the Afghans became, the more they were shunned. The bright spot for the Afghans under Taliban rule was the cessation of civil war and relative stability; the dark spot came with retreat from modernity, the application of one of the severest forms of Islamic law in combination with Pushtunwali, and the growing cancer of training camps for Muslim fanatics that spread from Afghanistan to Central Asia, Africa, and especially to the West. The impasse broke with September 11, 2001. The military engagement of the United States and its allies in Afghanistan shows every sign of lasting for an indeterminate period.

Throughout the early part of 2000, Ralph Magnus continued to keep a close eye on Afghan events and to discuss what could be salvaged. Would a nation emerge after such a prolonged period of suspicion, treachery, and lawlessness? Would the well-intentioned or controlling nations of the world throw up their hands and declare Afghanistan ungovernable?

In late summer 2000, Ralph called to say that his heart had weakened again. His decline came rapidly and by November he was dead. His many Afghan friends mourned with the rest of us. He did not live to see the fruits of terrorism, which had incubated in Afghanistan, affect his own country so devastatingly ten months later. And he did not see the American-led coalition, which set itself the task of rooting out bin Laden, bombing Afghan towns and villages, and destroying the unrepentant Taliban in punishment.

Ralph Magnus was a compassionate man who had a deep love for Afghans; after the television images had faded, he would have worked hard to see to it that Afghans would continue to receive attention, even if help needed to be tailored to their historically difficult political culture. He would have joined me in the hope that those intending to reconstruct the region would let history and not hysteria become a guide toward understanding what is possible and what is not. Thus, in a sense, Ralph has continued making contributions to this revision of our joint book even though he did not have a writing role in the last chapter and the updated chronology. This book is still dedicated to the Afghans and now also to the memory of one of their best American friends.

Eden Naby

Chapter One

Introduction

Visiting Kabul, the Afghan capital, in 1929, the French journalist Andree Viollis, one of the few Westerners in the city, was struck by the devastation wreaked upon the palace of the overthrown monarch, Amanullah, by revolutionary forces.[1] In that year the preliminary phase of Afghanistan's thrust into the international setting ended. Today, Kabul is once again a city of destroyed palaces, museums, public buildings, and private homes and of breakdown in public service and order.[2] Writing from Kabul, journalist John H. Burns captures the essence of the desolation of this fascinatingly remote but pivotal part of Central Asia.[3] The difference between the two periods of destruction lies more in the prolonged period of conflict than in the profile of the protagonists: In the first case an internal rebellion led to the destruction. In the second case outside invasion so destroyed order in society that hope for reconstruction of the nation continues to recede. A secondary difference, but one that gives the situation in Afghanistan far greater significance worldwide today than in 1929, is the opening of all of Central Asia to interaction not only within the region but also with the global community. More than ever the territory occupied by the diverse groups that have been brought together to form the country called Afghanistan forms a vital link in Asia, because from east to west it connects Iran with the Indian subcontinent, and from north to south it ties the former republics of Soviet Central Asia with Iran, Pakistan, India, and the world's shipping lanes.

Travelers, empire builders, archaeologists, spies, researchers, traders, diplomats, teachers, and seekers of spiritual or drug-induced fulfillment have flocked to Afghanistan whenever conditions have allowed. Many of these visitors jotted down memoirs and wrote books, in many languages, from the earliest historical period of the Greeks and Romans to the Chinese, Arabs, British, Russian, and French. The many rich archaeological sites throughout the country attest both to its position as a crossroads of culture and to its hospitality to diversity and contemplation. Afghanistan's many valleys and mountains have provided places of refuge for those who have experienced religious persecution or others who have wished to preserve

1

their culture, away from the overwhelming cultural tides that have swept over the region throughout history. Towns such as Kabul, Kandahar, Herat, and Balkh resound through history as remote and slightly dangerous places.

Despite this varied past and ethnic multiplicity, which can compete with any region of the world for its richness, after nearly two decades of armed conflict, Afghanistan evokes in the last decade of the twentieth century a sense of poverty and fanaticism. Is this impression true? Why have the Afghans become scattered as refugees throughout the world? What drives the Islamic forces in the country? What avenues exist for betterment of the situation? Why is Afghanistan so important for regional stability? Why has this mountainous country fascinated so many people in the past? What do its people, culture, and resources offer the world?

In this volume we will introduce you to the people of this country, to the diversity within the unity of its culture, and to the reasons—past, present, and perhaps in the future—diversity fosters conflict. Some regions and cities are important in world history because they have served as cradles of culture—Athens, Jerusalem, Paris, and Rome are among these. Others stand out because of particular economic assets. The oil-rich Gulf states, the gold and mineral resources of Siberia, the concentration of technological assets in Silicon Valley, and the tourist resources of Florida are among these. But some parts of the world attract attention because of their political importance within the region. Afghanistan is one of these. Hence as we deal with the many facets of the area and the people in order to identify them and make them understandable, we will pay particular attention to the political developments in this country, since in its political aspect it was the focus of attention of the superpowers in the post–World War II period, and long before that, the focus of contending powers in the heart of Asia.

Features of Physical Geography

The geography of Afghanistan, encompassing 245,000 square miles (about the size of New Mexico and Arizona together), features a wide variety of terrain. Afghanistan is located on the eastern part of the Iranian plateau, an elevated region of Asia that rises in western Iran from around the Zagros Mountains and drops down into the Indus valley region at Afghanistan's eastern borders. The ecology of this country, dominated by mountains and deserts, a few fast flowing rivers, and narrow mountain valleys, demands intensive labor to support human existence. Bisecting the country roughly into a northern and a southern part is the Hindu Kush range, which extends out of the Pamir mountain range clustered to the northwest. The Pamir range, often called the roof of the world because of the many mountain ranges that converge near it, lies at the intersection of four countries—Afghanistan, Pakistan, China, and Tajikistan (the former Tajik Soviet Socialist Republic). An

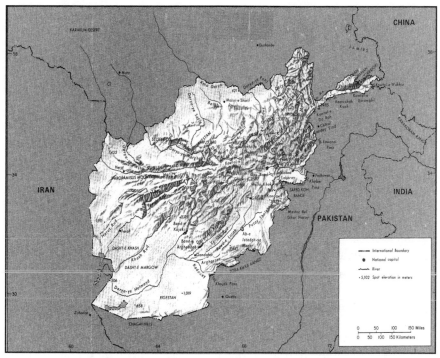

MAP 1.1   Afghanistan's topography (From Richard S. Nyrop and Donald M. Seekins, eds., *Afghanistan: A Country Study,* Washington, D.C.: Department of the Army, 1986)

appreciation of how high this region of the world is may be gained from the knowledge that K2 (also called Dapsang and Godwin Austen) lies within this region and is the second highest mountain in the world, while Mount Everest rises out of the nearby Himalayas. The highest mountain within Afghanistan, at 24,557 feet (7,485 meters), is the Nowshak.

Afghan river systems drain in three directions out of the Hindu Kush and the smaller southern mountains of the Sulaiman range. The rivers and melting snows of the northern slopes eventually drain into the Amu Darya (known to the ancient world as the Oxus River and to Arab geographers as the Jayhun River). This river begins as the Panj River, currently dividing Afghanistan from Tajikistan, and becomes the Amu Darya, one of the two major river systems of Central Asia. The Amu Darya flows into the Aral Sea and forms Afghanistan's international border with Uzbekistan. Both of these countries, but especially Uzbekistan, along with Turkmenistan, drain the river for irrigation, especially for new, marginal semidesert areas used for cotton cultivation. The excessive use of the waters of the Amu Darya for agriculture as well as the use of chemical fertilizers and pesticides has gradually caused the desiccation of the Aral Sea and the alarming pollution of the area around it.

Of the central rivers and streams falling exclusively within Afghanistan, the most extensive and significant is the Arghandab, which flows into the Helmand, located along the southwestern slopes of the Hindu Kush. The Helmand flows west and south and makes its way into the inland swamps and lakes called the Hamun area, which consists of three large, shallow, and brackish lakes. The Hamun area, once the breadbasket of the region, forms part of the border of Afghanistan with Iran, disputes about the distribution of waters notwithstanding. The Hari Rud also flows westward, and it waters the agricultural fields of the Herat area; when it takes a northern turn toward Turkmenistan, it forms part of the Afghan-Iranian border. The eastern rivers mostly connect to the Kabul River, which makes its way to the Indus River near the town of Attock (in Pakistan). In the age of Afghan Empire two centuries ago, the Indus formed the border of the Afghans with the Indians. Today Afghan political territory stops at the Sulaiman range.

Afghanistan's mountain ranges, like the Karakorum and Pamir ranges, were formed relatively late and are thus young mountains. As such they are rugged rather than contoured, and by virtue of climate, elevation, and human activity, they are also relatively barren rather than thickly forested. A low-flying passenger plane crossing over the mountains offers to the eye a palette of colors ranging from purple to orange, depending on the angle of the sun and the season. Again, the Afghan terrain as well as its climate are reminiscent of the American southwest.

Balancing the heavily mountainous terrain of the east, the west contains desert and semidesert regions. In some places Afghan deserts meet the deserts of Iran, and together this region contains one of the most inhospitable parts of Asia. The Dasht-i Margo, a stony desert north of the Helmand River, and the Registan ("sandy place") of the southwest form the true deserts of the country, although most of the rest of the land is arid and many other parts are semidesert.

A land cut by so many mountains but lying at the crossroads of Asia in the heart of the old silk routes between Chinese and Mediterranean civilizations demands human ingenuity for travel and transport. World-famous passes with inns, trading settlements, shrines, and water sources dot the landscape. The most famous of the passes in Western lore is the Khyber Pass, which allows traffic to flow between the plateau and the Indian subcontinent. The Khyber Pass, with its rocky and narrow passage punctuated with carved remembrances of retreating or victorious British Indian regiments and Afghan villages fiercely clinging to narrow flat patches between mountains, has entered the memoirs of many travelers, from Xuan Zong, the eighth-century Buddhist monk who carried sacred texts from India to China, to journalists covering the Afghan war against the Soviet invaders.

Other higher passes, such as the Shibar, connect Kabul to the northern plains. This treacherous road, passable only by horse and camel until 1931, has been replaced largely by the Salang Tunnel (11,100 feet), which turned out to have had enormous strategic importance during the war against the Soviet army. The stretch of Afghan territory that points toward China lies almost entirely in the Pamirs. Though of political significance, this Wakhan corridor is covered by ice and snow for much of the year.

Geographic Zones

Afghanistan may be divided into eight geographical zones distinguished by both population clusters as well as terrain and climate. All of these zones, with the exception of the central one, extend outside Afghan political boundaries. Below we will see how the population clusters are related to similar groups outside Afghanistan. Here we will summarize the eight geographic zones and discuss the way that Afghanistan fits into the region. Beginning from east to west, the eight regions are (1) the high altitude Wakhan, (2) the mountain valleys to its south beginning with Badakhshan southward to the Panjshir and Nuristan, (3) the semitropical lowlands of Kunar, Logar, Jalalabad, and Laghman, (4) the southeastern mountain regions, including greater Paktia, (5) the plains and foothills of the Kandahar region, (6) the central mountains of greater Hazarajat, (7) the northern plains known as Afghan Turkestan, and (8) the western regions around Herat. Though Afghan province names have preserved some of the appellations of these zones, political demands vastly multiplied the number of actual provinces to twenty-nine before 1978.

Political designations aside, all but the central zone extend well beyond Afghan borders into the political entities that surround Afghanistan. Again starting with the northeast corner, the terrain of the Wakhan extends into Tajikistan and into China's Xinjiang Uighur Autonomous Region. The native inhabitants of the Wakhan extend as well into both neighboring areas; that is, the Wakhi, an Iranian (not Persian) linguistic group, dwell outside Afghan borders in close proximity to similar groups, such as the Ishkashimi, the Sarikoli, and others.

The next zone, the Badakhshan to Nuristan region, contains some of the same people as the Wakhan, and similarly the inhabitants flow across international borders into China, Pakistan, and especially Tajikistan. As in Afghanistan, across the political border in northern Pakistan similar small groups also have sought refuge from the majorities of the lowlands in similar mountain strongholds. Linguistic and cultural affinities exist across the political border. The third zone, the semitropical area marked by the large central city of Jalalabad, shares its terrain and population with parts of Pakistan's Northwest Frontier Province, especially with Peshawar, to which it is connected through the Khyber Pass. The Pushtuns (in this region belonging to the "Pukhtun" half) traversed this zone into what is now Pakistan as invader, trader, smuggler, and most recently as mujahid and as refugee. In like manner, the fourth zone, elevated and more mountainous, has also seen Pushtuns cross back and forth in traditional semipastoral and other cycles with limited encumbrance from political borders. In both the third and fourth zones some Pushtun tribes are divided by the international border.

Zone five is composed of extensive agricultural lands that receive waters from the southern slopes of the Hindu Kush range and northern parts of the Sulaiman range. A heavily populated area with dominant Pushtun tribes and smaller Baluchi tribes to the west, geographically this zone opens to Pakistan's province of Baluchistan, where the nominal political dominance of the Baluchis is being challenged by large Pushtun pockets, especially because of the nearly permanent Afghan refugee presence. The Chaman Pass over the low hills dividing Afghan and Pakistani territory in this zone allows for far easier passage for the ethnic groups divided by politics than elsewhere, a factor that has facilitated the shipment of armed motorized convoys from Pakistan to Afghanistan throughout the war, in contrast to the use of pack animals through the narrow mountain passes of the north and east.

Zone six includes the central mountain region and takes its name from its chief inhabitants, the Hazara (and some related groups). With poor agricultural land and isolation from the trade routes and modern roadways that enriched the areas closer to international borders, the Hazaras have historically been targets of oppression because they are different from others in Afghanistan on several important planes. They speak a distinct Persian dialect, and unlike most Afghans, they adhere to Ja'afari Shi'ism, the state Islamic sect of Iran. Although there are some small pockets of Hazaras in Iran, no geographical link ties the two communities to each other.

Zone seven, however, borders Iran and as late as the 1860s was disputed between Iran and Afghanistan. Traveling by land from the Iranian city of Mashhad to the Afghan city of Herat, one can observe the terrain change dramatically only in one respect: The gently rising hills on the Iranian side have a semidesert vegetation cover, whereas the Afghan ones are barren. The availability of natural gas and petroleum for cooking and heating in Iran, rather than differences in culture, account for the green vegetation on one side and the barren hills on the other. Otherwise, the customs and language are similar on the two sides of the border, although the Afghan side includes many Pushtun landowners, this being one of the few areas of the country where large absentee landlords provided the justification for the Marxist land-reform decree of 1978.

Zone eight, called Afghan Turkestan by western writers throughout the nineteenth and twentieth centuries, carries this apt name because the land to the south and north of the Amu Darya consists of similar terrain and is inhabited by the same Turko-Iranian people. In fact, this part of Afghanistan became joined to Kabul politically several times over the past two centuries but has frequently broken away in times of instability. The current period of instability is no exception, as Mazar-i-Sharif, its chief city, has become the stronghold of an Uzbek warlord who has threatened Kabul regularly. That Mazar lies on a vital trade link for Iran, Uzbekistan, and Tajikistan and encompasses road connections with Pakistan and India—straddling as it does the road to the only substantial bridge from Afghanistan to Central Asia—makes the Turkic and Tajik culture of this zone a constant problem for any government in Kabul. Likewise, the rich agriculture of zone eight, in both foodstuffs and cotton as well as natural gas, gives it some of the same attractiveness as the countries it borders in Central Asia—Turkmenistan, Uzbekistan, and Tajikistan. Given the acute centrifugal forces created by terrain, cultural diversity, cultural affinity across international borders, and two decades of conflict, the central government's ability to hold all parts of Afghanistan together without regional insistence on autonomy is tenuous.

Agriculture and Irrigation

Approximately 12 percent of Afghan territory allows for cultivation, both irrigated and nonirrigated. Therefore, despite a relatively small population before the war (about 14 million in 1978), shortage of agricultural land is a perennial problem, made even more acute in the aftermath of war by mined fields and destroyed irrigation systems. Throughout its history, Afghanistan has been an agricultural society in which only a small percentage of the population has also supported itself as intermediary or long-distance traders. A climate that in some parts is subtropical (in eastern Afghanistan around Jalalabad) and centuries of construction of water channels of considerable ingenuity have combined to make the Afghan farmer productive, particularly in the cultivation of fruits and nuts. Fresh and dried Afghan fruit has formed a staple of local diet and export for centuries. Given the relatively low area of arable land, however, Afghans, particularly in the southeast, depend heavily on a semipastoral existence based on the raising of sheep and goats. Moving to higher elevations in summer and down to the semideserts in winter, clans traveled back and forth seasonally in set territorial patterns that evolved from years of negotiations and disputes among neighbors. The preferred beasts of burden for such movement, camels, donkeys, and rarely horses, are being replaced by motorized vehicles. Nonetheless, the production of meat and dairy foods depends on free-range grazing rather than ranch-style feeds for animals. Afghanistan's semi-arid and unirrigated grain fields are suitable for such use, although overgrazing has become a problem, as has the extension of irrigation into former pastoral lands, facilitated through the construction of dams and canals. Since the 1920s, when the Persian lamb (*karakul*) herds in northern Afghanistan expanded as a result of the immigration of Uzbek and Tajik refugees from Soviet Central Asia, the trade in cultivated furs has added considerably to Afghan exports. Cotton, another adaptation from Central Asia after the 1930s, became the "white gold" (*spinzar*) to broaden the list of Afghan exports.

The importance of irrigation in Afghanistan—and to Central Asia to the north and Iran to the west—may be highlighted by three features: the *qanat* system, the depopulation of the area in the aftermath of the Mongol invasion, and the deliberate destruction of irrigation systems by the Soviet military. The *qanat* or *kariz* system of irrigation is unique to the eastern Islamic world and may be found in active or defunct form from the foothills of the Zagros Mountains to the desert oases of Chinese Central Asia. Essentially the *qanat* system has as its purpose the carrying of snowmelt and underground water from foothills and mountains across semidesert areas to agricultural fields. To do this with as little evaporation as possible, the water is carried underground in streams that are dug and maintained by means of wells placed every twenty feet or more (depending on the soil) connected by underground channels. The water flows to the "mother *qanat*," usually near a village, from where it may be used as a domestic source of cool water and diverted to fields. Maintenance of the wells and channels must be a constant community activity, and specialized *qanat* plumbers, called *muqannis*, hire out for these services. The line of wells and channels can stretch for miles. From the air, one may observe sometimes two and perhaps three lines stretching toward one village, an indication that some lines have collapsed and adjacent lines have been dug as replacements. Any well in the functioning line can also be used as a water source by travelers or shepherds.

Regular maintenance of these irrigation systems demands stability and cooperative communal activity. The Mongol invasion destroyed both of these and in fact depopulated swaths of agricultural communities, especially around Herat and Kandahar. In many areas the desert has claimed once-fertile fields. The remains of *qanat* systems and thriving communities provide evidence of the extensive irrigated land prior to the Mongol invasion, as do historical accounts of high levels of crop production in the area called Khorasan, which encompasses much of present-day western Afghanistan.[4]

In the period before the Soviet invasion, the irrigation system of the past was being replaced in large part by actual and planned surface irrigation systems in conjunction with dams that could serve the dual purpose of flood control and energy production. Only partially successful as irrigation methods (due to drainage and salinity problems), the dams became important sources for electricity generation. With the Soviet invasion and the subsequent civil war, the destruction of dams became a deliberate means of warfare. As a result, this new irrigation system has become a victim of war and invasion, as had the *qanat* system before it. An added by-product of war has been the deliberate destruction of agriculture through the cutting down of fruit trees and vines, and the mining of agricultural fields along roadways, both undertaken to reduce hiding places for guerrilla attacks. When one considers that nut trees (walnut, for example) take almost two generations before harvest, the costs of the wanton devastation of agriculture in the past two decades becomes more incomprehensible.

Demography

Few scholars agree on the intricate details of Afghanistan's population statistics. As in its gathering of other statistics needed for planning development, the statistical arm of the Afghan government was always weak, and population figures in particular may have been exaggerated in order to increase the per capita distribution of international funding through United Nations agencies.

A fundamental difficulty has been the lack of any reliable census, and hence estimates of the total population before 1978 varied from 10 to 20 million. The most reliable estimate is based on a 1972–1973 national demographic survey of the "settled" as opposed to nomadic population, which yielded the figure of 14 million.[5] The government conducted a census in 1978, which, though planned earlier, actually took place after the coup d'état of April 1978. The figure reported from this census was 15.5 million, but doubts about the actual national coverage placed its results under suspicion. The figure reported to the United Nations stood at 17 million before the Soviet invasion, and other sources report 18 million in 1978.[6]

Afghans formed the largest number of refugees worldwide throughout the 1980s. Repatriation from both Pakistan and Iran has been problematic because of internal conditions in Afghanistan, where the devastation of the southeast in particular has discouraged the return of villagers. One in nine houses in the villages was deemed uninhabitable throughout the country in 1993, and in Nangarhar province (east) only 60 percent were habitable. Of the approximately 15,000 villages of the country, about 13 percent of those located in the southeast have problems with mines in agricultural land, irrigation systems, around houses, and at access roads.[7] Resettlement in the north, the northeast, and the southwest has proceeded more successfully than in the west, and especially in the southeast and east of the country. Because of the prolonged period of war, some Afghans in early adulthood have known only refugee camp life or life in foreign countries. Some have become resistant to repatriation because of the urban destruction that has come with civil war. Therefore, reliable estimates of the population in the country will probably not be available for some time to come. The most successful repatriation and conditions of normality are occurring and will continue to occur in those rural areas that are removed from the core of fighting. Repatriation of critical members of educated and professional classes may never occur, as many of these families have relocated successfully to Europe and the United States, and despite their continued sympathies and concerns with their homeland, they would find return with their families both difficult and risky. Consequently, a reconstituted Afghan population is beginning to show signs of continuing agricultural employment patterns as in the past, when 85 percent of the population worked mainly in agriculture or agriculturally related professions. The emerging urban population, which relies on either direct government employment, small industry, or the small private sector, may begin to come from a whole new set of rural to urban transplants with little relationship to the urban elites of the past.

Demographically, the Pushtuns represent the largest of the Afghan ethnic groups and form at least 40 percent of the population of the country. The Tajiks are the second-ranked ethnic group, comprising about 20 percent of the population. The next three ethnic groups are roughly equal in size: the Hazaras, the Uzbeks, and the Aimaq. In addition, there are Turkmens, Kazaks, Qizilbash, Wakhis, Nuristanis, Baluchis, and Kyrgyz as well as Sikhs, Hindus, and Jews. In fact, the eminent Afghanist Louis Dupree listed twenty-one Afghan ethnic groups.

Located generally in single ethnic villages clustered together around more mixed towns, Afghanistan's ethnic groups have been associated with their own locations, although location names have not represented ethnic or tribal groups, except in the case of the Hazaras, whose region is broadly called the Hazarajat, and the Wakhis of the Wakhan corridor. The various provincial designations, redivided and renamed over the decades, do not refer to ethnic groups but rather either retain medieval Islamic regional names (Jowzjan, Takhar, Herat) or are revivals of pre-Islamic names uncovered through archaeology and ancient studies (Kapisa, Bamiyan, Paktia). When population shifts have occurred, as in the case of Central Asian refugees settling in Afghanistan after tzarist and Soviet expansion, they too have tended to cluster together. Their relationships with existing members of their own ethnic groups as well as others have ranged from uneasy (as in the case Uzbeks from Ferghana with native Uzbeks around Mazar-i-Sharif) to difficult (as in the case of the Kyrgyz, who took control of Wakhi territory). To fracture this ethnic solidity of various regions, Kabul has tried a variety of methods, especially transplanting Pushtuns into the north of the country. Ethnic integration has rarely occurred, and in the aftermath of war, the regions to the north have reverted to the old single ethnic patterns, especially in rural areas.

Urban settlement patterns differed demographically from those of rural areas. In this regard, Kabul must be considered on a different scale from provincial capitals. The national capital was the most ethnically mixed city in the country because of government employment, trade and commerce, educational facilities, and cultural institutions. Still dominated by Pushtuns, the interethnic language Dari held sway in formal and informal interaction, largely because of its role in public administration, as in the rest of Central Asia. This forced tribal people into bilingualism, and in some areas, such as Kabul, it gradually led to a decline in the knowledge of Pushtu. The decreased use of Pushtu did not arise from the preponderance of any other group in the capital or in employment there. Other cities and towns, from large important ones such as Herat, Kandahar, Mazar-i-Sharif, and Jalalabad, to lesser ones like Ghazni, Gardez, Kunduz, and Baghlan, feature the ethnic culture of the region as their main characteristic.

Ethnic Groups, Languages, and Structures

The name Afghanistan means the land of the Afghans, in the same pattern as that of some of its neighbors, where the country name is derived from that of the real or purportedly real majority ethnic group. Thus Afghanistan fits into the "stan" model like Kazakstan, Uzbekistan, Kyrgyzstan (Kyrgyzia), Tajikistan, and Turkmenistan, all currently existing states that rose from former republic status after the disintegration of the Soviet Union in 1992. Historically there have been many other names along this pattern, such as Turkestan, Uighuristan, Baltistan, none of which have international status today.[8] Among the existing country names that refer to a single ethnic group, Afghanistan is the oldest. The term is not without controversy, however.

The medieval and popular meaning of *Afghan*, and one retained in Soviet scholarship through the 1970s, referred to what we today call Pushtu/Pukhtu. Though the origins of the term Afghan remain unclear, its use as part of a country name dates from the eighteenth century, when Pushtun tribes began to carve out a region of Central Asia as their sovereign base. At first the Pushtuns headed toward Delhi, and in the process they began to consolidate all Pushtuns behind them. Thus Afghanistan, as a term, more or less accurately reflected the controlled area; it consisted mainly of ethnic Afghans/Pushtuns.

As the British Indian empire began to expand, however, it cooperated with Afghan enemies, in particular the Sikhs, to reduce Afghan territory and to place many ethnic Pushtuns under Sikh and then under British rule. Throughout the nineteenth century, British Indian military units were occupied with trying to control the recalcitrant Afghan tribes, who may or may not have preferred rule by other Afghans but certainly opposed that of the British. The frontier Pushtun tribes continue to bedevil Afghan-Pakistani relations today, since the Pakistanis have inherited the British mantle in this region.

With the loss of territory to the British in the east, Kabul turned to less challenging areas to control. It took another century for all of the areas within the international borders of Afghanistan to give nominal allegiance to Kabul. By expanding westward and northward, however, the Pushtuns became rulers over non-Pushtuns. Consequently the term Afghan underwent a political transformation into that of a multiethnic people rather than of one ethnic group. As a corollary to this, the term Pushtun/Pukhtun gained prominence as the name of an ethnic group. Although this change occurred well over a century ago, the amalgamation of many ethnic groups under the term Afghan occurred slowly, largely through such integrative factors as public education, the conscript military, the media, and public sector employment. These very integrative factors were among the first casualties of the war in Afghanistan. The period of civil war in particular has sharpened the cleavages among ethnic groups, making the understanding of the country's ethnic diversity critical to understanding its political crisis.

Pushtuns as the Primary Ethnic Group

The ethnic diversity aside, the Pushtuns form the most important and probably the most numerous ethnic group in Afghanistan. Because statistical measurements have been unreliable to begin with, then also complicated by war, the standard estimate is that 40 to 50 percent of the population is Pushtun, which in 1973 may have been about 6.5 million people.[9] The twin terms Pushtun and Pukhtun refer to the two main ways in which three consonants differ in pronunciation between the "soft" western dialect (Pushtun) and "hard" eastern one (Pukhtun). Additionally, the two groups also represent, roughly speaking, two separate confederations of tribes, the Abdali or Durrani tribes, based in the Kandahar-Herat region, and the Ghilzai, based in the Nangarhar-Paktia region, who, together with the eastern tribes in Pakistan, speak the Pukhtun dialect. Historically the two groups competed for political power and influence over those tribes that did not belong to either confederacy as well as over non-Pushtun ethnic groups. The tribes that belong to neither confederacy but are of this ethnic group (the Afridi, Khatak, Orakzai, Waziri, Mahsud, and so forth) were designated the "hill tribes" by the British, although increasingly they all easily come under the term Pushtun for the sake of convenience.[10]

Since 1747, the Abdali confederacy (which took the title Durrani, meaning the "pearl of the age") has provided the monarchs and the ruling oligarchy. The communist revolution, however, was led by members of the Ghilzai confederacy. And the titular president of the country after 1992 has been a non-Pushtun, thus making one aspect of the civil war ethnically based.

The other term that confuses the ethnic appellation of the majority ethnic group in Afghanistan has been used mainly in the subcontinent and among British Indian authors. Pathan, as in Sir Olaf Caroe's *The Pathans* or in William Spain's *The Way of the Pathans,* originates in the Indian corruption of the plural form of Pakhtu, the term Pakhtanah. Since at times the term Pathan and Pukhtun have been used exclusively for the eastern and hill tribes, and because it is the Pusthuns who live almost exclusively in Afghanistan and have provided the monarchial line, the term Pushtun will be used throughout this book to refer to the entire group of people, in order to avoid constant use of both terms.[11]

The language of the Pushtuns forms one of the major living Iranian languages of the world. As do Persian, Baluchi, Kurdish, and Ossetic, Pushtun belongs to the Indo-Iranian branch of the Indo-European family. Influenced in the west by Persian and in the east by Indian languages, Pushtu as a whole has a complex grammatical structure, evinces a heavy lexical borrowing from Arabic and Persian, and is written in a modified Arabic alphabet to accommodate the larger consonantal variety of its pronunciation. Because the pronunciation of the two main Pushtu/Pukhtu dialects occurs only in speech, readers of both comprehend a single written language.

Many Pushtuns acquire Persian, in its Afghan variant Dari, as a second language. For many males belonging to the western confederacy, Pushtu/Dari bilingualism is the norm. For non-Pushtun Afghans, however, the acquisition of Pushtu has proved both difficult and unattractive, despite decrees to force all government employees to know Pushtu and despite its being the national language of the country. Reinforced during the Da'ud period of the 1950s, this stress on knowledge of Pushtu for government officials began during the regime of Prime Minister Hashim Khan in the late 1930s. In the constitution of 1964, both Dari and Pushtu were designated official languages, but Pushtu was singled out as the national language. This dual language situation burdens Afghans with double publications of government documents, two educational systems, and a constant struggle to maintain the position of Pushtu, at times seemingly artificially, especially in the north of the country, where Pushtu speakers often formed the minority government officials, bankers, or administrators, quite out of place in an ethnically foreign area.

The characteristics of Pushtuns form the stuff of stories and tales from Rudyard Kipling to George MacDonald Fraser.[12] The seventeenth-century Pushtun poet and warrior, Khushhal Khan Khatak, depicts the acme of Pushtun manhood as brave, love-smitten, honorable, and heroic. He writes,

The very name Pushtun spells honour and glory,
Lacking that honour, what is the Afghan story?[13]

Whether influenced by previous writers or inspired by the mujahidin themselves, many Western authors writing of the Afghan war against the

Soviet army also portray the Afghan (mostly Pushtun) fighter in similar light.[14] But anthropological work, especially that conducted since the 1960s, sheds further light on Pushtun culture. Among significant features of Pushtun life are the practice of Islam, mainly in its Sunni aspect among nearly all Pushtuns, the nonhierarchical structure of tribal groups, and the Pushtun code known as the Pushtunwali. All three features have come to contribute significantly to the persistence of the Afghan resistance to the Soviet army at first, and then to the stubborn inability of the Pushtuns either to agree among themselves on how a new government should be formed or to work with like-minded ideological groups to end the civil war.

The structure of Pushtun tribes is intertwined with the entire development of the Afghan polity. Less so is the explanation of Pushtunwali, although this too has helped to determine what the Pushtun will fight for and how he will do so. Here we will summarize these issues, and in Chapter 4 we will examine Afghan Islam.

Pushtun tribal structure originates in part in the mythology of the lineage of the Afghan tribes, a mythology that may have its roots in unwritten history. Despite the fact that their language today belongs in the Indo-European family, Pushtun tribes trace themselves to the ten lost tribes of Israel, who, it is alleged, ended up in Ghor (western Hazarajat) after their captivity in Babylon. The written source for details of this genealogy is a sixteenth-century manuscript that tells of Afghana, a grandson of the Biblical king Saul. Later, the whole Pushtun ethnic group sprang from the Bani Afghana descendants, who became fighters for Islam under the Prophet Muhammad. Afghan (Pushtun) tribal divisions are traced then to three sons of the leader of these early mujahid. Thus the Abdalis are descendants of Sharkbun, and the Yusufzai are descended from Kharshbun. The Ghilzai, while accepted as Pushtuns, according to this legend, do not belong to the male-descended line from Bani Afghana but rather come from a female of that line and a descendent of Zohak, who in Iranian mythology is a merciless creature of evil.[15]

As with any society in which identity is linked strongly with tribal and family genealogy, the tracing of tribal origin and the questionable descent of the Ghilzai already creates mutual suspicion among the Pushtun groups. Since the Pushtun tribes in rural areas tended toward endogamy and a preference for cousin marriages, the cohesion of the tribe is supported by blood lines both known and fantasized.

Pushtun tribal structure resembles less a pyramid than a trapezoid; that is, the governance of a tribe or a clan depends not on one person but on a consortium of active male members whose standing is determined by birth, stature, and accomplishment. In this respect, the hereditary nature of rule in tribal groups such as the Baluchis is modified among the Pushtuns to reflect the considerable freedom of males born within the tribe. As anthropological studies have underlined, the political dimensions of such tribal structure allow for diffusion of political power and disorganization. Observers of the Afghan confrontation with the Soviet military who have been cognizant of this basic structural underpinning of Pushtun society, have been more able to understand the inability of the Pushtuns to present a unified military or political stand over recent decades.

The Pushtuns are overwhelmingly Sunni of the Hanafi school of law, although there are a few isolated Shi'a Pushtuns among the eastern tribes. Their traditional interclan or tribal interaction is based in part on the tribal legal system of Pushtunwali and in popular political participation through the tribal assembly (*jirgah*).

Tajiks and Related Dari-Persian Speakers

Tajiks, the category of diverse settled people who speak Afghan Persian or Dari, are widespread in northern, northeastern, and western Afghanistan. Related to the Tajiks are the Farsiwan (also known as Parsiwan), although they form a separate ethnic group that shares language traits with them, as do the Qizilbash and the Hazara. Of these four related groups, the first two adhere to Sunni Islam of the Hanafi school of law as do the majority of the Pushtuns. The latter two groups profess Shi'a Islam of the variety promoted as the state religion of Iran.

The issue of language designation has become an appendage of the nationalist issue throughout Central Asia, but nowhere is the artificiality of language separation more apparent than between Dari (Afghanistan), Persian or Farsi (Iran), and Tajiki (Tajikistan). Born of the same classical tradition, these three forms of Persian differed more in colloquial speech than in written form, until the institution of Tajiki as the national language of Soviet Tajikistan. At that time, after a series of intermediary steps, a modified form of the Cyrillic alphabet was adopted for the language in place of the original modified Arabic alphabet, which continued to be used in Iran and Afghanistan. The writing system, plus political proscription, drove Tajiki toward elevation of dialect to literary usage and away from Persian. Afghan insistence that their Persian develop separately from Iranian Persian led to the exaggeration of spoken-language differences between the two countries, mainly lexical, as well as the attachment of the term Dari (meaning court language, a reference to the provincial courts of Central Asia where Persian was used). Under such conditions was Afghan Persian allowed to stand beside Pushtu as an administrative language while the status of national language was reserved strictly for Pushtu. Until the Marxist coup leaders tried after 1978 to introduce Pushtu as the interethnic language of the country through a nationality cultural policy reminiscent of Soviet nationality policies, Dari had been the unchallenged interethnic language of Afghanistan. It appears that it will continue to serve in this function, even during the period of resistance and civil war.[16]

Tajiks have served as administrators in Central Asian courts as well as in Afghanistan. Belonging to an ethnic group that has not even retained memory of a tribal past lost in antiquity, Afghan Tajik loyalty patterns evolve around village and family. Without the genealogical and tribal distinctions of the Pushtuns, Tajiks theoretically can better integrate among themselves. Having been largely shut out of the military officer class as well as of high-ranking leadership positions in the government, Tajiks have had only limited opportunities to produce leaders. Only twice in Afghan history has a Tajik succeeded in gaining political power—first in 1929, and then in 1992. In the first case, the leader arose because of personal charisma, but he had no training or experience in holding political power; and in the second case, the Tajik leader gained his position by having established his qualifications during the course of war and confrontation. In both cases, a slowly coalescing Pushtun backlash to Tajik ascension to power toppled Tajiks from a position of political power over Pushtuns.

Hazaras

The Hazaras, located in the central part of the country, number about one million. Hazara social structure revolves around a headman, chief, or *malik*, locally called *mir*, whose status rises out of both landholding and hereditary stature and who is often associated with descent from the line of the Prophet Muhammad. They have suffered because of their Shi'ism and discrimination against them, by Pushtuns in particular, and through Afghan history they were often used as slaves and servants. The Hazara facial features demonstrate their Mongol racial origins, which comprise an added physical barrier to their integration into the Afghan power structure. Although most Hazara belong to the dominant Shi'a sect, some among them belong to the Isma'ili sect (see Chapter 4), and a small number are Sunni. The locale that they inhabit in the Hazarajat is both isolated and barren; when agriculture has suffered, as in the case of the 1972–1973 drought, famine has driven many Hazara to Pushtun areas and, in the past, into harsh conditions of servitude.[17] However, because of their isolation, except for internal struggles baited by Iran's revolutionaries, the Hazarajat has remained relatively free of the destruction from the Soviet invasion and the Afghan civil war (see Chapter 6).

Qizilbash

Distinguished from other Afghans by descent from the troops of Iranian armies of the eighteenth century as well as by their exclusively urban settlement pattern, the Qizilbash form the single most literate group in

Afghanistan. Their Shi'ism also sets them apart from others, as does their use of Dari. Having suffered attempts at forced conversion to Sunni Islam, the Qizilbash's prospects for continuing in active public life appear slim in the newly emerging Afghan society.

The Turkic Ethnic Groups

Before 1978 four Turkic-speaking groups resided in northern Afghanistan, from Maimana in the northwest to the Wakhan in the northeast. All four groups had coethnics on the Soviet side of Central Asia. Shortly after the Marxist coup d'état, the Kyrgyz departed Afghanistan, almost en masse, leaving the Wakhan corridor once more to the native Wakhis. Having arrived in Afghanistan as refugees from Chinese communism in 1949 and 1950, the Kyrgyz have finally settled in central Turkey, where they have traded yurts for brick apartments. Other Afghan Turkic groups have a longer history on Afghan soil, although many among them fled to Afghanistan to avoid tzarist rule or the substitution of Islam with atheism under Bolshevik rule.

The numbers of Turkic people, sometimes exaggerated by their coethnics for political reasons, include one million Uzbeks, 200,000 Turkmens, and about 15,000 Kazaks. Variously engaged in pastoralism or agriculture, the Uzbeks and the Turkmens consider themselves jointly "Turki" speaking, although most men are bilingual in Dari, the interethnic language of the north. Uzbeks are mainly detribalized, whereas the Turkmens retain tribal associations. The Turkmens, including tribes such as the Teke, Salor, and Yomut, are also traditionally associated with the fine wool carpets in which they specialize.

Other Ethnic Groups

Among the fifteen or more smaller groups in Afghanistan, approximately another twenty languages and dialects are spoken that span several language families, from Dravidian to Mongolian. Literacy in these communities, to the extent that it exists, is measured by use of Persian but rarely Pushtu. The interaction of these communities with others, insular by virtue of terrain and endogamy, may expand if a central government emerges that can enforce integrative state functions such as education, conscription, and the expansion of various media, all of which would spell in time the end of these linguistic and social communities.

Lifestyles

The ways in which the nearly two decades of war have and will effect lifestyles in Afghanistan remain to be determined as the situation shows

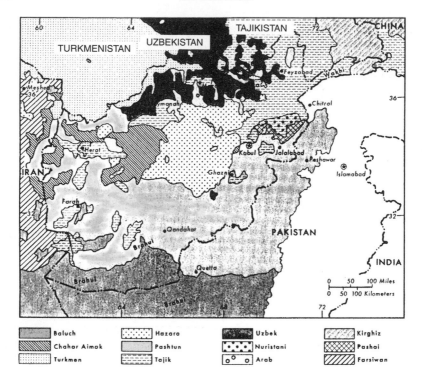

MAP 1.2   Ethnic groups in Afghanistan and adjacent areas (From Richard S.
Nyrop and Donald M. Seekins, eds., *Afghanistan: A Country Study,* Washington,
D.C.: Department of the Army, 1986)

signs of settling into a warfare mode. Some patterns of the past may shift,
especially with regard to urban-rural migration, integrative forces such as
education, and the effect of families divided inside and outside the country.
Nonetheless, certain tendencies will continue to govern lifestyles as they
have over the past centuries.

The varied terrain, the diverse ethnic groups, the nomadic versus the settled patterns, and urban versus rural settlement comprise the main reasons
for the lifestyle diversity in Afghanistan. In some areas stone and wood are
plentiful and thus available for construction of habitation. In others climate
requirements call for roof construction that is better able to withstand
heavy snowfalls. But the basic elements of the Afghan lifestyle depend on
family relationships, multigenerational living patterns, dependence on agriculture, symbiotic living with the natural world, including domestic animals, and a sense of permanence, not of the individual but of the community. Loyalty patterns begin with family and extend to village or tribe, and
then to ethnic group. The extension of loyalty to country has not achieved

universal acceptance as has allegiance to Islam, which is imbedded in the community traditions rather than in the intellect or the written word. The definition of gender roles lies at the heart of the maintenance of these lifestyles, as does respect for wisdom, which is generally associated with age in both sexes.

Physical structures of habitation reflect lifestyles in various parts of the country. In their traditional areas, rural Pushtun settlements feature *qala*s (fortified extended-family dwellings), built of fired or sun-dried bricks, with curved roofs overlaid with flat roofs. The room complexes are constructed to face inward into a courtyard, and the backs of the rooms form part of the ten-foot or higher compound wall, whose single gateway, used by man and beast, is firmly bolted at night. Each primary family unit will have some quarters allocated to them, primarily for sleeping and storage of personal items. But kitchen and toilet facilities are shared, as are food storage areas and guest quarters. Operating more or less strictly on principles of age respect, the oldest competent male and female fulfill their respective and well-defined gender-associated duties. Women tend to children, help with the harvest in the fields, look after domestic animals, and engage in crafts and home furnishing activities such as quilt making. Younger men and women run the kitchens. Men maintain the construction, conduct purchase and sale activity, shepherd flocks, plow, plant and handle irrigation, and generally do work that requires public exposure. It is not unusual to find as many as 100 people of many generations inhabiting one large *qala*.

In a typical village, several *qala*s may be scattered in proximity, set in the middle of irrigated fields. Roads, shops, and public buildings are rudimentary. In eastern Afghanistan, where the arm of the government reaches only rarely, the *qala* provides security for families and their animals. Many *qala*s have a small mosque (and bath) incorporated into the walled and turreted compound. In more secure areas, such as around Kandahar and Herat, domed or vaulted single-story buildings made of sun-dried bricks form the basic architecture of village and town dwellings. Several of these structures may be attached within a single walled compound that houses as many as three generations of a family, though usually not as extended a family as in the *qala*s. Wealthier families will also have a separate structure that functions as a male guest house. Fruit trees as well as a small stable for domestic animals (chickens and cows) may be found at a farther end of the compound near the toilet. Storage areas for food and fuel are a critical part of any domestic structure, since such items must be gathered or purchased and stored for use for an entire year. Sources of clean water can include a well in the compound, but in the countryside can also include streams or the *qanat* system. Space heating, needed in seasons when outdoor activities are limited, calls for the use of small braziers using charcoal, around which a number of people can sit, leaning on cushioning formed from bedding stacked against walls, sometimes with a quilt covering the legs and feet of all. When a brazier is placed in a shallow hole in the middle of the room, a low table over it covered with a quilt and a tablecloth can serve as a cozy sitting, eating, and study area, ideal for evenings of storytelling.[18] The *kang,* found in eastern Afghanistan, is a heating system widespread in Central Asia and familiar in the Chinese countryside. This system, which may be heated with brush as well as wood, is composed of a raised platform on which most winter activity takes place, including sleeping, eating, and resting. Underneath the platform is a funnel system for smoke and heat, fed by a fire tended from the inside or the outside. A version of the *kang* may be seen in the traditional built-in Russian stove, which served numerous purposes. Poorer families simply have less elaborate versions of what wealthier ones enjoy.

With greater openings to the outside world, local habitation patterns have shifted dramatically, at least in the large towns and cities. Family relationships still dictate the modes of privacy, but internal plumbing, often dependent on a private well run electrically, represents a chief departure from the past. This feature sets rural and urban families apart, as they do the more modernizing families from others. Other factors, such as refrigeration, kerosene cookstoves, electric lighting, and kerosene or coal-fired single-room stoves, also begin to separate lifestyles, both among the rural and the urban.

By and large, the main form of Afghan domicile follows this pattern. Other variations of settled domestic constructions also occur as well as some specialized constructions adapted especially for narrow valley dwelling, as in Nuristan, where the roof of one structure may be the yard of another. With few exceptions, the use of wood is limited by availability and durability, and brick, baked and dried, forms the chief basic building block.[19]

Special to the Pushtuns were tent dwellings used by pastoral nomads, who, having taken advantage of the expansion of Kabul's authority to the northern plains, could be found encamped in most parts of the country. Black tents, made of goat hair, were to be found in vaulted and peaked form throughout the country, in summer and winter. Using a minimum number of wooden poles in their tents, these pastoralists move to higher and lower elevations depending on the needs of their flocks. Other tent dwellers, the Jugi, who are not pastoralists but itinerant peddlers and fortune tellers, use cotton tents.

Another semipastoralist ethnic group, the Turkic groups of the north and northwest, use the yurt system of temporary or movable dwelling. Dependent on more wood than does the tent of the Pushtuns, the yurt consists of thin branches elaborately connected with ropes that can be rolled together when the yurt is ready to be moved to another pasture area. The yurt is round with a smoke hole at the top, and the exterior is covered with layers of thick felt matting made of sheep wool. The interior may be covered with embroidered wool cloths and carpets. In outline, the yurt resembles the domed permanent structures of village dwellers of the north.

Town and city architecture of the period after World War II follows patterns borrowed from the West and uses glass and concrete in high-rise structures. In northern Afghanistan as well as in some buildings in Kabul the heavy-walled and massive Russian style of public building construction became prevalent, especially in buildings dating from the 1950s. Unlike Soviet buildings, however, which were generally heated by means of a city-wide central heating system, Afghan buildings had individual heating systems, which were not always suited to these massive structures. The adaptation of indigenous form for public buildings is rarely seen except in the construction of mosques, palaces, and bazaars. Mosques frequently achieve the spacious, quiet, and cool atmosphere of their central prayer hall through the use of the squinch and dome, which are similar in principle to the domestic construction of the west and north. The use of glazed tile to decorate the exterior of buildings is limited mainly to Herat and Mazar-i-Sharif, but interior decorative techniques using shaped plaster and mirror are widespread, as they are in Iran and Central Asia.

Towns serve as market centers for villages as well as provincial administrative centers. As such, they include market areas, both wholesale and retail, sometimes all within a bazaar complex (as in Khulm and Kandahar) but sometimes simply in a series of shops. A feature of markets in Afghan towns is that retailers are clustered by product rather than being scattered among shops selling other products, a rule that tends to hold true with the exception of localized small grocers. Close to the single-product section of a market may be found a mosque and a teahouse, both associated in the past with guilds for particular crafts such as jewelers, potters, or metalworkers. Inns, catering almost exclusively to merchants, also appear in proximity to bazaars and usually have warehouses associated with them as well as stables in the back for pack animals. Government hotels with parking spaces are gradually replacing these inns, and since they serve a multiprofessional setting, especially for government guests and administrators, they are usually built near public offices.

Many older Afghan cities have old and new towns that reflect changing lifestyles over the decades. Although the walled family compound continues in popularity, apartment buildings constructed in Russian-style complexes with single systems for heat, water, and plumbing have become the stepping-stone dwellings for government and military workers before they acquire private compounds. Laid out along wide motor-vehicle-accommodating roadways, the apartments and family compounds contrast with the narrow lanes of the old parts of towns, where dreary mud walls are broken only by narrow wooden doorways leading into crowded but surprisingly lovely courtyards closely planted with fruit trees, flowers, and vegetables. Urban life offers proximity to schools, office jobs, electricity, and opportunity, but the problems of clean water and sewage systems, overcrowding, and food acquisition have not been resolved in Afghan cities and towns.

Worldview

The Afghan worldview at the start of the twenty-first century and for several decades thereafter will be shaped by the Soviet invasion, the civil war, and the regional and international diaspora. With Afghan insularity torn by war, and with the necessary and unwanted intrusion of outsiders as well as the Afghans' own exposure to new settings either as internal or external refugees, a large proportion (perhaps as much as half) of the Afghan population cannot resume life as it was before 1979. How far these events will thrust the Afghans into interaction with the world outside remains to be seen, but that the effects will reverberate in the countryside as well as in the towns and cities cannot be in much doubt.[20]

Inasmuch as exposure to the outside world effects worldview, Afghans may adopt a worldview that appreciates better the technical advantages of other societies. However, because their regional neighborhood has altered during the past two decades as well, their confidence in pressing for the retention of Islam-based Central Asian values may provide the basis for a greater discernment between the worthwhile and the useless offerings of the outside world.

The fortunes of war have determined the outcome of the struggle between modernizing elites and traditionalists that raged throughout the twentieth century. The traditionalists have won by the force of arms and persistence in remaining in the country or returning to it, and the modernizing elites either must regroup for a comeback or find a niche within the revivalist Islamist or traditional factions. However, there seems little prospect of such a niche's being transformed into a secular imitation of Western values and worldview, as it seemed from the 1950s to the 1980s.

Given the changes in the region, especially in the former Soviet Central Asian republics, Afghanistan must either play an active regional role both politically and economically or disappear into emerging politically powerful states in its neighborhood. By necessity, therefore, it will be drawn into closer regional integration, which in turn will bring elements of the worldview of Pakistan, Iran, and Uzbekistan into Afghanistan. The worldview of all these areas contains strong Islamic elements whose evolving definition for the foreseeable future will include technical modernization within a context that emphasizes small-unit loyalty (as in family, village, and tribe). The internalization of democracy based on a Western individualism rather than traditional Afghan Islamic communalism, gender-blind social interaction, and the elevation of the individual above society, do not appear to be part of the emerging regional or Afghan worldview.

On an interethnic level, the recent political upheavals have leveled the playing field in interethnic relationships, perhaps to the permanent disadvantage of the Pushtuns. Tajiks and Uzbeks in particular, buoyed by many years of virtual self-rule as a result of Kabul's inability to administer directly in the north and west, and by the acquisition of independence by co-ethnics in Central Asia, show few signs of accepting Pushtun political superiority.[21] The positive impact of this development may be a more equitable eventual distribution of power, economic opportunity, and social integration. The negative impact may well involve continued civil war, increasingly conducted with other ethnic groups united against the Pushtuns, who insist on reestablishment of the status quo ante.

The worldview of the Afghans therefore will be determined less by their centuries of history, as it had until recently with the upholding of the values of the medieval past, than by the trauma of the most recent decades and the eventual resolution of the problems created by the upheaval. That Afghans will adopt a changed worldview, one based on broader knowledge and a stronger appreciation of the acquisition of knowledge, appears to be the main positive outcome of the chaos and destruction that the country has experienced.

Chapter Two

Afghan History to 1973

Afghan history before the politically critical period beginning in 1973 may be divided into five periods. During the two earlier periods no entity by the name Afghanistan existed, but because the territory lies at the crossroads of many cultures and of Asian migration routes, its earliest human history is rich in art, architecture, and archaeological remains. These two earliest periods may be broadly categorized as pre-Islamic and Islamic. It was only during the latter three periods that Afghanistan began to assume its contemporary form. The country began to appear during the eighteenth century and emerged at the end of the century as a budding empire spreading west and south. During the course of the nineteenth century the empire declined rapidly, and Afghanistan became a client state of Great Britain. This status ended in 1919 with the emergence of an independent monarchy. In July 1973 the monarchy gave way to a republic, which continues to struggle to take shape with as yet limited success. Nonetheless, the precedents of the Afghan monarchial past remain the cornerstone of the country's continued existence. The five historical periods are as follows:

The pre-Islamic period, 500 B.C.E. to 700 C.E.
The medieval and late medieval Islamic period, 700 to 1709
The period of Afghan Empire, 1709 to 1826
The "Great Game" or European imperial period, 1826 to 1919
The period of the independent monarchy, 1919 to 1973

Pre-historic archaeology together with oral history that was committed to writing during the medieval period as legend, epic, and myth, casts considerable light on the early culture and politics of the area. Rich archaeological sites, such as the Greek city Ai Khanum, located at the upper reaches of the Amu Darya, the Kushanid site at Sorkh Kotal, and the massive Buddhas of Bamiyan, are among the many remains that confirm Greek and Seleucid, Roman, Arab, and Chinese references to this area. For most Afghans before the age of Western archaeology, these sites held no significance, either because they were all but buried or because oral traditions had ascribed mythical or biblical/Koranic significance to them.[1]

Beginning in the seventh century, the spread of Islam eastward toppled local rulers and swept northeast into Central Asia and southeast into the Indus valley. Over the span of three centuries, adherence to Islam gradually diffused from the ruling classes to the peasants, so that by the period of the Ghaznavids in the tenth century the population had become largely Muslim. Exceptions existed in the form of local Jewish communities, some Buddhist strongholds, and the animists of the eastern mountains. The latter were known as *kafir* (infidel) until they were converted by force in the late nineteenth century.

The continuity of the medieval Islamic period is conspicuous in three factors: the use of Afghan territory and population as propagators of Islam in India, particularly but not exclusively under the Ghaznavids, the destruction wrought by Mongol armies in the thirteenth century, and the recurrent invasions of Turkic Central Asians into this region. The last and most successful of these conquerors, Babur (d. 1531), the poet-soldier progenitor of the Moghuls of Delhi, exemplifies the historic geopolitical role of Afghan territory as the link between Central Asia and the Indian subcontinent. Despite changes in forms of government, ideology, and even the configuration of ethnic groups and international boundaries, this role of Afghanistan as the vital link and intersection of the Asian landmass gives the land a significance far beyond its troubled road to political and economic development. In purely political terms, location puts Afghanistan on a par with its neighbors. When it finally emerged in the eighteenth century, however ephemerally, as an empire led by a local rather than an invading ethnic group, the desired expansion toward India simply followed the pattern set in the previous historical periods. The struggle of Afghanistan in the contemporary period may be regarded as the struggle to retain the autonomy gained in the eighteenth century rather than revert to its role as the anonymous crossroads of Asia. In this chapter the focus is on the three historical periods up to 1973, when the paradigm established in the eighteenth century began to weaken. The final section of the chapter provides an evaluation of the legacy of Western imperialism, expressed as colonialism and neocolonialism, and the contribution of this heritage to xenophobia, isolation, and the consequent slow integration of Afghanistan into world trade and development systems.

The Afghan Empire

The Afghan Empire rose in the eighteenth century at the intersection of three rival Islamic empires, each of which was undergoing a period of de-

Detail of gate of Congregational Mosque of Herat (Ghorid, twelfth century). (R. H. Magnus, 1970)

Citadel of Herat (largely destroyed in fighting, 1978–1992). (R. H. Magnus, 1970)

Congregational Mosque of
Herat. (R. H. Magnus, 1970)

Tomb of Mir Wais Khan Hotaki
(d. 1715), founder of Ghilzai
Afghan empire, Kandahar. (R. H.
Magnus, 1969)

Tomb in Kabul of Amir Abdul Rahman (r. 1880–1901).
(E. Naby, 1965)

cline—the Uzbeks under the Astrakhanid (or Janid) dynasty, the Iranians under the Safavid dynasty, and the Indians under the Moghul dynasty. These regional neighbors had divided Afghanistan among themselves for centuries. Before this time, however, the Afghans themselves had furnished ruling dynasties who sat on the Muslim thrones of India. One of these was the Lodi dynasty of the sultans of Delhi defeated by Babur in 1526 and replaced by his own Moghul line. Another Afghan ruler in India, Sher Shah Suri, overthrew Babur's son and successor, Humayun. He ruled northern India for fifteen years until his death allowed Humayun's return from exile in Iran. Afghans, as merchants and military men, continued to form an important component of the ruling class during the Moghul empire.

The Ghilzai Empire, 1709–1738

In 1709 Mir Wais, the leader of the Hotaki tribe of Ghilzai Pushtuns in Kandahar, threw off his allegiance to the Safavid Shah in Isfahan, Iran. The direct cause was oppression by the court-appointed governor of Kandahar, a Georgian transplanted from Safavid lands on the Black Sea. A second source of irritation was the dominance over the Safavid court of radical Shi'a ulema, who were trying to impose Ithna 'Ash'ara Shi'ism (see Chapter

4) on the fervently Sunni Afghans as part of their controversial and largely successful bid to impose Shi'ism throughout Iran after it became the state religion in 1501. Earlier Shahs had rejected religious persecution, but under the influence of the noted Shi'a theologian Shaykh al-Islam Muhammad Baqir Majlisi, Shah Sultan Husayn (d. 1726) resumed active persecution of Sunnis. In the view of a leading scholar of Safavid Iran, "the repression he [Majlisi] instituted can be counted as an important cause of the discontent of the Sunni population of Afghanistan, which led to the Afghan invasion and the fall of the Safavid dynasty."[2] Mir Wais, the Afghan tribal chief, had been a hostage at the Safavid court, but he used the occasion of a *hajj* to obtain a *fatwa* (a religious legal opinion) from the Sunni ulema in Mecca to justify his revolt against the Safavids on religious grounds.[3]

Mir Wais's son and successor in 1715, Mir Mahmud, launched a daring invasion of Iran in 1719 and succeeded three years later in defeating and massacring the members of the Safavid family after having conquered their imperial capital, Isfahan. For all practical purposes this spelled the end of the most illustrious dynasty in the Islamic history of Iran. The Afghans went on to defend Iran against an invading Ottoman army, but their empire in Iran soon disintegrated because of internal quarrels, including the assassination of Mir Mahmud (who is denigrated in Iranian history as insane). Instead of having an Afghan dynasty on the Iranian throne, the Turkmen general and tribal leader, Nadir Shah Afshar, revived Iranian power and drove the Afghans out of Iran in 1729. He ruled for a time in the name of a Safavid prince until he became confident enough to forgo this legal fiction in 1736 and proclaim himself Shah. As Nadir Shah, he marched his army in 1738 through Kandahar (thereby eliminating the Hotaki dynasty), which lay on his path to conquest of the Moghul empire in Delhi the following year.

The Sadozai Durrani Empire, 1747–1826

The Pushtun tribes of the Abdali confederation had taken advantage of the success of the Ghilzai revolt in Kandahar to establish their independence from the Safavids in Herat. As Nadir Shah Afshar rose to power, they joined his army and received as reward the lands taken from the defeated Hotaki Ghilzai in Kandahar. The Abdali confederation was the traditional rival of the Ghilzai.

Ahmad Shah Durrani, 1747–1773. Following the assassination of Nadir Shah Afshar as he camped near Kandahar on his booty-laden return from India in 1747, Ahmad Shah was elected ruler of the Afghans after a nine-day Loya Jirgah (Great Assembly) of Afghan tribes in Kandahar. Ahmad Shah changed the name of his own tribal confederation from Abdali to Durrani (meaning the pearl of the age) and ruled until 1773. During his reign, he conducted many expeditions to India in search of gold and glory. He fulfilled his Islamic obligation by defeating the Hindu Mahrattas on the field of Panipat in 1761 and thereby freeing the Moghul emperor, whom he replaced on the Delhi throne. Within his own territory, Ahmad Shah Durrani extended his authority over virtually all of the Pushtun tribes, over whom he ruled as a first among equals through a jirgah of the leading khans.[4] His success in war, piety, justice, wise political leadership, and conformity to the traditions of the Pushtuns won him a great deal of popular support, and his name became revered in Afghan history as the father of his country, Ahmad Shah Baba.

Through judicious employment of the military strength of the Pushtun tribes as well as of the adventurers and *ghazis* (raiders against infidels) attracted by his wars against non-Muslims, he established a conquest empire stretching from Mashhad and Nishapur in present-day Iran to Kashmir, Baluchistan, and the Punjab in India. His rule over the Pushtuns differed significantly from his rule over non-Pushtuns of the empire. Among the former he seemingly never forgot his origins as an elected tribal chief, whereas among the latter he was a foreign ruler exacting tribute. His greatest achievements lay in his realization that the only way to rule the Pushtuns was by consultation in jirgahs and that one of the most effective methods of maintaining Pushtun tribal loyalty was to lead them in battle against non-Muslims to gain wealth and religious merit. In effect, his empire continued the long historical pattern of "conquest movements" of warrior chieftains especially important in Central Asia.[5] Ahmad Shah Durrani, the last of the Central Asia conquest movements rulers, is worthy of consideration among the great Central Asian warriors and political leaders, in the tradition of Genghis Khan, Timur, Babur, and Shah Abbas.

The Later Sadozai Rulers, 1773–1826. The Afghan Empire survived substantially intact through the twenty years of the reign of Ahmad Shah's son, Timur Shah. He moved his capital from Kandahar to Kabul in order to weaken the power of other Durrani sardars (princes) but also to be closer to the Punjab, his richest province. After Timur Shah's death in 1793, his many sons (more than twenty) clashed in disputes and eventual civil war. Distant provinces began to break away, and at home rival Durrani tribes, particularly the Barakzai, challenged Sadozai authority. The Barakzais had supported the Sadozais in the election of Ahmad Shah, and as reward their leader, Painda Khan, had become hereditary vezir (second in power) of the empire. Later, under Ahmad Shah's grandson, Zaman Shah, Painda Khan was executed and the Barakzais turned into hereditary enemies of the Sadozais.

The empire disintegrated in the early years of the nineteenth century, just as the Sadozais began the process of establishing relations with the British empire in India by signing the first Anglo-Afghan treaty in 1809. Political power became highly fragmented for a decade. The sons of Timur Shah, Shah Shuja, and Shah Mahmud fought each other for the dubious prize of a rapidly shrinking empire. Shah Shuja eventually went into Indian exile, and in 1818 Shah Mahmud gave up the contest to revive the empire and withdrew to a small principality in Herat. From this period through 1826 the Afghan Empire splintered into small principalities ruled by members of the Sadozai and Barakzai clans while non-Pushtun areas moved toward ethnic autonomy.

The Heritage of the Afghan Empire

Internally, the mutual distrust between the Ghilzai and Durrani confederations, which certainly predated the eighteenth century, was reinforced by the fact that they each had established a valid claim to imperial leadership of the Afghans. The Ghilzais' destroying the Safavid empire was a truly remarkable military achievement and something that the powerful Ottoman sultans themselves had been unable to accomplish in two hundred years of wars. The Ghilzai empire, however, was particularly short-lived. The Ghilzais' own homeland in Kandahar was reconquered by a shah of Iran. The Durrani empire lasted three times as long, nearly sixty years. Ahmad Shah's victory at Panipat is legendary as a success of Islam against Hinduism, and his establishment of the Durrani confederation in power resulted in its supplying all subsequent Afghan monarchs. The Durranis, however, faced continual, major revolts by Ghilzai tribes, with one as late as 1937.

On the Indian subcontinent the role of Afghans as champions of Islam continued to resonate in tradition and history. Muslims of the subcontinent looked to Afghanistan for leadership following the demise of the Moghuls after the rebellion of 1858. King Amanullah attempted to fill this role in 1919 by fulfilling the wish of the participants in the "Hijrat" movement to live under Muslim rule. These Indian refugees nearly overwhelmed the Afghans, who could offer them very little other than land (near Jabal us-Siraj, at the foot of the Salang Pass). Their subsequent neglect by the Amanullah government left a bitterness among Pakistanis some sixty years later when Pakistan served as refuge for Afghans during the Soviet occupation.[6]

Relations between Iran and Afghanistan as well have been influenced by the imperial past, most particularly in the mistrust between Sunni and Shi'a. The foundation of both the Ghilzai and Sadozai empires had been based on declarations of independence from the shahs of Iran, whereas that of the Ghilzais was directly related to the religious issue.

Iran and Afghanistan have shared largely the same culture and history. Dynasties based in Afghanistan, such as the Ghaznavids, have ruled much of Iran at times, and Iranian-based dynasties (Safavids) did the same in Afghanistan at other times. The wars of the eighteenth century, however, added a particular legacy of distrust and antipathy, which made it difficult for twentieth-century problems to be solved sensibly. The treaty on the division of the Helmand River basin waters, agreed upon by the two neighbors just before the overthrow of the Afghan monarchy, became the object of violent attacks from both Afghan nationalists and Marxists who labeled it a betrayal of Afghan interests. Even the common linguistic and cultural heritage became a divisive issue as Afghanistan banned the import of Iranian books, journals, and films, fearing that their availability and popularity would eclipse Afghan Dari and Pushtun writings. The legacy of mistrust shows signs of continuing into the twenty-first century at a juncture in the history of the region when each country, for different reasons, desperately needs the good will of the other.[7]

The empire of Ahmad Shah established an image, reinforced by official sponsorship and repeated in schoolbooks for generations, of an Afghan "golden age." Afghanistan then had a legitimate Islamic government under a noble, just, and brave ruler, which resulted in a wealthy and glorious empire. It became an article of faith that Afghans would never again submit to foreign rule and that their own rulers must be elected by and responsible to the entire nation, as represented in the Loya Jirgah. To be sure, these assumptions about their country were largely a myth, but with some basis in fact. The strength of the myth is attested by the royal family claim, to the end, that the Afghan monarchy was elective.[8] The Marxists, once they realized that there was little hope for a Marxist revolution, attempted to return to the mythical origins of Afghan history by holding their own Loya Jirgahs and hoping thus to gain traditional legitimacy. Some traditionalist mujahidin parties and leaders have called for the convocation of an Islamic Loya Jirgah to unify the jihad, a demand opposed by revolutionary Islamist groups as an un-Islamic and, in effect, barely disguised call for the restoration of defunct systems and the monarchy.[9]

Perhaps the most significant legacy of the Afghan Empire was that its end provided the historical basis for the division of the Pushtun tribes into those inside and outside Afghanistan. Under the empire, the Pushtuns had been united. All Afghan rulers from Dost Muhammad (1826) to President Sardar Muhammad Da'ud Khan (1973–1978) harbored a special relationship to their coethnics on the other side of the border. Peshawar had served as the winter capital of the Sadozai rulers until its loss to the rising Sikh kingdom. The irony of seeking shelter in Peshawar during the Soviet invasion rekindled for many Afghans the sense of loss of this same territory 150 years earlier.

The Muhammadzai Dynasty and the Great Game (1826–1919)

The most prominent of the Afghan leaders emerging from the decades of chaos at the close of the Sadozai empire were individuals and groups of princes from the Barakzai tribe. Three clusters of Barakzai sardars, all of the Muhammadzai clan, eventually took power in what remained of the Afghan Empire. Each cluster operated from a particular base in Kandahar, Peshawar, and Kabul. From this clan descended all subsequent kings of Afghanistan.

Amir Dost Muhammad Khan: 1826–1838, 1842–1863

The head of the Kabul Barakzai clan, a son of Painda Khan, gained the upper hand over his rivals in Kandahar and Peshawar. By 1826 Dost Muhammad Khan had reunified a considerable portion of the old Durrani Afghan empire. After his army won a victory in 1837 over the Sikhs at Jamrud, located between Peshawar and the Khyber Pass, he adopted the Islamic title *Amir ul-Mu'minin* (Commander of the Faithful), the title of the first caliphs and one used by the Ottoman sultan. The title "Amir" preceded the names of Afghan rulers until 1919, when "Shah" (king) was reinstated.

The exiled Shah Shuja, intending to regain the throne he had relinquished in 1809, conspired with the powerful Sikh state of Maharaja Ranjit Singh. The British, however, who were worried about the tzarist Russian ability to manipulate the Iranian Qajar shahs as surrogates for the conquest of Afghanistan, began sending a series of diplomats and spies into the region to gain intelligence. The most colorful of these, Captain Alexander Burnes, arrived at the court of Dost Muhammad in Kabul. Burnes, favorably impressed with the amir, recommended an alliance, though this proposal was rejected by his superiors in Calcutta. Dost Muhammad preferred British friendship but wanted them to force Ranjit Singh to restore Peshawar to Afghanistan, a bargain the British would not make since it meant opposing their Sikh allies. Along with its heartland in the Punjab, the Sikh empire included most of the Pushtun-inhabited territory in what is now the Northwest Frontier Province of Pakistan, as well as Kashmir.

When Dost Muhammad received the Russian envoy, sent by the tzarist ambassador to Tehran, in a friendly manner, Burnes left Kabul. At this juncture, the British decided to support Shah Shuja's claims to the Afghan throne. Through alliance with the Sikhs and the British, Shah Shuja overthrew Amir Dost Muhammad in 1839. Dost Muhammad, defeated and abandoned, accepted exile in British India. A British Indian army garrisoned Kabul and other major cities south of the Hindu Kush, and the British political adviser to the shah operated as de facto ruler. Within two years, a powerful revolt against the British broke out under Dost Muhammad's son. The British decision to cut subsidies to the Pushtun tribes in order to save money encouraged the tribes to join the rebellion, and since they controlled the lines of British communication between Kabul and Kandahar as well as Kabul and the Khyber Pass, the tribal uprising proved fatal to the British army.

The British retreat from Kabul during the winter of 1842 was disastrous. Shah Shuja as well as Captain Burnes were killed. The Sadozai line ended when the last provincial ruler, in Herat, was killed, but the line continued through female descent by marriage with the Muhammadzai clan in a branch known as the Musahiban family. From this branch came the last two kings of Afghanistan, Nadir Shah and his son Zahir Shah.

When the British recaptured Kabul the following summer, they freed their prisoners, and before they withdrew from Afghanistan they went on to punish the Afghans by expeditions against Pushtun tribes and the burning of the great covered bazaar of Kabul. Kabul is the only major traditional Central Asian city without the traditional covered bazaar. The British allowed Dost Muhammad to return, and he spent the next twenty years in reunifying Afghanistan. The Anglo-Afghan treaty that he signed with the British in January 1857 for mutual respect and friendship grew out of continued British worries about Russian expansion and Afghan fears of Russian-backed Iranian aggression. When the revolt against the British broke out in India the following May, Dost Muhammad remained faithful to the treaty despite severe pressure from public opinion. In turn, after much foot-dragging, the British intervened to force Iranian troops to withdraw from Herat. Dost Muhammad went on to conquer Herat just before his death in 1863.

Amir Sher Ali (1869–1879) and the Second Anglo-Afghan War

Civil war followed the death of Amir Dost Muhammad as his twelve sons battled for the throne. Eventually Amir Sher Ali consolidated his rule over Afghanistan. Sher Ali attempted a number of Westernizing reforms in education, government, and the military. A government civil and military school taught Western courses in English (with Indian Muslim instructors). He supported military workshops to supplement the arms aid he received from the British, and the regular army was doubled in size to 37,000. A postal service was established, and two lithographed newspapers appeared among ruling circles. Sher Ali attempted to continue his father's good relations with the British with a visit to the viceroy in 1869.

By this time, however, the Russian advances in Central Asia had reached the Amu Darya. The Amir was interested in Central Asia and sent several embassies to the Bukharan khanate, though it had already become a Russian protectorate in 1868. The Russian advance aroused constant British fears. The British view of Afghanistan that led to the second Anglo-Afghan war was expressed by the viceroy to India, Lord Lytton, as follows: "Afghanistan is a state far too weak and barbarous to remain isolated and wholly uninfluenced between two great military empires. . . . We cannot allow Sher Ali to fall under the influence of any power whose interests are antagonistic to our own."[10]

In 1878 Amir Sher Ali received and negotiated with a Russian envoy but rejected a British ultimatum to receive their envoy. The British army moved into Afghanistan, occupied Kabul, and deposed the amir, who fled north and soon died. The British replaced him with his son Amir Yaqub Khan, who had to sign a new treaty with the British at Gandamak. Afghanistan agreed to receive a British embassy and to give up several frontier districts (including those controlling the Khyber Pass). Gandamak, however, was an ill-fated location for a treaty of "eternal peace and friendship" between Afghanistan and Great Britain: It was there that the British army had made its last stand on the retreat from Kabul in 1842.

The second Anglo-Afghan war reflects a greater appreciation by the British of the complexities of warring with the Afghans and attempting to dictate their leadership. To be sure, the British Indian army was severely defeated at Maiwand (outside Kandahar), but the situation was salvaged by Sir Frederick Roberts (later Lord Roberts of Kandahar), who marched from Kabul to Kandahar and subsequent victory there. The political result of the this war resembled the earlier one: The British realized the futility of direct administration of Afghan affairs and withdrew. They wrote to invite Abdul Rahman Khan, a nephew of Amir Sher Ali living in exile in Tashkent, to grasp the reins of power that he desired, provided he could establish his rule effectively. This was precisely what he accomplished over the next twenty years. Thus at the culmination of both their nineteenth-century Afghan wars, the British sought rulers who could establish a government stable enough to make Afghanistan a barrier to the Russians while not posing a threat to India. Such was the case in the reigns of both Amir Dost Muhammad and Amir Abdul Rahman.

Obviously, we cannot include within the scope of this study the long and complex history of the "Great Game" of European imperial rivalry in Central Asia, of which Afghanistan was an important chapter, but not the exclusive story. The reader should refer to the chronology in Appendix C. The history of the Great Game has been analyzed many times, often with the use of the writings of the participants themselves as well as official documents: Alexander Burnes, Amir Abdul Rahman, Lady Sale, Lord Roberts, and others left written observations. Nor are novels about the Great Game lacking.[11] The historical patterns from this era seem to reappear with regularity in the following century and continue to have significant consequences for the Afghanistan of today.

The "Iron Amir": Abdul Rahman Khan, 1880–1901

The success of Amir Abdul Rahman in maneuvering among the pitfalls created by the Great Game lay in his firsthand experience of tzarist rule in Central Asia and his ability to combine a pro-British policy with an ability to prevent British interference in the internal affairs of his country. The threat from Russia, extending along Afghanistan's entire northern border, was ever present. In 1885 the threat turned to fact when an Afghan army was routed by Russian troops at Panjdeh oasis, located between Herat and Merv. This threat made the choice of foreign supporters all the more imperative for any Afghan ruler. Unlike most Afghan rulers, Abdul Rahman's direct experience of Russian governing of Muslims in Tashkent had deepened his understanding of the realities of the threat to Afghanistan. From his experience he concluded that British interests in Afghanistan were on the whole defensive and thus could be achieved through the maintenance of Afghanistan as a buffer state, whereas the Russian interests were offensive and could only be achieved by use of Afghan territory for the invasion of India.

The amir used the generous and regular British subsidies and weapons to suppress his many internal enemies. Simultaneously he denounced all contacts with foreigners as un-Afghan and un-Islamic. Primarily, he succeeded in this contradictory policy because he was able, energetic, a good commander, and utterly ruthless. He gained the sobriquet "the Iron Amir" because he appeared not to hesitate to kill, exile, terrorize, and otherwise subdue all his opponents. His success was so extensive that he established a model of a centralized state in Afghanistan, which was supported by the introduction of the political theory of virtual divine right to rule based on the defense of the land of Islam (the *Dar-ul-Islam*). The absolutism of this form of government had not hitherto been espoused in Afghan history. In the past, the amir had acquired his legitimacy by being acknowledged as the first among equals. With Abdul Rahman came the theory of the divine rights of kings.[12]

Even a ruler as self-confident as Abdul Rahman was careful to justify all his innovations as necessary to Afghanistan's unity and power in the face of the imperialist threat. The gradual consolidation of European imperialism on Afghanistan's borders, and Abdul Rahman's acceptance of a buffer state role, inevitably resulted in the formal demarcation of Afghanistan's borders. Although these largely coincided with the actual state of political power at the time, the border between British India and Afghanistan, the so-called Durand Line of 1893, proved to be fraught with the seeds of future conflicts. It formally divided the Pushtuns into two roughly equal parts with a total lack of consideration of their own tribal organization, history, or geography.

Internally, Abdul Rahman began to build local industries, suppress tribal revolts and, in particular, unify the country through a policy of ruthless internal imperialism. His principal instrument in this process became a powerful army based on conscription (and largely paid for with British subsidies) instead of the traditional military system based on khans furnishing their tribal contingents for a particular campaign or the levy system of feudal tradition. In this policy of internal imperialism, he followed the traditional practices of forced population transfers as well as voluntary movement encouraged through government land grants. Tribes from his own ethnic group of Pushtuns were settled along the northern borders. Here they could, theoretically, serve as guardians of the borders with Russia. The lords of the marches (*marzban,* meaning in Persian border keepers) were a time-honored tradition on the Iranian plateau.* Simultaneously, the Pushtun presence could serve as a discouragement to rebellion by local Turkic and Tajik populations in what was known as Afghan Turkestan.

The actual extent of Abdul Rahman's modernization efforts was limited by his distrust of all foreign advice. Even those few Europeans who were employed for specific purposes, such as managing arms factories or conducting geological surveys, were treated as actual or potential spies. In fact, the educational system remained wholly traditional. Sher Ali's experiment in rudimentary modern schooling was not continued. The Afghan historian Hasan Kawun Kakar points out that the only school actually established by the amir during his twenty-year reign, despite his statements in favor of modern education, was a *madrasa* (Islamic theological school) for 200 students in Kabul. He supported modern education in theory, but in practice responsibility for it was relegated to the future and his "sons and successors." For the present those Afghans who obtained a modern education had to do so outside the country, and so they remained in exile. The practical result of the amir's xenophobic position was isolation.

Perhaps his policy of isolation was the best one available to him in his day. The limitations imposed on the foreign affairs of Afghanistan by the British required Kabul to deal with Delhi, which in turn was suspicious of any foreign activity in the country. In the competition with Russia, it feared the use by Russia of third-country surrogates to undermine British control. In like manner, the tzarist regime controlled as much as possible British attempts to undermine its position in tzarist Central Asia. Accounts of British agents employed to travel in Central Asia attest to such activity. The isolation of the entire region was in no small part a result of the politics of the Great Game played by Russia and Britain.

In any case, there was no one foolhardy enough openly to challenge Abdul Rahman's ideology of isolation and internal consolidation. He had an all-pervasive system of informers and secret police, which some say was modeled on that of the amir of Bukhara while others hold that it was modeled on that of the Russian Empire. The secret police, the prisons, the torturers, and the executioners might well have represented a traditional and modern mixture, but there was no doubt that they were efficient in enforc-

---

*The English term *marzipan* comes from the practice of exporting almonds to the West through the medium of the march lords.

ing the amir's will on his subjects. The amir wrote his own propaganda pamphlets, and his official views and explanations of the Islamic justification for the absolute rule of the monarch continued to be taught in Afghan schools for generations.

In the end, Abdul Rahman was successful in his central preoccupation—the consolidation of internal rule. He died in bed of natural causes while still ruler of Afghanistan. His was an achievement accomplished only once in the previous hundred years, and not at all in the nearly one hundred that have passed since his death. He even managed to pass his throne on to his son and chosen successor, Habibullah. Afghanistan, despite the Amir's personal and private association with the British, remained in most respects independent at a time when virtually the entire Muslim world had come under the rule or indirect control of one or another European imperialist power. Abdul Rahman left a decidedly mixed legacy. He was certainly a key figure in the foundation of modern Afghanistan. However, he ruled through rampant despotism, terror, and cruelty. The news of his death in 1901 was greeted at first with skepticism, then followed by rejoicing.[13] The reckoning for his foreign and domestic policies remained for his son to pay.

Amir Habibullah Khan, 1901–1919

Either the reign of Habibullah's father, Abdul Rahman, the originator of a strong central government and unified state, or that of Habibullah's son, Amanullah, who moved boldly to adopt full-scale modernization and national independence for the state as his goals, is usually considered to be the beginning of modern Afghanistan. In fact, the most crucial decisions on the road to modernization in Afghanistan were taken in Amir Habibullah's reign. The first of these, modern education in both civilian and military subjects, began at this time and employed foreign teachers. The first institution established was Habibiya College in 1903. Headed initially by an Indian Muslim, it was modeled after the twelve-year secondary colleges for boys in British India. A few years later, the Royal Military College was established employing Turkish instructors, and in 1914 the groundwork was laid for a public education system with the foundation of a teacher's training college. Later institutions established in the 1920s and 1930s provided the backbone of the governmental and military elite bureaucracy of the state.

Habibullah's second contribution to modernization was a liberalization of the political system that allowed for the return of key Afghan exiles, who in turn encouraged other reforms. Other modernization efforts undertaken by the government included construction of the first modern hospital and the first hydroelectric plant. Factories and roads were improved, and trade with both Russian Central Asia and British India increased manyfold.

One of the returned exiles, Mahmud Beg Tarzi, was the son of an exiled Durrani sardar (and poet) who had adopted the pen name "Tarzi" (the stylist). Mahmud Tarzi had been educated in the Ottoman Empire, where his father had died in 1900, and had even served as an official in the Ottoman administration of Damascus. On his return home, Tarzi became head of the translation bureau and founder and editor of a modernist and nationalist newspaper, *Siraj ul-Akhbar-i Afghanistan* (The Lamp of the News of Afghanistan), which was published from 1911 to 1918. The Afghan press dates from this period. In this newspaper Tarzi advocated modern education and political views that remained influential as the basis for subsequent debate among Afghanistan's modern intellectuals and that were influential as well among the awakening reformers of Central Asia.[14]

Since he was working for the government (under the nominal supervision of Crown Prince Inayatullah), he effusively praised Amir Habibullah's policies. However, a good deal of his criticisms of social inequalities, injustice, and ignorance in Afghanistan in fact were veiled criticism of the amir's regime. Tarzi came to have a special relationship with the amir, since two of his daughters married two of Habibullah's sons, Amanullah and Inayatullah. The source of his other influence on the two princes came from his service as their private tutor and mentor. In a larger sense, through his published ideas, he became the tutor of a whole new generation of modernizing elites. The Afghan modern nationalist movement owes much to his direct inspiration, even if some of its early leaders had begun their careers under Abdul Rahman. After Amanullah reached the throne in 1919, Mahmud Beg Tarzi became his foreign minister and chief adviser on domestic policies as well as in the fields of education and modernization in general.

Tarzi's editorials, despite their being in a government newspaper, were highly critical of Western imperialism and particularly of the British. He rejoiced in the Japanese victory over the Russians in 1905, because it represented an Asian triumph over Europeans, and in the Chinese republican revolution of Sun Yat Sen that overthrew the Qing dynasty. During World War I, however, his anti-British and pro-Ottoman policies drew protests from the British, particularly when they leveled criticism at the amir's neutrality policy. Habibullah resisted internal pressure and attempts by the Ottomans and the Germans to draw Afghanistan into the war by supporting anti-British activity in India with the hope of restoring the lost Afghan Empire.

Eventually, Amir Habibullah paid with his life for his policies. The liberalization, education, and modernization of even a tiny elite spawned an opposition movement. These "Young Afghans," who demanded an end to royal absolutism and the establishment of a constitution, reflected a trend reaching from Turkey to China. Although few in number, they were strategically located within the government, and even within the royal family itself. Within a few years, plots were discovered against the amir. He executed and imprisoned a number of would-be reformers.

World War I put an intolerable strain on the policy of pro-British neutrality that the amir had inherited from his father. This one issue drew together otherwise incompatible elements, from the tribal and religious conservatives, led by the amir's brother Nasrullah, to the modernist-nationalists, led by Tarzi and Amanullah. The situation became even worse after the war. The entire Muslim world was aroused by the Western allies' harsh treatment of the remnant of the Ottoman Empire, which also led to the abolishment of the caliphate. At the same time, the Bolshevik revolution had resulted in chaos in Central Asia, seemingly creating an opportunity for Afghanistan to extend its influence to peoples who had thrown off Russian imperialism. In February 1919 an assassination attempt against Habibullah was successful.

The reign of Habibullah set the pattern of Afghan politics until the end of the Afghan monarchy: It became the prime modernizing agent. This role called for a precarious balance between the demands of the modernizing elite for more rapid progress and greater political participation and the conservative and religious concerns of the vast majority of the population. At the same time, the dangers of foreign imperialism resumed, despite the recognition of Afghanistan's independence and the establishment of regular diplomatic relations with the major European powers as well as with the few independent Middle Eastern states at the time. Within a few years, Soviet imperialism extinguished the bid for freedom by the Central Asians, and Afghanistan found itself once again in the role of a buffer state between British and Russian interests.

The Period of the Independent Afghan Monarchy

Between 1919 and 1973, Afghanistan may be included in the category of constitutional monarchies, with the understanding that the monarchy functioned under three different constitutions (1923, 1931, 1964) and that the role of the legislative branch, in all but the last ten years, was mainly to endorse programs presented by the king or his close representatives. The other significant difference in this period from the one before lay in Afghanistan's foreign affairs. Still fettered by its geographic position between opposing and powerful neighbors, and without direct access to shipping lanes, Kabul nonetheless gained the freedom and responsibility to shape its foreign policy independently.

This period of independence coincides with the beginning of the decolonization period throughout the world, but especially in the Muslim world. The upheaval of World War I and the doctrine of self-determination merged with nascent nationalism to encourage hopes for European withdrawal from colonies. Over the next fifty years these hopes were realized for most countries from Morocco to India, with only exceptional resort to arms, as in Algeria. Afghanistan, never colonized, was among the first Muslim states to gain independence. Ironically, as it gained its independence, its close northern neighbors, Russian colonies, disappeared into the Soviet state, not to be decolonized until the end of 1991.

King Amanullah, 1919–1929

Amanullah defeated his uncle, the conservative Nasrullah, in his attempt to seize the throne. He then proclaimed a jihad against the British in May 1919, which led to the third and last Anglo-Afghan war. That same month, General Mustafa Kemal Pasha (Kemal Atatürk) began the Turkish War of Independence following the Greek occupation of Izmir. Kemal Atatürk served as a model for action by many progressive leaders in the Muslim world, including Amanullah. After fighting of only a few weeks' duration, Amanullah's war ended with the Treaty of Rawalpindi. Amanullah succeeded in securing full national independence for Afghanistan, which was his most significant foreign affairs achievement. At the end of the jihad, Britain gave up supervision of Afghan foreign relations. In turn, Afghanistan forfeited British subsidies. It also gave up British guarantees with regard to foreign aggression at a time when growing Soviet power began what would be decades of pressure on the country.

Amanullah harbored ambitions of his own to realize the pan-Islamic ideals of his father-in-law. These included sending aid, including troops, to support the besieged amir of Bukhara engaged in a struggle against the Red Army and local Bolshevik sympathizers. When the Bolsheviks reestablished Russian military control of Central Asia, Amanullah withdrew active support. The Afghan treaty with the Bolsheviks in 1921 attempted to continue diplomatic pressure to assure the independence of Bukhara and Khiva, both reconstituted as republics under national reformist and Bolshevik leaders. Through this treaty, Amanullah also tried to press for the return of Afghan territory seized by the Russians at Panjdeh in 1885. The Soviet state ignored all three clauses of the treaty. For his part, Amanullah gave refuge to the ex-amir of Bukhara, publicly entertained Ibrahim Beg, a leading mujahid commander of the Central Asian insurgency against the Red Army that the latter branded *basmachi* or bandits, and provided safe haven for thousands of Central Asian refugees fleeing Bolshevik rule over the next decade.

On the domestic front, Amanullah's efforts were concentrated on overhaul of the state to make it conform to his vision of a modern state. Some of his ideas set abiding standards to challenge the Afghan polity for the rest of the decade; others, more superficial, raised the ire of conservatives to an extent that was not outweighed by the actual benefit offered by the changes he espoused. The highlight of his reform program was the drawing up of a constitution in 1923 that, although reworked several times, established the basis for the formal structure of the government, set the role of the monarch within a constitutional framework, and attempted to regulate state-Islam relations. Despite Amanullah's adoption of virtually the entire program of the modernists, there were still some malcontents who formed a secret society, the Hizb-i Niqabdar (Veiled Party), to plot Amanullah's overthrow and the establishment of a republic.[15] To be sure, many conservative Afghans felt their monarch's reforms moved too fast and too far. The influential Islamic figure in the country, the Hazrat-e Shor Bazaar, threw down the draft of the 1923 constitution before Amir Habibullah in a public durbar, calling it the work of communists and not of Muslims. The army commander, General Nadir Khan (a member of the Musahiban family who had also returned from exile under Habibullah), also felt that the reforms moved too rapidly for the Afghan context, with overreliance on Turkish officers ignorant of Afghan realities. Nadir received ambassadorial rank to Paris, a diplomatic exile, and later chose to remain there on his own. Even Tarzi, the inspiration for the reforms, felt that events were getting out of control. A tribal revolt in Paktia province pitted the army against tribesmen, but the army succeeded only when supplemented by another tribal contingent belonging to the hereditary enemies of the rebellious Paktia tribes. The constitution was amended in 1924. However, after Amanullah's grand tour of European and Middle Eastern capitals in 1927 and 1928, he returned determined to advance his modernizing agenda without regard to caution. In so doing he moved directly against the ulema and the Sufi leadership alike, arresting the Hazrat Sahib, Fazl Umar Mujaddidi, and executing the chief *qazi* (religious judge) of Kabul together with four other ulema on charges of treason. Amanullah finally managed to alienate the most powerful forces in the country, including the military, the religious leaders, and the Pushtun tribes. In late 1928 Amanullah's structure collapsed. The triggering event was another Pushtun rebellion, this time of the Shinwari tribes east of Jalalabad. A prominent Tajik freelance soldier operating north of Kabul, known pejoratively as Bacha-i Saqao (son of the water carrier) routed the ill-equipped, ill-paid, and poorly led Afghan army garrisons and besieged Kabul. Amanullah fled south toward Kandahar, but abdicated in favor of his brother Inayatullah, who also soon abdicated. The royal family owed its safe exit from Afghanistan to an airplane provided by the British following negotiations with the Hazrat Sahib.

Amanullah made many lasting contributions to the institutionalizing of the Afghan central government. He is celebrated as the liberator of the country, and Afghan independence day, dating from 1919, has been a widely observed national holiday, although his name and work went unacknowledged in public or print during the next four decades. Slowly, in retrospect, he has developed into a symbol and hero of modernists. The return of his body after his death in Rome in 1960 for Afghan burial did not meet with opposition.[16] Trying to fashion a public image of themselves as modernist Afghan nationalists, even Afghan Marxists such as Hafizullah Amin and Babrak Karmal paid homage to Amanullah as the martyr for modernism.

Amir Habibullah II: The Son of the Water Carrier, 1929

The nine-month rule of Kabul by Habibullah Ghazi, a man of undistinguished birth from the Kohistan area north of the city, marks the only instance of the Afghan monarchy's passing to a non-Pushtun, in this case a Tajik. In the period since his downfall, Habibullah was not simply ignored in Afghan history, like Amanullah, but he has been denigrated and maligned so that even his name is unrecognizable by most Afghans. He is known instead as Bacha-i Saqao, a reference to his mean birth into a poor family. Knowledge of his period is limited, and his person and motivation lie buried with him, his associates, and those who oversaw his overthrow and hanging. His short period of rule is credited with neither reform nor stability, although there may be evidence that his government gave reinvigorated support to the anti-Soviet resistance movement in Central Asia. This support turned to a summary hunt of anti-Soviet leaders by the Afghan military once Habibullah II was replaced. The extent of Russian and British machinations in the overthrow and replacement of both Amanullah and Habibullah II may remain unknowable. But the rule of Habibullah II confirms both the severity of the ethnic divisions in Afghanistan and the difficulty of changing attitudes and worldviews of an isolated and a perhaps rightly suspicious people.

In his accession speech, Habibullah II vowed to reverse the social reforms instituted by prior rulers, especially those in marriage customs, education, and the status of women. He accomplished most of these goals, instituting a severe veiling of women resembling the Central Asian heavy veil and trousers rather than the billowy Indian and Iranian veils. The attack extended to cultural institutions such as museums and libraries, which were sacked. Government workers, especially those closely associated with Amanullah, became victims of beatings, imprisonment, and exile. Students from the new schools came under suspicion. Other measures he instituted addressed the political changes during the Amanullah period, especially abolishing conscription, lowering taxes, and returning the courts and schools to the jurisdiction of the Muslim ulema and *fuqaha* (judges). Within a few months his regime made some attempts at leniency by permitting a newspaper, some foreign-language schools, and a receptivity to reforms that did not violate Islamic principles.[17] The economic instability, the growing disaffection of the Pushtun tribes who had initially backed him, and Soviet and British fears of an unstable Afghanistan combined to bring about the end of Habibullah II's rule. Controversy about his personal end lends to the emerging idea that he was a character of personal courage, honor, and charisma but with neither the training nor the experience to rule a divided land.

Nadir Shah, 1929–1933

When Nadir Khan became Nadir Shah (king) on October 16, 1929, a new line of Afghan monarchs began; although they numbered only two, their combined reigns lasted well over forty years. Belonging to the Muham-madzai Durrani clan but of the Musahiban family, the line had close ties within the Pushtun confederation but was hard pressed from the start to control the eastern tribes with whose help it had defeated Habibullah II. Nadir Shah bore the burden of having returned to Afghanistan in 1929 through India, and thus he could be branded a British puppet, a favorite term of opprobrium for anyone deemed unacceptable in Afghan politics. He was not labeled a Soviet puppet, though he signed a nonaggression treaty with the Soviet Union in 1931 (at the ten-year anniversary of the 1921 treaty) and had driven the leading Central Asian resistance leader into waiting Red Army encirclement in 1929. The balancing act for the Musahiban family after 1929 was focused on instituting social and political reform at a pace rapid enough to please reformers but slow enough not to arouse conservatives. At the same time, Afghanistan's geographic posi-tion—a land-locked buffer between two great empires—called for vigilance in playing one against the other or seeking a third party to balance the two.

Die-hard Amanullah supporters, whether they were actual supporters or merely using his prestige to advance their own interests, created an under-current of distrust between the modern elite and the dynasty during the four and a half decades of Musahiban rule. An assassin who belonged to the Young Afghans and had been studying in Germany killed the king's brother, who was ambassador in Berlin. A plot to overthrow the monarchy and replace it with a republic was uncovered and resulted in the execution of a former Amanullah minister of war in 1932. Finally, while visiting a school in Kabul in 1933, Nadir Shah himself was assassinated by the adopted son of Ghulam Nabi Charkhi, a prominent Amanullah supporter who had been executed for treason in 1932.

Plagued by intrigue from both urban elites and tribal leaders, Nadir Shah had little time to constitute any major action other than promulgating a new constitution in 1931, reopening some schools, laying the groundwork for restoration of the state treasury and other institutions, and assuring suc-cession to the throne to avoid another civil war.

Zahir Shah, 1933–1973

Nineteen years old when he succeeded his father, Zahir Shah's long rule was marked not by his own initiatives as monarch but by the cohesion of his extended family, which administered the country mainly as prime ministers. Two uncles and then a first cousin held that post. When his reign ended, it came about without any family bloodshed. His first cousin, the former prime minister, declared a republic and became its first president. A decade later, Zahir Shah became the focus of attention once again as a compromise figurehead to replace the crippled Marxist leadership in Kabul in order to provide a period of stability for the competing resistance leaders. Despite his relative inactivity during his actual reign, his beneficial influence on Afghan political development may yet come to pass, as to many Afghans and observers he appears to be the sole acceptable unifying figure despite his advanced age.

From 1933 through the end of World War II Afghanistan was effectively under the rule of Sardar Muhammad Hashim Khan, an iron-fisted uncle of the king. The proliferation of newspapers and journals, though under strict censorship, nonetheless allowed for the impassioned exchange of ideas among Kabul elites on the problems of modernization and the relationship of Islam to society and the individual as well as Islam and modernization. Archaeological research, conducted mainly by the French, began in this period to reveal the richness of the Afghan past. This emerging view of the pre-Islamic period encouraged secular perspectives among intellectuals and modernists who saw in the past a vehicle for two related issues: the restoration of Afghan glory and a diminished role for religion. Already inclined toward regarding Islam as inherently antithetical to progress, an idea fostered by the colonial experience of the Islamic world, the value attached by representatives of European colonialists to the pre-Islamic past reinforced an increasingly negative attitude toward Islam, particularly as a social force. These notions remained topics of discourse among the elite but did not penetrate to the general public until the attempted social reforms of the period after 1958.

Afghan nationalism drew on the past and the stable present as it grew. Although Pushtu academic pursuits were pressed under Hashim Khan, in fact both Dari and Pushtu advanced in the public educational system that laid the groundwork for higher education for men and women.

Meanwhile the Afghan economy advanced with the introduction of banking institutions to partially replace bazaar money changers; new agricultural exports developed; and transit trade through Soviet Central Asia increased as relations with the Soviet Union began to be built on barter arrangements. As a neutral country in World War II, Afghanistan had been unique in suffering neither occupation nor devastation. Rather, like Central Asia, it became a place of refuge for many, even Central Europeans, who provided some important technical assistance, cheaply, for development.

Moreover, World War II offered little opportunity for spending cash, and Afghanistan found itself with a fat treasury at the end of the war.

Under the administration of the second royal uncle, Shah Mahmud Khan Ghazi, political relaxation domestically and expansion of foreign ties, especially with the United States, dominated the political agenda. Intent on infrastructure development, Kabul looked for ways to improve agriculture, especially irrigation, and for that third-party balance to its geographic dilemma stemming from its being neighbors with the Soviet Union and the British or the replacement states on the Indian subcontinent.

Shah Mahmud Khan was encouraged by young modernizing Afghans in the government to liberalize the political system in order to make his own mark as the originator of true democracy. Consequently, the political controls that had assured a docile parliament were relaxed in 1949, and the reformists entered the Assembly as one-third of its members. As soon as the laws were passed establishing a free press, newspapers sprang up overnight. Many of the newspapers called for an agenda that included an elected constitutional government responsible to the Assembly, an end to corruption, improved living conditions, and an end to government-established import-export monopolies by local capitalists (dating from the 1930s and 1940s). At the same time, the press officially supported the institution of the monarchy.

Soon a student union emerged at Kabul University. Students produced satirical plays against the abuses of the royal family and the misuse of Islam to sustain injustice. Many of these liberal elements belonged to a broad movement known as Wish-i Zalmayan (Awakened Youth), which had been established in 1947 and supported, initially at least, by an important royal cousin, Sardar Muhammad Da'ud Khan. Possibly the most radical program of action appeared in the newspaper *Nida-ye Khalq* (Voice of the People), published by Dr. Abdul Rahman Mahmudi.

By 1951 the government had become alarmed at what it saw as the excesses of the reformists, and it closed the student union. In 1952 the government arrested about twenty of its critics in the press and halted their publications.

The next prime minister under Zahir Shah belonged to the king's own generation and was not only a first cousin but a brother-in-law as well. Da'ud, who took his post in 1953, shared many aspirations with the reformists: He felt that the government was too conservative, the new capitalists too powerful, and the religious establishment too reactionary. To accomplish the reformist agenda, he planned to harness the energies of the dissident intellectuals by employing them to run the new government programs. To assure the smooth transition to a modern society, Da'ud planned to avoid having what he perceived to have been Amanullah's critical error—a weak military—and so he needed a large infusion of funds for training and equipping a modern army. Modernization, both military and socioeconomic, required foreign aid and advisers, a program for which he hoped to gain broad public approval by showcasing the military program as supportive of the legitimate demands for Pushtunistan, an issue that generated sympathy, especially among the eastern Pushtun tribes, who had seen the political aspirations of Pushtuns ignored during the British withdrawal from the Indian subcontinent in 1947. Because of Cold War geopolitics, Da'ud's first choice of a donor state, the United States, fizzled, and he was forced to turn to the Soviet Union for aid and advisers. Thus, as the Cold War alliances were drawn in the Middle East after 1954, Afghanistan was ignored by the West but inexorably nurtured by the Soviet Union. More and more of Afghanistan's trade became tied to military aid repayment plans, and relations with Pakistan deteriorated.

Under Da'ud's leadership social reforms, particularly with regard to education and women's issues, were instituted that affected the lives of most Afghans but relatively few women outside Kabul. With some participation by the United States, a highway infrastructure tied major Afghan cities together and with Pakistan. The Soviet effort dwarfed that of other countries, although in the field of education, U.S. help was particularly significant.

By 1962–1963, however, Da'ud's autocratic methods as well as his continued clash with Pakistan over the Pushtunistan issue had made him a liability to the government. When he left office in 1963, a new constitution under consideration banned close members of the royal family from holding such a powerful position. Through the constitution of 1964, the document's formulators also attempted to institute measures to prevent the concentration of political power in a single person. This more democratic constitution ushered in the last ten years of Zahir Shah's reign, which represent a period of feverish political activity by a democratically elected legislative branch, heavily contested elections, and the rise of multiple parties, a free press, and some political instability. Throughout this period expectations rose that Zahir Shah would grasp the monarchial reins to help shape the direction of government. He approached his constitutional responsibilities with indecision and procrastination. In 1973 Da'ud seized power, this time abolishing the monarchy altogether and ruling as president of a very shaky coalition brought to power by elements that included the Marxist wing of Afghan politics. The ten-year hiatus between the two periods of Da'ud's rule witnessed the rise of openly Marxist parties in Afghanistan, the details of which appear in Chapter 5. Here we will examine the socioeconomic events of the period between 1964 and 1973.

Socioeconomic Developments of the Liberal Democratic Period

The impetus for transforming tradition-bound societies into a closer likeness of European and other Western societies did not come under serious challenge in the Middle East until the 1980s, largely as an outcome of the

Iranian Revolution. Before that, the directional choices, confined to broadly Marxist or Western orientations, allowed little or no questioning of the efficacy of modernization by imitation.

In Afghanistan, too, the modernization model accepted very early in this century came secondhand through the Ottoman Empire and then Kemalist Turkey. Trickle-down modernization, paced to create the least amount of political disruption, provided the norm under the Zahir Shah monarchy. Confident that his control of the country allowed bolder dictates in the socioeconomic area, Prime Minister Da'ud launched a threefold program for socioeconomic change that continued despite the adoption of a new political format through the constitution of 1964: central planning, based on five-year plans beginning in 1956 (1957–1961, and so on), infrastructure development with foreign aid, and expansion of the educational system from elementary through higher education. In all three areas, the socioeconomic changes that were generated led to problems of their own, especially in the expansion of education, as job creation did not keep pace with graduates of secondary schools and universities. As in the Soviet Union itself, the Ministry of Planning, run increasingly by Soviet advisers, devised growth and development schemes devoid of reliable statistical information. The area of infrastructure development, successful in large measure, relied heavily on foreign aid and increased the foreign debt. The basic nature of the Afghan economy, relying as it did on agriculture, did not change except in two areas. The first was that the government began to plan for collective farming, as in the model Soviet farm in Jalalabad, rather than encourage private farmers. The second entailed the launching of several mineral resource exploitation projects, particularly in coal production (with American aid at Dara Suff) and gas production (with Soviet aid at Shibarghan). In addition, secondary smaller industries based on the processing of agricultural products began to become profitable, the most important of which was a sugar, cotton, and textile industry (at Baghlan and Pul-i Khumri) and a canning industry (at Kandahar). The lack of internal statistics has been a regular planning problem, but one estimate placed the number of industrial workers in the entire country at fewer than 10,000.[18] Irrigation and power production projects in place in 1966 yielded 192,000 kilowatts in all, but projected hydroelectric capacity tied to irrigation held great promise.

Agriculture, on which three out of four Afghans depended during the 1960s for their livelihood, improved steadily so that except for a period of two years of severe back-to-back droughts (1972–1973), Afghanistan had been self-sufficient in food production before the Soviet invasion. Steadily Pushtun tribesmen from Paktia to Farah began to benefit both from expanded irrigation projects and from the introduction of better seeds, fertilizers, and pesticides, all standards of the Green Revolution that was in the process of transforming the subcontinent. In fact, chemical fertilizer production in northern Afghanistan held considerable promise. At the royal/public experimental farm outside Kabul, dairy, fruit, and crop projects began to benefit agriculture throughout the country, especially in Pushtun areas, where political restrictions on transit trade and the need to replace rifles with tractors encouraged the governors to improve agriculture. Silk production, based on mulberry tree planting, and wool fiber from sheep in particular, both traditional products, began to be encouraged through the increased possibilities of export of both craft items and unprocessed fiber. The market for *karakul* skins, though dependent on fashion and hence somewhat fickle, continued to provide revenue, and the export of leather quality skins contributed as well.

Four other factors that began to enter the economic equation were the considerable growth of the tourist industry, the corruption multiplied through the expansion of opium poppy cultivation, the very large proportion of the national economy devoted to the military (creating a debt to the Soviet Union), and somewhat later, the increase in migrant Afghan workers earning their income in the oil-rich Middle Eastern states.[19] These four factors of the economy turned into serious problems after the Soviet invasion and have not abated since then.

Social change occurred slowly, with the divisions in society increasing between urban and rural areas. The differences between the two were based less on economic levels than on the changing worldviews of urban elites that began to separate them from the conservative countryside. With rare exceptions (in the Herat area), agricultural landholding in Afghanistan involved many small landlords rather than absentee landlords with tenant farmers. Therefore, the Western worldviews adopted by urban elites had little to do with economic differences between urban and rural dwellers. Nor did this pattern shift with economic changes, since much of the five-year plan budgets were devoted to the rural agricultural sector (29 percent in the third plan, 1967–1972) and to countrywide infrastructure (communication and transport) development.[20]

In visible ways, Kabul especially drifted further from the realities of the social context of the countryside. Encouraged by the extended royal family, women not only continued to receive secondary education in large numbers at girls' schools, but they also formed an increasingly large proportion of the coeducational university student body. Their widespread employment in government offices in the capital as well as their appearing in public without veils (since 1959) and running for public office (in 1965) set them apart from their counterparts in provincial towns, where the most conspicuous public employment of women was as teachers in girls' schools.

The expansion of the educational system also tended to set Kabul apart from the rest of the country. Boarding school education at the high schools, teacher training schools, and university level education were all concentrated in the capital, helping only in part to meet the educational needs of the provinces. Students whose families lived in the city or who could stay with relatives in the city benefited from education beyond the sixth grade. Social custom prevented many girls from the provinces from living in dormitories even when this was the sole means of gaining advances in education. The inequities of educational locale came to be addressed very late in the monarchial period, and then only inadequately. Even when high schools and a medical faculty were established in provincial capitals, the educational needs of the Afghans living in the villages and small towns could not be met. The problems of centralized educational facilities multiplied at other levels of public access to integrative institutions: The same situation existed with regard to hospitals and banks, both run by the government. For these reasons, although some integration of the country was achieved on the economic level, on the social level Kabul and the countryside became increasingly out of tune with each other. The consequences of this unsynchronized social development were complicated by the ethnic diversity of the country: Pushtun access to power and privilege in the capital translated into privileged appointments to government sector employment. Since so few economic and legal resources were invested in private sector development, government employment of educated youth—from engineers to doctors—depended on connections to ministries and governors. In this respect, the ethnic pecking order that placed Pushtun Durranis at the top operated to the disadvantage of others, from the military on down to provincial officials. Individuals belonging to the Pushtun ethnic group, often detribalized, manned posts in northern provinces where populations consisted of Tajiks, Uzbeks, and other non-Pushtuns. The rule, in effect since 1938, that all government employees must know, or study, the national language of Pushtu, rankled non-Pushtuns when in many areas Dari served as an adequate interethnic language.

The Legacy of Imperialism

The impact of a historical legacy can be determined by the ways in which history is recalled and reprocessed. With family and community being as coherent and cohesive as they are in Afghan society, historical memory, even if preserved differently than in more literate societies, nonetheless plays an important role in the perceptions of people and in their concept of their identity.[21] Afghanistan's legacy of imperialism has entered the schoolroom textbook and historical writing as well as formal entertainment in nonliterate settings. An evaluation of this legacy can help to explain the attitudes of Afghans toward foreigners and toward the Soviet invasion and why Afghans are both susceptible and resistant to outside interference. In light of the heightened paranoia about Afghan Muslim fighters developing into a source for international guerrilla fighters, it is well to recall the words of one of the earliest British visitors to Afghanistan in 1832. Struck by the absence of prejudice by Afghans against Christians, he writes, "It is a matter of agreeable surprise to anyone acquainted with Mahomedans of India, Persia, and Turkey, and with their religious prejudices and antipathies, to find that the people of Kabul are entirely [devoid] of them. In most countries few Mahomedans will eat with a Christian; to salute him, even in error, is deemed unfortunate, and he is looked upon as unclean. Here none of these difficulties or feelings exist. The Christian is respectfully called a 'Kitabi' or 'one of the Book.'"[22] A century of imperialism has changed attitudes toward Westerners in many corners of Afghanistan.

The Imperialists Aims

From the early years of the nineteenth century, the British had begun to establish their dominion over the Indian subcontinent as the successor to the moribund Moghul empire. Even though a shadowy Moghul ruler still remained in the Red Fort of Delhi, he retained his post under British protection. They continued to fear that some other European power would attempt to snatch this prize from their grasp—certainly, this is what had motivated the French expedition to Egypt in 1798. Although Bonaparte's attempt was defeated by the British, the French resumed efforts through military and diplomatic missions to Iran and the Ottoman Empire.

The Russians, simultaneously, resumed their historic "civilizing" mission of wars against their Muslim neighbors, including the Ottomans, the Iranians, and the various khans and amirs of Central Asia and the Caucasus. Briefly, following the Treaty of Tilsit, from 1807 to 1812, the Russian and French empires allied. The danger posed from such an alliance to British interests in India prompted the British to send out embassies to the states on their northwest frontier. One of these was the first embassy of a European country to Afghanistan in 1809.

The Anglo-Afghan treaty of 1809, though not very important in substance, set the pattern for the long and tortuous history of Anglo-Afghan relations that lasted until the British withdrew from their Indian empire, the jewel in the British crown, in 1947. The British wanted to stabilize their northwestern frontier with a treaty with the Afghans. But the Afghans were locked in internal struggles of succession. By the 1830s the Russians had joined the contest for influence in Afghanistan. Initially, their opening came because of their privileged positions as advisers and patrons of the Qajar dynasty of Iran, but later it developed as that of a powerful neighbor in Central Asia.

Afghanistan posed a dilemma for imperialists: The internal divisions of the country presented tempting opportunities for intrigue and influence.

But even when this influence was backed by military force, the divisions of the country meant that any alliance created as many enemies as it did friends. Moreover, Afghan supporters of the imperialists could and were tainted as allies of infidels.

The Afghan Rulers and the Imperialists

From the point of view of Afghan rulers, the ideal strategy for a weak state, which Afghanistan became after 1826, was to balance the interests of the rival imperialists and serve in the role of a buffer state. Through this process they might obtain formal guarantees of assistance to preserve their independence from other imperialist pressures and, just as important, support for themselves and their chosen successors against rivals. The latter was of vital concern for the rulers, for the diffuse nature of political authority extended to the entire royal clan and, in the absence of the law of primogeniture, wars of succession became civil wars. In these wars, outside material support and ultimately the recognition by the British of the rule of a particular sardar could guarantee success, although sometimes only short-lived success. In turn the ruler would give up some control over foreign policy, and even over borders, for the British would not give a blank check to provoke a war with a European enemy and then demand support.

The Legacy of the Cold War

Afghanistan became the ultimate and final victim of the Cold War. Desperate to play both sides against each other for the benefit of his country—or as he put it, light his American cigarette with Russian matches—Da'ud as prime minister moved Afghanistan into a debilitating military and economic dependency on the Soviet Union and paid a high personal price when he tried to reverse directions during his presidency between 1973 and 1978. During the period of the monarchy after World War II the success of the Afghans in remaining neutral in the Cold War, as they had in the war itself, became dependent on both their geographic position and their ethnic problems: Pakistan's control of Afghan access to the sea drove the Afghans to increase trade with the Soviet Union so that by the end of the 1960s about 50 percent of their trade was locked into Soviet dependency. The inconvertibility of the Russian ruble forced barter agreements over which Afghan leaders exercised very limited control in terms of quantity, enforceability, and prices that were equitable on a world scale.

In the area of military dependency, once Afghanistan became shut out of Western-led regional defense agreements, its options were to have no military or to turn to the Soviet Union. Unlike many developing countries whose military buildup led to dictatorial control of its own population, during the monarchy in Afghanistan the military was not used in this way.[23] Indeed, it was only during the Soviet invasion that the army, however inadequately, came to be used as an instrument of internal state power. Afghanistan's own Cold War with Pakistan over the issue of Pushtunistan, in which the two superpower adversaries backed their respective military allies, drove Afghanistan to its military and financial debacles. In this respect, the U.S. decisions of the 1950s, made in Cold War confrontation, should come under scrutiny as the leading cause of Afghanistan's military dependency and its subsequently being a casualty of this dependency.

Chapter Three

Geopolitics
Then and Now

"Amir Abdul Rahman well understood the international political situation of his day."

—Burhanuddin Rabbani[1]

The political significance of Afghanistan exercised few minds in the West before December 27, 1979, when the Soviet army began its airborne, armored, and infantry assault southward across the Amu Darya from Central Asia into Afghanistan. Soviet troops came across the Hindu Kush, over concrete roads they had constructed as part of their aid to Afghanistan, to occupy key strategic points inside the country. Yet, only a hundred years before, as readers of Rudyard Kipling's story "Kim" are aware, Afghanistan had been at the center of the geopolitical rivalry of the Great Game, which was summarized in Chapter 2. The rivalry between the colonial empires of Britain and Russia had spread during the nineteenth century across the Asian continent from the Bosporus to Manchuria. Great Game rivalry still accounts in great part for the political boundaries and relationships within Asia as we enter into the twenty-first century. The destruction and chaos in Afghanistan at the close of this century attest as much to the legacy of Great Game politics as they do to the callousness of Russian attitudes toward the Afghan people and the willingness of the rest of the world to brush aside the events that transpire in this vital point at the heart of Asia. In the historical past, when the silk routes passing through the territory enriching cities like Balkh and Herat, this geographic position had functioned to the advantage of the inhabitants. When stability does return to Afghanistan, a return of economic prosperity may yet occur as the country resumes a role as a transit point for Asian trade. For good or for bad,

Afghanistan's geographic position has contributed the single most important element to the shaping of its history, its ethnic diversity, its economy, and its political situation in the region and increasingly in the world.

Prosperity and Diversity Along the Silk Road

The "mother of cities," as Balkh, the legendary trading town in northern Afghanistan has been called in history, stands abandoned today, surrounded by a crumbling but impressive outer wall in the middle of a vast, well-watered plain. Broken glazed tiles, potsherds, and the foundations of bazaars, inns, and mosques attest to its lost fortunes. The latest structures date from before the Mongol conquest when it was destroyed, as were many other prosperous sites in Central Asia. After that devastation, the entire region took several centuries to recover, but Balkh never did. Instead, some twenty miles northeast stands Mazar-i-Sharif, a shrine town, located close to the paved road that almost rings the country. But the paved road has never matched the riches and cultural exchange enjoyed by cities like Balkh that were located on the travel and trade routes collectively called the Silk Road. Tied together through middlemen of many ethnic, religious, and linguistic groups, these routes carried short-distance and long-distance trade, especially of the prized fabric of China—silk—to the Mediterranean and beyond.

Even before Portuguese capacity to circumnavigate the African continent and thus expand, hasten, and cheapen the cost of trade with the East, the Mongol invasion had crippled many areas of Central Asia—although the intent of the Mongols was to promote trade as long as there was no local resistance to the expansion of their empire. In Afghanistan and its environs, there was resistance. Shahr-i Golgola, near the tallest free-standing Buddhas in the world, lies witness to the vengeance of the Mongols as it stands "rattling" in the wind after paying the cost in human and material destruction for being the site where a grandson of Genghis Khan was killed.

At its height, and still during its partial eclipse following the Mongol invasion, the Silk Road crossing Afghanistan brought with it Buddhism, Christianity, Islam, the Persian language, and empires, one of which, that of the Kushans, centered itself in Afghanistan (Sorkh Kotal is one of their major archaeological sites). The rulers of the empires all appreciated the importance of stability needed for maintaining economic prosperity. A Ghaznavid ruler is famed for admonishing an overzealous general for bothering ordinary farmers and traders, knowing that on their work was built the richness of his capital of Ghazni. In this early history Genghis Khan's hordes stand as the chief destroyers, and they held that distinction until the Soviet invasion.

To the crossroads position of Afghanistan may also be attributed the ethnic and cultural diversity of the country and the region. Although the division of ethnic groups stems from the drawing of international borders by the tzarist and British empires in the nineteenth century, the geographic position of Afghanistan on the migration routes of Iranian tribes, Indian Aryans, and Turkic and Arab groups peppered the land with small ethnic groups hidden and protected by the myriad valleys and mountain ranges. Although in the contemporary period Islam lends a level of homogeneity to the population of Afghanistan, in fact its population of under 20 million represents many ethnic groups whose linguistic and physical diversity ranges from Mediterranean to Indian to Mongolian in origins. The Iranian linguistic family is the most heavily represented and includes Pushtuns, Tajiks, and Baluchis. The migration of Iranian tribes, dating to at least 1000 B.C.E., gives Afghanistan a strong cultural affinity with present-day Iran. Moreover, the widespread use of Persian in its Afghan form, Dari, ties together a number of ethnic groups that have a tenuous relationship with the descendants of the tribal groups of two millennia ago. For example, the Hazara, Mongol-related historically and physically, use a Persian-based language and profess Shi'ism.

The next wave of southward moving tribes was generally Turkic in background, although the Huns (called Hephtalites in these eastern regions) may represent a non-Turkic group that has left no discernible trace among Afghans. The Turkic groups, appearing in the Afghan area about the fourth century C.E., formed at least one important dynasty based in Afghanistan, that of the Ghaznavids (tenth–twelfth centuries). Turkic groups in Afghanistan have been heavily influenced by Persian culture, as were the Ghaznavids. It was not until the appearance of the Uzbeks in Central Asia in the sixteenth century that the Turkic elements in Afghanistan began to retain a Turkic linguistic feature. This basically Uzbek presence in northern Afghanistan was supplemented by a further migration of other Turkic and Tajik groups who fled the tzarist conquest of Central Asia and later the Bolshevik presence. The Stalinist agrarian collectivization of the 1930s brought yet another influx of Turkic people, as did the dawn of Chinese Marxism. Therefore, though the Turkic presence in Afghanistan is small proportionally, it represents a long-term and continued southward pressure by many different groups, some of whose core populations are not located in geographical contiguity to Afghanistan. The Kazaks and the Kyrgyz, for example, are wholly migrant communities dating from Russian expansion, and the Uzbeks and Turkmens have grown in numbers and diversity as a result of continued migration. For some Turkic groups Afghanistan became a temporary sanctuary as they moved on to India or the Ottoman Empire. This diaspora of Central Asians is represented in the Ottoman successor states, especially Jordan and Saudi Arabia, as well as in Turkey. Prominent in merchant classes and in the military, this Central Asian diaspora took a keen interest in the Afghan resistance, both in its promise as a successful anti-Russian and anti-communist action and as inspiration for similar activity by other Central Asians under Soviet rule.

Geopolitics has led to movements out of Afghanistan as well. Small pockets of Afghans, generally Pushtuns, live in Tajikistan and in Uzbekistan. These groups, numbering in the hundreds, are almost exclusively descended from Afghan communists who migrated northward during the 1920s. In Tajikistan they are located in the old political center of Hissar.[2] Added to these numbers are the thousands of Afghans who were sent to Tashkent, Dushanbe, and elsewhere in the Soviet Union for study after 1978. Many sought this opportunity because it allowed them to escape military service and the hardships of war. Others are the children of the privileged Marxist elite who, either for the safety of their children or to engage in illicit trade (some reputedly in narcotics), sent family members to the Soviet Union.

Some of the diversity of the Afghan population is related to trade rather than migration. Hindu and Sikh communities, small and scattered, represent trading communities, as do Pushtun communities outside the Northwest Frontier Province on the Indian subcontinent. These trading communities are found only in urban areas. The Jews of Afghanistan, related to Bukharan Jews, also were found in urban areas, such as Mazar-i-Sharif and Kabul, rather than involved in agriculture. Some of these small communities have become depleted through emigration because of the war, or, as in the case of the Jews, through emigration to Israel even before the war.

Afghanistan's terrain offered refuge for persecuted groups and isolation for other ethnic groups that would have lost their language and culture had they lived within easy access of cities, roads, and centralized institutions. The Nuristanis as well as Wakhis and other Pamiri people, the latter found in Afghanistan, Tajikistan, and Pakistan, remain largely unintegrated because of their physical isolation, a position they retained in order to maintain their separate religious traditions and languages. The diversity of people lends to the disunity of the state, as do the physical geographic impediments to integration.

In the sixteenth century transport from Europe to Asia by ship became possible and eventually preferable to the overland transfer of goods. The many intermediary merchants, the inn keepers, the caravan drivers, the scribes, the money changers, the food vendors, and the thousands of others whose livelihood depended on the overland trade suffered as a result. Why carry bolts of silk by camel from eastern China through Turkestan, Khorasan, Afghanistan, Iran, Mesopotamia, and Syria to Venice when it could be crated aboard ship at an eastern Chinese location, such as Macao or Canton, and unloaded in Venice? Gradually trade after the sixteenth century became far more localized, mainly along a north-south axis from Central Asia through Afghanistan and on to the Indian subcontinent. Iran, which at this same time began a vigorous campaign to make Shi'ism the state religion, clashed with the Sunni world surrounding it. This clash of sects gained further fuel from the entry into Central Asia of the Uzbeks, whose suspicion and distrust of Iran feeds on legends of cruelties and wars between these two ambitious and competing groups that contributed to the Turko-Iranian culture of Central Asia. These changes in the geopolitics of the region began to isolate Afghanistan and allow the rise and spread of Pushtun domination over a large expanse of the region, especially in the south.

Its isolation exacerbated by the geopolitics of the Great Game, Afghanistan tottered on the edge of becoming solely a quaint, culturally untarnished, outpost of Asia. Though destroyed by war for the two decades since 1978, it may enter the next century located within a region relatively free of the polarities that have controlled its international destinies since the nineteenth century. Central Asia and the Indian subcontinent function once more without colonialism. The end of the Soviet Union may equalize the playing field for all, assuming that China does not rise as an imperialist threat in the region. The crossroads position of Afghanistan may yet become a positive factor once again in its geopolitics in a revival of prosperity to compete with that of the time of the Silk Road.

A Dangerous Neighborhood

The Afghans, with long memories and larger stakes, were well aware of the precariousness of their position during the period of colonial expansion. What happened in the century between 1879 and 1970 was a twofold stabilization of the situation in the country—internationally and internally. Internationally, the rival empires of tzarist Russia and Great Britain agreed to accept Afghanistan as a buffer territory between their respective empires in Central Asia and India. However, a buffer would do little good unless it was itself stabilized internally. This need created a common interest between the Afghan leadership, centered in the Muhammadzai lineage of the Barakzai tribe, and their two imperialist neighbors.

The hastily made, and in many cases informal and unspoken, arrangements to achieve stability managed to survive the shocks of two world wars, the Bolshevik revolution, and the end of the British Indian empire. In the post–World War II era the United States, to a much more limited extent than had the British, replaced the British Empire as the major international force balancing the southern side of the geopolitical equation in opposition to the Soviet Union.[3] In the following decades the postwar situation came under more strain with shifts in the international, regional, and internal environments.

Internal development of modernization within Afghanistan had created significant differences within a ruling modernizing elite and its supporters, which had gradually broadened beyond the ruling family and tribe. More specifically, an openly Marxist element emerged in the formation in 1965 of the People's Democratic Party of Afghanistan (PDPA or *Khalq* "Masses" Party). New alignments in the region had increased the power of India, aligned by treaty with the Soviet Union, and had greatly weakened the Pakistani role as the regional successor of the British Indian empire assuring Afghanistan's geopolitical position as a buffer state. But farther to the west, in Iran and the Arabian Peninsula, the rising financial power and to some extent even the military power (in the case of Iran) of the oil states created a new factor potentially capable of restoring the balance. Afghanistan's leadership moved quickly to try to use these regional changes to their country's advantage.

Internationally, however, the superpowers' perceptions of imbalance became more dangerous for the very existence of Afghanistan. The British had always been aware of the regional importance of Afghanistan as the keystone in the defense of their imperial position in the Indian subcontinent and the Persian Gulf. In contrast, even at the height of the Cold War the United States never considered Afghanistan to be within its politico-strategic definition of "the Free World."[4] It was eventually deemed worthy of major expenditures of U.S. economic assistance in the competition with the Soviet Union for influence in the "Third World." But by the 1970s, in the wake of the debacle of U.S. policy in Vietnam, even this limited interest declined.

The Soviets, for their part, had drawn exactly the opposite conclusions with regard to Afghanistan's geopolitical role within the region. The weakness of Pakistan, the tempting resources of the oil states of the Middle East, and the United States distancing itself from foreign commitments, all raised the possibility of major, or even decisive geopolitical gains on the Soviet southern flank through the utilization of Afghanistan's central position. To these temptations was added a dangerous new development. President Sardar Muhammad Da'ud Khan (president 1973–1978) was attempting to change directions in foreign policy. After two decades of growing dependency on the Soviet Union, he planned through aid from the oil-rich Muslim states to continue economic development without becoming totally reliant on the USSR.[5] The stage was set for the last foreign adventure of the Brezhnev era (and of the USSR itself), the invasion of Afghanistan and what was to become, in the words of the last Soviet leader, Mikhail Gorbachev, the "bleeding wound" for the Soviet Union.

Afghans themselves have always been keenly aware of their location, its dangers and costs, and the potential benefits of their situation. Depending on the political situation in the surrounding region, and to a large extent depending on their own political unity or disunity, they have been able to play a number of different roles on the regional and even the world stage since the emergence of their state in the early eighteenth century.

At first the Afghans were a dynamic and expansionist empire, the last successors to the Central Asian imperial tradition of the Kushans, Huns, Ghaznavids, Seljuks, Mongols, Timurids, and Uzbeks. For more than fifty years in the mid–eighteenth century they conquered and briefly ruled successively both Iran and northern India (as far as Delhi). However, the nineteenth-century expansion of European imperialism put an end to this recurring cyclical pattern of Asian history. Instead, Afghanistan became one of the major focal points of rivalry between the two great European empires in Asia. The Russians were expanding overland eastward and southward while the British expanded northward from their trading bases along the Indian littoral, until they dominated the entire subcontinent by the middle of the nineteenth century. The British were checked, however, in attempting to extend this domination to Afghanistan in the course of two wars fought during the nineteenth century (1838–1842 and 1878–1880). Thus in the final decades of the century Afghanistan became stabilized into a wary and wily neutrality, attempting to preserve its independence while at the time extracting the maximum benefits at the least cost from its stronger neighbors—largely by playing on its own strategic geopolitical location. This continued for the following century, until April 1978.

Geopolitical analysis, as developed in the theories of Alfred Thayer Mahan, Halford Mackinder, and Karl Haushofer, is easily subject to abuse and oversimplification. It attempts to consider the spatial aspects of any political pattern, especially through hypotheses explaining or predicting the distribution of power and political potential among states. The key to making these theories useful lies in understanding that they deal with assessments of potentialities, and these "are essentially probabilistic, even though they may be expressed in deterministic or near deterministic rhetoric."[6] One of the most sophisticated recent attempts to apply these concepts on a global scale is that of an American, Roy S. Cline. Cline has coined the term "politechtonics" to discuss "the formation and breakup of power groupings, mainly regional in makeup, that determine the regional balance of influence and force in today's international affairs."[7] In the 1970s he identified a total of eleven regional groupings worldwide. For our purposes, it is important to note that Afghanistan bordered on four of these groupings. Cline included Afghanistan in South Asia (where it borders on China), the Middle East, and the USSR/East Europe regions. Clearly, this is a position of immense strategic potential.

The Geopolitical Background of the Soviet Invasion

After the British announced in 1968 that they intended to withdraw their forces from the Persian Gulf, the Indian Ocean, and southeast Asia, the Soviet Union demonstrated its own strategic intentions by beginning to keep a naval force permanently deployed in the region.[8]

Throughout the 1970s the Soviet Union followed a consistent strategy of increasing its political, military, and economic presence in the region, establishing bases in South Yemen, Somalia, and Ethiopia as well as having access to port facilities in India, Iraq, Libya, and Syria. It concluded treaties of friendship, containing security clauses, with India, Egypt, Iraq, the People's Democratic Republic of Yemen, Somalia, Ethiopia, and Syria. A major Soviet political objective in this period with regard to Afghanistan was to obtain Afghan backing for Brezhnev's proposals for an "Asian Collective Security System."[9] Since the Afghan government believed this to be, in fact, an anti-Chinese alliance, they refused to support it. In general, these "friendship" treaties were soon followed by large amounts of military aid, equipment, training, and advisers. Eventually this "forward" policy of the USSR included participation in regional conflicts (at times using Cuban and East German proxies), including the "war of attrition" between Israel and Egypt, the Ethiopian-Somali war over the Ogaden, the Ethiopian war with the rebellious province of Eritrea, and the "Dhofar rebellion" in Oman.

Along with increasing direct and indirect Soviet involvement in the region, there were a number of other events that tended to enhance both the importance and the vulnerability of the oil resources of the region. During the 1973 Arab-Israeli War the oil-producing states gained control over the use of their resources from the international oil companies that had dominated the industry through the concession system since its foundation. These countries asserted their unilateral ownership rights to set prices and rates of production, and even to determine the destination of crude oil produced from their territory. The major international oil companies quickly became little more than technical contractors and commercial middlemen.[10]

After a brief attempt following the Bolshevik revolution to use Afghanistan as a highway for the export of revolution to India, the general policy of the Soviet Union became defensive for the next two decades. This position was motivated largely by fears of possible British intervention against their own southern flank. Following the death of Stalin in 1953, the Politburo leadership under Nikita Khrushchev began a new orientation in seeking the extension of Soviet influence to the new nations of Asia, Africa, and the Middle East.[11] Military and economic aid along with political support in regional conflicts were provided on a state-by-state basis. This was done without regard to the internal politics of the regional regimes, or even to their treatment of local communist parties. Afghanistan was one of the first, and on a per capita basis, one of the nations most favored by this new Soviet policy. It served as a valuable "demonstration project" to show that the Soviet Union provided useful and "disinterested" aid to its poor and backward neighbors, without ideological or political conditions. The fact that Afghanistan was a traditional monarchy and actually bordered on the Soviet Union was continually cited in both official communiqués and propaganda as proof that Soviet aid (unlike U.S. aid) came without strings and did not interfere in the internal politics of recipient states.

Under the leadership of then Prime Minister Sardar Muhammad Da'ud, the Royal Government of Afghanistan took advantage of the new Soviet policy to carry out its own economic development plans and to modernize its army and air force. At the same time, however, the Afghan government was eager to balance this aid with assistance from the United States, other Western states, and international agencies. Not only was more development thus made possible, but this help was also valued as a means of avoiding exclusive dependence on the Soviet bloc. Thus in the late 1950s and early 1960s, Afghanistan became a peaceful battleground of the Cold War, with the Soviets and the Americans in rivalry based on the value of their respective foreign aid programs.[12]

By the early 1970s, however, the overall extent of U.S. economic aid lagged and became far more selective. Afghanistan was no longer a priority of foreign policy, especially when compared to U.S. commitments in Southeast Asia. In keeping with its tradition of *bi-tarafi* (without sides) in foreign policy, Afghanistan began to turn to regional states to provide balance to its development. These states, principally Iran and Saudi Arabia, responded with commitments that would have dwarfed the entire Soviet aid program over the previous two decades. President Da'ud, in a political quid pro quo, moved toward an accommodation with Pakistan over the issue of Pushtunistan. This conflict periodically had brought their relations to the breaking point since the independence of Pakistan in 1947. This movement began in a private meeting of President Da'ud with Pakistani Prime Minister Zulfikar Ali Bhutto. It was arranged by King Khaled of Saudi Arabia at the funeral of King Faisal in 1975.[13] This accommodation, along with the suppression of internal communist (PDPA) influence already begun by President Da'ud, was the price set by the Middle Eastern monarchies for their aid. Da'ud, who had grown annoyed with the increasing arrogance of the "disinterested" Soviet Union in its aid program, was now more than willing to pay this price.

By the end of the 1970s, the international geopolitical balance around Afghanistan was approaching a turning point. On the one hand, the economic resources of the Middle East had become increasingly vital to the West, and on the other hand these resources were becoming more vulnerable to Soviet pressure. Regionally, backed by these same economic resources, Afghanistan was moving toward a new Middle Eastern alignment that would free it from dependence on the Soviet Union. At this critical juncture, the communist coup of April 27, 1978 (or the "Saur Revolution, as it was titled by the Marxists, from the name of the Afghan month), in which President Da'ud was killed, seemingly assured that the Soviets would not lose the strategic position they had patiently established through an expensive effort over the previous twenty-five years, ever since the then prime minister Da'ud himself had invited them into the country to provide economic and military aid.

In scarcely a year and a half, by late 1979, Afghan geopolitics became still more critical for the USSR. The Islamic revolution in Iran had removed the Shah, hitherto seen as the strongest regional obstacle to Soviet ambitions. With the approval of the revolution's leader, Ayatollah Ruholla Khomeini, the United States was being humiliated by the imprisonment of its diplomatic personnel as hostages in their own embassy in Tehran. In Pakistan, instability followed the trial and subsequent execution of former prime minister Zulfikar Ali Bhutto by the martial law regime of General Muhammad Zia-ul-Haq. U.S. aid to Pakistan had been cut off earlier because of suspicions about its development of nuclear weapons, and the U.S. embassy had been burned by a mob after the occupation of the Holy Mosque of Mecca by religious fanatics in Saudi Arabia. Even in Turkey, fighting between ethnic, religious, and political groups strained the very foundations of the secular and pro-Western Kemalist republic.

By contrast, within Afghanistan the situation had shifted dramatically against the Soviet Union. Instead of exploiting a compliant regional ally under a Marxist regime to help advance its interests, Brezhnev faced a situation fast approaching chaos. The new regime's cadres, few enough to begin with, were divided into hostile factions in the process of busily trying to murder one another. More important, the resistance of the Afghan people, based on national, social, and religious grounds, was increasingly successful in challenging the authority of the PDPA regime in the provinces. The army melted away to less than half of the strength it had before the coup. The remaining military units fought each other, mutinied, or deserted wholesale to the opposition. The loss of control over the countryside, where 85 percent of the population lived, meant that the annual draft of conscripts would not be reporting the following autumn. This news, which successive Soviet military observation missions confirmed, added a new element to Soviet calculations. They had to consider the preservation of the communist regime from a humiliating defeat, a defeat all the more ignominious in that it would be happening in a country actually bordering the Soviet Union. Moreover, it would be viewed by both clients and enemies as a defeat for a military that had been advised, trained, and equipped by the Soviet Union. Finally, there was the assessment of the attitude of the United States. The Americans, to date, had reacted with indifference to the political-military role staked out by the Soviet Union, even when this went so far as the establishment of a communist regime. When added to U.S. problems and preoccupation with Pakistan and Iran, the political risks and costs of military intervention on behalf of communism in Afghanistan appeared acceptable to Moscow.[14]

After a century of having played, in various guises and eras, the role of a buffer state, Afghanistan moved once again into the center of world politics. In the decade of the 1980s its geostrategic position, much to the sorrow of its people, was once more considered crucial by regional and world powers.

The Politics of Physical Geography

A century ago, the internal dividing line of mountains and desert in eastern Afghanistan was widely believed to be impassable by modern, that is, European, armies. There was, however, some concern on the part of the British that the route through western Afghanistan (Herat, Farah, Kandahar) skirting the end of the Hazarajat, and from there over the Bolan Pass to Quetta in Baluchistan, might prove to be a feasible route for a Russian invasion of the Indian subcontinent. Hence the constant strategic concern of the British in the nineteenth century was to keep the Russians (and their occasional allies, the Persians) out of Herat. It was in large part this concern that motivated the British policies that immediately occasioned the two nineteenth-century invasions of Afghanistan by the British. Eventually the British came to accept that although the strategic frontier of India might well be the Hindu Kush and Herat, it was too difficult physically to occupy Afghanistan in the face of inevitable Afghan resistance. A unified and stable Afghanistan and a ruler who agreed to forgo relations with other foreigners, when coupled with the natural barriers of geography and the human barrier of the strongly Muslim and well-armed Afghan tribes, would be sufficient to secure the defense of India's northwest frontier. Constant observation and intelligence were needed along with some periodic political pressure to make sure that the Russians (or later, the Turks or Germans) did not obtain enough political influence in the court of Kabul to turn its rulers into willing allies. The danger lay in that the Pushtun dynasty in Kabul was historically oriented toward India. It considered the Pushtun-inhabited border areas toward the Indus River as lost provinces of their empire.

Geography, however, is not a constant; its political significance is continually being altered by human intervention. Thus a number of modern developments after the 1950s had the effect of altering the accepted strategic wisdom of the previous century. Most important, a network of modern roads was constructed around and then through the Hindu Kush range to replace fair-weather passes that had previously impeded military movement. A beltway around the central core of the Hazarajat was connected with modern paved highways to the natural physical geographic exits from the country: Three in the north led to the USSR, two in the east to Pakistan, and one in the west to Iran. These were constructed with aid funds and engineering from both the Soviet Union and the United States. It was thus

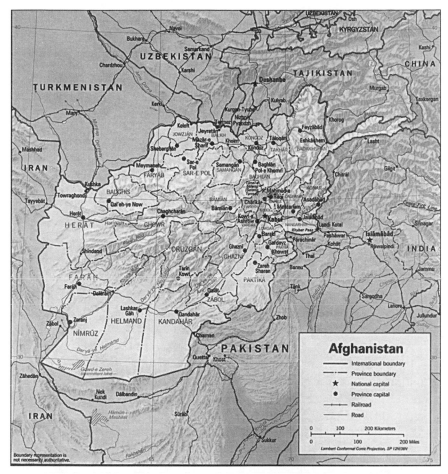

MAP 3.1   Afghanistan, political (Central Intelligence Agency Atlas, 1993)

briefly possible, for about a decade before 1978, for a traveler to enjoy a pleasant day's drive of 390 miles from the Soviet border on the Amu Darya to the Pakistani border at Torkham in the Khyber Pass. In the west it was possible, though it was 150 miles farther, to travel from the Iranian border at Islam Qala to the Pakistani border at Chaman via Herat and Kandahar. During the Soviet occupation these trunk roads sustained the occupying forces and served as the major targets of mujahidin attacks and Soviet mining. Bridges constructed over the Amu Darya by the Soviets (at first on pontoons, but then replaced beginning in 1982 by permanent construction) replaced ferries. War-damaged roads in 1992 had turned the journey of forty minutes between Jalalabad and the Khyber Pass border at Torkham into a four-hour nightmare of potholes, craters, blown bridges, and culverts.[15]

There was no similar construction of east-west roads in the Wakhan region to connect Afghanistan to China. The passes there are snowbound nine months of the year and the terrain daunting for construction. Besides, thus far, China's interest has been focused on Pakistan rather than Afghanistan. However, just south of this corridor with Afghanistan, the Chinese-constructed Karakorum Highway connects China to Pakistan through the Pakistani-occupied part of Kashmir. The road over the Khunjarab Pass has had a strategic impact on the entire region, including Afghanistan. Training camps in the Xinjiang Uighur Autonomous Region of China and arms for the resistance came through the pass.[16]

During the same period, a number of modern airports were opened with, as in the case of road construction, aid from the rival superpowers. Two of these, Bagram to the north of Kabul and Shindand to the south of Herat, were Soviet-built military air bases. Kabul's airport, which has a military section, was modernized and expanded, and the Americans built a large international civilian airport at Kandahar. The Kandahar airport, intended to serve as a major terminal for international air traffic, never saw much service beyond local flights, a source of Afghan dissatisfaction with the United States.[17] Smaller regional airports were built in major provincial centers, such as Kunduz, Herat, Mazar-i-Sharif, Bamiyan, and Jalalabad.

The Geopolitics of the Jihad

In the nineteenth and early twentieth centuries, Afghanistan acquired a special religious significance throughout the entire Muslim world reminiscent of its significance among Muslim states in the latter part of this century. Its significance stemmed from the fact that it was one of the few Muslim states not directly colonized by expanding European imperialism. Its status came to be symbolized by the towering figure of Sayyid Jamal-ad-Din, "al-Afghani" (1838–1897), perhaps the leading politically active Muslim of the past century who enjoyed international stature. Although he lived for a time in Afghanistan, where he had come to advise the amir, it is generally accepted by scholars outside Afghanistan that he was Iranian by birth and education.[18] Whatever the circumstances of his birth, Sayyid Jamal-ad-Din regarded himself as a citizen of the Islamic world as a whole and not of any particular Muslim state. His adoption of "al-Afghani" as his pen name reflected his belief that Afghans symbolized the anticolonial struggle. Moreover, because the Afghans lived on the fringes of the sectarian and political countries with which the more western-situated Islamic people were embroiled, they would be less controversial throughout the Islamic world as true defenders of Islam. Afghans have been slow to accept Sayyid Jamal-ad-Din as Iranian and in fact gave him an elaborate reinterment in Afghanistan as an honored native son.

Amir Abdul Rahman Khan, caught in the geopolitics of the Great Game, felt that Afghanistan's political situation precluded any attempt to fulfill the broader pan-Islamic politico-religious role for the Afghans envisioned by al-Afghani. Instead of turning the Afghans into the champions of Islam in opposition to the imperialists, he effectively capitalized on his local role as the defender of Islam inside Afghanistan. This allowed him to present religious justification for the enhancement of his power over the traditionally unruly tribal society, independent ulema and Sufis, and diverse ethnic groups. Only a unified country, he argued, could hope to resist the power of the Europeans. His jihad was thus waged against political rebels and Shi'ites (whom he regarded as non-Muslims) as well as against the last remaining pocket of non-Muslim *kafirs* (animist unbelievers) in the mountains of Kafiristan (Nuristan).

From 1978 on, Afghanistan's Islamic culture propelled it again into the center of regional and international struggle. The member states of the Organization of the Islamic Conference (OIC) and all Muslim states not obligated to the USSR through treaty overwhelmingly backed the resistance while those states that had a client relationship to the Soviet Union tried to stand with Kabul's Marxists. Cooperation within the OIC with regard to aid to the Islamic resistance of the mujahidin invigorated the organization despite the split in its ranks caused by fears of the export of the Iranian Revolution. By the mid-1980s the Afghan resistance had become a victim of the rivalry between Iran and Saudi Arabia (in cooperation with Pakistan), the two regional competitors for leadership of the Islamic world. This competition extends now to Central Asia and threatens to prolong the civil war in Afghanistan (see Chapter 7).

The Islamic nature of the Afghan resistance as a declaration of jihad—one of the most successful ever waged by a Muslim country—alarmed another regional player, India. With close military and economic ties to Moscow, a large Muslim population regarded with suspicion, and contention with Pakistan over Kashmir, India wholeheartedly supported the Afghan Marxists. This support took the form of political work in the Non-Aligned Movement, of which Afghanistan was a founding member, as well as media support and support in other international bodies. India also continued to maintain normal relations with Kabul as it became increasingly a pariah among other states and at international bodies. With the fall of the Marxist regime, and indeed the collapse of the Soviet Union, India's favored position in both Central Asia and Afghanistan has suffered.[19] The repercussions from India's backing of the loser in the Afghan jihad may continue as the issue of Kashmir periodically creates military crises with religious overtones.

No geopolitical assessment of the jihad in Afghanistan can be complete without an evaluation of the effects of the Afghan situation on the Muslim areas of the Soviet Union. Although the full impact of Afghanistan on Central Asia remains to be understood as the Central Asian republics clarify their identities with regard to Islam, the experience of individual Central Asians serving with the Red Army in Afghanistan has had some observable cultural effects. Thousands of Central Asians who served as interpreters and spies had their first opportunity to experience a Muslim culture, learn the Arabic alphabet, and meet obstinate, armed resistance to Russians. A result in no small part of this factor, since 1991 the Uzbek press in particular has revived memory of anti-Bolshevik resistance during the 1920s, and in a historical revisionist move many authors recall to public memory that earlier resistance as freedom fighters and true nationalists on the model of the Afghan resistance.[20]

Moreover, the sense of defiance fostered by the Afghan resistance fueled anti-Moscow activity as far as Estonia, Poland, and Chechnya and as close as Tajikistan. Setting aside the extent to which the Russian debacle in Afghanistan contributed to the moral bankruptcy of Soviet Marxism, the fact remains that the breakup of the Soviet Union has removed direct Russian presence from the immediate neighborhood of Afghanistan, with the exception of Russian troops in Tajikistan. Therefore, after nearly two centuries of constant distress about Russian threats, Afghanistan is free of this geopolitical concern.

The Geopolitics of the Islamic State

Two geopolitical factors stand out in the current post-jihad era of Afghan politics. First, the international situation has been dominated by the collapse of the Soviet Union and its replacement by the now formally independent (but still dependent economically and militarily) Central Asian states in the Russian-dominated Commonwealth of Independent States (CIS). At the same time, the "victor" of the Cold War, the United States, has continued its precipitously declining interest in Afghanistan in particular and in the region in general. This process became evident after the signing of the Geneva accords of 1988. After the Reagan-Bush administrations and their fascination with events in the Soviet Union and the CIS, U.S. interest shifted to focus on resolving Cold War issues rather than confrontation with an old enemy. Therefore, the United States, which had led the battle for justice for the Afghans, abandoned their cause at the end, when the dual problems of formation of a strong interim government and the accountability of the Soviet Union for the reconstruction of Afghanistan should have been of paramount interest to all those countries, especially the United States, which had shown such humanitarian and military concern for the Afghans. The U.S. withdrawal from resolution of these issues is nowhere better symbolized than in the lack of a diplomatic presence in Kabul. Justified from the security point of view, the U.S. position contrasts sharply with the continued maintenance of such representation by Pakistan, Iran, Turkey, and Saudi Arabia. Instead, the United States has relinquished its role to the United Nations, whose efforts since 1988 have been singularly ineffective.

Second, with the lessening of superpower involvement, the vacuum has been partially filled by greater scope for regional involvement in Afghan politics; Pakistan, Iran, and Saudi Arabia, and Uzbekistan since 1992, have, individually or in combination, tried to influence Afghan events with predictably disastrous results. The regional participants compete with one another throughout the region but have focused on Afghanistan and to some extent on Central Asia, which were regarded as clean canvas for the regional political artists.

Thus far this regional involvement has not brought the stability obtained in the competition by the previous set of rivals, the British and tzarist Russia, nor that of the Soviets and the Americans, who balanced each other's efforts with some benefit to the Afghan people. Individually and collectively, the regional powers are too weak in their own right and too distracted with internal and external problems to be effective in their stabilizing mission. They are also rivals for regional dominance and thus continue to support their particular Afghan favorites despite formal agreements. There is the additional factor at present of continued political involvement from the north of a new regional power, now in the form of the nominally postcommunist regime of Uzbekistan, which supports (along with the Russians) its own player on the Afghan political scene—the ethnic Uzbek general, Abdul Rashid Dustam, and, for fear of Taliban success, the ousted President Rabbani.

Hope for resolution of the Afghan civil war therefore includes a strong geopolitical dimension even after Soviet withdrawal. The complexion of this dimension has changed from a confrontation of East and West to the kind of Islamic state that can emerge in Afghanistan. Given that the issue of the role of Islam in all Muslim states remains fluid and potentially disruptive, the likelihood that current regional powers will reach any positive results remains slim.

Another avenue of hope lies in the stake that regional countries have in Afghan stability in order to take advantage of trade opportunities with Central Asia. The formation of the Economic Cooperation Organization and its inclusion of Afghanistan, offered for the first time since the sixteenth century the possibility for contiguous states to work together to construct infrastructure and build networks that would necessarily cross Afghanistan. Mazar-i-Sharif might yet function as the Balkh of old had on the Silk Road. Though prospects remain slim for regional cooperation, Pakistani profits from the import, and then the export, of Turkmen gas and petrochemical products appears to offer at least western Afghanistan some opportunities (see Chapter 7).

Chapter Four

Traditional Afghan Islam

In 1896, after overseeing the conquest of the non-Muslims of Kafiristan, Amir Abdul Rahman was given the title Ziya ul-Millat wa ad-Din (The Light of the Nation and of Religion). Thus this Afghan ruler who had contributed most toward bringing the traditional religious establishment under state supervision became instrumental in assuring that all lands allotted to Afghanistan by the end of the nineteenth century were predominantly peopled by Muslims. In the case of the *kafirs* of eastern Afghanistan, Sunni Islam became the accepted public faith. Despite concerted efforts to convert the Shi'ites to Sunni Islam, however, many who could left the country, a few converted, and the rest remained on the fringes of Afghan society clinging to their own interpretation of Islam. Today, at least two forms of Shi'ism, Ithna 'Ash'ara (Twelvers) or Imami, and Sabi'a (Seveners) or Isma'ili (Khoja branch) exist disharmoniously beside the dominant Sunni profession of most Afghans. With the exception of a small number of Jews related to Bukharan Jews of Central Asia, Sikhs, and Hindus, Afghanistan has been one of the most uniformly Muslim states in the entire eastern Islamic world. Yet, as David Busby Edwards has pointed out, the scholarly studies of religion in Afghanistan contain more information about Buddhism, a pre-Islamic faith of the area, than about Islam.[1] Indeed, even those studies of Islam in Afghanistan that have been undertaken have been conducted by anthropologists, whose efforts have led to considerable information about communal relationships and folk practices but little about the formal structure of religion. Yet traditional Islam, which includes the formal structure of religion, has played a key role in shaping events in the twentieth century.[2]

Located at the crossroads of south and central Asia, the land that became Afghanistan by the late eighteenth century had not only been traversed by Islamic armies early, but it had also served as the launching pad for zealous Islamicized rulers who sent their armies into areas farther east and south, especially toward India. Its geographic position and mountainous terrain also gave much of northeastern Afghanistan status as a place of refuge for those needing to flee because they were regarded as heretics. Thus the Badakhshan region, stretching into the Pamirs, provided refuge for Isma'ilis, the extreme Shi'ites who posed a real and imagined threat to Sunni rulers since the eleventh century. The central belt of mountains, the Hindu Kush, became the traditional homeland of the Hazaras, the largest Imami Shi'a group in Afghanistan. With the exception of a small enclave of Pushtuns who are Shi'a, a small group of Hazara who are Sunni and others who are Isma'ili, and the special case of the Qizilbash, also Shi'a, the other Muslims of Afghanistan are Sunni. In this respect, Afghans resemble the Muslims in areas to the north (Uzbeks, Tajiks, Turkmens) and the south (Baluchis, Punjabis, Sindis) as well as the Muslims of India. Like much of the worldwide Muslim population, the *madhhab* (school) of Sunni Islam that they follow is the Hanafi, which is the most juridically liberal of the four Sunni systems. Into every Afghan constitution until the Da'ud constitution of 1977, this adherence to Islam in its Sunni Hanafi form has been prominently included.[3] Islam therefore binds Afghans to their neighbors (as through the Organization of the Islamic Conference) as well as together across the otherwise bitter divide of ethnic groups.

In this chapter we present traditional Islam within the context of recent history, and as a contrast to both modern Islamists and antireligious ideologies such as those of Marxists and other far leftists. In the scheme of this volume, traditional Islam is represented by the symbolic term "mullah," but for our purposes it encompasses all Afghan political players who were specifically not bound within Marxism or conscientiously and deliberately Islamists. Most Afghans would fall within this category whether they are Sunni or Shi'a. That is, while their level of religious observance might differ, former King Zahir as well as most tribal leaders, village elders, teachers, students, and others would fall within this category. As traditional Muslims they would observe birth, marriage, and burial customs, the basic admonitions of the faith with regard to monotheism, worship, family law, and to a lesser or greater extent, dietary laws, and observance of fasting and holy days. Perhaps even more important, they would be steeped in the lore of Afghan Islam, which includes not only popular stories about the life of the family of the Prophet, saintly tales related to Sufi figures, and memorized verses but also traditions associated with holy places such as the sepulchre in Mazar-i-Sharif, believed to stand over the remains of the fourth caliph Ali.

Although there are basic factors to address such as the relationship of traditional Sunni and Shi'a and the role of the non-Muslims and of the Isma'ilis, more important here is that as the war politicized so much of Afghan society, it magnified the importance of traditional Islam as a political force even though it had otherwise played a relatively minor political role among Afghans in general. Before entering into an analysis of the role

Tajik baker with Afghan nan in his Herat bakery. (R. H. Magnus, 1965)

Workmen in the tile restoration shop at the Congregational Mosque of Herat. (R. H. Magnus, 1970)

Author (E.N.) with Pushtun girls in a village outside Jalalabad in her *60 Minutes* disguise after the Soviet invasion (E. Naby, 1980)

Camels delivering wood supply in Mazar-i-Sharif, overseen by Hazara housekeepers. (E. Naby, 1964)

Pushtun boys on a picnic, Wardak province. (R. H. Magnus, 1970)

of traditional Islam vis-à-vis Marxists and Islamists, it is useful to examine Islamic institutions, the basic belief system and its propagation, and Sufi orders and other forms of confrereship, to the extent that information about these aspects of traditional Islam is available for Afghanistan.

Islamic Institutions and the State

Sunni Islam has historically been nonhierarchical and noncentralized. Because dispersed authority has made the incorporation of Sunni Islam into the centralized, authoritarian state complicated, in several instances, in the modern period, state authority has created a hierarchy in order to wield greater control. This was done in the Ottoman Empire as well as in the Soviet Union after 1941.[4]

In Afghanistan, the isolated valleys and oasis towns as well as ethnic and linguistic differences among people lent themselves well to the observance of Islam without the need to communicate in a hierarchical line with leadership. In this respect Imami Shi'ism and especially the Isma'ili sect are far more structured than is Sunni Islam.

For rural Afghans, who constituted well over 80 percent of the population before the Soviet invasion in 1979,[5] the main Islamic institution with which they were associated was the mosque (*masjid*), often a simple one-room edifice in the village. Larger towns had mosques in each quarter or *mahal*. The mosque would be served by a mullah (or more formally put, the imam), a man who led the prayer, presented a sermon on Fridays especially, recited or read from the Koran, officiated at life-cycle services, adjudicated disputes, and taught boys how to read the Koran. His income came from payment for services, including teaching, and the maintenance of the place of worship would be part of communal responsibility or assumed by a rich patron. The system of charitable foundations (*awqaf*), which in past centuries supported religious and charitable work and property, had been eliminated in Afghanistan by Amir Abdul Rahman. Only the property immediately adjoining a mosque or shrine was exempt from this confiscation. Mullahs were married if able, but not consecrated in any way as are clerics in other faiths. Through their moral position they wielded considerable influence in their communities and were treated with deference according to their piety.

In addition to the village mullahs, who were not particularly well versed in either the faith or otherwise, others in the community also commanded respect associated with their religious position. Families that traced descent from the Prophet, sayyids, or *khwajazadas* are relatively endogamous and carry the titles *sayyid*, *khwaja*, or *mir* before the name of males in the family. They are treated with deference and enjoy influence but do not perform any formal function. Those involved either as teachers or students in the religious schools (*madrasas*) were titled *mawlawi*, although this title applied in some parts of Afghanistan to leaders of Sufi orders, and elsewhere the term can refer to judges. The *mawlawis*, whether teachers and students or members of Sufi orders, were quite influential because of their network of associations. We will discuss the Sufi orders later, but for now the titles by which Sufi leaders are known are useful to note: *pir, eshan, mawlawi,* and *khalifa.*

The term ulema, literally meaning the learned ones (singular alim), applies to Muslim scholars formally trained at many levels. Their standing in the community is determined in large part by their level of training. The institutional system that produced the ulema in the past was the madrasa, which young men could attend either after having studied with a mullah in a mosque school, or, for the higher socioeconomic levels, after about ten years of study with a family tutor (*nazim*). After the Mongol invasion in the thirteenth century and the subsequent decline of Central Asian cities, the madrasa system in Afghan areas never recovered (as in Balkh, for example), except in Herat, which served briefly as capital for a branch of the

Timurids. Herat still boasted six madrasas in the nineteenth century, and Peshawar had a few more. Lesser madrasas existed in Ghazni, Maimana, and Kandahar well into the 1970s. However, since there were no madrasas of wide repute in Afghanistan, after basic training motivated scholars would undertake travel to one of the madrasas of Bukhara, such as the Mir Arab Madrasa, or to India, especially to the Deoband school after it gained reputation by the late nineteenth century as a theologically traditional institution with new educational methods. As political restrictions began to prevent Afghans from traveling to Central Asia, improved travel opportunities allowed for access to the great learning institutions of Egypt and Syria. By the mid–twentieth century, study at al-Azhar in Cairo was not unusual for Afghan Muslim scholars, whereas two generations earlier they might have gone to Deoband or Bukhara.

The curriculum of the madrasas, while fixed around theological and juridical studies, underwent some change over the years to include mathematics and medicine (Yunani/Greek) as well as increasingly language-specific poetry. In Afghanistan, Central Asia, and India, Persian poetry provided the backbone of literature even among non-Persian-speaking communities such as Uzbeks, Pushtuns, and Punjabis.[6] By the late nineteenth century, in many influential corners of the Islamic region around Afghanistan, the need to revamp the traditional education system was recognized, and this movement eventually destroyed the importance of the madrasas as general institutions of learning. The Deoband school became a compromise model of education, as did the Jadidist system of education introduced in Samarkand, Tashkent, and Bukhara. But in most areas, in the aftermath of the wave of social and political reforms of the 1920s, madrasas as institutions of education for elites gradually came to be replaced by publicly funded, largely secular schools. In Afghanistan the need for special training in law, the military, and foreign languages as well as the modern sciences led to a diminished role for the madrasa system beginning as early as the reign of Amir Abdul Rahman. By the 1960s, when political confrontation began to emerge in Afghanistan, the madrasa was already relegated to the role of seminary, in contrast to the university and other preparatory schools. It should be noted, however, that government-funded schools served the educational needs of a small proportion of the population, mainly urban. Although many among the Islamists and Marxists received their education within the government system, to the extent that the bulk of the population was literate at all, it benefited from mosque schools and from madrasas. The traditional Islamic leadership, the ulema, relied almost exclusively on this system.

Historically, the students of the madrasas served as *qazis* (judges) or as *mufti* (canon lawyers), although poets and historians might also emerge from their ranks. As long as Afghanistan was ruled mainly by *shariʻa* (Islamic law), the opinion of the *qazi* and the *fatwa* of the *mufti* formed the rule of law. However, after civil codes were introduced in 1925 under King Amanullah, the position of judge came to change, albeit very gradually. Even before that, however, Amir Abdul Rahman had brought the power of the state to bear on the entire ulema establishment, from the local mullahs to the *qazi* and *mufti*. He not only subjugated the mullahs to the state but also adjusted the method of religious education by introducing a special madrasa in Kabul to train students in law who would enter the bureaucracy and the judiciary.[7] Later, the introduction of public schools, though never pervasive at the village level, nonetheless further eroded the religiously run educational system. Thus by the 1960s the entire traditionally educated religious establishment had already been shaken from its historic position as provider of the sole institutional system of education. By extension, the educational role of the ulema had also been reduced, at least in Kabul. Their communal leadership status, however, was enhanced as the Kabul governments increasingly became radicalized after 1973.

The responsibility for education among the resistance has fallen both to the remaining ulema, although progressively fewer were trained after the 1950s, and to government teachers who cooperated with the resistance. In conditions of war, however, education has suffered, even in the best-administered areas. Education beyond literacy has been difficult to acquire within Afghanistan because of the military recruitment of both teachers and students, and in the refugee areas education became dependent on the prescriptions of the political parties that took charge of administering the camps. Under these circumstances, while traditional Islam merely survived, the radicalized Islam of the Islamist groups prospered as they used the opportunity provided by the camps to indoctrinate while teaching basic literacy. The requirements of the war for efficiency and organization inherently worked to the advantage of the Islamist political parties. The outcome of the breakdown of the educational system has been that Afghanistan's literacy rate has dropped. Despite the civil war, however, in pockets of the country, among returning refugees and those who never left, schools are being reinstituted. In Herat, Badakhshan, and Kandahar resistance leaders, in cooperation with a combination of local teachers and mullahs, run schools. In Mazar-i-Sharif the ethnic Uzbek militia leader Abdul Rashid Dustam (promoted to General in 1992 by President Sibghatullah Mujaddidi), appears to have established schools to which the Iranian government has offered textbooks.[8] The likelihood is that when a new school system reemerges, it will continue the system of public education, but one in which, however, Islamic education and teachers trained in Islamic theology and practice will make a greater contribution than before 1973.

In a purely Islamic society, the prevailing juridical institutions administer the law according to the *shari'a*, with modifications for nonintrusive local custom. This ideal system, as juridical systems are wont to do, to some extent becomes entangled in the demands of politics, depending on the degree of authoritarianism of the state. In Afghanistan both sets of conflicts existed in the administration of the *shari'a*, despite the lip service paid to the traditional Islam of society. Customary law, the Pushtunwali of the Afghan tribes, stood contrary to the *shari'a* on many issues, especially on *badal*, the generational blood feuds among Pushtun tribes, and on the usurpation of land belonging to a rival. Since Afghanistan had been ruled during its history as a country by Pushtuns, backed by tribal military levies, the code of the Pushtuns prevailed widely in their confrontations with other ethnic groups, especially the Hazara, as well as among Pushtuns themselves. The coexistence of the Pushtunwali with the *shari'a* was achieved only through the arbitration by mullahs and other ulema, whose community stature allowed them to bridge the chasm between the two sets of laws.[9] Indeed, the Pushtunwali specifically allows for mullahs to intercede to modify the code in special instances.[10] Political interference also came from the rulers, locally or centrally. Abdul Rahman, for example, regarded himself as the sole arbiter in law when the *shari'a* was unclear on an issue or when he favored a more repressive *shari'a* school (such as the Maliki) over the more lenient Hanafi school.[11]

The first Afghan constitution (1923) ushered in the period of reliance on statutory law, although statutory and *shari'a* law have since then shared the bench, albeit unevenly and with difficulty. Despite the removal of King Amanullah and the repudiation of many of his reforms, the country continued to function under a constitution as well as sets of civil laws. The *shari'a* never fully replaced the conviction of the need for civil law, except briefly during the nine-month rule of Habibullah Ghazi II (Bacha-i Saqao).

During the period of national consolidation that followed the restoration of a Pushtun monarchy, the Faculty of Law and Political Science was created (1937), which enjoyed French government support. Later this faculty became part of Kabul University (1946). The inclusion also of the Shari'at Faculty into the university allowed the government to press for the replacement, by attrition, of the *mawlawi* judges as university graduates became available. The goal for the manning of the judiciary as envisioned in the constitution of 1964 and the legal codes drafted in 1967 was to recruit university graduates and candidates with a balanced knowledge of both the *shari'a* and secular civil law. Madrasa graduates continued to enter the judiciary, but the balance was clearly in favor of university graduates. By the 1960s the Shari'at Faculty had become a training ground for Islamists, thus making it difficult for the traditionally educated candidates from the madrasas to compete successfully for the positions available. From the perspective of the government, however, the problem of balance was between that of *shari'a* training and training in statutory law, not the plight of madrasa graduates. Dissatisfaction among madrasa students became focused on the government.

The last prime minister under the monarchy, Muhammad Musa Shafiq (1972–1973) appeared to many, in both the modernizing government camp and the traditional Islamic camp, to embody the compromise jurist who would ease the problem of *shari'a* versus statutory law. Shafiq had trained with a *mawlawi* and then had studied at the Shari'at Faculty, followed by al-Azhar and then Columbia University, where he studied Islamic and comparative law. His career was cut short by the Da'ud coup of 1973, and he was taken from arrest to execution by the Nur Muhammad Taraki regime.

The leaders of the 1978 coup ruled by decree. Within seven months of the coup, the government issued eight decrees aimed at revolutionizing social and economic relations throughout the country. During that period, the ability of the government to enforce its decrees eroded rapidly, especially in the countryside. As resistance followed repression, civil judicial activity collapsed. It remained to the various parts of the country to govern themselves. As legal scholar Mohammad Hashim Kamali aptly concludes: "Instability and lack of continuity in the legal and constitutional order of Afghanistan tend to re-enforce the vital role that Islam and its Shari'a play as stabilizing influence amidst conflicting changes imposed by different regimes."[12] Thus the reintroduction of exclusive *shari'a* rule tempered by local custom (*adat*) during the 1980s among the resistance in those areas free of Kabul's control is an indication of the continuity of traditional Islam as well as its reliability. In Herat there was a sufficient number of ulema to allow for two sets of courts—a preliminary court as well as a court of appeals. In all, during the period of resistance the Afghan countryside appears to have fallen back into the traditional pattern of law regarding daily living, and *shari'a* adjudication was accepted in matters ranging from land use (cultivation of the land of those who became refugees) to taxation.[13]

The situation in the country since the resistance entered Kabul and the communist regime ended appears to have followed the juridical patterns established during the 1980s in places where the resistance was in control—that is, *shari'a* law provides what stability exists while the civil war rages. How a new Afghan central government deals with issues of constitutional and civil law remains to be seen. However, setting aside the differences between the Islamists and traditionalists, there is a strong likelihood that institution of *shari'a* law will take the dominant position vis-à-vis statutory law.

Of the traditional Islamic institutions affecting Afghan society, education and law are the most basic. Other systems, such as village authority organization, landholding patterns, money and banking systems, and gender issues rely heavily on local custom, often enforced by interpretation of Islamic law. In the course of the confrontation that developed with the accession to power of the communists, traditional Islamic groups did not

coalesce as organized groups until the ineptitude of the execution of reforms bestirred local people to oppose the central government. Otherwise
the reforms themselves might have been justifiable even along Islamic lines,
especially land redistribution in areas such as Herat and Kandahar where
absentee landlords were a problem. The literacy program was derailed because it was imposed without regard to custom (mixing of the sexes in one
class, forcing the elderly into classrooms, bringing into the community
strangers to administer and teach, rather than recruiting local people), and
without local input, rather than because of intrinsic opposition from traditional Islamic elements to secularized literacy classes. However, anticipating
opposition from traditional elements, the government of Nur Muhammad
Taraki and Hafizullah Amin made many arrests of traditional leaders in far-
flung parts of the country.[14]

With the Soviet invasion, opposition to Kabul strengthened even among
traditional Islamic elements who might not have been affected earlier—
those people who might not have understood the Marxist rhetoric of the
communists and felt threatened by it, and recognized that a Kabul government dependent on Soviet troops (even if some were Central Asians) presented an alien demeanor. A loosely organized party began to emerge that
brought together this regionally diverse and amorphous traditional Islamic
element. The party called the Harakat-i Inqilab-i Islami (Islamic Revolutionary Movement), headed by the leader of a madrasa, Mawlana Muhammad Nabi Muhammadi, was at first the numerically largest party among
the resistance. Its loose organization and lack of commitment to a radical
ideology was attractive as traditional Islamic elements became active fighters. The party eventually fell victim to two problems, both stemming from
its looseness: It was easily infiltrated by government and leftist individuals,
and it was unable efficiently to supply arms to its fighters. Therefore, while
it continued to function as a moderate, pro-monarchy, pro-*shari'a* party, its
members drifted away to other Islamist parties, especially in Herat. In addition to Mawlana Muhammad Nabi Muhammadi, others involved with the
traditional educational system also led resistance movements throughout
the war, such as Mawlana Muhsini, Mawlana Baqi Ahmad, and others.

Although traditional Islam was under constant and direct pressure, as
government continued to encroach on it through the educational and judicial institutions, as a result of the invasion it was strengthened and to some
extent radicalized. Had the invasion not occurred, that is, had Afghanistan
continued as a constitutional monarchy opposed by Islamists alone, would
traditional Islam have become as politicized as it did? Would it have found
a modus vivendi with a compromising government, such as one headed by
Muhammad Musa Shafiq, and followed the relatively smooth path taken
by Pakistan in this regard? Can traditional Islam step back from being a
participant in the establishment of strict and idealistic Islamic institutions?

The answer may lie in looking at the belief system in traditional Islam before the years of war.

The Belief Systems and Their Sociopolitical Implications

Analyzing the relative importance of the several aspects of Sunni Islam in the system of belief in Afghanistan is complicated by two major factors: (1) Afghanistan includes a particularly diverse population that has existed for much of the period since 1747, without either the centralization or a communication system to develop uniformity in a common code of belief. (2) Because of the paucity of literacy-based institutional means for the transmission of a formal system of belief, practice and belief vary. With these caveats in mind, the formal system of belief may be understood through a consideration of the salient features of each of the three different Muslim groups in the country as broadly known, and then a closer look at the particulars and peculiarities of Sunni Islam in various parts of Afghanistan.

Important in the consolidation of the country or the "internal imperialism" as practiced by the Amir Abdul Rahman were the belief communities of Afghanistan, which permeated political and economic relations. Grasping religious authority for political action provided the amir with justification for pacifying active opposition, as in the north, or extending authority, as in the east and central areas of the country. The communal divisions of the country did not change substantially between the period of the amir and the postcommunist period, when these differences have become a critical element in the civil war. The heightened politicization of Shi'a (Imami and Isma'ili) and Sunni Islam, within Afghanistan and in the region, contributes to the groups' inability to find compromise, in Kabul and the countryside.

Shi'ism in Afghanistan appears in two doctrinally distinct forms: Imami (Ithna 'Ash'ara or Twelvers); and Isma'ili (Sabi'a or Seveners) belonging to the Khoja rather than the Bohra branch. For the most part, the two Shi'a groups do not interact and, with some exceptions, are separated into distinct ethnolinguistic, geographical, and historical identities.[15] The overlap, too, is significant to an understanding of contemporary politics.

The Imami Shi'a

During the mid-1970s Imami Shi'a as a whole numbered roughly 1.3 million, consisting mainly of Hazara and Farsiwan, with smaller groups of Qizilbash and Pushtuns.[16] The advanced training of Imami Shi'a leadership took place in Iraq, at the madrasa of the shrine city An-Najaf—where many Iranian Shi'a leaders also trained, and not in Iran where Iranian Shi'a clerics receive most of their training.[17] The mother languages of most Afghan Imami Shi'a are dialects of Persian/Dari (Hazaras, Farsiwans, Qizilbash), whereas the religious language is primarily Arabic, the language that binds together all advanced Islamic writing regardless of ethnic group.

Some identity issues are important to understanding the position of the Shi'a in Afghanistan. The socioreligious concept of *takiya* (dissimulation) is significant: *Takiya* allows practitioners of Shi'ism to dissimulate their religious affiliation if they need to protect themselves against oppression based on religion. Thus the Qizilbash in particular, who live in urban areas, are able to take advantage of this concept, as can the rural dwelling Farsiwan, whose dialect and appearance do not distinguish them in particular from Sunni Persian speakers such as the Tajik.[18] The Hazara, however, display distinct Mongoloid features, which sets them apart from other ethnic groups and therefore do not allow them to pretend to be what they are not.

The catechism of Imami Shi'ism, and the practical outcome of these concepts in precommunist Afghanistan, includes the following:

1. *Authority:* In formal Shi'ism, the concept of the living Imam holds that the mantle of the Prophet Muhammad passed within his hereditary line through his daughter Fatima and thence through the male line beginning with the Caliph Ali, Fatima's husband. The twelfth Imam, Muhammad al-Mahdi, disappeared in 940 C.E. (the Greater Occultation), but he is the Mahdi ("the one guided by God") who will return. In his absence, the Shi'a hierarchical structure allows for wide latitude of interpretation of earthly and spiritual matters, whence comes the conflict inherent in Shi'ism between temporal authority and the Shi'a hierarchy. In Afghanistan, where, unlike in Iran, Shi'ism has never been the state religion and where Shi'a populations often live in isolated terrain, authority has grown out of social context rather than formal religious structure. During the years of war, exposure to revolutionary Shi'ism from Iran brought to the surface the conflict in authority stemming from religious sanction and traditional practice.

2. *Martyrdom:* The suffering of the Imams, especially of Husain, the younger son of Ali, at the hands of his rivals for the Caliphate in 680 C.E., has translated into a passion that exhibits both spiritual and physical implications for Shi'a communities worldwide. Spiritually, martyrdom becomes a potent motivation for religious war, less for the rewards of paradise than in imitation of the martyrdom of the Imams. Physically, the annual commemoration of the seventh-century martyrdom, either through procession and performance or through memorial services during the first ten days (Ashura) of the Islamic lunar month of Muharram, rejuvenates the Shi'a commu-

nity's separateness from its Sunni neighbors, whose forces opposed Imam Husain. By allowing the Ashura performance and procession in the Hazara Shi'a quarter of Kabul during the 1960s, the Afghan monarchy signaled its respect for this community, which had been long persecuted, especially by the Pushtuns.

3. *Descent:* Because of the Imamate concept, the position of those claiming descent from the Prophet in general is more important in Shi'ism than in Sunni Islam. Sayyids, or the descendants of the Prophet when addressed as *mir* or *khwaja,* serve a wide purpose as traditional leaders, often filling positions that in Afghan Sunni Islam might be held by Sufi leaders. Shi'a Islam has generally frowned on Islamic mysticism, especially in periods of orthodox hierarchical authority. Sayyids also supplied the ranks of those seeking higher religious education, mainly in Iraq but also in Iran. A madrasa-trained person, sayyid or not, acquired the title *shaykh.*

4. *Juridical authority:* The supplementary texts (Hadith and commentaries on the Koran) accepted in Shi'ism differ from those in Sunni Islam, as the Shi'a place greater emphasis on the traditions of the Imams derived from the basic tenets of Shi'a belief that are rooted in the Imamate concept. For this reason, the Hanafi *shari'a* law and courts ascendant in Afghanistan, both de facto and later de jure, as applied to Shi'a, have appeared unfair in later years. By 1977 jurists opted to avoid defining the legal school to be adopted, at least in the constitution, in order to mollify Shi'a circles.

When the Khalqi regime came to power the Hazaras rebelled very soon after the Nuristanis. Since both lived in relatively compact and remote areas of the country, they succeeded in maintaining continual autonomy during the war. The Hazara resistance organized under traditional Shi'a leadership (Sayyid Ali Beheshti and the Shura-i Inqilab-i Ittefaq-i Islami-i Afghanistan [Revolutionary Council of the Islamic Union of Afghanistan], the Shura for short), but dissension soon pitted Shi'a against one another when a dedicated Shi'a Islamist group arose. The Sazman-i Nasr-i Afghanistan (Victory Organization of Afghanistan, commonly referred to as NASR), headed by Mir Husain Sadeqi, stressed the radical Shi'a line of Iran's Ayatollah Khomeini. In one of its tracts, it defines order of (spiritual and temporal) authority as follows: "The authoritative governing of the Muslim world and the rule of law (*vilayat-i faqih*) is continued through the line of the Imamate in the Age of Occultation. The aim of belief is in the leadership of jurists and responsible, pious and faithful Muslims who deserve obedience after God and the Prophet."[19]

Fighting between the aggressively Islamist NASR and the more traditional Shura destroyed any peace that the Hazarajat might have enjoyed because government and Soviet troops did not menace it. As NASR gradually distanced itself from Iran, new, pro-Iran groups arose in an escalatingly Islamist pattern. In the absence of outside forces, the civil war that raged in the Hazarajat pitted traditional Islam against radical Islamists. Thus the civil war in the Hazarajat became a prelude to the civil war that inflamed the rest of the country once the communist government in Kabul had been subdued.

As Olivier Roy points out, the resistance in the Hazarajat was complicated not only with the shifting relationship with Iran but also by the sociopolitical situation in the Hazarajat, which was "feudal."[20] Other Imami Shi'a, the Farsiwan and to some extent the Qizilbash, proved more effective in the fight against the Russians because they were less subject to the vagaries of Iranian politics and to internal communal conflict, as seen in the Hazarajat between traditional society and the revolutionary and Islamist forces.

The Isma'ilis

The position of the Isma'ilis of Afghanistan is little discussed in works about Afghanistan, and not at all in analyses of the last two decades. Their role in northeast Afghanistan continues to provide a critical weight not only in Kabul's interaction with the Dustam faction in Mazar-i-Sharif but also in Kabul's relations with Dushanbe in the course of the Tajik civil war and refugee situation that began in summer 1992. The Isma'ilis of Afghanistan are part of the relatively large and compact body of the followers of the Agha Khan. After centuries of splintering, missionary work, persecution, and decline, by the mid–nineteenth century the Isma'ilis reemerged divided into the two main branches in existence in the eastern Islamic world: the Nizari Isma'ilis (called Khojas, followers of the Agha Khan) and the Musta'lian Isma'ilis (called Bohras or Bohoras).[21] The communities in the Wakhan, Badakhshan (both divided between Tajikistan and Afghanistan), Chitral, Gilgit, Hunza (located in Pakistan), and the eastern Pamirs (falling within Chinese borders) form a closely knit community that, despite international borders, maintains communication among locales.[22] This community includes speakers of many different languages, mostly within the Iranian family of languages. Persian has become the language of religious writing, and it is the language that allows communication among a broad segment of the male population. Thus, as they have acquired the written national languages of the countries in which they reside, Russian and Tajiki in Tajikistan, Chinese and Uighur in the Xinjiang Uighur Autonomous Region, Dari/Pushtu in Afghanistan, and Urdu in Pakistan, Persian has served to tie them together. In Afghanistan, the northeast Isma'ilis speak languages named after the valleys and mountains in which they reside. These are Shugni, Ishkashimi, Roshani, and Wakhi among others. Although this is the only ethnolinguistic grouping in Afghanistan that is Isma'ili, the Isma'ilis of Afghanistan are not confined to this northeast area, nor to these small mountainous groups. Isma'ilis are to be found north of the Salang Pass among both Tajiks and Hazaras. Their numbers in Afghanistan are difficult to estimate, but before the Soviet invasion the total population numbered no more than perhaps 250,000.

Isma'ilis, also called Seveners, take their name from Isma'il, the seventh Shi'a Imam and son of Imam Ja'far al-Sadiq. In the eighth century, when Isma'il died, a faction refused to accept his brother as Imam and insisted that his son be accepted as the true Imam: thus the split with the main Shi'ites over descent in the Imamate. This splinter group came to be commonly called Isma'ili or Seveners as opposed to the Ja'farites or Twelvers, who form the main body of Shi'ism.

Over the years, doctrinal and political dissension has resulted in the emergence of many more sects among the Isma'ilis, mainly as a result of disputes in lineage. The Druze of Lebanon and Israel are one such sect. Many sects disappeared, but those that have survived have been marked by a belief in the authority of the living Imam, who in the case of the Isma'ili sect of Afghanistan and Central Asia is the Agha Khan. The Bohras of India believe that the Imam went into Occultation—that is, a linear descendent of Isma'il, the seventh Imam, disappeared and is the awaited one, the Mahdi, in similar fashion to the main body of Shi'ites, with a difference about the particular descendent of the Imam who went into Occultation and is awaited.

Nizari Isma'ilism, with which we are concerned here, is distinguished by the two major doctrinal tenets:

1. *The Living Imam:* This concept implies two distinguishing characteristics for the Nizaris. First, that the Living Imam is the arbiter of spiritual and temporal issues in the life of the community, and second, that the community is constructed in a pyramidal hierarchical structure. The hierarchical structure allows for greater authoritarian control than might otherwise exist as well as a greater possibility for concerted communal action, supported by a network that is not necessarily visible to an outsider.

2. *The* zahir *(apparent) and the* batin *(hidden):* This concept allows for escalating levels of sophistication in the faith and for the accommodation of mystical (Sufi) concepts, such as the final unification with the first intelligence, as well as esoteric understanding of the cosmic order.

Over the centuries, because of persecutions—and perhaps also because of interpretation of doctrine—secrecy and dissimulation have surrounded the communities of Isma'ilis, especially those in northeast Afghanistan. Living in often ethnolinguistically exclusive unisect villages, their neighbors have accused the Isma'ilis of fantastic digressions from normal Islamic practice and of cabalistic ritual. Added to the fact that textual materials were hidden (and literacy in general declined after Alamut—the stronghold of the sect in northern Iran—was destroyed by the Mongols), Isma'ilis were frequently shunned as heretics by Imami Shi'a as well as by Sunni Muslims.

Under the reorganization of the Nizari community by Agha Khan III (1877–1957) and the current Agha Khan IV (Shah Karim al-Husayni), Isma'ilis have concentrated on education, trade, and agriculture. Because of his doctrinally sanctioned authority to direct the community at large, Agha Khan III appointed Sayyid Nadir Shah Husain as the head of the Isma'ili community in Afghanistan. He held this post for more than four decades, until his death in 1971. His sons, well educated privately, served in prominent positions, and Sayyid Shah Nasir Naderi, the son who succeeded as Sayyid-e Kayan (community head), served as vice president of the People's Assembly in Kabul in 1968. After being imprisoned by successive coup leaders in 1973 and 1978, he was freed in 1980 by the Parchamis, the branch of the Communist Party that took power after the Soviet invasion, and left for London. His brother, Sayyid Mansur, is acting head of the community in his absence, and another brother has served as deputy head of the Hazara community. A third brother, Major General Sayyid Ja'far Nadiri, joined the Uzbek General Dustam in opposition to the Burhanuddin Rabbani regime in Kabul and operates out of Mazar-i-Sharif. The family has also been active in forming commercial enterprises.[23]

Observers of the resistance have commented on the lack of cooperation from the Isma'ili community in the struggle against the communist governments in Kabul as well as against the Soviets. In part, this community-wide reluctance may be ascribable to the self-preservation instincts of a persecuted group, though Pakistani sources claim to have intercepted explicit instructions from the Agha Khan IV to his followers in Afghanistan to support the communist regime.[24] Should the general perception among the now victorious mujahidin be that the Isma'ilis function as a hierarchical instrument against them, with instructions from the outside, the future for Isma'ilis in an Afghanistan that is run by traditional or Islamist groups may be quite grim.

There may be other evidence too that would demonstrate Isma'ili sympathy with the communist regime, or at least unwillingness to help the resistance. Sultan Ali Keshtmand (b. 1935), a founding member of the PDPA and member of its Central Committee in 1965, held successively more responsible posts in the party and the government, especially during the Parcham ascendancy. The highest placed Isma'ili serving in the governments formed by the PDPA, Keshtmand was prime minister (1981), then first vice president

(1990). His sister was the second wife of Tahir Badakhshi, the Parchami renegade who headed Sitam-i Milli (Against National Oppression), the pro-minority, anti-Pushtun communist party. The two men were both arrested in late summer 1978 when activists of the rival communist Khalqis were rounded up. Badakhshi's arrest led to the kidnapping and assassination of U.S. Ambassador Adolph Dubs in February 1979. Under Hafizullah Amin, Badakhshi was executed (October 17, 1979), but Keshtmand was released. Pushtun sources have continued to accuse Keshtmand of anti-Pushtun and pro-minority sympathies, which the Soviets manipulated to create ethnic tensions.[25] Keshtmand's wife, Karima, was secretary of the Democratic Organization of Afghan Women, a Soviet-style women's organization used to spearhead the mobilization of women in support of the PDPA.[26] It is not clear that the Sitam-i Milli drew its estimated 300 members from among Isma'ilis, but the group's strength was consolidated in Badakhshan, where it was virtually annihilated in 1980 by mujahidin and by government/Soviet forces, though not in cooperation with each other.[27]

The traditional Isma'ili authority structure as well as their small numbers make the community a target of suspicion, even if its members only remain on the sidelines. As pointed out earlier, however, Isma'ilis span the Afghan-Tajik border. Interactions across the border have become increasingly easier as the Afghan and then Tajik civil wars have led to extragovernmental border crossings. A future division of Afghanistan (in the fashion of Yugoslavia) into Pushtun, Tajik, Uzbek, and other parts could allow Afghanistan's Isma'ilis to entertain thoughts of a future in which they joined more completely with their co-religionists in Tajikistan. It is such a tendency that may fuel fears of the coalition in Mazar-i-Sharif between the Uzbek militia leader Dustam and the brother of the Isma'ili leader of Afghanistan referred to earlier. Suspicions such as these by Afghans hampered the efforts of the United Nations refugee aid organization, Operation Salaam, which was headed by Prince Sadruddin, the uncle of Agha Khan IV and a respected international civil servant. Afghan leaders voiced suspicion that Operation Salaam was cooperating with the communist regime in Kabul and belittling the mujahidin struggle when Prince Sadruddin disapproved of a Thai mine detection project, which used dogs to locate mines, on the grounds that he was overly concerned for the animals. To many Afghans, this highly Westernized Isma'ili appeared to value the lives of dogs more than Sunni Afghans.

To avoid unintended affront to local governments and thus raise animosity toward the Agha Khan or his followers, the office of the Agha Khan IV has moved very carefully in Central Asia, where his followers have been agitating for his direct leadership and help since the late 1980s. The cross-border situation of the Isma'ilis illustrates one more complication in the Tajik-Afghan interaction and will receive further attention in Chapter 7.

The Sunnis

Just as the Sunni Muslim population worldwide is the largest of all Muslim sects, so too in Afghanistan, and in Central Asia as a whole, the Sunnis form about 90 percent of the Muslim population of the country. Yet this is a community that has no central structure and whose core doctrine allows for decentralization—despite attempts by Kabul, from the reign of Amir Abdul Rahman onward to the rule of Muhammad Najibullah, to impose a hierarchical structure on Sunni Islam in order better to control religious activity.[28] Genuine cohesive units in this community are achieved through group mechanisms other than the hierarchical ecclesiastical structure. Secular bonds, through tribes, geographic regions, and ethnic-linguistic groups, provide for the basic sources of cohesion.

Two exceptions to this are the madrasa and the *khanaqa* (Sufi hostel) networks, built around religious institutions, which allow for some amalgamation, although often even these two institutions, in practice, function within limited boundaries. Loosely structured as the Sunnis may be, Afghanistan is rich in Sufi brotherhood traditions as well as loyalty and philosophical networks built around religious teachers by their students. Moreover, the two systems are not mutually exclusive. In the Sufi orders (*tariqat*) a similar relationship exists between the spiritual leader (*murshid*) and the adept or devotee (*murid*). These two networks—that of the madrasa built around the teacher and students, and that of the *khanaqa* around a *murshid* and his various *murid*—allow for intrafamily structures, which sometimes have even become intraregional. As the Afghan resistance fought year after year, the discipline of party organization that appeared to hold the traditional or moderate parties together began to wear thin, and splinter groups built on ever-smaller networks appeared. Splintering was less of a problem for Islamist parties, in which a defined ideology provided method and goal for continued work. Yet the basic tenets of belief as well as the guidelines—that is, exegesis, traditions, and schools of law—do not differ between traditionalists and Islamists.

To clarify the distinguishing doctrines within Sunni Islam, a return to the history of the first century of the faith may be helpful.

Caliph and Imam.   The concept of caliph and imam differ considerably for the Sunni from the Imami Shi'a and the Isma'ili. For Sunnis, neither the term caliph nor imam implies authority acquired as a special representative of the divine, through the circumstance of lineage or the transmission of esoteric knowledge. The two terms were used interchangeably for the first four caliphs. Imam denotes a leader (of prayer) and caliph means deputy, as in deputy of the Prophet. Theoretically, election based on merit, rather than divine selection or bloodline, determined who became the caliph. The caliph had no doctrinally sanctioned infallibility, as the term implies in Shi'a doctrine.

After the death of the last of the "Rightly Guided Caliphs" (the first four, Abu Bakr, Umar, Uthman, and Ali), the caliphate (Umayyad) became political and dynastic, with several competing centers in Damascus and Granada, then in Baghdad (Abbasid) and in less important splinterings in the west. Gradually both the aura of piety associated with the caliph and his temporal power eroded and became symbolic rather than real. In the aftermath of the Mongol invasions, the last of the Abbasid dynasty of caliphs disappeared from both the religious and secular scene. The Ottoman sultans, temporal rulers, never held the title of caliph officially until it was vested in them in 1922 after the abolition of the sultanate by republican Turkish leaders. Two years later the same Turkish National Assembly that had bestowed the title in the first place abolished the institution of the caliphate. Among the populace however, the caliphate represented vaguely a religious station and was associated with the Ottoman sultan. But neither rebellion against the caliph in the eighth century in western Afghanistan nor against the Ottoman sultan in the twentieth century in the Hijaz could be easily branded as a heresy.[29]

Examples of the imposition of ecclesiastical hierarchy to promote temporal goals abound in the modern period. In the Ottoman Empire, the institution of Shaykh ul-Islam became an attempt by the state to impose a hierarchical structure within Sunni society in order to control and rally the populace to support a particular policy. In tzarist Russia, beginning in the late eighteenth century, as Muslim areas were conquered, "muftiats" were organized that, theoretically if not actually, could be controlled through the Ministry of Religious Affairs, that is, from the top down. In the amirate of Bukhara, which in sociopolitical terms most resembled Afghanistan during the premodern period, religious organization before and after its conquest by tzarist armies was effectively headed by the *qazi kalan* (literally, the "great judge") in a hierarchical system that controlled the juridical, educational, and worship institutions.[30] Although the amir of Bukhara ultimately appointed the *qazi kalan* and was himself the final arbiter in life or death sentences (hence the bloody image of the amir), the official exercised considerable power and could not be removed easily, since the amir neither had nor claimed religious power.

By contrast, in Afghanistan, Amir Abdul Rahman introduced the concepts of the ruler as defender and champion of the faith, ruler by "grace and will of Allah," and the dual role of leader and interpreter of Islam and Islamic law.[31] Specifically, he proclaimed that none but he could declare holy war (*jihad* or *ghazawat*), a necessary precaution since he faced rebellion from many quarters in his kingdom. For example, a *fatwa* for *jihad* against the amir issued by a religious figure sympathetic to one of his enemies plunged the amir into war with Ishaq Khan in the north. Declaring himself the sole personage with the right to declare a jihad was designed to guard against this possibility. As the "Iron Amir," he was able to enforce his will. But he did not have the ability to convince either the mullahs or his subjects of the actual right of succeeding monarchs to claim such privilege, despite the many tracts he wrote and published.

In the same manner, once the communist government perceived the moral power that the mujahidin acquired through the popular acceptance of the call to jihad raised by the resistance, it too brought out its state mullahs to declare jihad against the resistance. By branding resistance leaders as tools of the United States (and Israel), Kabul hoped to succeed in bringing the power of traditional Islam to bear upon its enemies. Changing the flag of the country back to its original colors (green, black, and red) from solid red, changing the name of the PDPA to the Watan (Homeland) Party, claiming to have built mosques, and convening Islamic conferences were all part of the late awakening of the Khalqi and then the Parchami leaders to the problem of being recognized as the vanguard of atheism. The exclusion of the Kabul regime of the PDPA from the Organization of the Islamic Conference, and the seating of mujahidin representatives, beginning with the Taif (Saudi Arabia) conference, sealed the branding of the PDPA as anti-Islamic throughout the region. Although the resistance took full advantage of the discrediting of Kabul among traditional Muslims and Islamists altogether, the very doctrines of Sunni Islam, as well as the divisions of Afghanistan into other Islamic sects prevented the recognition of the authority of a single religious leader.

Thus the practical outcome of the concept of caliph and imam for Sunni Afghanistan was that no undisputed religious authority, either in law or in theology, was accepted by all. The title imam was rarely used and *khalifa* (caliph) could be applied to an assistant bus driver or to the deputy and designated successor of a Sufi *pir*. This usage, however, should be distinguished from that of Khilafat, which distinctly referred to the Ottoman caliphate and came to play a role in Afghan and Indian politics during the 1920s.[32]

Equality of Believers. Despite socioeconomic differences and ethnic inequalities, Afghan Sunni Islam fundamentally allows for the equality of all males. Once slavery became truly outlawed and lost support in custom by the early 1920s, even Shi'a Hazaras began to gain some equality in society, at least before the Sunni encoded constitutions and written laws. The sensitivity to non-Sunni Hanafi views led to the dropping of the specification of Sunni or Shi'a for high office holders by the time the constitution of 1977 was adopted.[33] By allowing for the accommodation of other Muslims, the framers of that constitution underscored Afghan nationalism as an important criterion for leadership. This gradual relaxation of the insistence on Sunni Hanafi codes of law illustrates the moving away from the rigidity of the 1923 constitution, which had gone so far as to brand as heretics members of the Ahmadiyya sect prominent in Pakistan, a step that had opened the door to their persecution in Afghanistan.[34] By contrast, six decades later, Hindus and Sikhs lived in Afghanistan and were able to maintain their places of worship.[35]

Juridical Authority. The concept of law based on the *shari'a* is fundamental to Sunni governance in Afghanistan, and up to the Soviet invasion it had not been completely eliminated from the judiciary system. The four schools of Sunni *shari'a* had been codified by the ninth century but remain open to a degree of interpretation, albeit more limited than in the Shi'a Ja'farite school. Trained in *fiqh* (Islamic jurisprudence) at madrasas, at the Shari'at Faculty, and at the Faculty of Law and Political Science, Afghan *qazis* by the 1970s were intended to combine statutory codes, Hanafi codes, and custom in order to arrive at legal decisions. As noted earlier, however, the breakdown of civil society during the war led to the institution of *shari'a* courts in the countryside wherever personnel have been available.[36]

The victory of the mujahidin over the communists appears to indicate a reversal of direction in the administration of law toward the wider adoption of the *shari'a* as the basis for a future legal code. This situation raises again past problems. To what extent must courts be staffed and run according to the Hanafi code? Can there be countrywide codes based on the Hanafi code that apply to Sunni and Shi'a alike? Will non-Sunnis (or non-Muslims) be treated equally before the law? And can a future constitution treat all Afghans equally in terms of access to governmental positions or elected office? To what extent will Islamists succeed in strict application of the *shari'a* and its interpretation to apply to complex issues such as foreign investment? Will the concept of *awqaf* (charitable foundations) be reinstituted, though it has not functioned since the time of Abdul Rahman? Will traditional or moderate Muslims succeed in confining the application of *shari'a* to family law?

So long as the armed conflict among the Afghans continues and the legitimacy of a unifying government is not accepted, the issues arising from doctrinal concepts cannot be confronted. Yet the warring factions are engaged in a struggle that is in part predicated on their positions on issues, such as the degree of secularism and the degree to which one set of laws is applied to the entire society. Such a situation is complicated by raw ethnic and personal rivalry for power. The absence of a monarch or a religious hierarchy that can command respect or allegiance may doom prospects for the revival of a unified Afghanistan, and one that is free from interference by strong neighbors on many sides.

Loyalties and Identities

The labyrinth of surviving pockets of traditionally functioning groups in Afghanistan that has made the country a fascinating mosaic in the past also has made the task of nation building formidable throughout the modern period. The effects of the war on nation building may in the long term prove important, in the sense that the displacement of millions of people may have created a need for a broader self-identity that did not exist in remote villages. Nonetheless, the breakdown of integrative institutions, and the enforcement of regional, ethnic, and tribal identities resulting from the demands of guerrilla fighting, has eroded national sensibilities. The extreme political positions—communist and Islamist—while politicizing many, are also squeezing out of political life those traditional Muslims whose loyalties, though strong to Islam, were becoming more secularist. Many of the best-trained technicians, educators, administrators, and specialists among them have settled abroad, and there is little prospect of their contributing to Afghan reconstruction. The limited educational facilities afforded to those in external or internal exile, together with the breakdown in educational systems altogether, has halted the slow drive toward universal literacy that existed before the war. In addition to the sheer destruction of infrastructure, a generation of Afghans has been deprived of nonviolent conflict resolution modes. There are strong indications that the Afghan population has grown by as much as 15 percent in the countryside, and if all the rural refugees return, numerous problems of land ownership and adequacy of arable land will arise.[37]

The internal dynamics of loyalties and identities are undergoing radical change, even as the entire region has entered a period of reorientation and reidentification. From the Tajik opposition groups, tenuously united against the Dushanbe regime, to the political leaders of Pakistan, changes in international borders are feared and eschewed.[38] Since the region as a whole shares with Afghanistan an underpinning in traditional Islam, the homogeneity of Islam, which does not accept ethnic nationalism as a barrier to the unity of Muslims, may play a major role in forming new regionally based identities. Therefore, the dynamics of change that will effect Afghanistan are both internal and regional.

A schematic of Afghan loyalty patterns within the context of Islam helps to illuminate the conflicts that arise in citizens' identifying with the Afghan state or giving it loyalty once the alien (labeled "infidel") force has been removed.[39] As may be seen in Figure 4.1, despite the preponderance of adherents to Sunni Islam, the Shi'a are isolated, and the ethnic groups in general display regional separation. Given this separation and the low level of urbanization in the country as a whole, the opportunities for shared experiences and loyalties are relatively few.[40] Indeed, ethnic loyalties and identities remain high despite the Islamic homogeneity of the population. The

FIGURE 4.1   Ethnopolitical Chart

Ethnic Group[a]	Sect	Political Inclination	Region
Pushtun (7 million)	Sunni; small Shi'a	Pro-Kabul communist Anti-Kabul communist Traditional resistance parties Harakat-i Islami Hizb-i Islami (Khalis) Islamist resistance parties Hizb-i Islami (Hekmatyar)	South, east, west
Tajik (5 million)	Sunni; Isma'ili	Jami'at-i Islami (Rabbani) Pro-Kabul communist Sitam-i Milli	North, northeast, north central
Hazara (900,000)	Shi'a Isma'ili	Hizb-i Wahdat Pro-Kabul communist NASR	Central
Uzbek (1 million)	Sunni	Pro-Kabul communist Northern Afghanistan Jami'at-i Islami Passive	North, bordering Uzbekistan
Turkmen (150,000)	Sunni	Pir Gailani's Mahaz-i Milli	Northwest, bordering Turkmenistan
Nuristani (100,000)	Sunni	Self-imposed isolation	East

[a]Note that many of the Dari/Persian-speaking groups have been collapsed into the category "Tajik," which can be broken down into Tajik, Farsiwan, and Aimac. See Louis Dupree, *Afghanistan* (Princeton: Princeton University Press, 1973), pp. 59–64.

coalescing of Uzbeks (and Isma'ilis) around General Dustam in Mazar-i-Sharif is evidence of three realities: (1) Uzbeks have remained relatively aloof from close cooperation with any of the resistance parties, even the Jami'at-i Islami (Islamic Society), which, though Tajik-led, attempted to become ethnically diverse. (2) Uzbeks have felt the attraction and inducements of closer ties with Uzbekistan, especially after 1991, when Tashkent became the capital of an independent state, and one that is closely attuned to the welfare of coethnics along its borders in both Tajikistan and Afghanistan. (3) The concept of a united Islamic revival stressed by the Islamist parties, while attracting individual Uzbeks, has not overcome the strong sense of ethnic identity among the Afghan Uzbeks.[41]

The shaping of Afghan traditional Islam over centuries may have received a definitive change in direction as a result of the fourteen years of resistance. Islamist sympathies, born among intellectual youth during the 1960s, are being espoused today by graying men whose scramble for temporal power has led them into alliances with former enemies, as in the case of the alliance of convenience between the extreme Islamist mujahidin leader, Gulbuddin Hekmatyar, and General Dustam. The civil war has highlighted not only the ethnic rivalries in the country, but the inability of the Islamist ideology to overcome ethnic divisions. Therefore, although the Islamists labored, fought, and sacrificed to overcome the communist regime in Kabul, they may find themselves discredited, with the sympathies of the Afghan people and the region's Muslim countries swinging once more toward the remnants of the traditional Islamic leaders. Pir Gailani, Mawlana Muhammadi Nabi Muhammadi, and other traditional forces located in Pakistan may prove to be beneficiaries of the failure of the Islamists to provide a stable government. That the force of neither traditional Islam nor of Islamist revivalism has been sufficiently strong to overcome ethnic identities and loyalties has been manifestly demonstrated in the aftermath of the fall of Kabul to the resistance in 1992. It remains to be seen whether a new push by traditional Islamic groups, such as the *taliban* (the term normally applied to Islamic seminary students) who have formed in Pakistan in order to restore order from the civil war waged among the various factions, will succeed where Islamist zeal has failed to overcome ethnic divisiveness.

Sufi Orders and Other Forms of Confrereship

As may be noted in Figure 4.1, religious loyalty was a strong feature for adherence among some Pushtun and Turkmen groups to Sufi leaders of the resistance. The two most prominent Sufi orders of Afghanistan, the Naqshbandiyya and the Qadiriyya, have played a special role in the Afghan resistance, proving that the Sufi-related aspect of traditional Islam did indeed play a role in the resistance to communism. The revelation that in Tajikistan the Qadiriyya as well as the better known Naqshbandiyya also has contributed to the leadership of the Tajik Islamic Revival (Renaissance) Party may point to the far greater breadth of both of these Islamic mystical movements.[42]

The nature of Sufi *tariqat* organizations creates a network among adherents. The *tariqat* allow for political action, although the primary function of these orders remains religious. The Naqshbandiyya *tariqa,* particularly identified with Central Asia, where it began during the fourteenth century, especially promotes the concept of "living within society" rather than being removed from it in a monastic way. This concept has allowed Naqshbandiyya Sufis in particular to participate actively in sociopolitical movements throughout regional history. Among members of this brotherhood may be counted historical political leaders such as Mir Ali Shir Nawaiy

(1441–1501), the prominent Timurid vezir (and poet) of Herat, as well as many activists of the past century throughout the Islamic world. In Afghanistan, Naqshbandiyya leadership is divided among several *pirs*, but prominent among them is the Mujaddidi family, who led a branch of the Naqshbandiyya that was developed in India during the sixteenth century and imported into Afghanistan. The patriarch of the family, titled the Hazrat Sahib-e Shor Bazaar (in Kabul), proved to be the kingbreaker during the reign of King Amanullah. Perhaps as a precautionary move, among the first victims of the Taraki regime were the male members of this family, including the patriarch, ninety-six of whom were killed in prison in 1979. The knowledge of this event spawned widespread alarm among the remaining family members, who had already fled into exile during the period of President Da'ud.[43] Returning to the area, they organized the political party known as Jabha-i Najat-i Milli Afghanistan (National Liberation Front of Afghanistan), under the leadership of Sibghatullah Mujaddidi. The party drew much of its support from among Mujaddidi followers in Pushtun areas, especially in the Laghman area. Sibghatullah Mujaddidi served as the first elected president of the Afghan Interim Government in 1989 in Peshawar, then in Kabul when that city fell to the resistance. His party has supported centrist political positions, including the temporary return of Zahir Shah, the last Afghan king, who lives in exile in Italy. A compromiser whose party played a greater political than military role in the course of the resistance, Sibghatullah Mujaddidi and this branch of the order fall squarely within the scope of traditional Afghan Islam. Regional support for the group came from traditional Islamic governments in the region, especially from Saudi Arabia, but not from the Wahhabi elements in the Gulf region or from Pakistan.[44]

Many other Naqshbandiyya activists in the resistance joined the Harakat-i Islami (Islamic Movement), which recruited widely among graduates of the Islamic seminaries, where Naqshbandi Sufism has always thrived. Initially numerous, the Harakat splintered and was easily infiltrated by Maoists. Nonetheless, it remained strongly grounded among both Sufi and non-Sufi traditional believers. It should be noted that not all Sufi brotherhood members remained within the traditional Islamic parties; a number of them joined the Islamists as well, especially the Jami'at-e Islami of Burhanuddin Rabbani.

In addition to the Naqshbandiyya, very active in the resistance has been the leader, or *pir*, of the Qadiriyya order, Sayyid Ahmad Gailani, known respectfully as Affandi Sahib. Heading the Mahaz-i Milli-i Islami-i Afghanistan (National Islamic Front of Afghanistan) since 1979, Gailani is the sole leader of the Qadiriyya in Afghanistan and much revered among Pushtuns, in the Kandahar area in particular. As an active member of the monarchial government, and intermarried with it, the Qadiriyya, as repre-

sented by Gailani and the Islamic Front party, have supported the return of
Zahir Shah and have attracted many otherwise disaffected intellectuals
from among the expatriate community. The Qadiriyya party therefore includes both peasant fighters in the field and commanders and members who
come from urban, educated backgrounds. For many of his tribal followers,
Gailani, a former businessman, is elevated to the position of a living saint.
By and large these groups would consider themselves within the scope of
traditional Islam, although it should be noted that among the resistance
this party was regarded by the Islamists as particularly compromised because of its secular nationalist rather than religiously based orientation.[45]

In the Central Asian region in general, in addition to the formal *tariqat,*
there are particular charismatic Sufi leaders, falling roughly under the appellation *darvish,* which implies a religious mendicant, usually not trained
in a madrasa but endowed with religious power that gives him authority.
Such figures become known to the outside world when they enter the political arena. References to their political activities against colonial powers exist in tzarist and British Indian accounts. Among these are Muhammad Ali
(referred to as Madali in Russian sources), and the Faqir of Ipi, Haji Mirza
Ali Khan (d. 1959). The first led the 1898 Andijan rebellion against Russian military and rural settlements, unsuccessfully, and was tried and
hanged. Western study of his motives and of the composition of his followers is based on records of the tzarist commission sent to investigate the rebellion. The commission was unconcerned about Islamic potential for opposition and generally ignored any Sufi or other network or connection
with the outside world.[46] A second Central Asian Islamic-based anticolonial movement was led by the Faqir of Ipi, a figure described by the British
as one of the "frontier mullahs," who instigated the Waziri tribes on the
British side of the Durand Line to rise against the British during the late
1930s and World War II. There is no evidence that these local leaders operated within a formal Sufi *tariqa,* but both were imbued with a mystical
presence that allowed their followers to rise against the superior arms and
organization of colonial armies.

The second kind of network is more closely related to the Islamists than
to traditional Islamic groupings. These are the organizations of reformers,
such as the Ikhwan-ul Muslimin (Muslim Brotherhood) and the group
called the Wahhabi. Both movements originate in the Arab world, Egypt
and Arabia respectively, and date to the late nineteenth and early twentieth
century. Although new to Afghanistan, having arrived in force during the
1960s or later, within the Arab world Wahhabism has become part of traditional Islam in Saudi Arabia. In Afghanistan, the two ideologies functioned
in opposition despite the passion of both for Islamic revival. Associated
with "Islamic fundamentalism" in Western and communist views, the Muslim Brotherhood inspired the Jami'at-e Islami, and the Arabs who fought

against the communist regime in Kabul from their base in the Kunar valley may have had an informal understanding with the Hizb-i Islami (Islamic Party) of Gulbuddin Hekmatyar. They enjoyed formal connections with the party of Abdul Rasul Sayyaf, who received most of his support from Wahhabi-oriented Arabs in the Gulf region.

Despite the cooperative network among members of Sufi *tariqat*, the cooperation of individual Sufis with the Islamic revivalist political parties, that is, the Islamists, is an important dynamic of the Afghan resistance. Especially because Sufi *tariqat* cross ethnic boundaries and geographic regions, Afghan leaders are bound by several loyalties and identities. Thus a Tajik or Uzbek member of a Naqshbandi *tariqa* might as easily join an Islamist as a traditional group, such as that led by Mujaddidi. By the same token, former president Najibullah, who for many epitomized the cruelty and illegitimacy of the communist regime, was politically protected by elders of the Ahmadzai tribe, despite clear ideological differences between a communist and a traditional Islamic group. Sheltered with the former president in the Kabul UN compound (1992–1996) was his Hazara bodyguard, who had remained loyal. Tribe and ethnicity as well as Islamic and ideological politics therefore continue to determine political action.

The Future of Traditional Islam

Afghanistan remains today as it was in the last century, a conglomeration of ethnic groups loosely tied within state boundaries by means of traditional Islam. Despite the religious homogeneity, important sects—the Ithna 'Ash'ara and the Isma'ilis, both with much stronger hierarchical organization—function alongside traditional Sunni Islam. From a state perspective, attempts have been made through the constitution to reduce discrimination against non-Sunnis and non-Pushtuns. Nonetheless, during the period of communist rule and resistance to the Soviet invasion, when central government became dysfunctional, ethnic and sectarian affiliations and loyalties emerged that splintered the traditional Islamic front. Islamist and communist ideologies both attracted multiethnic and multisectarian followers. But as the Afghan civil war has redrawn lines of battle, ethnic affiliation has proved too strong, possibly even for the Islamist forces. Traditional Islamic forces may be able to step into the chasm of uncertain legitimacy and political power evolving around the Sufi orders or respected religious teachers. A further examination of these issues appears in the next chapter, which discusses the mujahidin and the interrelationships of the fighters with the traditional and Islamist parties.

Chapter Five

Marx
Among the Afghans

"All of us came from the old society. No matter what we are now, in the past, we all belonged to the bourgeois intelligentsia."
—Chou En-lai (1962)[1]

On July 17, 1973, a palace coup brought Afghanistan out of the monarchial and into a republican form of government. The coup enjoyed the support of Afghan Marxists but brought to power the former prime minister and royal cousin, Sardar Muhammad Da'ud Khan, who was not a Marxist. The road to Afghan Marxism ended in tragedy for many of the leading participants in the coup and for the Afghan nation as a whole. For a people caught between wanting to return to the peaceful days of the monarchy and needing to move forward in their political and ideological development, the Afghan civil war may have resolved only the issue of Marxism—that is, its total defeat—but not yet its replacement ideology or even agreement on a republican form of government. Part of the failure of Afghan Marxism lay in its inability to transcend its limited base among urban intellectuals. The other cause for its failure is related to the many years of Afghan suspicion of its northern neighbor and hence, for many, the sense of betrayal when Afghan Marxists embraced that very same neighbor. When the Marxist experiment finally ended in the spring of 1992, few parts of the country had been spared the ravages of war. By that time the legacy of Marxism had all but disappeared in most of Asia, including in the Soviet Union.

The Origins of Reformists and Marxists

The failure of reformists and Marxists in Afghanistan lay in the fact that they both attempted to create a national-democratic revolution in a country that was not yet a nation. Marxists went further by attempting a revolution in a countryside where reform had barely penetrated. This does not mean that there were not, in 1978 or indeed in 1908, Afghans who were clearly nationalists and reformers, and even the beginnings of political movements that can be called nationalist. These movements, however, were confined almost entirely to a minuscule elite located almost exclusively in the capital of Kabul if they were not posted on government assignments in the provinces. The leading representatives of Afghan nationalism, such as Amir Abdul Rahman, King Amanullah, Mahmud Beg Tarzi, and Sardar Muhammad Da'ud Khan, were monarchs or members of the royal family. Some of the latter, especially King Amanullah, were acknowledged by the Marxists themselves to be their heroes and models. In their eyes, their own alliance with President Da'ud failed because the president himself did not live up to his past promise as a nationalist and modernizer.

The origins of Afghan reformists came from the modern educational system first introduced by Amir Habibullah with the establishment in 1903 of Habibiya College, which was modeled on the twelve-year secondary schools (for boys) that the British had established in India. The military college soon followed, staffed by Turkish instructors. The beginnings of a public school system included the foundation of a teacher training college in 1914. Schools for girls as well came to Kabul during the 1920s, and some years later a medical faculty, the basis for Kabul University, was founded. The modern-educated graduates of these schools became the backbone of the governmental and military bureaucracy of the state.

Simultaneously, this modern educational system became the breeding ground of opposition movements demanding fundamental changes in the political system and essentially calling for the establishment of participatory democracy. These opposition movements began with the "old constitutionalists" at Habibiya College, thirty-eight of whom were imprisoned and seven executed in 1909 on the charge of plotting a coup against Habibullah. This "National Secret Association" (*jamaat-i-siri-yi-melli*) was organized into cells of ten members each. It included members of the existing bureaucratic elite at the royal court, the *ghulam bacha* or pages at court, some Durrani sardars, and even a few commoners (two watchmakers and a filing clerk were among those arrested). Their goals included the founding of a constitutional monarchy, full independence from Britain, and a "new culture" for Afghanistan.[2]

The modernist opposition movement did not end with the repression of the "old constitutionalists." It soon reemerged as the "Young Afghans," led by the greatest modern liberal thinker of Afghanistan, Mahmud Beg Tarzi, and his pupil and son-in-law, the future King Amanullah. Tarzi arrived in Afghanistan from Ottoman exile at the age of thirty-six. Soon afterward, he began a campaign at court to reverse Afghanistan's internal and external problems, which he judged to be caused by its backwardness and isolation. He remained at court under two monarchs for nearly three decades and took as his main task the broadening of the perspective of the elite public through a newspaper that became extremely influential throughout the region. This publication, from 1911 to 1918, spread the ideology of Islamic modernism, emphasizing the need for modern education in particular. Another theme that Tarzi avidly promoted was anti-imperialism—in Afghanistan's case, directed at the British. Among Tarzi's many translations was a five-volume history of the Russo-Japanese War by the Ottoman chief of staff. The Chinese Revolution of 1910 was also hailed as an example of modernism and national liberation. Finally, Tarzi was an Islamic modernist and thus promoted the view that there was no incompatibility between Islam and either nationalism or modernism. On the contrary, these were necessary to fulfill Islam. It was thus a religious duty to serve the homeland, the government, and the king. Only through modernization could Afghanistan hope to defend itself against European imperialism.

From this unsteady beginning, which was marked by repression of political movement on the one hand and promotion of reformist discussion on the other, Afghanistan headed into the 1920s led by King Amanullah, an impatient idealist. The constitutionalists could now emerge into the open. Indeed, their ideas were adopted by Amanullah, included in Afghanistan's first constitution, and they themselves became prominent in his government. Tarzi became foreign minister, and his ideology was embodied in reform programs in education, the military, and economic and social development. These included progressive social measures such as women's rights and education, including scholarships abroad (in Turkey) and the opening of secondary schools for women.

Despite his adoption of virtually the entire program of the modernists, there were still some among the Young Afghans who formed a secret society, the Hizb-i Niqabdar (Veiled Party) to plot Amanullah's overthrow and the establishment of a republic. On the more conservative side, the leading Islamic figure in the country, the Hazrat-e Shor Bazaar, rejected the new constitution as the work of communism and not of Islam. Amanullah's actions, which threw his father's cautious approach to reform to the winds, quickly bred political rebellion and antireformist backlash that in 1929 cost him his monarchy.[3]

The failure of this first reformist period illustrates the wide divergence among Afghans with regard to reform, especially social reform. The failure of reforms also drove the Young Afghan movement back underground.

Nadir Shah and his brothers, when they had restored the Pushtun monarchy some nine months later, were by no means reactionaries; they had supported Amanullah and the broad objectives of the reform program espoused by Afghan modernists. But above all they had to be realists. Most of the modernists supported Nadir's family as representing the best chance for stability and the eventual resumption of modernist reform. Other reformists became embittered by the defeat of Amanullah and continued to regard him as the rightful king and Nadir Shah as the conservative usurper. King Amanullah remained in exile in Rome but was by no means resigned to his fate. The die-hard Amanullah supporters, whether they were actual supporters or merely using his prestige to advance their own interests, created an undercurrent of distrust between the modern elite and the dynasty over the next four and a half decades of Musahiban rule. An assassin belonging to the Young Afghans took the life of Sardar Aziz Khan, the king's brother and father of the young Sardar Muhammad Da'ud. Another Amanullah supporter was executed in 1932, charged with plotting to set up a republic, and, finally, Nadir Shah himself was assassinated in 1933. The underlying mistrust between a segment of the educated elite and the dynasty remained, however submerged, as modernization resumed at a cautious and selective pace.

Soon after World War II, Shah Mahmud Khan Ghazi, who assumed the role of prime minister, was encouraged by young modernizing Afghans in the government to liberalize the political system in order to make his own mark as the originator of true democracy. Consequently, the political controls that had assured a docile parliament were lifted in 1949, and the Seventh Parliament reflected the relaxed atmosphere that allowed about one-third of its number to be freely elected reformists. Although the institution of the monarchy was unquestioned, many reforms, mainly political in nature, were adopted. Many of the liberal reformist elements formed part of a broad movement known as Wish-i-Zalmayan (Awakened Youth) established in 1947 and supported, for at least a time, by Sardar Muhammad Da'ud. The newspaper *Nida-ye Khalq* (Voice of the People) was established by Dr. Abdul Rahman Mahmudi, with possibly the most radical program of all, but still within the boundaries of democratic reform. Mahmudi announced the formation of a political party, *Khalq* (Masses), which functioned mainly among the students of Kabul University.

The groups and individuals associated with the "liberal Seventh Parliament" period form a bridge joining the era of the Young Afghans of the 1920s, the partisans of "New Democracy" in the 1964 constitution, and the Marxists of the 1970s. In the view of the Pakistani left, the liberal constitutionalist movement of the 1950s was "the flowering of the tender plant whose seeds Amir Amanullah Khan had sown against such odds twenty years earlier."[4] Among the reformists of this period were the historian Mir

Ghulam Muhammad Ghubar, who had been a leader in the "Young Afghans" and publisher of *Watan* (Fatherland), and Mir Muhammad Siddiq Farhang, a self-described democratic socialist who was editor of *Watan* and later one of the seven drafters of the liberal constitution of 1964 and leader of the left democrats in the lower house of parliament (1965–1969).[5]

Some in this group of reformers went to prison when new restrictions against them were activated: Mahmudi was imprisoned, and then released by the king during the next liberal period in 1963, only to die a few months later. He became a martyred hero of the left, and his relatives continued his work during the liberal constitutional period (1963–1973). The Maoist far-left journal and political movement known as *Shula-ye Jawid* (Eternal Flame) developed from among his relatives and supporters. Nur Muhammad Taraki, a largely self-taught writer and journalist who later became the first president of the Marxist Democratic Republic of Afghanistan (DRA), was the major contributor to *Angar* (Burning Embers). And Babrak Karmal, another future DRA president, at that time a leader of the Kabul University Student Union, was imprisoned until 1956.

With the possible exception of Mahmudi, it is difficult to identify any of these leaders as ideological Marxists, although in all probability Taraki had become a member of the Communist Party of India during his work as a clerk for the Afghan Fruit Company in Bombay in the 1930s. In a larger sense, however, the period of the Seventh Parliament epitomized the influential position of the Afghan intellectual reformers and modernizers vis-à-vis the politician members of the extended royal family. This tension, which had begun during the 1930s, continued through 1978, when the Marxists eliminated the royal family altogether.

During the 1950s, however, native Marxist and liberal ideologies were still vaguely formulating protests of a democratic-liberal bourgeois type possible in a constitutional monarchy. The groups espousing them devoted most of their energies to describing the abuses of the traditional system (most of which had little to do with the government), but their proposed solution to social and economic problems arising out of traditional society looked to elected government and a constitutional monarchy as panacea. Some of their energies also became diverted to the foreign-policy issue of Pushtunistan, which became contentious when the Afghan government was unsuccessful in pressing for a voice for the Pushtuns of British India during the breakup of the Indian empire into Pakistan and India. The publisher of *Angar* in particular, Faiz Muhammad Angar, a wealthy Kandahar landowner and an official in the economics ministry, was a strong supporter of Pushtunistan.

The leading Afghan historian of the modern period, Hasan Kawun Kakar,[6] however, holds that the constitutionalism of the reformers of the 1950s was merely tactical and that almost all of the modernists were at heart republican, not Marxist. More important than their actual effects on the public (which in any case included a minute fraction who read their limited and short-term publications) was the reaction of the government. Although none were killed and most released once they had promised to desist from their activities, the purge instituted against these political activists reinforced the distrust between intellectuals and the royal family. Many of them felt that liberalization had been merely a tactic employed by the government to flush them out so that the regime could observe the strength and numbers of its enemies. A minority engaged in self-criticism and concluded that they had been insufficiently focused and had suffered from scattered goals. This minority further concluded that when they had another opportunity they would be ready through preparations for a revolutionary movement based on the "scientific" principles of Marxism-Leninism. Thus a number of private informal "study groups" came into being toward the end of the 1950s.

The conclusions reached by the royal family/government pointed to the need to liberalize, but not through the means advocated by its reformist critics. Da'ud, who became prime minister in 1953, shared a number of the values of the liberal intelligentsia. He wished to lead a new generation of the royal family in renewing Afghanistan's social and economic modernization at a rapid pace. In short, he wished to become the new Amanullah of a royal-led revolutionary movement. This of course required a good deal of money for the major infrastructure projects he had in mind along with a reorganized military. As a military man himself, he realized the army's weakness and did not wish to repeat the bitter and chaotic ending of Amanullah's experiment.

This policy would inevitably mean a large infusion of foreign aid and, especially, foreign advisers, including advisers in the military itself. Such a policy constituted a radical break with Afghanistan's tradition from the beginnings of modernization. To justify the military changes to a suspicious population, in particular the Pushtuns, on whom the officer ranks relied, the demands for Pushtunistan were raised as a rallying point. Da'ud hoped that such aid could be obtained from the United States, which already had been approached with little success by the Shah Mahmud Khan Ghazi government. The United States had the advantages of being far away and of having no imperialist past to overcome in Afghan eyes. It was the height of the Cold War, however, and the Americans were interested in a "northern tier" alliance in the Middle East to prevent a repetition of what had happened in Korea in 1950. It was difficult to get further north than Afghanistan in the northern tier, but the problem was that Afghanistan was also next to the Soviet Union and on terms of active hostility with its neighbor Pakistan. Thus, even before Pakistan became a formal ally of the United States by signing the Mutual Security Agreement of 1954, the U.S.

military reached the conclusion that Afghanistan was too distant to be defensible by U.S. action should the Soviets repeat the aggression they had encouraged in Korea.

Da'ud then turned to the Soviet Union for the required aid, recognizing that it was a gamble. The regime would have to modernize fast enough, with Soviet aid, to satisfy the new forces in society before those forces became powerful enough to seize power through revolution. The gamble failed two decades later. In September 1977, two months after the Soviet-enforced reunion of the two wings of the Afghan Communist party, Muhammad Na'im, Da'ud's brother and adviser, remarked to Abdul Samad Ghaus, the deputy foreign minister: "You know the gamble is lost. We played our hand but lost. Sooner or later a small minority will seize power and, by the force of arms, will rule over the entire people. Of course Communism will never be accepted willingly by the Muslim people of Afghanistan. But, I see rivers of blood flowing. . . . " The "gamble," of course, referred to the decision in the 1950s to trust in Soviet assurance of Afghanistan's survival through massive economic and military assistance while maintaining friendly relations with the royal government.[7]

The Soviet Union and Afghan Marxists[8]

Several problems come to mind in describing Afghan Marxism. The first and most important, and still relevant today, is the "authenticity" of the Afghan Marxists. To what extent were they independent actors versus agents under Soviet direction, at least in their major activities? Were they perhaps demanding clients trying to blackmail their supposed principals? Were they indeed ever Marxist in the sense of being dedicated to revolutionary change in their society, or did they merely see Marxism as the vehicle for power and personal advancement? This is a vexing problem, given their fulsome praise of every action of the Soviet Union and their claim to carry on the progress of the Great October Revolution. It is also complicated by the reality of personality as a basis for action. For a philosophy supposedly based on impersonal economic forces to be examined "scientifically," Marxism in practice often seems to be inordinately personalized, in general (as with Lenin, Trotsky, Stalin, Mao, Castro, Ho Chi Minh, etc.) and in Afghanistan (as with Taraki, Amin, Karmal, Najibullah). Perhaps this is part of the Leninist element, for any vanguard revolutionary party based on "democratic centralism" will inevitably revolve around the personality of the central leader, as Lenin himself realized too late with regard to Stalin.

Second is the problem of the Marxists' relationship to overall Soviet policy with regard to Afghanistan: Did the Soviets really care about using the Marxists to achieve their aims, either before or after the seizure of power in

1978, giving them a long-term strategic significance in the advancement of Soviet aims, or were they merely a tactical adjunct to the de facto control of a certain territory? If another relationship with Afghanistan or another method or conduit of influence were better suited to the control of this territory, in how high a regard would Moscow have held the position of Afghan Marxists? The entire picture of Marxism in Afghanistan has yet to emerge, possibly when surviving key Marxists address crucial questions openly and publicly.

Domestic development of the Afghan Marxists reemerged during the 1960s as political relaxation of public politics followed in the course of the liberal constitutional period. By the time of the 1973 republican coup, the People's Democratic Party of Afghanistan (PDPA) was a partner in government, although it was not the sole Marxist party functioning in Afghanistan. In the international context, the Afghan Marxists, emerging as they did out of reformist movements that gripped many of the intellectuals from the lesser developed countries, came under the influence of the Soviet Union while being also nurtured by the Soviet-backed Tudeh party of Iran. The role of the Iranian communist party in Afghan affairs began to emerge visibly in 1977, when Ehsan Tabari, a leading Tudeh member, helped, on Moscow's instructions, to broker the rapprochement between the Parcham and the Khalq, the two rival sections of the PDPA.[9] Afghan sources trace the beginning of Tudeh influence to an earlier period, the late 1940s and early 1950s, when Persian-language publications from this group began to come into the hands of young Afghans. It is well to remember too that when the Tudeh party was routed from Iran, many members took refuge in the Tajik Soviet Socialist Republic, Afghanistan's neighbor across the Amu Darya, whence many continued political and intellectual activity.

The extent to which Iranian communists played a role in Afghan developments, either through Iran or through the Soviet Union, is only part of the history of Soviet involvement with Afghan Marxist politics. This, in turn, is part of the overall Soviet pressure on Afghanistan. Among the many-pronged Soviet hands that probed the country since the 1920s were Soviet-armed Central Asians who were sent to help restore Amanullah to the throne in 1929. From the 1950s Afghans were recruited as spies from among the military and other students studying in the Soviet Union (mostly in Central Asia).[10]

Similarly, the Soviets' covert interest in the border areas continued. They were interested for a time in the Pushtun nationalist movement of Khan Abdul Ghaffar Khan in the Northwest Frontier Province as a true revolutionary movement, but soon denounced them as "servants of imperialism" rather than "Servants of God" (which was their official name in Pushtu). But they did not give up their long-term interest in the Pushtun tribes of eastern Afghanistan bordering on the tribal frontier of British India. The issue of Pushtunistan, and later Baluchistan, provided the means for them to insert a destabilizing influence in this region through the Kabul regime, especially during the first prime ministership of Da'ud.

The Liberal Constitutional Period (1963–1973)

Marxism came to Afghanistan by many routes beginning in the late 1950s and accelerated in pace through the liberalization of the 1960s. The broadest path, and ultimately the most important one, lay not in the ideological appeal to the discontented intellectuals that created the PDPA but rather through economic, educational, and military modernization, some, though not all, achieved with aid from Soviet sources. Cold War peaceful competition brought foreign aid from Western sources as well, with the United States the largest donor outside the Soviet Union. Afghan officials considered themselves quite clever in tapping various foreign sources in order to complete a project. Thus, for example, the film department of the Ministry of Information and Culture had an American technical adviser and American raw stock and cameras, and they had their film developed in the United States before the completion by the U.S. Agency for International Development of a film laboratory in Kabul. However, most of their technicians and cameramen were trained in the Soviet Union.

The royal government was well aware of the dangers of internal Soviet subversion through aid projects. It was careful to have the modernization of the educational system, from the university to the elementary level texts, in the hands of American advisers from the School of Education of Columbia University. The different faculties of Kabul University were advised by different Western experts, including Americans, French, and Germans (with the Shari'at Faculty having its agreement with al-Azhar of Cairo). The Soviets, however, complained of their exclusion from educational institutions, and the government allowed them to establish and equip a separate "Polytechnic" school, which later became a unit of Kabul University. There is a certain irony in the fact that American training produced Hafizullah Amin, the strongman who masterminded the Marxist coup of April 1978, and the Polytechnic school produced the prominent mujahid commander, Ahmad Shah Mas'ud.

Positions throughout the bureaucracy were infiltrated by "sleeper" agents under Soviet control (not even known to the PDPA) who abstained from political activity and competently performed their bureaucratic duties. However, after the coups of 1973 and 1978, these individuals suddenly appeared in leadership roles in their ministries, much to the astonishment of their former superiors and colleagues. They were placed in key positions such as minister of the interior, minister of commerce, and interpreter to President Da'ud. Once such a system was in place and coordinated by Soviet agents, it was impossible to detect in a bureaucracy as inefficient as that of Afghanistan. A very few individuals could lose files or arrange for the promotions of their friends and the demotions of their enemies with abandon. There were so many irregularities in the normal course of events as personal favoritism overrode regulations that even were they to be discovered, the motivation of these sleeper agents could be attributed to "normal" reasons. The route of Marxism through aid projects and advisers was in all probability more important to the overthrow of the old Afghan regime than was the communist party of Kabul intellectuals, especially in the case of the military. Of course the military was considered to be the most important of all the pillars of modernization. With the exception of the editor of the newspaper *Parcham,* Mir Akbar Khaibar (a graduate of the military academy and instructor at the police academy), virtually none of the public members of the PDPA had any professional military background. Many, including Babrak Karmal, had service as draftees. After the communist coup, several military officers claimed to have been covert party members for years.

Modernizing economic projects helped to create a growing constituency of discontented intellectuals. Until the 1960s, the pace of modernization projects created a shortage of graduates. Ministries and government agencies were given "draft rights" to a quota of graduates, who had little choice about employment. Of course graduates always had the "choice" of using family influence or sheer bribery to change their assignments. At least the earlier graduates had an assurance of some government position. But in the late 1960s, precisely when foreign aid began to decline, the educational system began producing a surplus at both the university and secondary school levels. Higher education graduates could not be assured "good" government jobs (which meant, in their eyes, jobs in Kabul), and the secondary graduates could not all be accommodated at the universities. Growing numbers of secondary school graduates had to be diverted to teacher training institutes and teaching careers.

One incident of the infiltration of Marxism into the bureaucracy is worth recounting in detail. In April 1975 President Da'ud returned from a visit to the Shah of Iran highly pleased by pledges of an Iranian aid program that would allow him to end his dangerous dependence on the Soviets and still achieve the modernization he desired for Afghanistan. He stopped in Herat, where he delivered an effective and impassioned speech (he was not a noted public speaker) promising to "sweep away" all foreign ideologies from the country. On his return to Kabul, he instructed the deputy minister of information and culture, who had experience in filmmaking and was trusted by the president, to edit the film of his speech for widespread distribution. That official went the same night to the film lab, where he viewed the newly developed footage. He felt that it would have a tremendous political impact.

However, the following morning when he called for the film to edit he was told that it had not come out, something was wrong with the American cameras. Having himself viewed the perfectly good film, he went directly to President Da'ud. "These people [the Soviet agents] are not just after influence; they are out to get you!" he reported. Da'ud replied calmly: "Don't you think I know this? Don't worry, I'll take care of them when it's time." There are several instructive conclusions to be drawn from this incident. The first is the speed of their actions in the hours between midnight and morning. The second is their decisiveness. They were either very well coordinated or had the training and authority to act on their own. Their boldness is also striking: Their action was easily detectable and in fact was detected, but they had confidence that they could get away with it. Finally, there was the overconfidence of Da'ud. He well knew that the Soviet Union and the local communists were a threat, but he relied on the loyalty, nationalism, religious feelings and anticommunism of the overwhelming majority of Afghans.

The relative ease of the coup of 1978 has never been satisfactorily explained. It is true that there were widespread failures of the government and even wider discontent among the intellectual elites. Some attribute the success of the coup to the generalized unpopularity of the Musahiban regime. In fact, the coup was a well-coordinated action probably far beyond the capability of the notoriously faction-ridden PDPA, whose leaders had been at daggers drawn for years. To examine the coup and the coup makers, it is useful to turn to salient points in the formation of the People's Democratic Party of Afghanistan and its two factions, the Khalq and the Parcham.

The question arises as to any Soviet influence on the founding of the indigenous Marxist party in 1965. If the Soviet Union was doing as well as it was doing in influencing the royal government through aid and political support, which in turn provided the opportunity to develop long-range infiltration into the military and the bureaucracy, why did it wish to have a local communist party? There were some contemporary observers and even later scholars who deny that the Khalq party was a communist party, holding that it was rather a reformist party in the broad tradition of twentieth-century Afghan modernization. The confusion is natural given the party's dual nature: its public platform, published in its newspaper *Khalq*, and its secret constitution, adopted at the party's founding meeting.

Publicly, the PDPA program called for the alliance of all progressive, democratic, and national forces to relieve the suffering of the masses. Although appeals to workers and peasants may be taken with a grain of salt, clearly a "national front" strategy was the only way of mobilizing the intellectuals, and in a country such as Afghanistan, they were the only feasible basis for a modern party. However, the messages of the party in newspapers and, most important, in the Wolesi Jirgah (People's Assembly), demonstrated that they had no real interest in a national democratic strategy. Their paeans for any Soviet action in the world or any development project planned for Afghanistan and their attacks on any action or aid project of the United States demonstrated that PDPA's primary allegiance was to the Soviet Union and not to Afghanistan.

It is impossible to know if Soviet agencies planned the actions of the PDPA; the split between Khalq and Parcham eventually proved to be real enough. Yet the Soviets moved with rapidity to take political advantage of it at the time. What is beyond doubt is that neither PDPA faction wavered in its fulsome praise and professions of loyalty to the Soviet regime and "the Great October Revolution." It is hardly possible to ignore the fact that the actions of the Karmal supporters (discussed later in this section), which made a crucial contribution to discrediting the constitutional regime, began at the first meeting of the Wolesi Jirgah. Despite that fact that the PDPA was not formally constituted until January 1, 1965, more than 3,000 demonstrators, mostly students, scarcely appeared spontaneously at the parliament building.

During the early 1960s several Marxist "study circles" were active in Kabul. One author mentions four or five of these: one run by Ghulam Dastagir Panjshiri (the brother and nephew of the then imprisoned Dr. Abdul Rahman Mahmudi), one formed by Shahrullah Shapur, another by Tahir Badakhshi, and a small circle around Muhammad Zahir Olfaq. All of these, except for the Mahmudi group, became prominent in the newly founded PDPA (Khalq), but the most important in the end were the two circles associated with Babrak Karmal and Nur Muhammad Taraki.[11]

These Marxist groups offered little criticism of the Da'ud regime before his dismissal in March 1963, despite the fact that Da'ud had had Karmal imprisoned and Taraki dismissed from his government position. The Soviets, too, had little to criticize in Da'ud's policies since, from a foreign policy angle, they called for close cooperation with the USSR and opposition to Pakistan. Had the situation changed in a liberal constitutional regime, however, the Soviets could have lost the entrée built up in the previous decade with Da'ud as prime minister. There was the danger that a reformed constitutionalist royal regime might prove attractive to the vast majority of modernist intellectuals, the core of the articulate dissatisfied. Such an eventuality, combined with the traditional deference of the rural population toward the monarchy, would have left the small Marxist groups irrelevant. The inclusion of provincial notables in government through free elections to parliament and elected provincial assemblies would eliminate another source of dissent and isolate the tiny minority of Marxist-leaning intellectuals from the new political system. On the left, there was also the danger that the "Maoist" group of the Mahmudis, now organized as the Shula-ye Jawid, would capture the leadership of the hard core of dedicated ideological Marxists. These were the dangers to the nascent pro-Soviet Marxists inherent in the introduction of a functioning liberal constitution.

Nur Muhammad Taraki continued his work as a local employee of the U.S. Information Service as a translator. Employment with a foreign mission (or even as a servant in a foreign household) required the permission of the Afghan security service. It was assumed as well to require periodic interviews and reports from those fortunate enough to receive such permission. Yet on September 30, 1963, Taraki left this secure and—by Afghan standards—highly paid position to begin full-time Marxist political organizing work. His biography states that he was also writing at this time, but this was not a position that could have paid a middle-class wage to any Afghan writer without an addition source of income that has not yet come to light.

The meetings that culminated in the foundation of the PDPA brought together most but not all of the Marxist-oriented intellectuals of Kabul. Democratic socialists led by Mir Muhammad Siddiq Farhang, who had been Karmal's superior as deputy planning minister, as well as the radical Mahmudi circle, remained outside. In theory, the constitution of 1964 had made political activity legal, but it was still in a twilight zone, as the promised political parties law was yet to be passed by the newly elected parliament. (It was passed but never ratified by the king in the years before in the coup of July 1973.) Within three months from the promulgation of the constitution, these separate leftist groups had prepared a twelve-page platform and an eleven-page party constitution. The platform praised all past reformers of Afghanistan since 1919, especially King Amanullah. It called for a national democratic government to be implemented by a united national front ranging from workers and farmers to small bourgeoisie and national capitalists. Only in its final paragraph did it mention "socialism" in relation to Afghanistan, although the words "democratic," "progressive," "freedom," and "national" appear in virtually every sentence. In the PDPA's secret constitution, however, it proudly claimed to be a party ideologically based on the "practical experience of Marxism-Leninism" and was thus the "vanguard of the working class and all laborers of Afghanistan."

Within a few months of its founding the party supported at least eight candidates in the 1965 elections to the first Wolesi Jirgah. Three of the candidates, including Karmal, were elected. Dr. Anahita Ratebzad, who won one of the seats reserved for women, was to become a formal party member later. An indication of the scope of the voting was seen in Kabul, undoubtedly the most sophisticated city, with the highest proportion of voters. Even there only about 15,000 of 40,000 eligible people voted. All of the future Khalqis, including Taraki and Amin, were defeated. One observer, quoting Mrs. Taraki as his source, writes that the nine-month-old party was able to finance its campaign after a visit by her husband to the Soviet Union.[12]

The elections were contested on an individual basis in the absence of parties. The press law had not yet been passed, which later allowed parties to wage "unofficial" political campaigns pending the adoption of the parties law. Candidates thus had to run on the basis of their individual personalities and reputations. Invariably, they stood in their home districts, where they could at least have name recognition and the support of their families and friends. The main form of campaigning consisted of presenting great *pillaus* (feasts) for the local notables and influential people. These were not inexpensive.

The founding meeting of the PDPA thus merged, at least on a tactical basis, numerous groups that had never been too close and whose relationships were to go from bad to worse in the following eighteen years, until the fall of the Najibullah regime in April 1992. This bloody record, including coups, purges, murders, torture, and assassinations, clearly indicates the deep divisions (to say the least) within Afghanistan's Marxist movement. Perhaps at the beginning of the unified party the Soviets had hoped that the divisions between the Taraki and Karmal groups could be submerged in a common struggle against the regime. There was little distinction ideologically or even tactically between the two leaders (who were elected by the PDPA as secretary general and deputy secretary general) either before or after their open break in 1966. Both were loyal to the national democratic party platform as published in *Khalq* in April 1966. Both were equally effusive in their praise of every past, present, or future policy and action of the USSR. After the party split each claimed to be the legitimate holder of the party's name and organization. The designation of *Parcham* (Banner) for the faction of the PDPA led by Karmal (from the name of the newspaper published from March 1968 to July 1969) was always unofficial. Karmal claimed that the Parcham faction and the PDPA were one and the same. Taraki, however, never received permission from the Ministry of Information and Culture (necessary under the press law) to resume publication of *Khalq* (or any other paper) once it had been closed at the insistence of the parliament for its criticism of the constitutional monarchy and Islam. Taraki was not a member of the Wolesi Jirgah either, a position that Karmal used to establish his claim as leader of the left in Afghanistan. Taraki and his Khalqi followers, however, could point to the fact that Karmal and Parcham received the special favor of the Royal Government of Afghanistan. In fact, he enjoyed the use of an official car and driver as well as a coveted apartment in the modern Soviet-built Microroyan complex, though he was supposedly just one of the more than 200 members of the Wolesi Jirgah.

Many observers have noted that the fundamental internal division in the party, besides being based on purely personal animosity, also reflected sociocultural differences stemming from the divisions between rural or very recently urbanized Pushtuns and the relatively sophisticated long-term residents of Kabul, both Pushtun and non-Pushtun. The "old-timers" had the advantage of an elite education at the prestigious Kabul secondary schools and at Kabul University as well as the contacts they had built up through their families' residence in the capital, and these advantages were reinforced by the Dari linguistic and cultural orientation of Kabuli elite (even those of Pushtun background). The new first generation of urbanite intellectuals, overwhelmingly of provincial tribal backgrounds, felt both envy and contempt for the "Persianized" Kabuli elite who monopolized good governmental positions and had betrayed the Pushtun linguistic and cultural heritage. Pushtun students in Kabul at the Pushtun secondary boarding schools were impressed with Hafizullah Amin's voluntary teaching and advice. They wished to study Marxism only from a fellow Pushtun in the Pushtu language. Despite the paucity of similar anecdotal information, we may assume that this dividing line among civilian students was mirrored in the military between the higher ranks and the junior officers. The higher-ranked military officers (colonels and generals) were virtually all Pushtun in origin, with the exception of a few Nuristanis, but came overwhelmingly from the "Persianized" Pushtun elite, whereas the junior ranks, more recent trainees, came from the provinces. The Soviets would have had ample information by this time, after almost a decade of military aid and training programs, on the susceptibility of the Afghan officer corps to both ideological and material methods of subversion. The division within the military necessitated a similar division in recruitment of the military to the PDPA, either as actual party members or as sympathizers. Given the separate security apparatus within the military, there were few if any open sympathizers with Marxist ideals, let alone party members, to be found. Hafizullah Amin was entrusted with the vital task of increasing the PDPA's presence in the military once the reunified party (July 1977) began seriously to plan for the coup of 1978.

The choice of Amin was no accident, and he aimed his recruitment efforts at precisely the same group of young Pushtun officers that had provided such a receptive basis for his recruitment efforts in the civilian educational sector. With the traditional military obsession with rank and merit-based promotions, the youthful officers were correct in their belief that the higher ranks of the military had no intention of diluting their dominant status until absolutely forced to do so.

Whether the Soviets had planned to create the sociocultural and linguistic division among the PDPA members, they were not slow to exploit its full potential. But when the need for unity in the face of dangers to the party arose and Soviet interests became clear in 1977, they moved rapidly to bring the party together for its new task of seizing power in its own name.

Between 1963 and 1973, the pro-Soviet communists had to compete with rival groups farther to the left, including a determined opposition of "ultra-leftists" and the pro-Chinese Shula-ye Jawid of the Mahmudis as well as the ethnic leftist group Sitam-i Milli (Against National Oppression). These non-Soviet Marxist elements came under attack during the following decades under both Da'ud and the PDPA. Many members were executed or driven into exile.

At the same time, the Khalq posed a "left" specter that the Parchamis could raise before the regime. This was an important influence on the king's decision not to ratify the political parties law passed by the parliament. In turn, the moderate socialist and liberal democratic supporters were thus prevented from legally organizing to support the new democracy of the constitution of 1964. As the "royal communist party" (the label derisively used by the Khalq), the Parcham was able to position itself with the royal regime as the reasonable left alternative close to the Soviets, and hence no threat to the monarchy. Babrak Karmal boasted of his close ties to the Soviets. He appeared at embassy parties with his arm over the shoulder of the Soviet ambassador, Alexandr Puzanov. On a more personal level, he would give out chits to friends and clients seeking medical treatment at the Soviet embassy's dispensary. Karmal expressed his devotion to Zahir Shah as the great leader of Afghan democracy in a speech to the Wolesi Jirgah. Of course, the monarch believed that the Soviet Union was in favor of good relations with his government.

For Karmal, however, his good relations with the king did not extend to the king's ministers. The first meeting of the newly elected legislature came in October 1965. It was to confirm the government of Dr. Muhammad Yusuf, who had been selected by the king to move from his successful role as the interim prime minister in the drafting of the constitution to that of the first prime minister under the new constitution. Few observers expected any trouble in the formality of obtaining a vote of confidence in the Wolesi Jirgah. Any opposition would be seen as an insult to the monarch, who in the Afghan tradition enjoyed the right to appoint his own ministers, regardless of the provisions of the new constitution. But this first meeting of the parliament turned into a disaster. A well-planned disruption by the PDPA members to protest against the Yusuf government was reinforced by a student invasion of the chambers. After the chambers were cleared, rioting continued the next day in the streets as the Wolesi Jirgah met without any outside observers under heavy security. By official count three people were killed when rioters, protesting their exclusion from the Wolesi Jirgah, were fired on by soldiers of Central Forces Kabul, under the command of Sardar Abdul Wali, son-in-law and a cousin of the king. This *sehum-i-aqrab* (25 October) incident served to poison the atmosphere of the entire constitutional period. Almost incidentally in the confusion, Yusuf's government won an overwhelming vote of confidence, but he immediately resigned, taking responsibility for the bloodshed. Despite its reputation among some foreigners, Kabul was not a violent city, and no such bloodshed had occurred in its streets since 1929.

Students were aroused and angry over the actions of the army. The political establishment was alarmed as well. It feared that political liberalization had gone too far at the expense of order. Thus, primarily but not exclusively through the actions of Babrak Karmal, the PDPA faction in the Wolesi Jirgah, the rioting of students, and the reaction of Central Forces Kabul, the chances for the success of the liberal constitution were greatly diminished or—as it appears in retrospect—extinguished.

The Parchamis received legal permission in July 1968 under the press law to publish the newspaper *Parcham*, and the Khalqis were turned down in their attempts to get permission to resume publication of *Khalq*. Babrak Karmal had been one of the most prolific contributors to both *Khalq* and *Parcham,* but he was never the publisher or editor of either. Taraki, however, had been both editor and publisher of *Khalq*.

Two important pillars of political liberalization were never implemented during the constitutional period, the political parties law and the provincial assemblies law. To the legalistically minded, the former deficiency made it impossible to form legal political parties, although the PDPA virtually ignored this technicality. The Karmal faction operated as a political party in all but name. Both Prime Ministers Muhammad Hashim Maiwandwal and Nur Ahmad Etemadi attempted to organize "government" parties. Maiwandwal's *Musawat* (Equality) party appeared on the verge of success, but ill health forced his resignation in 1967. Under the Da'ud-PDPA republic, he became one of the first casualties when, either inadvertently or deliberately, he was killed in prison in 1973.

The consequences of the lack of provincial assemblies is more difficult to assess. Legally it left the upper house of the parliament, the Meshrano Jirgah (Assembly of Notables), incomplete, since one-third of its members were to be elected by provincial assemblies. Some said that this made the entire constitution illegal, as the legislative branch was incomplete. Provincial assemblies were felt to be vital by members of the constitutional drafting committee. They would establish a formal political link between Kabul and the provinces and would give the people engagement in practical electoral politics at a level that they could understand, because provincial issues had a more immediate impact on their lives than did the distant politics of Kabul. Without the outlet that might have been provided through provincial assemblies, the local notables' only means of participating in the new liberal system was through membership in the Wolesi Jirgah at the national level. This led to clashes of cultures and interests that came to be viewed in stark terms by both the conservative provincial members and the modernist elites of Kabul. This division allowed the Parchami faction to place itself in the center of the political spectrum. They warned against provincial assemblies charging that they would be captured by the ultraconservatives and would become centers of local rebellion.

The Parchami could increase their influence with the modernist Kabul elite as the defender of the social reforms instituted by Afghan governments since 1919 against the ignorant traditionalists of the backwoods. To this Kabul elite, the left radicals, including Maoists and Taraki's Khalq wing of the PDPA, were the enemy on the left, and both the traditionalist mullahs (led by the Hazrat family of the Mujaddidis) and the Islamist political activists centered in the Shari'at Faculty of Kabul University formed the enemy of modernism on the right.

An evaluation of the overall impact of the two wings of the PDPA during the constitutional period (1965 to 1973) reveals them to have been a major factor in the failure of the liberal experiment. Their direct actions led the king to hesitate in his reform program in midstride. To be sure, the situation was a difficult one, and the record of modernizing monarchs in Afghanistan and elsewhere is none too brilliant. The communists were by no means the only enemies of the constitutional experiment. Many members of the royal family, not only Da'ud, resented their exclusion from political activity by means of Article 24 of the constitution. In the Loya Jirgah of October 1964 the constitution was amended to strengthen the prohibitions on political activity by the royal family to include activities in political parties as well as the holding of office. One of the unhappy royal sardars visited the U.S. embassy to warn of the danger from great khans and provincial religious leaders, which would in his opinion lead to anarchy as in 1929. Sardar Abdul Wali, who had been responsible for the disastrous firing on demonstrators by the armed forces outside parliament, was known to have political ambitions of his own. As for Da'ud, he rejected repeated requests from Zahir Shah for his political advice and influence in making the constitutional experiment a success.

The political system of the monarchy lost credibility at the levels of both popular and elite opinion in the wake of the two-year drought of the early 1970s. The paralysis of the government and legislature, the mediocrity and venality of the bureaucracy, and the lack of leadership from the monarch were unmistakable. In 1972 the U.S. ambassador, Dr. Robert G. Neumann, felt that it would not last another year. None, however, could predict who its successor would be. The Soviets, through the PDPA and the covert networks that they had established over decades, had ensured that they would be positioned to shape the future. When Da'ud approached the Parcham to join him in a coup against Muhammad Zahir Shah, the man who had dismissed him as prime minister, the Parcham did not hesitate, although the Khalq reportedly was against any alliance with Da'ud.

Sharing Power: The First Afghan Republic

What led to Da'ud's coup on July 17, 1973, and why did it have the support of the PDPA and of the Soviet Union? To what extent did Soviet action help the coup to succeed? The understanding of the international context in which the coup occurred is important to the explanation of why Afghan Marxists and their Soviet supporters joined with a royal republican to topple a long and relatively benign monarchy.

First, it should be clear that at that time Soviet domestic considerations played no part in the foreign policy decision, as they would later. The decision by the Soviet Union was based purely on foreign policy and possibly ideological considerations. In 1973 the Sino-Soviet conflict was at its height. The Afghan government of Muhammad Musa Shafiq refused to support the anti-Chinese "Asian Collective Security" organization pressed by Leonid Brezhnev as he attempted to ostracize China internationally and regionally. The second consideration stemmed from the politics of the subcontinent, which had historically held first priority in Soviet views of Afghanistan.

The political situation in Pakistan was still characterized by turmoil that dated from the agitation that had led to the resignation of President Ayub Khan in 1969. Equivocating about its alliance with the United States, Pakistan had given notice to the United States to close its communications intelligence base outside Peshawar, which was used for overflights in the Soviet Union. At the same time, it continued its Central Treaty Organization (CENTO) membership. Pakistan's questionable pro-Western stance was replaced with what must have been considered by the Soviets as a far more dangerous alliance, that of Pakistan with China. The Soviet Union responded in 1970 with an alliance of its own with Pakistan's nemesis, India. The stage was thus set for the events of 1971 leading to the civil war between East Pakistan (Bangladesh) and West Pakistan, the intervention of India in the civil war, and the independence of Bangladesh. Subsequently, the Pakistani military dictator, General Yahya Khan, resigned in disgrace and was replaced by the populist politician Zulfikar Ali Bhutto.

As discussed earlier, the general policy of the Afghan monarchy during the liberal constitutional phase had been to seek good relations with Pakistan and to downplay Pushtunistan. As a consequence, during the brief Indo-Pakistani War of 1965, Afghanistan not only remained quiet on the Pushtunistan issue but also discreetly helped Pakistan. Aid from both Iran and Saudi Arabia to Pakistan was especially important since the United States had proclaimed an arms embargo. The Afghans allowed vital components to be shipped by air to Kandahar and then trucked over the border to Pakistan. Pakistan Civil International Airlines received safe haven for its aircraft on Afghan airfields. However sincerely the Afghans felt about the just cause of their Pushtun brethren, they felt even stronger ties of solidarity with their fellow Muslim Pakistanis locked in confrontation with Hindu India.

Likewise, in the Indo-Pakistani War of 1971, the restraint of the Afghans with regard to Pakistan's weakness was even more evident. When Zahir Shah visited Moscow in early 1971, he and his advisers met as usual with the Soviet leaders in a general conference. Brezhnev then requested a private meeting with the Afghan monarch—so private as to exclude even an Afghan interpreter. The king emerged from the meeting clearly shaken. In his explanation later to delegation members and to his family, he said that Brezhnev had asked the Afghans to join with the Soviets and India in finishing the job of carving up Pakistan. Afghanistan's reward would be the Pushtunistan. The king had replied that Afghanistan could not attack a fellow Muslim nation, but Brezhnev persisted by stating that all the Afghans would have to do was to stand aside and let the Soviets transit through their country to accomplish their goal. Zahir Shah again refused.[13]

Friendly Iranian-Afghan relations were also progressing, from the Soviet point of view, at an alarming rate. The long-standing dispute over the Helmand River waters was seemingly resolved by a treaty signed on March 13, 1973. The king and his new prime minister (December 1972), Muhammad Musa Shafiq (the principal drafter of the 1964 constitution), had pushed the ratification of the Helmand Treaty through the two houses of the legislature by the end of May.

Internally, the unaccustomed activism of the Shafiq government and, especially, the strong backing it received from the king, left little room for any meddling that was bred from general discontent. It seemed as if the king had resolved doubts about the constitution. He gave Shafiq the confidence of royal support, and his active influence with the vast conservative majority of the Wolesi Jirgah gave promise of breathing life into the nine-year-old constitution. Indicative of the success of the new government was passage of the budget within two days after the vote of confidence on the government. This same budget had been submitted nine months earlier by the previous government but had failed to pass.

Speaking from exile in Rome in 1975, the former king agreed in retrospect that part of the reason for the coup might well have arisen from Soviet fears that the Shafiq government would succeed. At the same time, Zahir Shah absolved his cousin from blame, saying that he believed that Da'ud had acted to prevent an even worse situation if a communist coup had been attempted. Of course, he and his family were at that time being supported in their exile by Da'ud's regime (as well as by the Shah of Iran and the Saudis).[14]

The planning for the coup of July 1973 had begun well in advance of the appointment of the Shafiq government. It coincided with the rising domestic discontent over the ineffectiveness of the government's response to the drought of 1970–1971. It also coincided with the king's refusal of the Soviet offer to cooperate in attacking Pakistan. Soviet sources admit that the coup was planned and carried out with the aid of supporters of the PDPA, who "formed the left wing" of the regime. The PDPA had at least four of their members and close supporters serving as ministers. PDPA leaders who rose in importance later, such as Colonel Muhammad Aslam Watanjar, performed prominent military roles in both the 1973 coup and that of 1978.

The coup mounted by Da'ud against the monarchy included the political leaders of the Parcham faction as well as the military networks, which can best be identified as a mixture of Parcham, Khalq, and Soviet agents. Real control of the military side was directly by the Soviets. Pakistani sources assert that Da'ud secretly visited the Soviet Union before the coup and formally agreed to share power with the PDPA. Whether or not this visit actually took place, it is clear that the Soviets had direct contact with Da'ud in Kabul.[15]

Even without a formal agreement for power sharing, in Moscow's view Da'ud was preferable to the monarchy. For one thing, it was assumed that he would support an active anti-Pakistan policy with regard to both Pushtunistan and Baluchistan. In fact he did, promptly. His policy of friendship with the Soviet Union facilitated the infiltration of pro-Soviet agents into the highest levels of the Afghan governmental structure. As collaborators with the new president, they might be expected to influence or even control his foreign policy. The problem with this Soviet analysis is a lack of any consideration of Da'ud's character. The only influence on his policies was his brother Muhammad Na'im. A member of his former cabinet noted: "Sardar Da'ud never consulted with his own ministers. He gave orders. We were all treated as privates before a general."[16] Nonetheless, despite his known character, it could be assumed that the PDPA stood a reasonable chance of succeeding him (he was born in 1909) either upon his natural death or through a subsequent coup. In any case, the crucial issue of legitimacy of government was eased somewhat because Da'ud, a royal prince, headed the coup rather than a minority Marxist faction.

Most of the Khalqi faction of the PDPA, with the exception of some of its military members, remained outside the new regime, although they did not actively oppose it. They endorsed the Da'ud coup and Da'ud's stated policies, but they continued to call for the reunification of the party and its dedication to achieving a socialist future for Afghanistan. However, they were highly skeptical of the prospect of Da'ud's keeping his side of the bargain; they were correct in this assessment. The Parcham and the Soviets felt that they had already achieved their maximum feasible goal. Karmal initially held that Da'ud's revolution was *the* revolution, that Afghanistan was on the road to socialism, and that the PDPA had no need for continued partisan activity. The "royal communist party" now became the "republican communist party."[17]

Da'ud Sheds the PDPA

Both the Soviets and the PDPA soon had reason to question the validity of their assumptions regarding President Da'ud. By 1975 he had effectively eased well-known Parchamis out of office. He also began to move toward a rapprochement with Pakistan. In 1975, in a last-minute decision, he attended the funeral of King Faisal of Saudi Arabia. There, King Khaled brought together President Da'ud and Zulfikar Ali Bhutto in a private meeting with a view to their reconciliation. The Saudis wanted to form an effective anticommunist front in the Middle East and feared communist influence in Kabul. Both sides were willing to further explore this option.

Da'ud and his brother Na'im embarked on a round of foreign visits and consultations to Iran, Pakistan, and Arab countries (including Egypt). From Iran and the rich oil states of the Gulf, they obtained pledges of financial aid more than sufficient to free Afghanistan from economic dependence on the Soviet Union. In the wake of the oil embargo and price explosion of 1973–1974, these countries had the funds to devote to the region in efforts that would enhance security.

By 1976 regional efforts had succeeded in forestalling Afghan-Pakistani confrontation over Baluchistan, a brewing trouble spot, stirred by Soviet efforts. Bhutto and Da'ud exchanged friendly visits in Kabul and Islamabad. Da'ud sought to diversify the training of Afghan officers by sending some to Pakistan in addition to the USSR. During his visit to Pakistan, President Da'ud spoke at the Shalimar Gardens in Lahore in terms indicating that the Pushtunistan issue would soon be resolved. He electrified his audience by quoting from a poem of Pakistan's national poet, Muhammad Iqbal, praising Afghanistan as the "beating heart of Asia." During this tour of the magnificent Moghul gardens, Da'ud was diverted to a tent set up by Pakistan's military intelligence service, Interservices Intelligence Agency (ISI). The ISI had laid out an exhibit of photographs of clandestine meetings in Kabul between supposedly loyal Da'ud supporters, Soviet intelligence officials, and PDPA activists. At first, Da'ud was blasé, feeling that he already knew all of this from his own secret police. However, as he found that one after another of those he trusted were involved, his expression became increasingly animated and concerned.[18]

In January and February 1977 Da'ud held a Loya Jirgah to institutionalize his revolution through a republican constitution (some three and a half years after his coup). He barred participation to PDPA members both in the drafting of the constitution and in serving in the Loya Jirgah. This constitution officially moved Afghanistan into a more active semisocialist state. It called for the enactment of "deep fundamental economic and social reforms" and the "elimination of exploitation in all its forms and manifestations." Land reform was promised. Natural resources, key economic sectors, and big industries were to be nationalized, and all business was to be regulated with the goal of eliminating exploitation. For the first time in Afghan history, class divisions were formally acknowledged. Before this, all citizens had theoretically been equal. Now the second article of the 1977 constitution outlining its "fundamental objectives" stated that power was to be exercised by "the people, the majority of whom consists of farmers, workers, the enlightened people and the youth." The single-chamber legislature was to embody this principle with the requirement that half of its members be farmers and workers. Deference was given to the armed forces, who received a political role through the High Council of the Armed Forces. Da'ud was unanimously elected president by the Loya Jirgah for a six-year term.

Perhaps the most important provision of the 1977 constitution was its fortieth article, which dealt with the position of the one party, "the national revolutionary party," as "founder and vanguard of the popular and progressive Revolution of Saratan 26 of the year 1352" (July 17, 1973). This party had been founded in 1975 in an attempt to monopolize politics, thus excluding Da'ud's collaborators—the PDPA. However, the party's Central Committee was announced by President Da'ud in 1977 without consultation with anyone. It was widely criticized as a combination of Da'ud's old cronies and corrupt ministers. Da'ud was faced with resignations from his cabinet and had to persuade them to withdraw their resignations. The party was seen to be a temporary measure. It was created to reflect social demands and the low level of the people's political education until they attained their "natural maturity." It was then, presumably, that pluralism would be allowed. Although the national assembly was to be elected by "universal, secret and direct elections," candidates were to be nominated by the party. The PDPA was further marginalized.

The Reunification of the Parcham and the Khalq

If there was to be a single government party, then the two wings of the communist party, Khalq and Parcham, had lost the reason for their division with one as the "royal communist party" and the other as the "left opposition." The Parcham had also lost any reason for supporting Da'ud as its vehicle to political power. Reunification negotiations between the two wings of the PDPA had begun as early as 1975, but their course did not go smoothly. Khalq reproached Parcham for revealing their talks, which they had promised to keep secret. They published a long document giving their version of the party split and blaming it, not surprisingly, on Babrak Karmal.

The decisive action solidifying the Soviet decision to force the reunion of the two wings of the communist party in order to seize power directly came during President Da'ud's state visit to Moscow in April 1977. As a routine exercise, Afghan heads of state discussed issues of the multifaceted Soviet-Afghan relationship at the highest level. Advisers accompanied the political leaders for working-group technical follow-up talks with Soviet counterparts. On that state visit, as described by a participant, in the midst of routine discussions, Brezhnev spoke in crude and unexpectedly direct language to Da'ud. He warned Da'ud that Afghanistan was allowing too many foreign specialists, some from member states of the North Atlantic Treaty Organization (NATO), even in northern Afghanistan, an action not sanctioned by past Afghan governments. He claimed that these foreign experts were mere imperialist spies. Da'ud's reply to Brezhnev was equally blunt: "We will never allow you to dictate to us how to run our country and whom to employ in Afghanistan. How and where we employ the foreign experts will remain the exclusive prerogative of the Afghan state. Afghanistan shall remain poor, if necessary, but free in its acts and decisions." He then rose from his chair and began to leave the room, naturally followed by the entire Afghan delegation. Immediately Brezhnev, Aleksey Kosygin, and Nikolay Podgorny tried to intercept him. Eventually, President Da'ud paused and shook hands with his host, but he turned down Brezhnev's offer of a private meeting the next day. The technical working groups did convene the following day, but not the political leaders.[19]

The talks between the Khalq and Parcham factions of the PDPA reunion—ultimately successful, though as a truce rather than a peace—began in March 1977, the month before Da'ud's crucial last visit to Moscow. However, this time they were carried to their conclusion, which came in July 1977.

President Da'ud repeatedly made it clear that he wished to maintain friendly relations with the USSR and to be truly nonaligned. He would never be a party to the encirclement of the Soviet Union. In October 1977 Da'ud drew back from his decision to protest unapproved Soviet overflights of Afghan territory for their military supplies to the new Marxist regime in Ethiopia. But it was too late to redeem Soviet faith in his fealty to them: The Soviet leaders had decided that the risk of losing the entire investment of the previous twenty-five years (not only the communist party but also the secret cadres created within the Afghan bureaucracy and military) was too great if Da'ud succeeded in developing the country through the aid from the oil monarchies of the Gulf.

With Moscow's nurturing, the PDPA reunion formally took place in July 1977, with Nur Muhammad Taraki as party secretary and Babrak Karmal as the secretary of the Central Committee, as they had been twelve years before at the PDPA's founding. Membership in the Central Committee was divided equally between the two factions. Immediately they began to plan the ouster of the Da'ud regime. In Karmal's own words, expressed to an Indian scholar in 1980: "Russia wanted that there should be a revolution here."[20]

Work within the military, a key position, was assigned to the Khalq's Hafizullah Amin, in deference to his strong Pushtun ties and his position as Taraki's right-hand man. In this aspect, however, Parcham reneged on the agreement. They continued the activities of their own "military specialist," Mir Akbar Khaibar. Of course, much deeper throughout the military were those officers, unknown to either Khalq or Parcham, who were awaiting their orders from the Soviet State Security Committee (KGB) and Chief Intelligence Directorate (GRU).

Da'ud had betrayed his Marxist allies, in their view, by not sharing power with them and by being seduced by Arab and Iranian gold to give up the nationalist goal of Pushtunistan, which he had done more than any Afghan leader to support. Simultaneously, he was attempting to deemphasize the role of the Soviet Union both as a political ally on the Pushtunistan issue and as a model of modernity. The killing of Da'ud and his entire extended family as a deliberate part of the coup of 1978 grew out of the fear that his erstwhile Marxist allies had of him.

Marxists with Illusions: The Taraki-Amin Years (1978–1979)

The coup d'état of April 27, 1978, established a new pattern that was to dominate Afghan politics for the next decade and a half—a pattern of total dependence on the Soviet Union. However, the Marxist regime came to power with illusions that they were in control of their bilateral relationship—that the Soviets would accord them freedom of action in their revolutionary reconstruction of Afghan society. This, more than the soon to be demonstrated incompetence of the regime in providing even a minimal degree of effective governance, doomed it from the start. The Soviets, in fact, cared nothing for the revolutionary transformation of Afghanistan, but they cared a great deal about the control of Afghanistan, which could provide them a secure base (and valuable, well-armed allies) for further advances into more promising areas of the Middle East and South Asia. They wished above all not to lose what they had gained through decades of patient effort and considerable expenditure.

Whereas the old regime (including the five years of the Da'ud republic) had a keen understanding of the need for balance in both foreign policy and a domestic policy of gradual change toward a modern-day national state, the new regime felt that everything was now possible. They attempted to revolutionize society with a few orders from the center and a policy of ruthless brutality to eliminate any actual or potential centers of opposition. In this way, they drove away potential allies from among modernist elites and traditionalists. These elements had looked forward to a chance to rectify the favoritism and patronage that had limited their scope. Instead, the members of the Revolutionary Council and the cabinet were unknown and inexperienced administrators who previously had occupied second-rank positions.

The entire post–World War II period, from the first political reforms of the Seventh Parliament through the economic and social reforms associated with Da'ud's prime ministership, politicized in the constitutional changes of the 1960s and the return of Da'ud in the republican regime of 1973, exhibits a continuity of purpose despite its many detours. With the shift toward regional cooperation in the mid-1970s, coupled with the movement to settle the debilitating issue of Pushtunistan, Afghans could finally look to a future that would combine their traditional social conservatism and Islamic social values with a modern progressive leadership. Despite considerable opposition from conservative forces, and from the new Islamist movement, few doubted that President Da'ud was a nationalist who stood for independence above all. His dramatic movement toward accommodation with Pakistan demonstrated that his vision of Afghanistan's future was not merely an excuse for continuing Pushtun and Muhammadzai rule over ethnic groups and tribes. This regionally based foreign policy had been coupled with the even more popular policy of removing known communists from positions of power and influence. The communists had met with little popular response or sympathy to their plight of having been betrayed by the man whom they had helped to gain power. Indeed, Da'ud was admired for his ability to outmaneuver the communists, who were seen as incompetent amateurs playing against a master. The assessment of Da'ud was that his control of the internal political scene was solid enough to withstand the opposition it had clearly aroused among the Soviets. Da'ud correctly saw the limited political appeal of the Marxists, even to their natural constituency of the Kabul dissidents. What he failed to realize was the extent to which the directly controlled networks of the Soviets in the military and security apparatus had been able to undermine these vital agencies, which he, more than anyone, had established and nurtured. Soviet policy had always been cautious when supporters came to power through military coups, preferring rather to influence such regimes once they attained power. With the amount of influence they gained worldwide through military and economic aid programs, assistance missions, and training, it was dangerous to demonstrate that such programs could endanger the very regimes that had invited them.

The coup leaders in Kabul immediately set out to prove that they were what they were manifestly not—that is, a true social and political revolution of the masses in which the military had merely acted as the progressive vanguard for the majority. This situation reinforced the naive tendency of the Marxists, marginalized in Afghan politics and society as an antinational and atheist splinter of a broader modernist movement, to exaggerate their own role as leaders of a vast and unstoppable revolutionary movement.

Nowhere was the difficulty of transforming the PDPA into a ruling Marxist party more apparent than in its internal disunity. The leadership of the regime was divided between the Parcham and Khalq factions in the same way that leadership of the party had been balanced in 1977, but Taraki was not only president but also prime minister. He gave Babrak Karmal the post of first deputy prime minister, which could mean whatever the prime minister wanted it to mean. Abdul Qader, a Parchami air force officer who had been a key ally of Da'ud in 1973, was named minister of defense as reward for directing air attacks on the Arg Palace. However, he was not well placed to control the armed forces as a whole, in which the army, not the air force, was the dominant service. The air force, with the need for extended individual and technical training for officers, had a larger percentage of officers trained in the USSR, and proportionally a larger number of Soviet advisers, than other services. The foreign ministry was given to Amin, who was also the second deputy prime minister. Thus the Khalq faction took control of the most prestigious of all ministries, the ministry that would have the greatest amount of contact with the Soviets and the greatest role to play in fulfilling the Soviet aims for Afghanistan in South Asia through reviving the Pushtunistan conflict.

The major internal political program of the Soviet advisers concentrated on the non-Pushtun minorities of the north.[21] This is somewhat puzzling, given the domination of ethnic Pushtuns in the Khalqi regime and the fact that the non-Pushtun groups had never proven to be decisive in Afghan politics, either traditional or modern. It argues for the importance of Soviet guidance in the regime. They could scarcely be expected to create a series of ethnic republics, along the lines of Soviet nationalities policy in Central Asia and the Caucasus, in as centralized a nation as Afghanistan. But they appealed to minorities on the basis of cultural and linguistic equality to a greater extent than any previous Afghan government and, in the process, against the dominance of Pushtuns, both in the north and nationally. This step may well be seen as a defensive measure against possible Chinese interference through Sitam-i Milli sympathizers. The policy was influenced openly by the common linguistic and cultural ties among ethnic groups who had coethnics in the Central Asian republics of the USSR. As a practical measure, the majority of the civilian Soviet advisers came from among Persian, Uzbek, and Turkmen speakers, since there were scarcely a thousand ethnic Pushtuns in the Soviet Union. Muhammad Khan Jalallar, an ethnic Turkmen and former minister in the royal government and that of President Da'ud, had been a key agent of the Soviets in the government, reporting to them on Da'ud's efforts to free Afghanistan from its dependence on the Soviets. His subsequent career in high positions (including his return to his old post of minister of commerce from 1980 to 1989), despite his not being a member of the party, indicates that he enjoyed a strong influence on Soviet policy as a direct agent, as did his highly profitable business activities during the communist regime. Another high-ranking member of the government (and eventual prime minister) was Sultan Ali Keshtmand, the party's token Hazara, who was married to a sister of the founder of Sitam-i Milli, Dr. Tahir Badakhshi. Badakhshi had been a founding member of the PDPA in 1965. Keshtmand was a Parchami, and his ties to Badakhshi resulted in his arrest and torture when the split between Parcham and Khalq became open again later in 1978, although he managed to avoid execution, which was Badakhshi's fate in September 1979 when Amin assumed total power.

The Parcham was reduced to a supporting role in the Khalqi regime almost immediately; interviews and major pronouncements came from Taraki himself and, increasingly, from his number-one aide, Hafizullah Amin. Even though Babrak Karmal had been far more prominent in the public eye for years, he was unable to use his oratorical skills in rivaling the leading public positions of Taraki and Amin. Instead the newspapers, radio, and the increasingly important medium of television were dominated by a full-blown Taraki cult of personality. Amin deferred to Taraki as the "Great Leader" of the revolution, and Karmal and his fellow Parchamis were ousted from the government within months and sent into the traditional form of exile in diplomatic postings to Washington, Islamabad, Prague, New York, and so on, where they would be forced to operate under the control of Amin's foreign ministry. Soon they were accused of plotting a coup with their fellow Parchami Defense Minister Abdul Qader and others. All remaining prominent Parchamis were arrested, stripped of their party and governmental positions, and charged with treason. The Parchami ambassadors were recalled as well, but they judiciously chose exile under Soviet protection.

The most remarkable aspect of the renewed infighting in the party was not that it happened but that the Soviets did little for a long time to influence the outcome. Evidently, they felt that Amin and the strongly Khalqi military would prove to be a more effective instrument for Soviet control than the more urban elitist Parchamis. They had ample opportunity since 1965 to evaluate the two wings of the party, and they saw in Amin a strength and ruthless energy that was lacking in Karmal. The Parcham was ideal for influencing an independent government of Afghanistan and gaining the allegiance of the Kabuli cosmopolitan elite, but the Khalq was the party of the hard-core Pushtuns, much more useful in appealing to Pakistan's leftist Pushtuns led by Khan Wali Khan. They could not have been unaware of the rival networks, especially in the military, of the extreme Pushtun nationalists of Afghan Millat (Afghan Nation; also known by its formal name, the Afghan Social Democratic Party). A number of the military mutinies that soon began to sap the strength of what remained of the army in bloody, fratricidal conflict (many deserted or failed to report for their military service) were actions of Afghan Millat officers rather than Islamists.[22] The Afghan Millat allied itself to Pir Gailani's opposition movement. Amin was the man who could better keep the loyalty of the military. Amin and Taraki signed the new Soviet-Afghan treaty in Moscow in December 1978, virtually without reading what had been dictated to them. They also had performed well in their roles of supporting Soviet policy in the Non-Aligned Movement (a role that precluded them from publicly proclaiming themselves as communists).[23] However, the Soviets had the perspicacity not to put all their eggs in the Khalq basket, and kept alive the alternative of returning to the Parcham should the Khlaqis fail.

The confusion of interparty conflict and the need to provide some rudimentary provincial administration when the representatives of the old bureaucracy either were ousted or fled the country, made it difficult to develop any new policies to capture broader political support. It seems remarkable that the regime could have ignored the necessity of using the existing rural power structure of khans and mullahs, given the fact that the elements of the state bureaucracy were distrusted as appointees of the old regime. The communist regime felt so secure in its backing by the Soviets, however, that it attempted to eliminate the old rural social structures. The regime's Marxist interpretation of Afghan history led it to seek to avoid repeating the circumstances around the failure of King Amanullah's reforms in 1929. That failure, they held, had been brought about by an alliance between the traditional social and religious leaders and British imperialists. Because control of land is the key strength of any rurally based elite, attacking the traditional system of land ownership appeared to be the key to breaking the power of the opposition movement before it could get started. The hastily conceived and partially implemented land reform program was an economic disaster that brought chaos at all levels of society. Even after the end of the Amin regime, following the Soviet invasion of December 1979, Soviet scholars continued to defend the necessity of the land redistribution program. Criticism of Amin centered on his methods (force and failure to pay compensation), not the program itself.[24]

The strategy of land reform succeeded only in part against those who were its political targets. The Afghan resistance was not led by the former great khans and landlords, since many of these laid low or fled the country. However, the Khalq regime failed to take into account the innate conservatism of the farmers, their strongly traditional Islamic belief system, and the social role of landowners as leaders of village society. The removal of this level of leadership, which historically had provided the basis of Kabul's control over the countryside, meant that the new leadership of the opposition movements did not have to fight the existing rural power structures and the government at the same time. The lack of complete and accurate land records, the paucity of trained agricultural economists and financial specialists, and the wide disparity of landholding conditions from region to region, appears not to have been considered by the regime. The difficulties experienced in earlier land reforms in Afghanistan and neighboring Iran and Pakistan (as well as the agricultural problems in Soviet Central Asia) were well known to the communists, but in their view the necessity of a social coup in the countryside to accompany the political coup in the capital outweighed any possible rational economic calculation.

There can be no doubt that the crucial failure of the PDPA regime of Taraki and Amin derived from the lack of party unity. Aside from the clash between the Khalq and Parcham wings, the Khalqis formed separate factions, some in favor of Taraki and others in favor of Amin, and still others waited for Moscow to indicate its favorite local communist. However, it was clear that Amin had control of the military and security services, with the latter securely in the hands of his nephew, Dr. Asadullah Amin, while his own son led the party's youth organization.

Amin may have been relatively more an Afghan nationalist (or at least a national communist) than either Taraki or Karmal, as some sources argue. He did not have the long personal association with the Soviet leaders that the two top political leaders of the PDPA had, and he demonstrated special favor for the newly arrived rural Pushtuns with whom he worked in Kabul. Perhaps Louis Dupree puts it best in his remark, made when Amin was still in power, that "the reality is that the DRA regime acts in ways it *assumes* the USSR wants it to act, because it *assumes* the USSR will never abandon it."[25] Amin was not averse to exploring possibilities of securing U.S. assistance as well as Soviet. Given Afghanistan's officially "nonaligned" status, this was only to be expected and, indeed, would strengthen his role in the Non-Aligned Movement. It could also serve to weaken Pakistani support for the opposition movements starting to organize there. The United States had yet to launch a movement to support these groups, although it certainly listened to their representatives. Washington appeared still too preoccupied with the Iranian Revolution and the burning of the U.S. embassy in Pakistan to pay much attention to the situation in Afghanistan. Amin directly approached the Americans for aid but was not willing to give anything in return.[26]

Amin could have no illusions that the survival of his regime depended on the support of the Soviet Union and that support would be forthcoming for whoever was the most likely person to consolidate the revolution and use it to advance Soviet interests. With the growth of the resistance movements this came into question, but it did not immediately have any effect on Amin, as he was the foreign minister. After the dangerous uprising and mutiny of the Seventeenth Division in Herat in March 1979, which was accompanied by a massacre of Soviet advisers and their families, Amin became prime minister.

In September the clash between Taraki and Amin came to a head, and it was Amin who triumphed. The Soviets by now were persuaded that only a unified party could hope to establish control over the rapidly deteriorating situation. They persuaded Taraki, in a personal meeting with Karmal in Moscow, to restore the unity of the party by bringing back the Parcham leaders. However, Moscow's plan failed because Amin was warned beforehand of Taraki's plan to remove him. Amin struck preemptively, removing Taraki from office and having him suffocated in prison. The Soviets had to put the best face on this reversal, even when now President Amin had the temerity to ask for the removal of Ambassador Puzanov, who was personally implicated in the anti-Amin plot.

Still, Amin felt to the end that the Soviets would support him, for only he could deliver the military, and it was the military that was vital for securing the country against the counterrevolutionaries. Amin did not object to the growing Soviet presence within the military, with increased advisers down to the company level. He even allowed complete Soviet combat units into the country so that they could relieve the army of some of the task of defending Kabul and free it for offensive operations in the provinces. Even as the handpicked Soviet special forces moved to attack his presidential palace at Dar-ul-Aman, he was attempting to communicate with those very same forces for protection against what he believed to be a Parchami coup attempt.

Marxists Disillusioned:
Karmal and Najibullah (1979–1989)

The period of Soviet military occupation can be divided into two phases. In the first, from December 1979 until May 1986, the Soviet policy was war rather than politics. In the second phase, from 1986 to 1989 (a year after Mikhail Gorbachev came to power and Moscow realized that the war was militarily unwinnable), the policy shifted to a political one of "national reconciliation." In a larger sense, these distinctions are artificial. The reality was that the Afghan Marxists had no illusions that the regime could be independent when the country was occupied by the Soviet Fortieth Army. The Afghan communists were useful internationally, if ineffective inside Afghanistan, for they provided the fig leaf for the Soviet presence in the country. As the lopsided United Nations votes on the Afghanistan question demonstrated, the Kabul regime was not considered by the vast majority of the international community to be an independent government. It owed its very existence to the Soviet Union, not to any international legality (loose though the standards of such international legality were in practice). This international opprobrium was tempered only by the seemingly immovable obstacle of Soviet interests and the Soviet army. No one, even the United States, was willing to use force to change the situation. Therefore, it seemed that the regime would exist as long as the Soviets wanted it to last, since it was assumed that they could never accept a defeat, as the United States had eventually grudgingly accepted in Southeast Asia.

The political tasks set for the Karmal regime by its Soviet masters were inherently incompatible. Internationally, it was intended that the regime gain respectability so that it would appear to represent a genuine national government, albeit one closely allied to the USSR. The Soviets realized well enough that their invasion of December 1979 would arouse international protests, but they counted on the short-lived nature of the indignation of world opinion. Once the world realized that Afghanistan was a fait accompli, governments and public opinion would forget about it soon enough. In private conversations at the United Nations, they cited their previous experience with military interventions in Hungary and Czechoslovakia, which had aroused great indignation and condemnation in international forums but within a few years had failed to secure enough votes to be included on the agenda of the UN General Assembly.[27]

This Soviet expectation eroded gradually as it became necessary to increase the numbers of their "limited contingent" and to play the leading role in fighting as the effectiveness of the Afghan military declined precipitously as a result of increased desertions and internal conflict between the overwhelmingly Khalqi military and the new Parchami regime. Simultaneously, the transformation of the war from a civil conflict to an international one aroused the Afghan people to increased resistance, which gained more effective international support. The reality of war, symbolized to the world by the dramatic increase in refugees, made it impossible for the Soviets to practice political "damage control."

Internally, the new regime needed to maintain the loyalty of the PDPA through commitment to revolutionary change. But at the same time, it had to demonstrate to the overwhelming majority who rejected such change that reforms would now be carried out in a measured fashion, with respect for Afghan traditional values, and particularly for Islamic values and leaders. It was never explained how these national and Islamic values could be better respected and guaranteed through a Marxist regime instead of either the old regime, which they had overthrown, or the Islamically based opposition of the mujahidin. Above all, Babrak Karmal, who proudly boasted that Afghanistan was the most friendly country in the world to the Soviet Union, could never dispel the image of having arrived atop Soviet tanks, despite the much justified criticism of Amin's dictatorial rule. Karmal was unable to persuade any of the liberal reformers prominent in Afghan politics to join his government, however grateful they were for being freed from imprisonment. Mir Muhammad Siddiq Farhang was personally approached by Karmal to join the government. He was told, "Now we have an opportunity to do what should have been done after April 1978. We can rally all progressives, party and nonparty, who want to work for the welfare of the country." Farhang replied that this strategy might have worked if it had been attempted earlier, but now there was only one issue that counted for all Afghans, and that was the occupation by the Soviet army. Karmal immediately replied that this was his aim as well: "The Russians will be leaving soon, in a month or so."[28]

In 1981 Kabul revoked implementation of the land reform decrees for those who agreed to support the government by selling it their produce. However, this step had little meaning when there was no security in the countryside, since two-thirds of the country was under the control of the resistance and much of the rest was virtually constant war zones. District governors were forced to commute to their administrative centers by helicopter, and the actual administration fell gradually into the hands of local mujahidin councils and commanders. Without a presence in the countryside it was impossible for the government to secure accurate intelligence for military operations in the countryside. Efforts to obtain the support of the traditional leaders against the mujahidin floundered when the party could not assure that Soviet forces would suspend bombings of rural populations. One Baluchi leader reported that he had joined the government's convening of a Loya Jirgah in 1985 in order to have the bombing of his tribe stopped. The result was that the Soviets continued to bomb while the mujahidin marked him as an enemy. His only solution was to leave the country.[29]

As for the Soviets, their hope that their intervention would lead to a healing of the internal divisions of the party came to naught. The Soviets had underestimated the difficulty of this task. They assumed the PDPA to have sufficient discipline, once the Soviets had made it unmistakably clear that Karmal and the Parchamis were in charge, that party members would see the futility of continuing their feuds in the face of the hundreds of Soviet political advisers who now occupied the ministries, military units, and administrative institutions. The ideological continuity of the revolution was asserted by describing the new regime as the "New Phase" of the Marxist Saur Revolution. This description made it awkward for the Parchamis and Karmal personally, since they had to acknowledge being subordinate to Taraki at the time of the coup, when it had been Taraki who had ousted, disgraced, exiled, and tortured their leaders. The Khalq supporters still comprised a large majority of party members and had an overwhelming number in the military. They could scarcely be dismissed, and a number of Khalqis, including the military officers Sayyid Muhammad Gulabzoy and Watanjar, and even the dreaded head of the security services, Assadullah Sarwari, who had personally tortured Parchamis, were brought into the Karmal government in an effort by the Soviets to enforce party unity. Sarwari eventually was sent into diplomatic exile as ambassador to Mongolia. Gulabzoy had to be retained in order to control the strongly Khalqi Interior Ministry.

The separate state security organization, KhAD (Khadamat-i Ittila'at-i Daulati, State Information Service), was given to Dr. Muhammad Najibullah, a Parchami with personal loyalty at the time to Babrak Karmal, whom he had served as a bodyguard before the revolution. The military, to be controlled by Parchami political commissars, refused, in many places, to accept new Parchami commanders appointed from Kabul. Assassinations were commonplace in the ongoing war between Parcham and Khalq. Officially blamed on the mujahidin, everyone knew their real causes. The mujahidin took delight in spreading false lists of their "secret supporters" in the regime, confident that they would be used as ammunition in the intraparty feuds by one faction or another. The Soviet army grew justifiably distrustful of their Afghan colleagues, since any intelligence was doubtful: KhAD would report Khalqis as suspect while the military and interior ministries would do the same with the Parchamis. Eventually, the Soviet military came to believe no results of any interrogation at which they were not actually present.

There is no central theme or policy underlying the blood feuds of the Marxists except the struggle for power. They were reduced to the status of despised auxiliaries in their own country, as they were all caught up in the growing war against the resistance. Social programs could scarcely be expected to show any success in a regime that was under siege and lacked control of the country. The party grew in numbers, although the numbers seemed to vary widely from speech to speech. However, the new adherents (sought by the Parcham in particular so that they might eventually outnumber the Khalqis) were hardly dedicated revolutionaries. Idealism had given way to opportunism. The new members were even more concentrated in the large cities, and particularly in Kabul, as it was unsafe to reveal oneself as a party member where security was not especially strong. Party membership conferred many privileges—education, housing, food, liquor, and jobs—but it could be dangerous as well. The need for military recruits to replace deserters meant that young party members would find themselves in the military before they could enjoy the privileges of membership in the new elite.

All of Karmal's attempts to bring about party unity and enforce discipline floundered on the Khalq-Parcham fault line. The all-PDPA meeting in 1982 to promote unity turned out to be a disaster. Interior Minister Gulabzoy interrupted Karmal's speech and was backed by noisy demonstrations of support by Khalqis as he demanded an explanation for attacks on him and his ministry. The head of KhAD, Najibullah, rose to defend Karmal, and the meeting deteriorated into bitter attack and counterattack, and had to end before schedule.

Eventually, Karmal proved an embarrassment to Soviet policy as it began to emerge under Gorbachev after March 1985. In his first year in power, the new general secretary maintained and even increased the scale of war in Afghanistan, carrying out the strategy of attempting to seal the border along the mujahidin supply routes through the use of highly trained special forces. In the meantime he continued and intensified the policy of devastation in zones outside government control. The war in Afghanistan, however, did not fit into Gorbachev's overall policy of glasnost and perestroika. He felt that it had turned into a debacle for the Soviet Union and was too closely associated with the policies of the Brezhnev era and the renewed Cold War. Glasnost meant that it was no longer possible to keep the price of the war a secret, although the true casualty figures were never released. The replacement of Karmal became necessary to the reaching of a diplomatic solution through the Geneva negotiations. Though the Soviet Union did not abandon its policy of support for the PDPA regime, Karmal's identification with the USSR and the war made him an unlikely figure to gain support for the new policy of "national reconciliation" designed to appeal to the common desire for an end of fighting and a deemphasizing of Marxists as the sole political force in national politics. Non-PDPA individuals, commanders, and eventually even the leaders of the mujahidin parties (with the exception of Gulbuddin Hekmatyar) were welcomed to share power in a reconstituted Afghanistan. The PDPA, however, was envisioned as the leading party among many parties.

As a practical matter, the role of the party in government and the military declined. Nonparty individuals were appointed to senior government positions, including prime minister. However, the party continued to dominate the security forces, interior, defense, and foreign affairs ministries, and the presidency. In the military field, the role of tribal and ethnic militias expanded beyond their original role of preventing the mujahidin from operating in their home areas. In addition to this passive role, the militias now obtained heavy weapons and large salaries and became a mainstay of the regime as they were deployed increasingly outside their home areas.

These new policies were not a total break with Karmal's leadership, but he was personally unacceptable to too many, both within the regime and outside it, to be the person to implement them. As they had in 1978, the Soviets opted for more energetic leadership, but a leader they could trust more than any Khalqi. The selection of Najibullah, head of the KhAD, was not expected, although he had risen within the party hierarchy to become one of the party's secretaries. However, he was a Parchami and a Pushtun. The security service was the government agency that had worked most closely with the Soviets, and thus he was well known and considered loyal to Soviet interests. It was also the most efficient entity in a regime not noted for its efficiency. There were demonstrations by Parchamis in favor of Karmal, who eventually was forced to leave the country for exile in the USSR, not to return until June 1991. Instead of ending intraparty factionalism, the removal of Karmal created a new faction of his supporters within the Parcham wing. Other party leaders saw the need to build their own factions as well, for if the Soviets had chosen to get rid of one so closely associated with them, they might well be tempted to make yet other changes. The Khalqis remained in their positions in the military. General Shanawaz Tanai, minister of defense, who had risen through the ranks of the military and the party as the most successful of the military leaders, took over the leadership of the Khalq. In 1990 he made a bid for power via a military coup. The attempt failed, but it led to the dismissal of most of the remaining senior officers of the Khalq faction from the army and the party. Tanai himself fled to the protection of the Hekmatyar faction of the mujahidin and eventually to Pakistan. The policy of blurring the lines between party and nonparty members brought new dangers for Marxist ideology. The more the regime identified itself as a national party to attract the resistance, the greater the chances that party members would regard the mujahidin parties as viable alternatives.

As Gorbachev moved toward ending the Soviet Union's military presence by means of a political solution guaranteed by the USSR, Pakistan, and the United States, the PDPA further divested itself of its Marxist ideology. In January 1987 President Najibullah announced a unilateral cease-fire (which was not observed), and in June the word "Democratic," widely associated internationally with Marxists, was dropped from the country's name. In November 1987 the first actual constitutional revision—as opposed to decrees or the "Fundamental Principles" of 1980—was made to delete mention of the PDPA as the revolutionary vanguard.[30] In 1990 the attempt to blend the party back into Afghan society turned full circle as its Marxist ideology was dropped along with its very name; it officially became the Watan (Homeland) Party. The Soviet Fortieth Army had departed by February 1989 as a result of the agreement reached at Geneva, and there was no longer any advantage to be gained for the party through advertising its past record. Two years before the fall of the Communist Party of the Soviet Union, the People's Democratic Party of Afghanistan ended its official existence after only twenty-five years of operation. From its proud origins as the vanguard of the revolution, it now attempted to maintain its position only in disguise.

The disguise did not fool the Afghan people. The resistance continued to refuse any deal in which the newly named party and its leader, Najibullah, would have a national political role. The borders were opened. To survive, the Kabul regime abandoned large areas of the country to the resistance but held onto a reduced territory. It concentrated on fortifying Kabul and other major cities and on keeping open the major communications routes. They could only succeed in this effort through continued massive infusions of Soviet aid (estimated at US$300 million a month), and direct support from

Soviet air force missions and from Soviet troops in civilian clothing who continued to fire thousands of SCUD missiles. They could survive as well because of reduced support for the resistance from their allies. These countries, including the United States and Pakistan, had secured their major aim with the withdrawal of the Soviets. Thus it was only after the end of the Soviet Union itself that the Najibullah regime fell. The Marxists never would have seized power in the first place, nor would they have held onto it for so long, without constant support from the USSR. In April 1992, fourteen years after the Marxists had taken power, the last of the Marxist Afghan presidents, Najibullah, fled to the protection of the United Nations in Kabul. His departure to New Delhi to join his family was blocked by his own Parchami commanded army, and he died at the hands of the Taliban.

Chapter Six

Holy Warriors, Mujahidin, and Fighting for Islam

"Chingiz Khan was not an enemy of Islam. Brezhnev has rolled up his sleeves to wipe the world clean of worship and prayer. He has instituted animosity to religion. Immortal praise to the mujahid nation who rubs the brows of this Chingiz of our time in the dust and who with their blood bring to a close his unjust and rapacious tyranny."
—Sayyid Makhdum Rahim, *Afghan Jehad* writer (1980)

The Afghan war against the Soviet Union put the term "mujahid" into the international vocabulary. Although there have been many instances of Muslims waging war against non-Muslims in the name of Islam, it was Soviet aggression in the climate of the Cold War that allowed respectability in the West for the concept of mujahid and its English-language translation as "holy warriors."[1] In the Muslim east, the holy warrior, whether mujahid or *ghazi* (one who wages a *ghazawat*, or victorious raid), was always a term of merit and legitimacy. Despite the fear of the spread of Islamic people, tactics, and ideals into the West that has begun to recast Western thinking about Muslim "defenders of the faith," in the east the concept of jihad, particularly if conveyed as *defensive* rather than *aggressive*, continues as a legitimizing concept, albeit not among Westernized and secular intellectuals. At the end of the twentieth century, to differing degrees, this is true among Muslims with as diverse a history as the Algerians, Muslim Palestinians, the Chechens, and the Bosnians. The concept of jihad has undergone transformation from the early Islamic centuries in that it is applied to defensive action rather than conquest of infidels or heathens, but it has maintained a positive, and righteous, aura. The anticolonial and anti-imperialist stirrings of the late nineteenth century, incoherent, disjointed, and easily suppressed, have emerged a hundred years later. The Afghan jihad provided a stage on which a spectrum of political ideas and religious convictions could be activated. These range all the way from Cold War greatpower manipulations to single-minded Arab Wahhabism.

The terms jihad and mujahid (and its plural, mujahidin) derive from Koranic Arabic, in which "jihad" applies to "those who strive" in the path of God rather than the more specific "those who fight" in the path of God.[2] Though in the West the mujahid has been taken to refer to men who engage in physical combat, Afghan sources have pointed out the broader, "those who strive" meaning and have applied it to writers, political activists, and women, particularly the old women who stayed behind in the countryside to provide refuge for mujahidin bands.[3]

Over a period of fourteen years (1978–1992) the mujahidin of Afghanistan underwent transformation from a small band of Islamist fighters inspired by a desire to institute the practices of revivalist Islam in their country to a disunited but dedicated citizenry from all walks of life who fought a technologically uneven war and, for all practical purposes, won. The period since the fall of communist Kabul to the mujahidin in 1992 has brought to the fore the many divisions both among the mujahidin and in the country as a whole. Complicated by intraregional rivalry and the disintegration of the Soviet Union, the civil war that has been waged among various factions of mujahidin has destroyed urban areas, especially Kabul, broken down normal trade and agriculture, and diminished the luster once attached to the term "holy warrior."

By the end of 1994 a new generation of Afghan fighters, bred and trained in orphanages and schools for refugees located in Pakistan, emerged to take the lead in trying to restore civil government. Whether they will in turn become yet another faction among the fractious mujahidin and continue the civil war remains in question. However, to distinguish themselves from the previous generation of religious fighters, they apply to themselves the term *taliban*, meaning students in general but more specifically students of Islamic madrasas. Thus the civil war has tarnished the term mujahid to such a point that it is eschewed by this newest generation of dedicated Muslims. It may well be that the Taliban represent not only Pakistani attempts to pacify Afghanistan but also a synthesis of the Islamists and traditional Islamic goals that has been tentatively called neofundamentalism.[4] Called popularly *mullah tulaban*, the emerging program of the Taliban indicates that their social policy will be strictly Islamic, that their composition and possibly their position is pro-Pushtun, and that they are anxious to open Afghan roadways to Pakistani transit trade with the new, desperately landlocked countries of Central Asia. But neither the concept of jihad nor the prestige of the object of the mujahidin should be dismissed hastily. The role that the Afghan mujahidin have played in recent Afghan events and their widely perceived miraculous victory over secularism and communism continue to have an impact on the confrontation between Muslim activists and their opponents. Therefore an assessment of the practical role that the mujahidin have played in recent Afghan events, particularly in their political formation and relationships within the mosaic of Afghan society, is important.

In this chapter we deal with two kinds of analysis: In the first we highlight the various ways in which the terms mujahidin and jihad have been applied in Afghanistan and in the region, the ways in which the Afghan resistance has succeeded or failed in making full use of the moral high ground afforded by religious sanction, and inter alia the reasons why religious zeal remains a potent, if not the only, arbiter of political action in Afghanistan and the region. In the second analysis we consider the three forms of "striving" or mujahidin action in order to reach conclusions about the relative effectiveness of each and the impact they may have on a future Afghanistan. The three mujahidin groups are the political parties, the field commanders, and the intellectuals and opinion leaders who urged on the jihad. The effects of all three, even the intellectuals, constituted the total effort to reverse the effects of the 1978 coup and its aftermath. Particularly as civil war began, the noncombatant participants in the war have become victims of betrayal and assassination, many being driven out of the region in search of safety. In the long term, the political, military, and intellectual wings of the resistance will have contributed together to the future of the country.

The Mujahidin Position and Kabul

Islamic politics played a key role in the confrontation between Kabul and the resistance. The terminology of "holy war" has strong cultural roots in the region and in Afghanistan in particular, evoking memories of colonial wars and imperial hegemony. The response is both emotional and intellectual. The articulation of the mujahidin's response played as much a role in their perseverance as did their successful acquisition of arms and regional support.

Historical Application of the Term Jihad in Afghanistan

Among the earliest of Afghan rulers to rally an army for attack under the banner of jihad was Mahmud of Ghazni, who led booty raids into the Indian subcontinent against Hindus during the eleventh century. Although not an Afghan in an ethnic sense, but rather a Turk, as a successful Muslim monarch Mahmud embellished his court with the trappings of Muslim Central Asian rule, including ornamental architecture and a court famous for its poets, Sufis, and philosophers, all writing in Persian. Since then, in Afghanistan and in the rest of Central Asia, jihad as a rallying cry has been used against non-Muslim colonists and invaders, against other Muslims considered heretical, such as Shi'a groups, and against any who have risen against the Muslim state of Afghanistan, without particular attention to ethnic affiliation. In some cases, the enemy, if Muslim, has counterrallied under the same rubric, as in the case of the Hazara Shi'a during the reign of Amir Abdul Rahman.

In the premodern and modern periods, the Afghan resistance represents the first case in which Islamic ideology has served as a rallying point for success against an outside, non-Muslim force. During the nineteenth and twentieth centuries, from North Africa to East Turkestan, when indigenous leaders tried to lead intellectual or military movements they faced not only far superior military adversaries but also local secular "modernizing" elements or entrenched oligarchies that allied together, and at times with outsiders, to defeat Muslim movements. The Mahdi movement in the Sudan (1880s), the Yaqub Beg rebellion in Kashgar (1860–1874), the Andijan rebellion in tzarist Turkestan (1898), and various intellectual and peasant movements in between, such as those inspired by Sayyid Jamal ad Din al-Afghani (1838–1897), all suffered from lack of a unifying direction. Moreover, Muslim revivalists became successfully branded as antimodern, and therefore, although they may have represented the inarticulate political and religious desire of many levels of indigenous groups to throw off foreign domination, their inability to find a modus vivendi with modernist trends caused them to lose momentum, and perhaps even more damaging for some, to retreat into isolated rural enclaves.

Incubated over several generations in small towns and madrasas of Afghanistan and at the great Islamic centers of learning, the Islamic revivalists thrived outside the political observance of central government. When they rallied again, during the 1960s and 1970s, their support came from the burgeoning, and newly educated, rural youth who craved social and economic opportunities that had already been commandeered by the offspring of secular urban elites. Coincidentally, by this time, for many Muslims secularist modernism, whether in Iran or in Afghanistan, had begun to show itself incapable of satisfying society on diverse levels: First, economic equity became increasingly diminished, and the gap between the wealthy and the poor grew wider as the wealthy began to connect with Western-generated sources of wealth (oil, cotton, Western franchises) while the poor remained tied to ever-diminishing returns on agricultural products. Second, the social safety nets previously provided by community (often mosque- or clan-based) had disintegrated as the state strove to control and eliminate institutions and leaders that might form a source of opposition. Third, the cultural divide between socioeconomic groups, seen as rooted in Westernization and rejection of local culture and custom, grew at an increasingly rapid pace with the advent of travel, communications, and the media. It is useful to note that in every case in which Islamic revivalism has succeeded, regardless of the range within the spectrum of Islamic traditionalism and Islamist idealism, the societal context has been either extreme secularism or pro-Marxism. Examples range from the rise of the Muslim Brotherhood in Syria and Egypt during the 1960s to Iran and Afghanistan in the 1970s and 1980s.

The emergence of an Islamic response has been accompanied with tactics associated with the concept of jihad. The cry of the Iranian Revolution of 1979 was directed against the "Great Satan" (the United States), the "Little Satan" (the Soviet Union), and against the *taquti* (Iranian quislings to local culture and religion—corrupt persons). Although rhetorically the United States became the focus of opposition (even after the freeing of the U.S. embassy hostages), the wrath of the Islamic government was activated against secularist Iranians, be they monarchist, democrat, or communist. Thus one sees the "striving for religion" being directed against fellow—but secularist—Muslims.[5]

In a similar manner, the Afghan Islamist movement began in the 1960s in response to the growing attractiveness of communist ideology for students and to the increasingly secular direction of the state. During the period of jihad, the Afghan resistance regularly lumped all its enemies, Afghan communist and Soviet expert and soldier, under the rubric "Russian." Thus the striving for religion, the jihad, was waged against indigenous Muslims and foreigners irrespective of their origins. Here, then, a further twist was added to the evolving application of the term jihad.

Although the term jihad has seen many transformations in the Afghan context, its application is broad in original Koranic usage and can include in the enemy camp born Muslims as well as non-Muslim opponents. For Muslims of this region, communism and Islam are regarded as implacable enemies and irreconcilably opposed despite efforts by Kabul to offer strenuous arguments to the contrary.[6] Even the platform of the Islamic Revivalist Party (IRP) of the former Soviet Union, though the party was driven underground in the Muslim countries of Central Asia, when drafted in 1990, specifically denied membership in the IRP to anyone who belonged to the communist party.[7] Through the activity of the Afghan mujahidin we see the term jihad, as currently interpreted, being applied in Central Asia, where mujahidin activity had hitherto been unobserved or, as observed in the 1920s and reinterpreted in the early 1990s, had lacked religious content.[8] For the Afghan mujahidin, Bukharan resistance to Bolshevik expansion in the 1920s was a failure as much of a weak Afghanistan in providing refuge and aid to the Central Asian resistance as to the betrayal of Islamic ideals by secular Central Asians cooperating with the Bolshevik state. For this reason the debt of the "mujahid nation" of Afghanistan to Pakistan for continuing aid to both the refugees and the fighters becomes critical in future Afghan-Pakistani relations. From one perspective it may be regarded as the Muslim duty of Pakistan to help Afghans, but from another, Pakistan deserves credit for fulfilling this obligation despite frequent poor relations between the two states in the past. From yet another perspective, Pakistan has used the Afghan jihad opportunity to enhance its international position as well as to enrich its oligarchy, and, desiring trade with Central Asia, it has sent in a trained force, the Taliban, to establish stability in the Afghan transit corridor. Despite claims by Afghan leadership and Pakistani officials that Afghans take independent action, it is clear that some influential Pakistanis have regarded the Amu Darya River rather than the Durand Line as the real border in the region. The presence of large numbers of Afghans in Pakistan, the integration of trade and much economic activity of the two countries, and the singular position of Afghanistan as Pakistan's link (and Iran's land link) to Central Asia, sets the stage for possible future conflict between the two as the good will generated by joint action for jihad diminishes over time.[9]

The Regional Application of the Term Mujahid

Observers of identity issues in the eastern Islamic world began in the 1970s to distinguish how indigenous people's self-identity depends on the circumstances and the interlocutor. Another school, mainly of indigenous origin, decries the emphasis on ethnic and sectarian difference in the region as indicative of outsider meddling. Just as controversy about terminology has existed side by side with the evolution of meaning discussed in the preceding section, so too has the proliferation of opposing groups claiming legitimacy as fighters in jihad.

Beginning in 1978, successive communist regimes in Kabul moved from portrayal of their Islamic-based opposition as "bandits" to the attempt to use the voices of Muslims worldwide to detract from the moral stance of the opposition and attract regional Islamic government to a directly negotiated resolution of the war. The opposition has remained adamant in its position that the Kabul regimes between 1978 and 1992 were both illegitimate and un-Islamic. Supported by the majority of the Organization of the Islamic Conference (OIC), the Afghan resistance succeeded decisively in this ideological struggle before achieving success in the field of battle. Undoubtedly, the actions taken by PDPA-led Kabul to introduce social reform by decrees in a clumsy and ill-planned manner helped the mujahidin cause by alienating all the mujahidin, whether they belonged to the Islamist or the traditional groups.[10] These actions, aimed at destroying local traditions and relationships in land ownership as well as gender relations, represented "Orientalism" filtered through a Marxist prism.

The urgency with which the Marxist leaders of the 1978 coup wanted to enact social revolution might have succeeded had they been able to rely on a strong military, as had Atatürk in Turkey and Reza Shah Pahlavi in Iran. But the Afghan conscript army did not recognize the Marxist rulers as legitimate, nor did they accept the condemnation of the growing opposition as mere bandits. As the Afghan army dwindled, the ranks of both the Islamist mujahidin and the traditionalist mujahidin were augmented. Indeed, the continued strength of the Islamist parties, both in the field and on the political front, owes much to their superior organization and to their foreign support. A hallmark of their organizational skill is illustrated in the conscious attempts they made to overcome both regionalism and monoethnicism in the party organization. The impetus for this effort came directly from their *ideological position* that Islam does not recognize linguistic and cultural divisions. As the war progressed, all the Afghan mujahidin groups fragmented into regional and ethnically exclusive groups despite Islamist ideology. Why this happened cannot be entered into here except in a very general way: First, the demands of guerrilla warfare require secure lines of communication both among the mujahidin and with their sympathizers among civilians and in the ranks of the army. Afghan society had not undergone sufficient homogenization and integration before the 1978 coup to allow trust to be extended beyond the village, tribe, and ethnic group—all the more so during conditions of war, when KhAD, the security institution, functioned as an instrument of terror and torture, especially under Assadullah Sarwari and later Najibullah. Therefore, ethnic groups coalesced within their region, and cooperation became more marked across traditional and Islamist mujahidin groups within the same region than among Islamists who belonged to different ethnic groups. The clearest example of this is the competition in the field between the forces of Burhanuddin Rabbani (Tajik) and Gulbuddin Hekmatyar (Pushtun), although both, as befits Islamists, maintained the appearance of leading a multiethnic following. Second, competition for outside support, be it in funds, arms, or recognition, ignited rivalry, especially when the Tajik Ahmad Shah Mas'ud garnered international attention largely because outside visitors found him accessible linguistically and personally. Few area specialists have mastered Pushtu, even among those who have studied Pushtun society. Most, however, know Persian, under which the Dari of Afghanistan can be subsumed.[11] The historic animosity between Pushtuns and non-Pushtuns surfaced as Mas'ud's fame grew, and this manifested itself in confrontation with the forces under Hekmatyar. In turn, the confrontation drove a further wedge of distrust among the Islamist mujahidin. Third, the suspicions within the region of Iran's intentions as a revolutionary Islamic state aroused suspicions about the susceptibility of related Afghan groups to sympathy with Iran. This meant that not only Hazara refugees and fighters received few funds except from Iran, but also that Rabbani and his followers came under some suspicion. Arab and American funds for the war, channeled through Pakistan, meandered toward Hekmatyar as a *Pushtun*, rather than Persian-speaking Islamist, despite his anti-American stand and the evidence that he demonstrated an intransigent authoritarianism reminiscent of the Ayatollah Khomeini's. The favoring of one Islamist over another deepened the chasm growing between the Islamist mujahidin, which only a few years earlier had cooperatively launched an unsuccessful attack against the Da'ud government.

The best hope for mujahidin unity, based on the specifically nonethnic and nonregional Islamist perspective, failed on the triple dangers of ethnic rivalry, envy, and distrust. If the Islamists could not unite, the challenge for the traditionally allied mujahidin was even greater without the passion for renewal that in some respects committed the Islamists to working cooperatively. These traditional mujahidin groups divided along ethnic lines as well as rural and urban lines. As discussed in the section on traditional Islam in Chapter 4, the picture was further complicated by urban/rural networks built around Sufi orders as well as tribal links. Among traditional mujahidin groups, the danger of regionalism and monoethnicism was even higher. This pattern may be observed in all parts of Afghanistan, even in the Hazarajat.

At the same time, in neighboring Iran the drama of Islam and politics pitted diverse Islamic groups against a secular regime that was unable to defend itself as pious and faithful to Islam despite attempts to brand the opposition as "Islamic communists." The initial success of both the Iranian Islamic uprising and the Afghan resistance came when traditional Islamic elements in society rallied against the central government. During the 1970s in both countries the radical Islamic elements, though dissimilar, had recruited among the youth and through radical means had tried to overthrow the government. In Afghanistan the Rabbani-Hekmatyar elements had tried to foment rebellion in 1975 by inciting the Tajiks of the Panjshir valley against Da'ud. Yet Da'ud's record did not show him to be anti-Muslim, although he was an avowed secularist. In the same way, the Mujahidin-e Khalq of Iran, having appropriated terms such as *shahid* (religious martyr or witness) for the many young men and women they lost in urban guerrilla warfare through 1975, still could not rally as massive a following against the shah as Ayatollah Khomeini could. Khomeini represented the pious and respected traditional center. In another uncanny similarity between Afghanistan and Iran, had the shah not been perceived as insulting the reputation of a holy man (with an article in the press accusing Khomeini of deviant sexual behavior), the momentum of public opinion against the shah might not have risen to destroy his base of support, especially in the conscript army. In Afghanistan too, when the PDPA under Taraki arrested the family members of the Mujaddidi in 1978, their action became symbolic for anti-Islamic action directed at the traditional center. Da'ud's crushing of the Islamists had not carried the same weight, nor did it have the same effect. For the twelve years after 1978 the PDPA, under two presidents (Karmal and Najibullah), tried unsuccessfully to overcome its initial negative image as an enemy of Islam.

In 1988, having made several attempts to rally regional Muslims to its side (through the Tashkent conference, the National Fatherland Front, and joint action with Soviet Muslim official bodies), the Kabul regime undertook one of its last major regional efforts to improve its Islamic image. Using the occasion of the convening of a conference dedicated to the Prophet Muhammad's birthday, Kabul issued a series of concluding resolutions. The topics of the resolutions are instructive, because they point to the elements within the spectrum of Islamic causes that Kabul (and Moscow) thought would gain favor regionally and among Afghans. The resolution topics were: (1) Settlement of all disputes by means of dialogue and understanding without bloodshed. (2) Support of the legitimate cause of the Palestinian people. (3) Resolution of regional conflict in El Salvador and Nicaragua and the end of discrimination in South Africa. (4) Implementation of a cease-fire between Iran and Iraq. (5) Stopping the war in Lebanon. (6) Declaration of the Indian Ocean as a zone of peace. (7) Witness to the numerous steps taken by the Kabul government to assure the well-being of Afghan Muslims through the creation of the Ministry of Islamic Affairs and Religious Trusts and the Islamic Science University, and the formation of the constitutional council to monitor compliance with observing and exercising Islamic shari'a. (8) Call on the Organization of the Islamic Conference to restore the Afghan (Kabul) position in the OIC. (9) Call on Saudi Arabia to provide a venue for talks that would terminate the fratricide in Afghanistan. (10) Promotion of the National Reconciliation policy in Afghanistan.

Despite the participation of Muslim individuals (not official delegations) from the United States, India, and Indonesia and official delegations from Libya, the USSR (Mufti Tajuddin), and Bulgaria, the resolutions of the conference reflect Cold War Soviet bloc positions shared by Kabul and Moscow at the time. Within this Soviet bloc there had been a consistent attempt to use Soviet Islam as both a model for Afghan Islam and as a cheering section for Kabul's communists. The multiple paper institutions created by Kabul to regulate Islamic activity followed the Soviet model, and the Tashkent conference of 1980, organized to condemn U.S. and Pakistani support of the mujahidin, attempted to present a solid Islamic front. In both these attempts Kabul failed to convince its focus audience—the region's Muslims. In large part the failure stemmed from regional and worldwide Muslim conviction that genuine Islam in the Soviet Union existed *de-*

spite official Soviet atheism and not because of it. Therefore, trying to bolster the Marxist regimes in Kabul by associating them with official Soviet Islam was a doomed effort from the start.

Despite Kabul's overblown Islamic rhetoric and activities, especially after 1987 when it became clear that the Soviet military presence would be withdrawn, Kabul did not carry its rhetoric so far as to claim a jihad. It claimed that the resistance forces were false Muslims but not that its own soldiers were mujahidin. Whereas the resistance regularly published brief biographies of its *shuhada* (plural of *shahid*), Kabul would not make similar claims. This is curious at first glance but explicable when examined in light of the bravado and the superiority of the negotiating position that it claimed. For the same reason that Kabul refused to negotiate openly with the mujahidin, correctly regarding this as an admission of the independent challenge of the resistance, so too its secularist and communist support would not allow its propaganda to extend to the labeling of its generals *mujahidin* or its dead *shuhada*. When in 1993, after the fall of Kabul, the interim president of the resistance allowed Rashid Dustam, the Kabul regime militia leader in Mazar-i-Sharif, to join the victorious mujahidin with the rank of general, many among the resistance leadership and rank and file regarded this inclusion of a government supporter as a betrayal of the true martyrs.[12] In an earlier case, when General Shanawaz Tanai fled to the Hekmatyar camp after his last unsuccessful coup attempt against Najibullah, the Hizb-i Islami of Hekmatyar could only excuse the sheltering of a communist general by claiming that he was a longtime sympathizer.[13] These examples serve to indicate the limits to Kabul's ability to claim Islamic legitimacy: Ideologically, it feared loss of support from its core atheistic and secularist supporters (including the Soviet Union), and realistically, it realized that within the Afghan population at large, where the Islamic stance was most critical, even the limited claims to piety were disbelieved. It may be too extreme to claim that Afghanistan's communist leaders were purely opportunistic and lacking in genuine convictions.[14] By the same token, cynical attempts to paint the mujahidin, even Hekmatyar, as without convictions are also deceptive exaggerations. Among each opponent's core sector, an unmovable ideological base existed that fueled suspicion and confrontation.

Within the region, since the start of the Afghan war, several local conflagrations have widely acclaimed the justice of their cause by declaring it a jihad: Saddam Hussein and Ayatollah Khomeini both made generous use of this term, although with Iran's many obviously religiously dedicated martyrs, its claim appeared to have a more convinced following. The Muslims fighting in Kashmir against Indian rule regard themselves as mujahidin, as do the Tajiks, especially members of the IRP, who describe themselves with the title of mujahidin. Azarbaijanis fighting Armenians in Karabagh have also used this religious terminology.[15] The most recent case, that of the Chechens, takes direct inspiration from the Afghan mujahidin because of the several similarities between the Chechens and the Afghans, both of whom were invaded by the Russian military. Not only did the Chechen receive materiel and manpower from the Afghans (mainly Arab "Afghans") and other Muslims but also the Chechen inspiration and determination to protect their independence appears to hark back to image of the Afghan mujahidin, if not particularly to the conservative or revolutionary ideals of the Afghan resistance.

The Success and Failure of Religious Sanction

In analyzing the Afghan resistance, sympathetic and antagonistic observers have been struck by the fragmentation of the mujahidin. For some, the strength of the underlying regional and ethnic divisions of the country vis-à-vis Islamic unity have appeared as an anomaly.[16] Others have so concentrated on the justness of one faction of the resistance that they have ignored the numerical strength of other groups as well as the legitimacy of their position.[17] Therefore, the evolution of the resistance, the redefining of Afghan nationalism and identity, and indeed the redefining of intraregional relationships have all been confusing when the Afghan situation is measured against a static model of the country and the region. If there has been a defining logic applicable to the Afghan region since the early 1970s, it is constant dynamism within a historically static and tradition-bound geographic people. We are concerned here with the dynamism of the resistance movement, of people from various walks of life whose mature years have become intertwined with the fate of the mujahidin, and of the young who will shape the next fifteen to twenty years.

The formation of the core resistance took two years and occurred in three stages. The Islamist factions, also called revolutionary Islamic groups, with their antecedents in the 1960s almost parallel to the communists, came from a social milieu similar to the Khalqi branch of the PDPA. Small-town and rural young men gained opportunities for higher education at the secondary boarding schools and at Kabul University. Here the young men became politicized and Islamicized under a small leadership that came from the same social setting but with a traditional Islamic background—Sayyid Muhammad Musa Tawana, Ghulam Muhammad Niazi, Abdul Rasul Sayyaf, Burhanuddin Rabbani, Mawlawi Hussein Jamil ul-Rahman, and Gulbuddin Hekmatyar, who continue to lead this movement, although Niazi died as a result of imprisonment and Tawana has taken a less public role as adviser to General Dustam rather than become factional leader.[18]

The coalescing of the Islamists into actual armed movement resulted at first in an abortive attempt to overthrow the Da'ud regime in 1975, backed by Pakistan. Unable to muster support among their rural kin, many involved in the effort ended up captured or in flight. While the Islamists licked their wounds in Peshawar, the PDPA coup occurred, and they were in a position to mobilize rapidly. Together with parts of the Hazarajat and Nuristan, the Islamists were the first to resist the establishment of the Khalqi regime under Nur Muhammad Taraki. Two Islamic revolutionary parties formed—Jami'at-i Islami-i Afghanistan and Hizb-i Islami-i Afghanistan, respectively, under Rabbani and Hekmatyar. Rabbani, older, al-Azhar-educated, and a Shari'at Faculty member, but of Tajik descent (from Faizabad), has come closest to formulating the political stance of the Islamic revivalist motivation and goals. Hekmatyar, a young (b. 1947) Ghilzai Pushtun, became involved in campus politics while at the engineering faculty of Kabul University and after 1973 escaped prison and went to Pakistan. Until late 1994, when the Pakistani government withdrew support for him after seeing that he would not be able to take a decisive role in a mujahidin-led government, Hekmatyar had led his party effectively in resistance politics, and his commanders had proved themselves loyal and successful in the field. A charismatic public speaker, Hekmatyar has vetoed continually the formation of a unified resistance by taking an uncompromising stand against secular resistance leaders such as Sayyid Gailani. A long-standing dispute with Ahmad Shah Mas'ud led to the ambush of important commanders under Mas'ud (1988) and later to alliance with Dustam against Mas'ud and his party leader, President Rabbani. The Rabbani and Hekmatyar forces began opposition to Kabul long before the coup of 1978, but in practice their movement gained prominence only after the un-Islamic character of the PDPA became apparent.

The second stage of the mujahidin formation began as the PDPA started to implement decrees aimed at altering Afghan customs and rules widely associated with Islam. The confiscation of private land and the negation of debt by decree engendered wide opposition, because these measures attacked the structure of agricultural production and the circulation of money in rural society. Added to these arbitrary actions came the arrest of the members of the Mujaddidi family. The formation of opposition to the PDPA during the spring and summer of 1979 from among rural traditional elements followed these actions. The alienation of the intellectuals began around this time as well, as large numbers were arrested and executed. It was in this second stage that most of the traditional resistance parties came into being.

The decisive step of intellectuals, nationalists, and government bureaucrats to join the resistance came only after the Soviet invasion on December 27–28, 1979. Some fled secretly while others made spectacular public exits.[19] This third stage energized the resistance, because it provided effective communication of the goals of the resistance to the outside world by harnessing the experience of Afghan intellectuals who fled into exile. The Afghan Information Center, the Cultural Council of the Afghan Resistance, and information sections of many of the political parties where intellectuals and diplomats worked contributed to dissemination of resistance information. The inability of the Kabul regime to retain the loyalty of these key ideologically uncommitted but fiercely nationalist urban elites after the Soviet invasion dealt a major blow to the effectiveness of their propaganda over the following decade.

The swelling of the ranks of refugees (*muhajirin*) also followed roughly the same time sequence as that of the formation of the ranks of the mujahidin. Refugees fled into Pakistan as fighting began in the eastern provinces and spread as the Soviet invasion led to the expansion of the war throughout the country. Refugees began flowing into Iran as well as Pakistan as fighting intensified around Herat, where, according to Afghan sources, 25,000 civilians were killed in one day alone. In the years after 1980, the refugee flow increased while the political parties fissured, and new leadership arrived to form parties that took advantage of the increasing funds for the resistance arriving from many sources, especially from the United States and Arab countries. Funds and facilities for refugees in Iran faltered while the politics of the Iran-Iraq War (1980–1986) allowed the usual donors to equivocate.

Despite the well-documented shift away from an antireligious stand that Babrak Karmal initiated, no reversal of resistance support occurred. Nor did the issuance of amnesty result in anything but a token return of refugees. In fact the wholesale destruction of villages, irrigation works, and agriculture led to further evacuation of the countryside, often to neighboring countries but also to the safer urban areas.

Among the many factors contributing to the formation of the resistance and the exodus of more than 5 million refugees, the atheism of the regimes in Kabul was only one, albeit an important one. Destruction of their homes and livelihood, fear of rapacious Soviet soldiers, the terror of summary imprisonment and execution, and general insecurity led to the refugee situation. Nonetheless, the factor that gave the resistance the will and passion to strive against the Soviet army was their Islamic faith. As the aftermath of the fall of the communist regime in Kabul has demonstrated, Afghan nationalism enjoys a weak base among the population. Nationalism, which may contribute to urban and intellectual endeavor, little affected the rank-and-file members of resistance bands. Despite the funds channeled to the resistance from abroad, most mujahidin lived difficult lives in caves and ruins without the comfort of home and family. Refugees, too, although they eventually benefited from basic medical help and education, which may not have been available in their remote villages, experienced extended disruption of home-oriented lives, spending more than a decade with little privacy or comfort. The deaths among Afghans easily reached one million, or one in fifteen Afghans. The number of maimed and those deprived of the ability to work, marry, and live normally is far larger. Yet the war continued until the Soviet army pulled out. Under civil war conditions, many refugees returned precisely because the threat to their Islamic way of life had been reduced. Together with monetary inducements for their return and means of return, and despite mined roads and farming lands, the steady return to the countryside indicates the anticipation of a political future that no longer threatens their cultural life.

The same assurance that encouraged the muhajirin to start to reclaim their homes beginning in 1989 led the Najibullah regime boldly to seek allies in the West to bolster its position. Using the U.S. cutoff of aid to Hekmatyar in November 1989 as a political stepping stone, Najibullah launched a campaign to exhort the United States to "join hands with him to checkmate the progress of the Islamic fundamentalists so that they may not be able to form or establish an Islamic fundamentalist government in Afghanistan."[20] Kabul's campaign to play on Western fears of Islamic fundamentalism, had it come in 1994 instead of 1991, might have fallen on more receptive ears (in view of the World Trade Center trials in New York City and popular identification of terrorism with Islam). Nonetheless, Najibullah's government correctly identified the area of uncertainty in the U.S. position toward the mujahidin. In a further appeal to secular and leftist sentiment, Kabul emphasized its women's organizational activities to contrast them with the widely feared "suppression of women" advocated by the Islamist and traditional groups. The Democratic Organization of Afghan Women (a Marxist-Leninist type of organization renamed in 1986 as the Afghanistan Women's Council) took the lead in publicizing fears among Westernized Kabuli women of a mujahidin victory.[21] By 1992, when Kabul finally fell to the mujahidin, both the UN push to include members or sympathizers of the PDPA (now renamed Watan Party) in an interim government as well as attempts to alarm the West about dangers from the resistance had come to naught. Pushed by the uncompromising position of Hekmatyar, the other Islamic parties from Peshawar had found it inexpedient to reach an understanding with Najibullah, and it did not seem possible then or since 1992 to invite the former king to take temporary leadership.

Viewed from the perspective of whether and how Islamic politics was a success or failure, three facts become evident: (1) Adherence to a conservative, nonsecular Islamic stance has allowed the mujahidin to persevere. (2) Attempts to co-opt the Islamic position or to raise alarm regarding its success did not rescue the Najibullah regime from failure. (3) Without an external (infidel) enemy (the Soviet military) or an internal, secular-atheist substitute, any semblance of unified mujahidin action has given way before ethnic rivalry and power politics. While disintegration may have been expected in the context of traditional Afghan Islam, the fact that the Islamist camps that showed promise of multiethnic revivalist Islamic hope also seems to have shattered into monoethnic components. The political situation during the civil war resembles the military situation of the late 1980s because of the apparent breakdown of interregional, intraethnic cooperation. The new hope seems to arise from rejuvenation of and return to religious sanction through the agency of the Taliban. Whatever their agenda may be, whoever their sponsors, direct and indirect, if the Taliban can claim the mantle discarded by the mujahidin, there is a good chance that Afghans will unite behind them. The success of the Taliban, however, will probably mean the establishment of a Saudi Arabian–style conservative Islamic government chary of revivalist innovation. Following that model, it may also employ autocratic methods less sympathetic to democratic institutions than either Pakistan or Iran.

The Three-Branched Afghan Mujahidin

Flamboyant, daring, or radical, the Afghan mujahid visualized in the West through journalistic accounts is more often than not the turbaned and mustachioed tribesman with a Kalashnikov or rocket launcher. Yet when the first stage of the jihad began in 1978, the fighters carried Enfield rifles, even rusting sabers, and few were organized into anything more than village units. By 1989, when the Soviet military left, field commanders communicated by satellite telephones, and Stingers were the elite weapon of the day. The fighter in the field had to be supported by an array of others, he had to be supplied, that materiel had to be donated or purchased, the donor had to be convinced of the justness or advantage of the mujahidin cause, and an army of journalists, diplomats, spies, and aid workers had to be kept informed and sympathetic. Though some attention has been given to the fighter and the organizers, the analysis has for the most part been uneven and based on spotty access. Little attention has been devoted to the gatherers and suppliers of information, a veritable quasi-administrative system run by Afghans in regional or foreign exile. The claims to fame and power put forth by political party leaders and field commanders notwithstanding, the running of a future government will fall upon the shoulders of the administrators. The success or failure of a future Afghanistan as an integral state or as one that has fragmented depends as much on the vision of the administrators as on other sectors of society.

The Political Organizations

The political organizations were located outside the war zone until 1992 when many returned to Kabul, and so they have been dissected often because of their more or less geographical accessibility.[22] The structure of the organizations is autocratic, with a leadership that gained legitimacy by virtue of factors other than elections. Because the organizations serve as extensions of the personality and position of the leader, they are known more frequently by the name of the leader than by that of the group. Remarkably, none of the leaders have passed from the scene for political or health reasons during the course of the entire jihad.

Attempts to form a united front against Kabul, which began in the spring of 1980, led to many realignments over the years. The single alliance that has lasted since then has been among the three political groups with a traditional Islamic hue: the Mahaz-i Milli-i Islami-i Afghanistan (National Islamic Front of Afghanistan, NIFA), the Jabha-i Najat-i Milli Afghanistan (National Liberation Front of Afghanistan, NLFA), and the Harakat-i Inqilab-i Islami (Islamic Revolutionary Movement). Regarded as moderates and representing traditional Islam (both Sufi and non-Sufi), ethnically these parties have been predominantly Pushtun, with only the Harakat attempting to include non-Pushtuns from the northwest and the north. Representative of their overall position is their consistent support for the return of Zahir Shah, at least as a symbolic, unifying leader. These parties have attracted urban elites, especially Kabuli diplomats and educated expatriates. The Harakat is the largest of the parties and has also splintered more often, losing sections to the Islamist parties (see Chapter 4). These parties were headquartered in Peshawar, where they were involved in fund-raising, the running of refugee camps, procurement of arms and munitions, and the politics of the resistance. During the civil war, some leaders remained in Peshawar, even after the mujahidin had taken Kabul.

Participating in the Islamic Unity of Afghan Mujahidin (IUAM) and, after Soviet withdrawal, in the Afghan Interim Government (AIG), the moderate traditional parties have contributed a stabilizing, generally pro-Western influence on the political negotiations. Sibghatullah Mujaddidi, head of NLFA, was elected the first president of the AIG on February 24, 1989, and later the first of the rotating presidency in Kabul in April 1992. Unlike his successor, Burhanuddin Rabbani, he vacated the post upon completion of his two-month tenure without seeking technical loopholes with which to extend his term. During his tenure Mujaddidi vigorously pressed for the AIG occupation of the Afghan seat at OIC and at the Non-Aligned Movement. Pir Sayyid Gailani, head of NIFA, was satisfied to remain in the background personally as long as his party was represented in any union or government. In light of the deteriorating conditions in Kabul and the uncertain results of the one-sided jirgah in Herat in December 1993, Gailani initiated plans for a more even-sided jirgah to convene in Jalalabad in October 1994. The meeting led to yet another formula for elections and a further agreement to remove all communists (namely, Dustam) from government posts.

Also falling within the moderate camp is the Shi'a Hazara party, Harakat-i Islami-i Afghanistan (Islamic Movement of Afghanistan), headed by Muhammad Asef Mohseni (referred to as Ayatollah in recognition of his advanced madrasa training in Iraq). Headquartered in Quetta (Pakistan) rather than Iran, Mohseni eschews aid from Iran, unlike other Hazara parties such as Sazman-i Nasr-i Afghanistan (NASR) and Hizb-i Wahdat.

Ranged between the Islamist parties and the moderates are a series of smaller parties that often act as swing parties in jirgah and shura. These parties, mainly Pushtu, also are regionally based. The most important are those led by Muhammad Yunis Khalis (b. 1919)—Hizb-i Islami–Khalis—and by Abdul Rasul Sayyaf (b. 1946)—Ittihad-i Islami-Barayi Azadi-i Afghanistan (Islamic Union for the Liberation of Afghanistan). The two parties differ in leadership style and personality as well as political position: Khalis has been distinguished by age and double duty as internal commander, and Sayyaf's eloquence coupled with Arab connections have earned him funds and reputation as hospitable to the controversial Arab volunteers among the Afghan mujahidin.[23]

Warily sharing the main Islamist camp are Gulbuddin Hekmatyar (b. 1947) and Burhanuddin Rabbani (b. 1940). Originating from the same movement in the 1960s, the two diverged in the 1970s and during the course of the jihad have gradually grown into implacable enemies. Aside from an increasing tendency to become identified as Ghilzai Pushtun and Tajik respectively, the two may also be identified as extremist and more compromising on various issues related to cooperation with other resistance parties and to the acceptance of communist government elements. Specifically, while strenuously objecting to participation in a union that included Gailani, Hekmatyar excused his ideological deviation when cooperating with the Khalqi General Tanai as well as with Rashid Dustam. Not trusted enough to hold a major post in any resistance union, nor trusting enough to enter Kabul when appointed prime minister in 1992, he has allied with whoever can bring down his chief rival, Burhanuddin Rabbani.

Of the two, Rabbani has a broader vision of an Islamic government for Afghanistan and the place of an Islamic Afghanistan within the region.[24] His Tajik ethnic background, however, has weakened his position and, in a replay of the Bacha-i Saqao history of 1929, has led to support for the Taliban movement among Pushtuns who otherwise might not have supported such a primitive political movement. Only the fear of the societal extremism of the Taliban allows Rabbani to maintain some trappings of the presidency he had held in Kabul. Many if not all of Afghanistan's neighbors continue to recognize his government, as witnessed by the Afghan seat he occupied at the ECO meeting held in Ashkabad in May 1997, more than a year after he was driven from Kabul.

Smaller parties—some splinters, others with specific programs—operated and continue to operate, vying for funds and turf, at the fringes of the active political parties that gained international recognition from bases in Pakistan. Some boast a military front, others claim only a political front.

Significant among these are Afghan Millat (Afghan Nation, derived from the name of its newspaper, though the party's formal name is the Afghan Social Democratic Party) dating from 1966, which advocates a united Pushtun stand, thus alienating Pakistan by raising the Pushtunistan issue. Its opposition to Hekmatyar has earned it defeat in the field and continual assassinations of leading members.

The Iran-based Shi'a groups of Afghanistan functioning among the Hazara include Shura, NASR, and Pasdaran as well as Mohseni's Harakat. Of these, the most traditional, Shura-i Inqilab-i Ittefaq-i Islami-i Afghanistan (Revolutionary Council of the Islamic Union of Afghanistan), is led by Sayyid Ali Beheshti, an elderly madrasa-educated notable. After 1982 he lost ground to the Khomeini-inspired Islamist NASR, led by Shaykh Mir Husain Sadeqi (b. 1930s). NASR's manifesto opens with the Koranic verse that refers to *killing* the household of Satan and the *taquti* (the corrupt) rather than the less radical references to "striving for religion."[25] NASR's violent methods earned it the enmity of other mujahidin groups, especially Pushtuns. Another Iranian-inspired group, allied with NASR, is the Sazman-i Pasdaran-i Jihad-i Islam (Organization of the Guards of the Islamic Jihad), which an Iranian publication on the political parties claims has activists in thirteen of the twenty-eight provinces of Afghanistan.[26] The same source lists only three specifically Shi'a groups: Hizb-i Irshad (Party of Help), Sazman-i Jawanan-i Islam (Organization of Islamic Youth), and Hizb-i Watan, which indicates that for the Iranians, the other Hazara parties were not exclusively monoethnic.[27]

In 1989 the Iran-based Shi'a groups, large and small, formed an alliance, Hizb-i Wahdat (Unity Party), which negotiated for considerable representation in the AIG, claiming that Shi'a represent 35 percent of the Afghan population. Wahdat claims to represent many ethnic groups and also claims to function along democratic lines, including elections for leadership positions. In June 1994, frustrated by yet another postponement of general elections by the Rabbani-led interim government, Wahdat held its own elections. In rivalry with Rabbani, it poses the second major threat to the return of exclusively Pushtun control of Afghanistan.

Also active on the political front are the two Turkic-based parties represented mainly by Rashid Dustam and Azad Beg. Both Uzbeks, they relied on support from among the Turkestani émigré community established in Saudi Arabia as well as the Tashkent government. Of the two, Dustam has emerged as the main champion of Turkic groups, despite his background of support for the former communist regime.

The Field Commanders

Conditions on the battlefield have demanded two attributes from commanders that are not required of the political party leaders. First, the commanders are a younger group of men than the political leaders, and second, the working out of compromises in the field has occurred with more frequency than in Peshawar or Geneva. The field commanders have therefore played a broader role than merely the military arm of the struggle: They have moderated the political stand of the parties, and, in conditions of civil war, they have created enclaves of peace and reconstruction while Kabul has deteriorated. The appellation of warlord applies to most, and the danger for the future lies in the field commanders' unwillingness to surrender political power in favor of a central government or democratic institutions.

By the end of 1994 five field commanders had gained control of major Afghan areas: Isma'il Khan controlled Herat and its environs, Rashid Dustam controlled Mazar-i-Sharif, Abdul Qader governed Nangarhar from Jalalabad, Jalaluddin Haqqani ruled Paktia from Khost, and Ahmad Shah Mas'ud administered the northeast while serving also as defender of Kabul. Although the party affiliations of these field commanders continue to be important, their military and political power has elevated their position within their respective parties such that their opinions and positions are more important than before. As the Taliban force swept from Kandahar toward Kabul, questions arose about whether the field commanders would join with the Taliban against their own political groups, or whether they would risk their power bases to engage the Taliban on behalf of their political parties. The likelihood that they would voluntarily surrender their long-hoarded and hard-won heavy weapons to the Taliban seemed doubtful. The field commanders came to be regarded with suspicion by the political leaders as their internal cooperative efforts began to lead toward the organized Council. By the same token, as one after another of the field commanders acquiesced to Taliban advance, they further alienated themselves from political leadership that was loathe to concede power. Some, such as Isma'il Khan, left the field altogether as the Taliban took control of Herat in 1996.

The field commanders began to meet independently under the rubric of the All-Commanders Council that established criteria for cooperation and future government. The first meeting of "internal mujahidin" was convened by Isma'il Khan and took place in Ghor in July 1987. One thousand two hundred commanders attended to discuss Kabul's reconciliation offer. Among the twenty resolutions adopted, only the first dealt with rejection of the Kabul offer, because "The right of determining the future destiny of Afghanistan lies with the heirs of the martyrs and with the Muslims of the trenches who are struggling in hot fronts and are ready to be martyred and nobody else is allowed to make decisions determining the fate of the nation."[28] Through the other resolutions, the commanders attempted to deal with overall coordination and administration issues. The seventeenth resolution appears particularly poignant in light of the continued maiming of

Afghan children and civilians by mines and the destruction of the country. It stated, "The Russians cannot safely leave Afghanistan without paying war reparations."[29]

The meeting of the commanders appeared to challenge the authority of the political parties, and to avoid such misunderstanding, the commanders reiterated that they were not challenging the authority of the Peshawar resistance leaders. In 1991, meeting in Quetta (to reduce the risk of assassination), the commanders' membership commission unequivocally declared that the aim in the creation of the council was to coordinate military activity rather than to distance commanders from political leaders.[30]

In order to deal with the increasingly grave problems of turf and lack of cooperation in the field (and in view of the assassination of Jami'at commanders by Hekmatyar's commanders), the Peshawar leaders issued instructions emphasizing the need for amicable and shari'a-based resolution of problems and the importance of staying focused on the real enemy.[31] Another meeting of commanders, held in Paktia in July 1990, attracted three hundred from twenty-nine provinces. At that time the commanders were careful to insist that no decision about the future of Afghanistan could be reached without the "leadership of the jihad" as well as the "Muslim people of Afghanistan."

The third All-Commanders Council met in a critical session of four days in Badakhshan in October 1990 in order to grapple again with problems of cooperation in the field. The six decisions taken represented steps needed for the reintegration of the country and establishment of security: devising a single strategy for military activity; dividing the country into nine zones to be administered by ulema, commanders, and elders; organizing administrative systems to secure supply routes; establishing of a joint office to harmonize the activities of the Council; calling on the Najibullah regime to step down; assuring amnesty (as previously announced by the AIG) to those who cooperate.[32]

With no means of enforcing its resolutions, and with competition for control of Kabul rising, by January 1992 the commanders in Wardak withdrew from participation in the All-Commanders Council. In early April, just weeks before President Mujaddidi entered Kabul, a number of field commanders took steps to assure themselves that Ahmad Shah Mas'ud was not planning to betray them by reaching a separate peace with Kabul through cooperation with Dustam and Sayyid Mansur Kayan. Mas'ud assured them, "We desire the formation of an Islamic government by safeguarding the territorial integrity of the country and national unity of all the jihadic forces in Afghanistan." However, with or without his consent, some of Mas'ud's subcommanders did join with the coalition of Uzbek and Isma'ili militia leaders when the latter rebelled against Najibullah's attempt to replace them with Pushtuns. Mas'ud became tarnished by this move, and despite his protests against ethnic divisions, the north of Afghanistan has in fact become divided from the south in the warlord situation that has ensued. The civil war ensued as efforts to form a united front both among the political leaders and the military commanders collapsed in suspicion and power grabbing after the spring of 1992. The excesses practiced by some commanders account in part for the welcome that the Afghan population showered on the Taliban as they made their way from Chaman to Kandahar in November 1994. With little likelihood of consolidation among field commanders and political leaders, the Taliban, even if Pakistani-trained and controlled, may represent, for many Afghans, the best hope for the end of civil war.

The Intellectuals and Administrators of the Mujahidin

When the prominent editor of *Afghan Jehad* took a survey of mujahidin publications in 1988, he listed thirty-four titles, issued in four languages (Dari, Pushtu, English, and Urdu), which did not include publications and newsletters published by Westerners. Though some of these publications were ephemeral, others could claim a history of a decade or more, having been transplanted from Kabul to Peshawar. When the Kabul press is included, the number of publications emanating from Afghan sources rises dramatically, in sharp contrast to the low literacy rate of the population. In addition to periodicals, the Afghan government and the mujahidin regularly published books in Dari, Pushtu, and English. The communist Kabul regime concentrated on justifying its cause through white papers and other political works often published originally in Moscow, whereas the mujahidin concerned themselves mainly with modern history, Islamic practice and political theory, memoirs, folklore, and poetry. Especially interesting among the latter are translations of works about Central Asia.[33]

Many of the authors, translators, and publishers of the mujahidin press came from the ranks of the political organizations. However, among the most effective and nonpartisan were the Kabul intellectuals, professors, and administrators who found themselves displaced in Pakistan. Less suited to the political work or to the field of battle, they remained in the region, though with much sacrifice of material comfort, and served the "striving for the sake of religion" with their special talents.

Mujahidin publishing focused at first exclusively on informing Afghans. Few among the party members or other intellectuals initially comprehended the importance of communicating with the outside world. This realization was driven chiefly by the need for material help for the war effort, the need to counteract the Moscow-Kabul information machine, and the maintenance of the refugees. Two nonpartisan editors, Sayyid Bahauddin Majruh and Sabahuddin Kushkaki, devoted their efforts toward keeping the English-reading specialist informed of the conduct of the war, political developments, the negotiations, and documents of import issued by the mujahidin. Both men augmented their publications with editorials and thus became spokesmen for the Afghan position, particularly with regard to negotiating a political solution to the war. Since the mujahidin were not allowed to participate directly in the UN-sponsored negotiations, their position was often lost among the diplomatic voices of Islamabad, Tehran, Kabul, Moscow, and Washington. Why the UN negotiations failed in all aspects except in arranging the untidy Soviet withdrawal is clear from a reading of the Afghan position.

Majruh paid with his life for his bipartisan coverage of events when he was assassinated on February 11, 1988, by unidentified persons. He is the best known of the intellectual *shuhada,* but others as well have been assassinated or driven into exile. Members of Afghan Millat, a party mainly of intellectuals, have died at the hands of assassins in Peshawar. A respected scholar of Islam, Mawlawi Zahedi Ahmadzai, translator of Sayyid Abul Aala Mawdudi and Sayyid Qutb into Pushtu, passed away during the years of war.

The Afghan Information Center (Peshawar), established by Majruh in 1981, and the Cultural Council of Afghanistan Resistance (Islamabad), begun in 1987 by Kushkaki, provided forums for the interpretation of Afghan events by Afghans themselves rather than through foreign journalists or specialists. The tendency to take Afghan events out of context and to concentrate only on information from politically biased sources because they are readily available are both problems that have bedeviled understanding of the Afghan war. The superficiality of the information about Afghanistan led to the wide disillusionment with the mujahidin and the disappointment in their inability to take Kabul after the Soviets left. The ensuing of civil war, predicted by many Afghans, area specialists, and some diplomats if the UN settlement ignored conclusions about a replacement government, appeared in the Western press as a sign of the instability of the mujahidin rather than a structural fault in the settlement. In the final analysis of the mujahidin confrontation with the Kabul-Moscow forces, the mujahidin only partially won the information struggle.

More important than the dissemination of unbiased information to the outside world was the service that the mujahidin intellectuals performed for the development of the Afghan ideas about nationhood, the place of Islam in a future Afghanistan, and the maintenance of current information about issues as vital as mine clearing and progress in irrigation restoration. Active on this front were the madrasa presses (especially Tawhid Madrasa), the Mujahidin-i Mustazaifin-i Afghanistan (The Oppressed Mujahidin of Afghanistan), and the Writers' Union of Free Afghanistan. Of the political parties, the Islamists were the main ones involved in book publishing, with both major parties interested mainly in history and Islam. Without the mujahidin publications, especially original documents, the level of suspicion among the mujahidin and the manipulation of that suspicion by KhAD/KGB and other interested security organizations would have taken a far greater toll than they did.

Afghan publications have virtually ceased since the mujahidin entry into Kabul. Shortages of electricity and paper, together with the shift of focus out of Peshawar, have left a vacuum, which is partly why there is a paucity of original material about Afghan events. In this information vacuum, journalists, United Nations diplomats and the often self-promoting publications of Afghanistan's neighbors fill the void imperfectly. Rallying the Afghan intellectuals again can only follow the return to relative stability in the country itself.

What Future for the Holy Warriors?

The mujahidin of Afghanistan learned to use sophisticated military technology in six years of war, going from Enfield rifles to Stinger missiles between 1978 and 1986. For a country ranked among the least developed, and with a literacy rate of only 30 percent, the uprooting and adjustments that have been imposed on the people have been overwhelming. Yet, through strict apparent and real adherence to Islamic precepts, the nation succeeded in its single goal of driving out the Soviets and their native promoters. Without belittling the role played by Cold War politics, a crumbling Soviet system, and disillusionment with leftist politics in the Third World in general, credit must go to the stubborn perseverance of the Afghan mujahidin. They have also paid the heaviest price of all—destruction, death, disabled bodies, and disunity. Perhaps the Afghan field commander best expressed the depth of the Afghan plight who gave as a condition for the release of Soviet prisoners of war, "If they do not have the money to ransom themselves, they are literate: Let each one of them teach ten of us to be literate." Truly this became a generation that sacrificed itself. A world that does not help to reconstruct their country and find meaning for their loss may pay the price in warriors for hire, which disrupts not just Afghan tranquillity but stability in many corners of the world.

Chapter Seven

Beyond War: Afghanistan in Post–Cold War Central Asia

The armed conflict that marked the 1980s in Afghanistan speedily transformed itself politically during the 1990s. But for civilians and some mujahidin, the level of fighting and destruction continued after only the barest of pauses. The resignation of Najibullah and his attempt to leave Kabul occurred fourteen years to the month after the staging of the Saur coup of 1978 that had brought the PDPA to power. Just as the PDPA in all of its stages had proved unable to govern the country, the fractious mujahidin, soon after their arrival in Kabul, could not agree on how to, or who should, maintain control. The Islamic jihad provided an effective model of legitimacy in the form of a broad alliance of virtually all Afghan groups, regardless of traditional or revolutionary orientation, or sectarian and ethnic identity. All had unified to fulfill their religious duty in rejecting a communist regime and its foreign atheist supporters. This alliance proved effective even after the withdrawal of the major (though not all) Soviet military units after the Geneva accords of 1988. However, the shift from a wartime alliance to a legitimate constitutional government has not proved to be an easy one. Certainly some of the difficulties can be attributed to outside interference. In addition, the assassination of Pakistan's President Muhammad Zia-ul-Haq in August 1988 removed the most capable of the Afghan mujahidin supporters at a critical juncture. Zia had held out to the last minute for the inclusion of a political transition to an Islamic government in the Geneva accords, but in the end yielded to U.S. pressure to come to agreement with Kabul and Moscow without the creation of a provisional government.[1]

MAP 7.1   Central Asia (Cartesia Map Art, Carto Data Bank, World)

To a larger degree, the failures of the Islamic state can be attributed to the paucity of guidance within Islamic political theory about concrete details of the construction of an Islamic government. Discussion of these issues brought out the divergences among the leadership that had been papered over during the jihad. These differing views were then grafted onto the reality of a traditionally diverse society that had its natural complexity multiplied manyfold by two decades of bitter internal and foreign conflict. One of the most significant sets of consequences of this struggle was the universalizing of popular participation in national politics on the one hand and the flooding of the country with modern weapons on the other.

The final collapse of the communist regime in early 1992 took place in the worst possible manner for the establishment of a viable successor. In the end the mujahidin did not win militarily, even though they clearly had prevented a communist victory. They had won the ideological struggle for public opinion long before—within a year of the communist coup. But the Geneva accords were a mixed blessing for the mujahidin. They had fewer enemies to fight, but they also received less help from their friends than did the Kabul regime from the Soviets.[2] In international standing, in fact, their position regressed. They were not a party to the accords, whereas the Kabul regime was. They had to rely on Pakistan and the United States to represent their interests.

The Kabul regime collapsed internally, following the withdrawal of Soviet support and the end of the Soviet Union. Its last "loyal" supporters, the ethnic and religious militias of the north, mutinied and formed an alliance with Ahmad Shah Mas'ud. This added to the complexity of the political dynamics a well-armed faction under the Uzbek General Abdul Rashid Dustam calling itself the "National Islamic Movement." Moreover, in and around Kabul, the remnants of the regular Afghan army and the numerous regime security forces concentrated to protect the capital proceeded to enter into alliances with mujahidin parties. These alliances appeared to have been formed on the basis of immediate political self-interest and defied any attempt to categorize them as moderate, radical, or Pushtun versus non-Pushtun. In the provinces, however, there was relative stability as most of political and military forces accepted the authority of the "general amirs" of the jihad and formed provincial assemblies of commanders and tribal leaders.[3]

Accompanying changes inside Afghanistan, the changes in the political dynamics and alignments in the surrounding region added another complication to the ability of Afghans to reform the government and restore order. The profound changes in the region make it virtually impossible to assess whether, had the region remained stable, the task of the Afghans would have been easier.

Most critical among the regional changes was the disintegration of the Soviet system and the rapid rise of independent Central Asian states, which soon had reciprocal effects across the Amu Darya border. Both Tajikistan and Uzbekistan, in different measures and ways, affected the stability of northern Afghanistan. Regionally, the emergence of the five Central Asian states as potential markets, freed economically from Moscow, quickly led to a change in the status of Afghanistan, which emerged as the most available transit route to Central Asia from South and West Asia. Iran and Pakistan in particular glimpsed, then grasped at this potential by building on their ties among the mujahidin to gain advantage. In the meantime interest on the part of the Central Asian states in the Afghan conduit was tempered with caution precisely because of the ideological victory of the Afghan mujahidin over Marxist secular rule. Since Central Asia itself did not undergo internal political revolution, those who had been privileged under communist rule continued to hold power and to fear the Islamic challenge to their position.

Internally, rather than to dwell on the dynamics of interaction among the various mujahidin groups, a position that leads to analysis emphasizing the fractious nature of Afghanistan's civil war, we concentrate instead on selected issues internally and regionally: (1) legitimacy, (2) Islamic politics, and (3) regional cooperation. Finally, we analyze the potential of internal catalysts for bringing about stability, and especially that of the movement known as the Taliban, in its internal and regional dimensions. The fluid but slow evolution of Afghan political and military events renders this last section subject to change. Nonetheless, analysis of the underlying issues should provide information for understanding ongoing developments.

Legitimacy

Haunting all Kabul regimes since the end of the monarchy in 1973 has been the specter of a lack of legitimacy of internal government. Since the fall of the Soviet Union the nagging issue of the legitimacy of Afghanistan's international borders has also entered the picture, an issue that ebbs and rises depending on the ethnic cross-border problems and the ability of the government in Kabul to provide incentives for border ethnic groups to remain within the fold. Internal lack of legitimacy feeds the fires of irredentism and thus exacerbates regional instability. At the same time, however, the questioning of Afghanistan's international borders arises from regional changes that have allowed for both hegemonic pretensions from Uzbekistan and frustrations about Afghanistan's inability to regain stability so that it can function within the economic framework of the region.

Internal Legitimacy

The struggle of the Afghan monarchy to establish legitimacy began with gradual acceptance of the rule of the Barakzai tribal clans over all Pushtuns and ended with the restoration of that rule in 1929 when challenged by a Tajik. Despite the contraction of monarchical rule in Pushtun areas as a result of successful challenges in South Asia, the expansion of Kabul's control over non-Pushtuns assured the existence of a multiethnic state in which the legitimacy of the monarch in Kabul was accepted without secular challenge. The transformation of the Pushtun tribal leader from *amir* (leader) to *padishah* (king) evolved in a regional context—Iran and the Central Asian amirates colonized by Russia—that gave no room for serious challenge. Moreover, the benign nature of monarchical rule under authoritarian royal oligarchies allowed for a relatively uneventful shift toward a constitutional monarchy that, while challenging governments, did not challenge the legitimacy of the monarch or the symbol of the monarchy. When Da'ud assumed the presidency in 1973 he cast aside more than two centuries of steadily growing legitimacy for the monarchy and replaced it with a republic system that has struggled for acceptance since then and has, in periodic moments of desperation, explored reestablishing some form of monarchy to assure unity.

The context of weak legitimacy can be overcome with ideology or longevity, or a combination of the two, which can lead to a measure of civil trust. Perhaps the best candidate for establishing a republic was Sardar Muhammad Da'ud because of the prestige he enjoyed personally and the continuity with the past that he represented. In retrospect, his period in power has proved to have been the most stable of all governments since 1973. His five years of rule were followed by short-lived regimes, Marxist and Islamist, whose tenuous legitimacy rests on ideology rather than past bases of Pushtun support and general acceptance over a long period of time. That any one of the PDPA leaders might have succeeded in establishing legitimacy by restoring stability is now a moot point: Each, especially Karmal and Najibullah, was tainted, one with having taken political power with the aid of Soviet tanks and the other with documented atrocities as head of the security services. In fact, however, neither leader was able to stabilize the political situation long enough to reestablish institutions that would project state validity and power. Their power base remained in military units of unreliable loyalty, whether the regular army or ethnic militias, in an indifferent and rapacious bureaucracy, and with no particular loyalty from tribal or ethnic groups. The gradual erosion of Kabul's ability to support programs and actions that flowed from the initial Marxist ideology undercut its credibility even among its ideological supporters.

Entering Kabul in 1992, the mujahidin suffered from two weaknesses that became the basis for the collapse of their case to establish themselves as having legitimate rights to form a state: First, despite years of expectation, their agreement for power sharing in Kabul was flawed. Second, the Islamist ideology that had allowed devotion to a cause even when faced with a magnitude of forces was shaken in the face of ethnic competition for political power. Combined with a regional context that has undergone the most significant ideological collapse of the century, the probability for the formation of legitimacy on the basis of Islamist ideology has eroded. One may speculate that had the mujahidin gained Kabul while the Soviet Union was intact, their external support might have been stronger and regional problems might have been far less severe. Arriving in Kabul when they did, however, they appear as political anachronisms in a regional context that has seen a shift away from Islamic ideology in post-Zia-ul-Haq Pakistan and post-Khomeini Iran. At the same time, the Soviet Union as a political and ideological threat has disappeared, making their neighbors less patient with Afghan problems (which include the most extensive minefields in the world). Reparations for war damages, the traditional method of funding reconstruction in the West, have not been seriously discussed with regard to the Soviet destruction in Afghanistan, since there no longer is a Soviet Union. At the same time, the international community, through the United Nations and nongovernmental organizations, is unable to administer effective reconstruction programs, whether in the technically simple task of mine removal or the more complex task of refugee repatriation.

The fact remains, however, that if there were a competent mujahidin government in Kabul, other difficulties in the region could be overcome in time. Without falling into the trap of blaming the victim for the crime, it is useful to examine how the mujahidin dissipated their chance to establish legitimacy after April 1992. The primary cause of mujahidin problems lies in their disunity and competition for power. The hydra-headed resistance forces turned into a dragon that threatens to swallow Afghanistan.[4]

In the late 1980s evidence of mujahidin groups' turning on each other and amassing arsenals for a future war began to accumulate. Particularly severe was the reaction of Hekmatyar's Hizb-i Islami to the expansion of the territorial base of action commanded by Ahmad Shah Mas'ud, the best known commander of the Jami'at-i Islami. Assassination, treachery, and revenge between these two forces spiraled, undermining Hekmatyar's credibility and contributing to his growing image as a spoiler among the resistance forces. Such action further fractured the always fragile ethnic cooperation among the mujahidin, since Hekmatyar was regarded as asserting Pushtun power against a Tajik. While competition between Mas'ud and Hekmatyar heated, other mujahidin leaders also continued bitter antagonisms rooted either in ideology or in ethnicity. Altogether, even on the eve of its entry into Kabul, the resistance could not produce a unified vision for a future Afghan government, nor a practical program for cooperative construction of a government. Rather, the plan for government simply grew out of the primitive power-distribution scheme instituted among the resistance in Peshawar, which functioned as a paper vehicle for aid acceptance rather than as the basis of a government-in-exile. The key to the plan, a rotating two-month leadership, assured brevity and ineffectiveness of power—which, moreover, betrayed the continued lack of trust among the leaders.

When it came time to enter Kabul, the plan for power sharing was little improved over the framework of the makeshift government-in-exile or previous manifestations of cooperative resistance action. The intentions of the resistance factions to retain power individually became clear when, even before the temporary president, Sibghatullah Mujaddidi, arrived in Kabul, each group consolidated its position in the city and its environs through the massing of fighters and weapons. To his credit, and despite voiced fears to the contrary, Mujaddidi did not usurp power but instead stepped down at the end of this two-month term to hand the presidency over to Burhanuddin Rabbani. Had the latter likewise remained true to the agreement, some semblance of stability and legitimacy for the resistance governments might have emerged. Rabbani, however, extended his presidential turn, first through an election held in December 1992 by an assembly boycotted by many parties (most important of which was Hekmatyar's), and then by reasoning that he needed to remain in power because of instability and civil war. As if this action alone could not undermine the legitimacy of his government in Kabul, Defense Minister Mas'ud, the former hero of the Panjshir, dissipated his own prestige by maintaining a mutually uncompromising position with re- gard to Hekmatyar that descended into naked ethnic war.

In hindsight, it is clear that the government-in-exile should have been more clearly envisioned, that the transition to a permanent government should have been better planned, and most of all, that plans for the disarm- ing of mujahidin and militias should have been laid, probably by the United Nations, in cooperation with regional and international powers. There were such efforts. But the rapid disintegration of the USSR, followed by the quick fall of the Najibullah regime after the ending of Soviet aid, rendered them moot. Remembering the historical context of the period, however, it is easy to see how attention and funds for Afghan reconstruction, in the broad sense, shifted quickly to the U.S. war in the Persian Gulf, to the Arab-Israeli peace accords, and to Eastern Europe as the Soviet period in Russian history closed. The renewed attention focusing on Afghanistan comes in a wholly altered context—that of Afghanistan as part of a region that must include Central Asia.

The legitimacy of the Afghan resistance as a claimant to the rule of the country was eroded not only by a disunited front and disunited action but also by the multiethnicity contained within the international borders of the country, both of which undermined the Islamic ideological fervor that, in regional perceptions as well as among traditionally religious Afghans, had cloaked the resistance with respectability. Though Pushtun chauvinism and minority ethnic irredentism had always lain in the background during the fourteen years of war against secular Kabul, it took the scramble for power to bring these divisive factors to the fore. When Rabbani came to power in the rotating power scheme, little opposition to his Tajik ethnicity surfaced. However, as it became clear that he would not leave power, fears arose of an attempt by Tajiks to seize power. Pushtun reaction was swift, leading perhaps to the mobilizing of other ethnic groups in opposition to Kabul. Thus Hazara factions as well as Uzbek groups, all erstwhile allies of Kabul, rose in constantly shifting alliances with Pushtuns to oppose Rabbani and his military strongman, Mas'ud. The loyalty of virtually independent Rab- bani commanders, as in Herat, came into question, as did Rabbani's inde- pendence from support by Moscow. A repetition of the oft-recalled 1929 events, when the Tajik who took power in Kabul was stripped of it by a Pushtun who restored the old monarchical traditions, turned into a realistic fear by Tajiks as the Pushtun Taliban advanced. Having fought so hard for the freeing of Afghanistan from Moscow's tutelage, the Tajiks would need strong regional guarantees before allowing themselves to be stripped of po- litical and military power by a possibly vengeful Pushtun force. Indeed, to foster or support a return to the pre-1978 ethnic dominance patterns, of Durrani Pushtuns at the tip of a pyramidal pecking order, would be folly.[5] The pattern of ethnic suspicion is repeated among Hazaras, Uzbeks, and probably among Nuristanis and Isma'ilis, all of whom inhabit regions less critical to the unity of the country in the immediate future.

External Legitimacy

The future of the restoration of a legitimate Afghan government to Kabul lies in three sources: (1) regionally guaranteed elections coupled with incentives to disarm all groups and form a regular army; (2) the convening of a Loya Jirgah to form a transitional government; (3) the return of the monarchy, either temporarily or on a permanent basis to provide either a transitional period or the mechanism for the formation of a legitimate government. A combination of all three may in fact provide the most workable solution. Imposing any of these solutions may have to be done without the cooperation of the chief rivals for power.

The legitimacy of Afghanistan's international borders is an issue that has recurred because of overlap of ethnicities along both sides of the borders, the relative clout of its neighbors, and Kabul's own reluctance in the past to accept its international borders, especially with Pakistan. During the crisis of the past two decades various factions have feared—or desired—the fragmentation of the country into separate territories allied to a neighbor.[6] Such fears are fed by rampant warlordism since the early 1990s that has resulted from the unacceptability of Kabul's power or rejection of its legitimacy. Though warlords exist without particular fealty to outside powers, the cases of the Uzbeks and the Hazaras involve instigation or alignment with neighboring powers.

In the case of the Hazaras, their Shi'a form of Islam has involved Iran in their politics from the first years of the war, leading to many successive factional formations within the Hazarajat that challenged existing power structures. The Hazara groups today are largely represented on the political scene by the Hizb-i Wahdat and its factions, which have variously fought in alliance with Hekmatyar, Dustam, and the Taliban. Located in a pocket of mountains fringed on all sides with nonsecessionist parts of Afghanistan, the Hazara cannot easily conspire for unity with Iran. They can, however, behave either semiautonomously, as they have in the past, or align with factions in the resistance. Their acceptance of Kabul's legitimacy would depend on how generous Kabul became toward them, especially in light of centuries of past grievances, particularly with regard to Pushtuns. They do not pose a critical threat to Afghan territorial integrity or legitimacy.

The Uzbeks, however, present a different problem. Although scattered in northern Afghanistan from Kunduz to Mazar-i-Sharif, the Uzbeks are economically successful but not numerically preponderant. Historically a part of the Bukharan (Uzbek) khanate, and much contested between the latter and Kabul, the Uzbek issue remained dormant until the independence of Uzbekistan created the option of reintegrating with Uzbekistan, the successor of the Bukharan state. Rashid Dustam, the militia leader who took charge of the Uzbek-inhabited areas, has received support from Uzbekistan, enabling him to conduct air bombardments of Kabul and giving him the ability to choke that city's trade access northward. Mazar-i-Sharif, moreover, as legendary Balkh before it, has the potential to serve as the transit depot for trade from Iran to Central Asia as well as trade from Pakistan. For this reason, Mazar-i-Sharif may be a sustainable autonomous enclave, both economically and politically, while remaining vital to transit trade in the region. These possibilities make Dustam a formidable opponent to Kabul and a clear challenge to it as the guardian of Afghan territorial legitimacy.

In somewhat similar manner, the Tajiks in the north and the Isma'ilis of the Wakhan corridor and other areas may form potential breakaway regions of the country. With a strong foothold in Kabul and a fairly well-organized and tested ability to administer northern areas (as through the Council of the North, which Ahmad Shah Mas'ud formed and which functioned for well over a decade during and after the war), the Tajik potential in Afghanistan remains strong. Neighboring Tajikistan, however, lacks the resolve and unity of Uzbekistan and is, with Kyrgyzstan, the weakest of the new Central Asian states. Despite Rabbani's attempts to mediate among the warring factions that have emerged there since 1992, the disintegration of Tajikistan remains a strong possibility.[7] For this reason the fate of the Tajiks of Afghanistan is not as easily hitched to Tajikistan as would be the Uzbek future to Uzbekistan. For similar reasons, the Tajiks in Afghanistan have become embroiled in the affairs of Tajikistan, divided between the Islamic Revival Party, which forms the backbone of the opposition to the Moscow-backed Dushanbe regime, and support for that regime, which may offer the main source of stability. Dustam and Hekmatyar—as well as Pakistan—have a stake in the efforts of the Islamic Revival Party, although Islamabad's interest dictates resolution of the turmoil in Tajikistan rather than the pressing of a more particular and disruptive agenda, as would be the case if the two Afghan leaders were able to play a more forceful role in the country.

The Isma'ili case is dependent on the Tajik case, although, as described in Chapter 4, Isma'ilis straddle borders across four countries and are not exclusive to Afghanistan or any new Central Asian state. Nonetheless, in Tajikistan, where Isma'ilis form a compact group in Badakhshan, as well as in Pakistan they enjoy numbers, cohesiveness, and the possibility of tapping into outside sources commanded by overseas Isma'ilis through the office of the Agha Khan. Although this does not constitute backing comparable to that provided Dustam by Tashkent, nonetheless in the perception of many Isma'ilis it allows them to consider transforming their territory into an actual politically autonomous entity in the context of a weakened Afghanistan and a weakened Tajikistan.

Aside from the emergent possibilities arising from the formation of Central Asian states, there are also latent threats to Afghan regional legitimacy that have existed in the past that continue today. These could come from Baluchi tribesmen as well as from possible Iranian designs on Herat, a city that Iran disputed with Afghanistan until a century and a half ago, and whose diversely mixed inhabitants resemble those of eastern Iran. Herat also lies on traditional trade routes to Central Asia, especially to Ashkabad. As Turkmenistan comes closer to fulfilling its potential as a major exporter of gas and oil, the importation of consumer goods and the export of its petrochemical products can make Herat an attractive transit city—which could add to the Afghan till. Herat can also drift toward closer ties with Iranian Khorasan, a reason for the Taliban push to control the city in 1996.

The Multiethnic Deterrent

Given the strong centrifugal potential along Afghanistan's periphery during the seemingly endless period of civil war, are there realistic chances for the fruition of irredentism? The answer still seems to be in the negative. The reasons lie not in Kabul's potential for reestablishing order and legitimacy as a capital but in outside factors within the region that guarantee its territorial integrity. No neighboring state, new or old, is prepared to press for or accept changes in international borders, no matter how much it may have pressed for these in the past. The most contentious issue, that of Pushtunistan, will remain dormant because of the practical resolution of the issue as a result of the war in a manner that no negotiations between Kabul and Islamabad could have done during long years of hot and cold negotiations. The Baluchi issue disputed with Pakistan falls into the same category. The newer cases in the north—the Uzbeks, Tajiks, and Isma'ilis—are being pushed into the background as Tashkent begins to appreciate the chaos that would result from any territorial shifts of boundaries. Having already rejected annexing Khojent and its environs during the heat of the Tajik civil war, it has squelched likewise any discussion of the reversion of Bukhara and Samarkand, and hence Surkhan Darya, to Tajikistan. Similarly, Iran's experience with Afghan refugees, coupled with its worries over Kurdish, Azari, Arab, and Turkmen minorities, virtually guarantees that it will not press for territorial annexation. Thus the multiethnicity of each state forms a deterrent to the use of ethnic issues to undermine the territorial integrity and legitimacy of the states in the region.

How does the multiethnic deterrent translate into the political picture in the region? First, it means that each state, particularly Afghanistan, must consider the well-being of its ethnic minorities in state formation and conduct so as to retain the goodwill of its neighbors and likely trade partners. The cumbersome mechanism of Soviet nationality policy never took firm root in Afghanistan and has not been successfully pressed elsewhere outside the Soviet system. The practical appeal of single-language education and bureaucracy attracts people, as does the clear need to acquire at least one international language. Trilingual education or bureaucracy, on the other hand, is impractical, as the Soviet experience in Central Asia had demonstrated. The problems these regions face therefore appear to include the integration of all ethnic groups into the economic and political fold while allowing institutions for the retention of social and cultural values and traditions. The new mechanisms for developing such a system must be configured regionally and can come from pressure for economic cooperation. A clear factor in the successful evolution of such mechanisms is the sublimation (and suppression) of chauvinistic ethnic behavior by majorities.

Second, the multiethnic deterrent has the positive potential for allowing cross-border communities to serve as bridges between states, provided the region settles into cooperative cultural and trade patterns. Despite the continual war, Afghan Tajik and Pushtun merchants plied their trade in consumer goods to Central Asia, bringing East Asian and Indian manufactured goods to private markets in Samarkand, Bukhara, Tashkent, and the Ferghana valley. Crude and small-scale, this trade emerged out of necessity. For several decades to come, it is likely that Afghanistan will remain a transit rather than a production base. Road, rail, and air transport as well as warehousing, though requiring specific and expensive outlay, nonetheless are within the capacity of the region to undertake given the desperate need of investors in Central Asia for multiplication of routes of access. Sole dependence on Russian routes has proved unstable, as illustrated in the case of oil and gas pipelines. Unless Afghanistan's transit possibilities are developed, the remaining alternative is China's eastern ports. To grant China the leverage to which such dependency would lead may be imprudent for states in the region (including Pakistan, though it is an ally of China) as well as for international funders and investors in Central Asia.

The multiethnic deterrent therefore has the added benefit of reducing the potential for conflict based on ultranationalism and of promoting cooperation among the states of the region. Although this may mean weak individual states, it could also mean a region in which cooperation, based on the aggrandizement of an Islamic past that included all these states, leads to collective prosperity.

Captured Soviet tank with
mujahidin crew from Hizb-i Islami
(Hekmatyar), Jalalabad.
(R. H. Magnus, 1992)

Mujahidin guards, Kabul
River bridge, Jalalabad.
(R. H. Magnus, 1992)

Mujahidin Governor Haji Abdul Qader Khan with staff, on the steps of the Royal Winter Palace, Jalalabad. (R. H. Magnus, 1992)

Afghanistan-Pakistan border at Torkham in the Khyber Pass. (R. H. Magnus, 1992)

Kabul River at sunset, Jalalabad. (R. H. Magnus, 1992)

Islamic Politics

As Afghanistan takes its place in the new state configuration of post-imperialist Central Asia, the potential challenge of ethnic conflict will be closely matched by that of religious conflict. In the ten states that currently hold membership in the regional Economic Cooperation Organization (ECO)—Turkey, Iran, Pakistan, Afghanistan, Azarbaijan, Turkmenistan, Uzbekistan, Tajikistan, Kazakstan, and Kyrgyzstan—in all but the last two, Islamic politics has played a role in the public political mindset. It could be argued that in Kyrgyzstan as well, areas outside Bishkek may become as susceptible to Islamic politics as parts of the Ferghana valley. Therefore, although Islam provides some commonalities among the states in this area, the threat that radical Islamic politics will spoil relations within and between states remains a concern. This concern verges on outright panic in the perception of outsiders such as those in Moscow, Washington, and even in Middle Eastern states under threat from radical Islamic forces, especially conservative monarchies such as Saudi Arabia.[8]

A second aspect of Islamic politics grows out of the Afghan situation directly and involves international perceptions of Afghanistan's Islamic politics. This perception has led to the depiction of Afghans as pariahs, to the fear of the spread of Islamic militancy from Afghanistan to Central Asia and beyond, and to the fear of international terrorism in league with drug production and trade. The struggle over Islamic politics thus shows little sign of ending with the Afghan war but rather has international repercussions that may last beyond the forging of regional cooperation and may even defy such cooperation.

Islamic Politics Within the Region

All the contiguous non-Arab states from Turkey to Pakistan have joined ECO. Membership has not been extended to Tatarstan and Bashqortstan nor to Xinjiang, all of which are eponymous Turkic entities but currently parts of Russia and China respectively. For practical analysis the ten member states of ECO may be ranked according to the level at which Islamic reformist/radicals have penetrated the power structure or threaten it. Figure 7.1 encapsulates these levels and also reflects the shift in direction that has taken place since the 1970s.

The assessment in Figure 7.1 is based on three factors: the extensiveness of the population that identifies itself as Muslim, the level at which religious practice is promoted or condoned by those who hold political power, and the level at which Islamic beliefs and practices have entered public institutions. Of all the states in the region, Afghanistan is the only one that continues to press for the adoption of universal Islamic practice, and Iran has begun to shift slowly away from this position, as has Pakistan. However, in both Tajikistan and Afghanistan the general political situation is so fluid that a move in the direction of greater secularization could develop. Despite the lack of any uniformity in the current condition of the regional states with regard to Islamic politics, the direction appears to be movement away from secular positions, converging toward combinations of secular and Islamic. In Turkey the process of democratic election has thus far increased the power of Islamic forces, whereas in Pakistan the opposite may be true. What the convergence implies for the region is not so much internal conflict, but rather a growing possibility in these states for reduction of the perception that Islam in politics is a threat to stability or success, and a corollary increase in dialogue along cultural lines and in regional confidence.

For states in the immediate region such as Saudi Arabia and the Gulf states, being shut out of the vast region of Central Asia poses a threat in prestige as well as a threat in seeing rival Iran achieve access and clout through pipelines and transit trade. In this respect, Saudi and U.S. interests converge. For this reason, despite Saudi Arabia's ability to invest money and Islamic respectability in the region, its power projection in Afghanistan is dependent on Pakistan as a conduit. Still, the official Saudi presence assures support for nonradical Islam which, despite Saudi history, does not engender radical reform of society. For this reason as well as for the funds and investment possibilities it offers, the Saudi presence is more comforting

FIGURE 7.1 Direction and Level of Islamic Politics in the Afghan Region

Country	1970s	1980s	Current Condition
Turkey	Secular/Military	Secular	Secular/Islamic
Iran	Secular	Islamic	Islamic
Pakistan	Secular/Military/Islamic	Islamic/Military	Islamic/Secular
Afghanistan	Secular/Secular Marxist	Marxist/Islamic	Islamic
Azerbaijan	Secular/Communist	Secular/Communist	Secular/Islamic
Turkmenistan	Secular/Communist	Secular/Communist	Secular
Uzbekistan	Secular/Communist	Secular/Communist	Secular (Islamic)
Tajikistan	Secular/Communist	Secular/Communist	Secular/Islamic
Kazakhstan	Secular/Communist	Secular/Communist	Secular
Kyrgyzstan	Secular/Communist	Secular/Communist	Secular (Islamic)

for Central Asia's secular rulers (and those of Chinese Muslim areas) than that of Iran.

International Perceptions of Islamic Politics

The climate of near hysteria that greeted the Iranian Revolution as the standard-bearer of radical Islam has subsided, only to be replaced in part by a fear of a steadily growing string of threats posed from Islamic areas since the decline of Moscow's global presence. Chief among the elements feeding these fears are the spread of anti-Western politics, the proliferation of arms and unemployed men available cheaply for hire to fight Islamic wars, the broad defining of Muslim resistance as international terrorism, and international drug production and traffic.[9] Together these threats have been pooled to present Islamic radicalism (and by easy extension Islam itself) as the enemy to replace the Soviet threat. The superpower bipolarity of the past has given way to the existence of one superpower, the United States, which sees itself under threat by Muslims. Hence a future unified Muslim region, such as Central Asia, can potentially come to be regarded as a threat not only in the eyes of some U.S. policymakers but also from the perspective of a Russia embroiled in proxy and direct war with Muslim ethnic groups (the Chechens and Bosnia) and Muslim radicals (Tajikistan). As illustrated in the case of the Chechens, oil-rich and critical sections of Russia could potentially become sympathetic to Muslim radicals or perhaps to membership in Muslim organizations—as benign as the Organization of the Islamic Conference or as radical as outgrowths of the old Muslim Brotherhood.

The international shift in perceptions of Islam, not entirely divorced from Islamic radical threats posed to the Palestinian-Israeli rapprochement in the Middle East, has led to several factors directly affecting Afghanistan and its region. First, Afghanistan has been virtually abandoned as a pariah. Funds for refugee repatriation, reconstruction, and the general peace process sponsored by the United Nations have gradually been reduced to the lowest level since 1980. Donors such as the United States have not simply cut arms supplies but also have come to find humanitarian aid for Afghanistan to be beyond "budgetary constraints."[10] The new priorities of U.S. and Western interests grow in part out of the end of bipolarity and the ascendance of regionalism. But a secondary and more sinister reason comes from retrospective analysis (mainly by those who opposed international support for the Afghan resistance) that maintains that supplying arms to the Afghans was a mistake.[11] This latter reason is directly related to the second factor affecting Afghanistan and its relationship to Islamic politics: An image of Afghanistan as incubator for radicals has developed to replace the image of the brave mujahid and his suffering but stoic family. This change in image evokes the fear that war-seasoned Muslim Arabs with Afghan exposure directly affect the security of ordinary Americans.[12] Revisionist thinking like this withholds from the Afghans any respect for the preservation of their national integrity in face of Soviet invasion, credit for discrediting a superpower enemy of the West as well as for contributing to the Soviet self-destruction and thereby to the initiation of a new period of U.S. strength and security. The inability of the United States to take the moral high ground in Bosnia has links to the revisionism with regard to Afghanistan as well as the problems of attempting to coordinate action with allies without the benefit of a clearly defined rival as in the past. The direct consequences for the Afghans is that they have been abandoned and are coming to be regarded as a threat.

Afghan arms and fighters have been linked to at least three low-level wars in the Muslim region. Small-time Afghan arms dealers plied their trade in Baku as the Azarbaijani government faced fire from Armenians in Karabagh, especially in 1993 and 1994. Afghan arms filter into Azad Kashmir. Most significantly, Afghan arms, fighters, and Islamic radicalism have escalated fighting along the Afghan-Tajik border. Some Afghan mujahidin groups have also engaged in training fighters, as in the case of Azarbaijan. In addition, China has protested Afghan propaganda and possibly weapons entering into Xinjiang, and the possibility that arms from the Afghan war reached Bosnia are reasonably good since they were less expensive than European weapons of similar quality. Without an effective international program, such as through United Nations negotiations, Afghans will continue to find arms (and drug sales) to be one of the few means for income production. The United Nations, however, has been ineffective in Afghanistan, with very few exceptions: Its involvement helped to focus attention on the need for withdrawal of Soviet forces, the moral support in the General Assembly and other UN organs maintained pressure for resolution of the invasion, and the United Nations work among the refugees coordinated international aid. But at the critical juncture when international coordination for a comprehensive rehabilitation program was needed, the United Nations has fallen virtually silent. The consequences of this ineffectiveness could spawn further Afghan-related problems for the entire region.

The serious Central Asian concerns about Afghanistan closely relate to Islamic politics rather than ethnic overlap or irredentism. Events in Tajikistan, particularly since 1992, have drawn in regional players, especially the Uzbeks. But more ominously for all former Soviet republics has been the presence of Russian forces on the Tajik-Afghan border following the unsuccessful attempt by the Tajik political opposition to oust from office the former communist leadership. The extent of ties between Afghan Islamists and the main core of the Tajik opposition remains shrouded, but the ties are clearly multifaceted: Hekmatyar's Hizb-i Islami has operated among future members of the Tajik Islamic Revivalist Party since the early 1980s, and Ahmad Shah Mas'ud has provided shelter and training for Tajik refugees and fighters since the fall of 1992.

In many ways, though not in its origins and raison d'être, the Tajik opposition correlates with the Afghan resistance. However, in both composition and context, the Afghan anticommunist movement drew on nationalism in the face of invasion for its inspiration rather the simple struggle for political power waged by Islamists and secularists against a secular/communist government. In this respect the Tajik situation resembles more closely the Islamist coup against Da'ud staged unsuccessfully in 1975 than the Afghan war beginning with the Soviet invasion in December 1979. The presence of the Russian 201st Rifle Division, however, draws Afghanistan into the internal Tajik struggle because Afghan territory is regularly shelled, air bombardment by Russian fighter planes causes damage on Afghan territory, and Afghan national integrity is threatened by hot pursuit of Tajik fighters. Russia's support for the Rabbani government when it was in Kabul, even if exaggerated to discredit him, may be regarded as an attempt to undermine Afghan (Tajik) sympathy or support for the Tajik opposition. Afghan long-term interests in Tajikistan have been recognized as lying in the restoration of peace in order to develop trade and remove the excuse for a Russian military presence in Central Asia. Dislodging Russia from Tajikistan appears to have evolved as the goal of the Uzbek government in Tashkent as well, after an initial period in which Islam Karimov's government worked in concert with Moscow to contain the Tajik opposition. Prospects for the Tajik Islamic opposition to gain political power in Dushanbe are dim even without the presence of Russian troops. The return to Tajikistan of the oppositional Islamic leadership may be possible only if it is willing to assume the role of a loyal opposition and confine Islamic politics to the limits of political party activity and the madrasa system. A long-term cooperative effort between the Tajik Islamists and the secular intellectual opposition operating from Moscow is as improbable as was cooperation between secular intellectuals and the Afghan Islamists for the two decades since 1975.

At the same time, Islamic politics in Central Asia may be credited with pushing all governments toward providing an increased public role for Islamic institutions and values where the social context demands it. The expansion of the madrasa system throughout small and large towns in Uzbekistan, the television time given to Islamic discourse, and the participation of the Islamic leadership in the electoral process all speak to the lack of obstacles for Islam in society. A modus vivendi may have been reached in Central Asia between government and Islam, particularly as, in every case, power in the Central Asian states appears to be firmly held by presidential leadership operating in the nondemocratic mold cast in the Soviet period. Whether the demand of its neighbors that it too stabilize in order to promote regional good will be heeded in Afghanistan may depend in some measure on how well Moscow's aims in the region can be reduced and reconstructed to serve a positive purpose.

Regional Cooperation

Interregional cooperation in what was called during the Cold War "the soft underbelly of the Soviet Union" came to be channeled through Moscow rather than directly between Baku and Dushanbe, for example. Within the confines of regimented cultural events such as an All-Union Kazak festival, opportunities for bilateral relations could occur as long as they were balanced with similar events from other eponymous areas of the old Soviet state. Relations of the "soft underbelly" with the "northern tier" of frontline states bordering the southern part of the Soviet Union were likewise circumspect. Reciprocity across the border with Afghanistan by Central Asia demanded planning and participation by Moscow. Even gatherings as innocuous as archaeological seminars originated centrally rather than from Samarkand or Ashkabad. The attendance and premier honor going to Russian or Moscow-based scholars was also de rigueur, as was the presence of spy agencies, on both sides. The passing of the mindset that crippled bilateral relationships within the region has brought an avalanche of proposals for regional relationships. Among the most promising of these have been those designed to promote trade within the region. While insisting on being a member of some of these, Moscow has been increasingly eased out of those involving the Central Asian region exclusively. It has reacted with threats.[13] As with oil and gas deals between members of the Commonwealth of Independent States (CIS) and Western companies, Russia also may have worked to derail agreements and upset agendas. However, the seeds for regional cooperation have been sown, and Afghanistan lies at the heart of the region.

The Economic Cooperation Organization focuses squarely on the region around Afghanistan. The latter was a late entry into the ECO—the tenth and last member to be accepted—less as a consequence of its insignificant economic sector than because of the absence of a government that could effectively hold negotiations. Pakistan endorsed at the first ECO summit meeting (Tehran, February 1992) a proposal for the formation of an interim government in Kabul without Najibullah and pushed to reject the membership request of the Republic of Afghanistan (ROA). Two months later the ROA had fallen. By autumn of that year, the Rabbani government led the first Afghan delegation to the ECO summit in Islamabad, thus completing the contiguity of the "northern tier" with the "soft underbelly."

Russia viewed ECO as a threat to the CIS umbrella created to retain Russian spheres of influence in the former empire. In October 1992 Vice Premier Aleksandr Shokhin attacked membership of CIS states in ECO, calling on them to choose between economic integration with Russia or their southern neighbors. At the same time, reliance on Russian trade routes and continued ruble dependency (in Tajikistan, for example) have not been wholly replaced by alternative air and rail routes to Europe and Asia and fully convertible local currencies. The process is slow, and as a consequence the Russian threat to CIS members was not entirely toothless. Coupled with the subsequent demonstration of Russia's ability to derail oil and gas agreements with Western companies (in Kazakstan and Azarbaijan, for example), in the absence of other forces, Russia's capacity to cripple regional efforts is considerable. However, its ability to promote local development is limited by institutional and financial weakness within Russia itself. As a result, the door for alternative action is ajar, if not wide open, for China, Pakistan, India, Israel, and by Turkish proxy, the United States. In this context the Chinese role becomes competitive with both ECO and its individual members as well as with Russia.

Afghanistan's economic participation in the region, and therefore its chances in the near future of raising its economy out of the abyss into which it has sunk, is subject to questions of how trade routes develop in the region: From which direction will trade routes for Central Asian exports and imports be most viable? Can Afghanistan and Pakistan or Afghanistan and Iran find the funds to build alternative routes and pipelines for Central Asian trade? Will Chinese routes through Central Asia and Iran link the region with the West and bypass Afghanistan before political stability allows for ECO or Pakistan to act?

Despite the several bilateral agreements signed between Kabul and Islamabad to facilitate trade, and Pakistan's communications and air connection agreements with all the Central Asian states, land connections must flow though Afghanistan either by way of the Khyber Pass–Kabul–Salang Tunnel–Mazar-i-Sharif and over the Khairaton bridge to Uzbekistan or through

Kandahar-Herat and on to Turkmenistan. Having witnessed its first major caravan of trucks bound for Turkmenistan captured outside Kandahar by lawless Afghans (October 1994), Pakistan has reason to be concerned about Afghan routes. Even after the fall of Herat to the Taliban in September 1995, which opened the road between Kandahar and the Turkmenistan border, the state of the paved highway after two decades of war is such that it requires extensive repairs before it can support any extensive traffic. But there are no viable alternatives. The Wakhan corridor, standing between Tajik Badakhshan and Pakistan's Northwest Frontier Province, offers no possibility for year-round transit, because of elevation and climate. Nor is any route from a future Pakistan-allied Kashmir any better. The proposed route from Osh (Kyrgyzstan) to Kashgar and then over the Karakorum Highway across the Khunjarab Pass is also both weather-dependent and treacherous. Therefore, Pakistan must concentrate on the Afghan alternative. Its political activity in the region appears geared to this end. Pakistan has long debated opening the alternate port of Gwadar on the Baluchistan coast to alleviate the pressure on Karachi, its only international seaport. The Central Asian trade would make this port development project cost-effective. Central Asian cotton export, already enjoying some markets through Pakistan, as well as petroleum and mineral resources call for complex storage and shipping facilities. The existing Chinese transport infrastructure with Central Asia has succeeded in diverting about 30 percent of Central Asia's trade away from Russia and through its rail and road networks through Xinjiang toward Shanghai. China's capacity for investment is far less dependent on outside sources than are those of ECO members collectively or individually. Iran, for example, has been stymied by the United States in its search for investment to build pipelines and road networks. Therefore, Central Asia's alternative to trade through Russia may be confined to the Chinese alternative for the near future. The political costs of dealing with China are high, since, among other factors, border disputes may have to be settled in China's favor. Central Asian states may not want to pay those and other costs in the long run.

The question of funds for route development depends mainly on Pakistan. Iranian hopes for building any infrastructure directly through Turkmenistan or through northern Afghanistan, though far simpler in terms of terrain and distance than those of Pakistan, have little chance of succeeding so long as the United States is bent on isolating Tehran and toppling the Islamic regime. China's promise of including Iran on the western leg of its revived Silk Road appears to be secondary to its wish to claim Central Asian trade. Therefore, Afghanistan's best hope for transit trade appears to be Pakistan, where the problems of investment for infrastructure may be resolved if Pakistan in turn can help resolve the Afghan civil war. The political stakes are high for Pakistan. Both its diplomatic efforts and its political efforts in Afghanistan appear to be motivated by the desire to stabilize Afghanistan less for altruistic reasons or for reasons of self-defense than because Afghanistan is Pakistan's link to Central Asia.

The Taliban Movement:
Internal and International Aspects

The term *taliban* is one of the plural forms of *talib,* which refers to a student in an Islamic madrasa. During the course of the long jihad, as we have noted, the rural areas of Afghanistan had remained largely outside of the control of both the Soviets and the Kabul regime. The madrasas attracted numbers of taliban and aspiring taliban according to the reputation and scholarly qualifications of their *mawlawi* (teachers).[14] The students lacked official subsidies, but rather lived on the charity of the community, often virtually as beggars obtaining a bowl of rice at one house and tea and bread at another, and washing their own clothes in the village stream (something no ordinary male villager would ever do on his own). In this setting the number of small madrasas grew, and hence that of taliban, who had always been a feature of traditional rural society. The informal network of these *mawlawi* provided the basis for the Harakat-i Inqilab-i Afghanistan (Islamic Revolutionary Movement) of Mawlana Muhammad Nabi Muhammadi, which had proven to be the most widespread of the mujahidin parties in the early years of the resistance. The taliban thus provided some of the best recruits for the mujahidin during the jihad. Accounts in the mujahidin journals produced during the jihad by the various parties of the lives of commanders (and the obituaries of *shuhada*) reveal that one of the most common backgrounds for commanders was that of small-town religious students, who had demonstrated particular zeal and leadership abilities. Their religious status, no doubt, was a boost to the young and talented among the taliban in overcoming the difficulty faced by youths aspiring to leadership positions in a society that accords to age and experience tremendous weight and respect.

The fourteen years of the jihad produced a similar phenomenon among the Afghan refugees in Pakistan. A considerable number of Afghan refugee orphans entered into the network of madrasas of the Northwest Frontier Province, especially in tribal territories, where they were supported as a charity by Islamic organizations. The Jami'at-i Ulema-i Islam (Society of Islamic Scholars, JUI), a long-established (indeed, founded before the state in 1945) Pakistani political party led by Mawlana Fazlur Rahman, went so far as to establish madrasas specifically for the orphans of the Afghan jihad. The JUI had its stronghold in the frontier Pushtun and Baluchi regions, where it regularly secured a greater vote in elections than did the more prominent Jamaat-i Islami founded by Mawlana Abul Aala Mawdudi. Its intellectual origins were in the Islamic University of Deoband (now in India), and its version of Islam has always emphasized strict Hanafi Sunni orthodoxy and the dominant role of the ulema.

The Jamaat-i Islami (JI) had been favored by the Zia-ul-Haq regime during the jihad as its principal Islamic contact with the Afghan mujahidin and, particularly through the Interservices Intelligence Agency (ISI), with Hekmatyar. The JI followers were bitter rivals of the Jami'at-i Ulema Islam. This situation continued during the first prime ministership of Benazir Bhutto (who was constrained to leave Afghan policy to the "heirs of Zia" in the military) as well as during the Nawaz Sharif government. However, in her second prime ministership, Bhutto came to rely on her father's old adviser for Afghan and frontier affairs, a retired military man, General Nasrullah Babar, whom she appointed minister of the interior. As commander of Frontier Forces for the Northwest Frontier Province in the 1970s, Babar had received the first Afghan Islamist refugees fleeing the Da'ud regime in the summer of 1973.[15]

Until 1994, however, Pakistan's policy in post-jihad Afghanistan continued to be governed by its long-standing relationship with Hekmatyar, along with a willingness to accept any compromise solution in the civil war that restored stability to Afghanistan should an outright victory by Hizb-i Islami prove to be impossible. Increasingly, either of these outcomes became more remote. Although power sharing formulas and peace plans through regional, Islamic, and United Nations auspices could be formulated and solemnly sworn to by the leaders, none could actually be implemented on the ground. The round of heavy fighting that broke out in Kabul on January 1, 1994, following Dustam's switch from alliance with Rabbani to alliance with Hekmatyar and the Shi'a Hizb-i Wahdat, did not bring about a military solution either, as Mas'ud's northern and state forces, with the advantage of air superiority and heavy weapons, maintained their grip on the capital. Mas'ud was unable, however, to drive Hekmatyar and the Wahdat-Dustam forces from positions in the suburbs and even from the southern and western quarters of Kabul itself. For its part, Pakistan was becoming desperate for a solution, since it regarded the opening of trade routes into Central Asia to be a priority national interest. A similar view in Uzbekistan had led President Islam Karimov to use his influence with Dustam to shift his alliance to Hekmatyar.

Kandahar was one of the provinces that had not taken a major part in the internal fighting after the victory of the mujahidin in 1992. A council of civic leaders, tribal chiefs, and mujahidin commanders had been formed under the nominal authority of a Jami'at-i Islami governor appointed by Kabul. But even here private armies existed throughout the rural districts under former mujahidin, tribal leaders, and commanders of tribal militias who had supported the Najibullah regime. Increasingly, numbers of these became little better than bandits setting up roadblocks to levy tolls and rob civilian travelers. Many became prominent as well in drug cultivation, production, and transportation. One of the largest of the tribal militias during the jihad had been the Achakzais of Ismat Muslim, who dominated the main highway from Kandahar to the Pakistan border at Chaman. Before Ismat Muslim's death during the jihad, he had switched allegiances from the mujahidin to the government, but always worked in his own self-interest. A number of his former commanders had continued these predatory activities along the road, taking advantage of the lack of any law or security to plunder and extort at will.

The circumstances that finally coalesced the taliban into a political force have been reported mainly through Pakistani sources. The movement began in the area around Kandahar. Throughout the course of the jihad one of the local mujahidin commanders in the province had been Mullah Muhammad Omar. A Durrani Pushtun (reported variously as either a Popalzai or a Noorzai), he operated from his base in the Arghestan district with a few hundred fighters. In the course of the jihad he was wounded and lost an eye and thus gained the nickname "Rund" (one-eyed). This wound enhanced his credibility, since it demonstrated that he had personally sacrificed for the jihad. Mullah Omar's base held some strategic importance, as it was located in the valley north of the Kandahar-Chaman road guarding the mountain passes across the low range of hills that parallel the road to the Pakistan border. He had fought with the Ismat Muslim militia for control of this road for years.

Following the end of the Najibullah regime, he returned to his religious role as head of a madrasa. But the chaos and lawlessness of the local warlords, bandits, and drug dealers disgusted him and a number of like-minded mullahs and former mujahidin. Finally, aroused by a particularly brutal highway robbery in July 1994 that involved an assault on women, Mullah Omar gathered a force of his taliban and former mujahidin to defeat and dispense summary justice to the miscreants. The effect of his action was electrifying to public opinion, and other local commanders rallied to these taliban. They captured the Afghan border town of Spin Boldak in October and Kandahar itself in November, having been invited by the residents. Soon afterward, after determining that the behavior of the JIA governor was un-Islamic, Mullah Omar expelled him from the city. Once the students (henceforth known as the Taliban) had captured Kandahar, they began to receive a number of foreign visitors, including John Monjo, the U.S. ambassador in Islamabad, and General Babar, Pakistan's interior minister. To further demonstrate that the road through Kandahar was now open, Pakistan sent a truck caravan to Central Asia, but it was halted by another bandit roadblock soon after leaving the city. The Taliban stepped in to keep the roadway open.

The Taliban movement spread rapidly throughout the southwestern provinces, gathering numerous volunteers, surrenders of arms, and the allegiance of entire provinces with scarcely a shot having to be fired. Before making any military advance, emissaries were sent to explain their program to the local people and leaders and to request their support, which was most often given enthusiastically. Mawlana Muhammad Nabi Muhammadi, Mawlana Yunis Khalis and Sibghatullah Mujaddidi endorsed their movement. In Pakistan, the JUI expressed its support and facilitated the movement of taliban from JUI madrasas in Pakistan in joining their Afghan brothers. Eventually they closed the frontier madrasas to studies and declared that all taliban should join the new jihad in Afghanistan.

The Taliban program was simple but astonishingly effective. They promised to end the fighting and to restore law and order under the shari'a. "Bad" commanders who had taken advantage of their position to enrich themselves were removed, but "good" commanders who were loyal to Islamic values were confirmed in office. Even former communists were accepted into the movement (but their conduct was closely watched). All heavy weapons were to be turned over to the Taliban. They were particularly vehement in their condemnation of the drug trade, which was not only against Islam but was also a major source of foreign influence and corruption in society through its vast profits. In contrast to what had become the usual pattern of Afghan leadership during the jihad, the Taliban instituted a truly collective leadership, although Mullah (now Mawlana) Omar is the head of the council. In national politics they declined to act as a political party, even when invited to do so by the United Nations representatives. Instead, they announced willingness to support any government that was achieved through the consensus of the political leaders and represented the will of the people.

The political views of the Taliban became clearer as they moved rapidly on Kabul. Ghazni fell at the end of January 1994, then Maidan Shahr, the capital of Wardak province, and finally even Hekmatyar's headquarters at Charasyab, a few kilometers south of Kabul, which he had occupied since April 1992. Hekmatyar retreated to Sarobi, strategically located on the Kabul-Jalalabad road, to preserve the core of his supporters. Although the Taliban were overwhelmingly Pushtun (estimated at over 80 percent), they treated the Hazara Shi'a of Hizb-i Wahdat very carefully. The majority of Wahdat under Ali Mazari had repudiated Iranian leadership and formed an alliance with Hekmatyar against the Rabbani/Mas'ud regime. However, the Iranians supported about one-quarter of the Wahdat (the Akbari faction) with money and weapons, and this faction supported Rabbani. Initially the Kabul government was cautious in their dealing with the Taliban. On the one hand, they had ousted the Jami'at governor of Kandahar, but on the other they had defeated Hekmatyar and driven him from the suburbs of

Kabul. This latter represented an important gain for the Kabul forces, an objective they had been unable to achieve in three years of fighting. The Taliban attempted to play a neutral role in Kabul by stepping between the Mazari and Mas'ud forces in order to separate them and by receiving the surrender of heavy weapons by the Hizb-i Wahdat. However, the takeover of the front lines proved disastrous as Mas'ud, in early March, took advantage of the situation to attack and drive both the Taliban and Wahdat (with a contingent of Dustam's Uzbeks) from the city. The Taliban felt that they had been betrayed by Mazari, and he was captured and executed by the local Taliban commanders. His body, returned to his followers in Ghazni, was taken for burial in Mazar-i-Sharif with high honors and amid great scenes of mourning. The new leadership of the Mazari faction, under Abdul Karim Khalili, continued in alliance with the Taliban and Dustam in their renewed common determination to oust the Rabbani regime from Kabul. In confused fighting in 1995 and 1996 the Mazari Wahdat faction fought against the Akbari Wahdat faction in league with Mas'ud's forces in the Hazarajat. This resulted in their winning, losing, and then regaining Bamiyan.

Despite their retreat from Kabul, the Taliban remained a potent force, entrenched at Maidan Shahr and thus blocking the Kandahar-Kabul highway. In the far west they advanced rapidly against Herat, the stronghold of the important Jami'at-i Islami commander Isma'il Khan. They initially hoped to gain Isma'il Khan's voluntary allegiance, but he had given refuge to a number of the commanders that the Taliban had expelled from Kandahar. As in their advance on Kabul, the move against Herat became more a political than a military victory as district after district declared in their favor. By early May they had surrounded the Shindand air base and approached Herat, but they were driven back by air reinforcements sent by Mas'ud. The Taliban suffered a major defeat at Farah Rud and retreated through Farah and Nimroz provinces into Helmand province, where they held for the summer.

In early 1995, the Kabul government attempted to regain international stature after their twin victories at Kabul and Herat. For the first time in years, the capital was not under fire or divided by hostile armies. The international airport reopened and a major diplomatic campaign was mounted to persuade foreign governments to reopen their embassies. This was to little avail, despite the dispatch of Dr. Abdullah Khan, deputy minister of defense, along with Mas'ud's brother Walid, to Washington. Washington remained firm in the view that, at best, it could accept the Kabul regime as a de facto government of part of Afghanistan, a country divided by a civil war. It was not a de jure government. It remained represented in Washington by a chargé, and the United States had no official representation in Afghanistan. Despite this lack of recognition, the U.S. ambassador in Islamabad and other American officials, including the assistant secretary of state for South Asian affairs, Robin Raphel, paid several visits to Afghanistan, where they engaged in talks with diverse political leaders, including the Kabul government. In officially stating the U.S. goals in Afghanistan, Raphel stressed the primacy of the establishment of peace and security through a political process under United Nations auspices. Other important aims stressed were support for reconstruction and the return of refugees, the combating of narcotics trafficking, and an end to the harboring of radical groups.[16] In 1995, at congressional hearings, Raphel spoke favorably of the Taliban. She mentioned their leaders' support, in principle, for a peaceful political process, in contrast to "factional leaders" who were "reluctant to relinquish their personal power for the overall good of Afghanistan,"—a thinly veiled criticism of President Rabbani.[17]

The United Nations reinforced the isolation of the Kabul government by making it known that it would not allow Rabbani's representative to take part in the regular session of the General Assembly. At a seminar sponsored by the United Nations Development Program held in Sweden in June 1995 to discuss Afghan recovery, the envoy of the UN secretary-general, Mahmoud Mestiri, stated both privately and publicly that he found President Rabbani's failure to keep any of his repeated promises to resign to be the principal cause of the lack of progress in creating an interim government of all parties prior to a peace agreement. Pakistan, for its part, showed a willingness to take yet another initiative toward a solution by inviting Sardar Abdul Wali, former king Muhammad Zahir Shah's principal adviser and nephew, to visit Pakistan and hold discussions with frontier tribes and representatives from Afghanistan—something it had never allowed during the jihad. He was received with high official honors and much popular enthusiasm on this tour. This naturally revived speculation about the return of the monarch to an active role in establishing a national government of reconciliation.

In a most embarrassing event for the prestige of the Kabul regime, fighter planes from Kandahar forced a landing there of a Russian cargo plane en route to Kabul with 3.4 million rounds of ammunition. The seven-member Russian crew was detained. This public revelation of undeniable direct Russian support in the continued civil war on the side of the Kabul regime (even though Kabul claimed it to be a purely commercial deal) led to widespread popular revulsion. In western Afghanistan the course of fighting between Isma'il Khan and the Taliban took a dramatic turn in late summer of 1995. After failing in an attack on the Taliban in Helmand, the government forces retreated rapidly along the road to Herat, which fell in early September. Isma'il Khan and a few hundred supporters took refuge in Iran. The government's repeated assurances that Kabul was secure enough to allow foreign embassies to reopen was belied by a mob attack on the Pakistani embassy (described later) after the Taliban victory in Herat.

The loss of Herat was a particularly dangerous event for the Kabul government, since it freed the Taliban to concentrate on Kabul, whereas earlier in the year they had been fighting on two axes, Herat and Kabul. From Herat, the Taliban established contact with Dustam's forces in the northwest and, between them, opened a direct access route between Pakistan and Turkmenistan. The Taliban advanced once again to the suburbs of Kabul, reoccupying Charasyab. Once again Mas'ud checked them, but Kabul came under fire yet again. Mestiri reopened his mediation efforts in three-way negotiations among the Kabul government, Mujaddidi's Supreme Coordinating Council, and the Taliban.

The military and political situation underwent dramatic and perhaps decisive change in 1996. Mestiri continued to shuttle between Kandahar, Kabul, Mazar-i-Sharif, and Jalalabad to confer with different Afghan regional leaders—the Taliban, President Rabbani and Commander Mas'ud, General Dustam, and Hekmatyar and Haji Abdul Qader. However, his plan, calling for a number of prominent Afghans from all factions to meet in order to install a provisional government, had no chance of success. The Rabbani regime liked it, since a clear majority (eighteen of twenty-eight) of the persons put forward to establish the interim government were favorable to him. The loose anti-Rabbani coalition of Hekmatyar, Mujaddidi, Hizb-i Wahdat, and Dustam, which formed the Supreme Coordination Council of the Islamic Revolution of Afghanistan (or SCC), together with the Taliban, were adamant that Rabbani would first have to resign and neutralize Kabul before any negotiations could begin. In light of Rabbani's refusal to accede this very point in all prior negotiations, conferences, and agreements, this effort also came to naught. Mestiri, worn by the cares and futility of his mission, resigned in May. UN Secretary-General Boutros Boutros-Ghali appointed as Mestiri's successor Norbert Holl, a German diplomat with experience in South Asian affairs. Although he has spent time visiting the diverse parties, the military situation has shifted considerably in the meantime.

From October 1995 onward, the Taliban had been entrenched in an arch reaching from the southwest to the area south of Kabul. A desultory war of attrition between them and the Rabbani forces commanded by Mas'ud occasionally flared up in the form of attacks and counterattacks on strategic hills or of long-range rocket bombardments and air attacks. In air attacks the Kabul government forces enjoyed a better tactical position, being based at Bagram air base, scarcely forty miles to the north, while the Taliban launched attacks from Kandahar, some 300 miles to the southwest. In the north of the country, fighting continued largely between Dustam and Mas'ud, with some participation by Hekmatyar commanders. In the west, some minor guerrilla attacks were conducted by Isma'il Khan's forces, now reequipped and based in Iran, but these forces suffered a severe setback with the death of Commander Alauddin, Isma'il Khan's best commander, who had been with him since their days together in the Afghan army before the communist coup of April 1978.

Hekmatyar's military and political situation, dramatically weakened because of his loss of Pakistani support, nonetheless allowed command of the strategic Sarobi district. From there he could block the road from Kabul to Jalalabad, and thence to the Pakistan border through the Khyber Pass, as well as control Kabul's electricity supply from the Maipar hydroelectric dam. Aside from this, some of his commanders located north of the Hindu Kush remained loyal, and he controlled the eastern province of Laghman. He also participated in the Nangarhar Shura, the provincial government composed of a coalition of several parties and dominated by governor Haji Abdul Qader of the Hizb-i Islami (Yunis Khalis).

The most serious blow to both Hekmatyar and the Rabbani forces came from the shift in their relations with Pakistan. Although diplomatic relations continued, Pakistan's position began to harden against the Kabul regime after its embassy had been attacked and burned in September by an officially inspired and directed Kabul mob, presumably in retaliation for Pakistani support in the fall of Herat to the Taliban. An Afghan employee of the embassy had been killed, and the ambassador and military attaché had been wounded. Pakistan demanded an official apology and money to rebuild the embassy, and it moved its wounded ambassador to Jalalabad. Perhaps worried at being marginalized militarily and politically, Hekmatyar began in February to shift his support to the Kabul government by allowing the road between Kabul and Pakistan to reopen. This rapprochement was facilitated by the leader of the JI of Pakistan, Qazi Hussein Ahmad, who came to Kabul to seal the shift in alliance. In May further reconciliation led to Hekmatyar's assumption of his former post as prime minister in the Kabul government beginning in June. This was the same position he had occupied in the Rabbani government from June 1993 until his attempted coup in alliance with Dustam on January 1, 1994. This time, theoretically, his position was strengthened, for his nominees to head the finance and defense ministries were installed. Unlike in 1993, Hekmatyar moved into Kabul and occupied the prime minister's residence, along with a thousand of his troops, while, as a precaution, he left the bulk of his men in their old positions in Sarobi. Other ministries were shared by Rabbani's Jami'at, Abdul Rasul Sayyaf's Ittihad, the Shi'a Ittihad of Shaykh Muhsini, the Akbari faction of Hizb-i Wahdat, and the Jami'at Tawhid wa Sunna (Society of Unity and Tradition), the ideological Wahhabi party dominant in the Kunar.

Once in power, Hekmatyar called for the dismissal of all communists and the strict enforcement of Islamic law. He ordered the closing of cinemas, banned music broadcasts on radio and television, advised women to follow Islamic dress codes, and ordered government workers to perform midday prayers at their workplaces.[18] He soon found that the life of a prime minister was not an easy one as one of his commanders, disappointed that he was denied a ministry, decamped for Sarobi with his troops. But the situation worsened still.

The Fall of Kabul to the Taliban

In September the Taliban launched a dramatic new offensive by moving east toward Jalalabad and ousting Haji Abdul Qader from the position he had occupied since the fall of the Najibullah government in 1992. Casualties were low on both sides, and the Taliban immediately moved to occupy Kunar and Laghman, with little resistance. They turned forthwith on Hekmatyar's forces at Sarobi, routing more than 2,000, who fled in confusion or joined the Taliban. Without pausing, the Taliban occupied Kabul on September 27, despite the fact that the capital had a purported 30,000 troops defending it. President Rabbani and Prime Minister Hekmatyar fled north of the Hindu Kush to Takhar and Kunduz provinces, respectively. This was the same kind of dramatic offensive that the Taliban had used to achieve the great victories of the past, from Kandahar to the gates of Kabul in 1994, and from Helmand to Herat in 1995. Thorough political preparation of whole provinces, including Kabul, led to victories with few casualties on either side as opposition melted away. Virtually their first move upon entering the capital was to deal with the last communist president (and secret police chief from 1980–1986), Najibullah, who along with his brother, General Shahpur Ahmadzai, had been given sanctuary at the United Nations compound for four years when their escape attempt on UN aircraft to India had been prevented by mujahidin troops. The two were publicly beaten and hanged from the traffic kiosk opposite the presidential palace in the center of Kabul.

Mas'ud withdrew to his old stronghold, the Panjshir valley, in relatively good order. The Taliban followed him, occupying the Bagram air base, Charikar, and Jabal us-Siraj at the foot of the Salang Pass and the entrance to the Panjshir valley. As they attempted to follow Mas'ud up the narrow valley, however, they fell into the same ambush that Mas'ud had used many times during the jihad. The Taliban were driven out of the Panjshir southward to within twenty-five miles of Kabul. There the front lines stabilized through the end of 1996, with the Taliban driving back Mas'ud's southward push. Hekmatyar remained in Kunduz, still claiming to be the legitimate prime minister independently of the Rabbani government. He attempted to reach an understanding with the Taliban, claiming that he had never opposed them or fought them. Mas'ud blamed the loss of Kabul precisely on Hekmatyar's failure to resist the Taliban at Sarobi.

Politically, a new alliance began to emerge in October as a consequence of direct negotiations between Mas'ud and Dustam at Khaletin, a small town at the northern entrance to the Salang Pass. The Abdul Karim Khalili's Wahdat faction, which until the previous month had fought to overthrow Rabbani, joined as well. The new alignment, composed of recently bitter enemies and former allies represents the instabilities of Afghan factions, especially during the civil war, when clear ideological positions have become blurred for many mujahidin parties. Dustam's opportunistic alliances since January 1992 have marked him as a particularly adept player. The Taliban and Dustam had cooperated against their common enemy, the Mas'ud-Rabbani government in Kabul. Once Kabul fell, however, Dustam was forced to reconsider his options. He could not but think that the Taliban, having conquered roughly three-quarters of Afghanistan in two years, would move against him next in order to complete their task. He probably also considered the grisly fate of his former communist leader, Najibullah, whom he had betrayed in 1992. Neither Dustam nor Mas'ud can survive in a country dominated by the Taliban, whose main purpose since their founding has been to end the warlordism of ex-communists and ex-mujahidin alike in order to restore the unity of the country under an Islamic government.

Solidifying their administration of Kabul, the Taliban formed a six-member Provisional Ruling Council, all mullahs, headed by Mullah Rabbani (unrelated to President Rabbani). From Kandahar, the Taliban leader, Mullah Omar, issued a decree dismissing all Afghan ambassadors and freezing their accounts. The representatives of Iran and Turkey remained in Kabul, but the Indian representation departed. The Taliban imposed strict Islamic code for women, demanding full veiling and barring them from work outside the home, and closing girls' schools. United Nations relief programs shut down briefly when some of their local workers were arrested but resumed upon their release.

Regional and International Reaction to the Taliban

The international response to the new balance of power in Afghanistan came swiftly. International news media descended on Kabul in numbers unseen since the fall of the capital to the mujahidin in April 1992. Much of the attention focused on the status of women under Taliban rule and the enforcement of Islamic codes of criminal punishment. Of note is the fact that there had been no similar international scrutiny of the human rights violations by the "national security" services under Mas'ud's control that had taken over the structures of Najibullah's KhAD, which fielded some 5,000 spies and agents in Kabul alone. Torture and labor camps for several thousand prisoners held in the Panjshir valley were widely believed to have taken place.[19]

The international impact of the Taliban victory was immediate and nowhere more alarming than in Russia and the Central Asian states of the

CIS. Alarmist newspaper reports warned "the freed jinni of the Taliban's Islamic fundamentalism, bursting out of its Afghan bottle, could threaten not only Tajikistan, but the other republics of Central Asia as well." General Alexander Lebed, the former Russian security adviser, warned that the Taliban planned to incorporate part of Uzbekistan, including Bukhara, into the Afghan state as well as to join with the Tajik Islamic opposition movement. "It might be necessary to help Ahmed Shah [Mas'ud] and Hekmatyar. To give them moral and material support."[20] General Boris Gromov, a member of the Duma and the last Soviet commander in Afghanistan in 1989, was more sanguine in his assessment: "The Russian leadership should not make any rash decisions. The ill-considered and rash decisions of the Soviet leadership in 1979 are what led to the current situation in Afghanistan. The Taliban do not have the strength to carry military operations over to the territory of Uzbekistan and Tajikistan."[21]

At the official level, an emergency meeting of the CIS leaders convened in Almaty, Kazakstan, on October 4 and 5, shortly after the fall of Kabul to the Taliban. Although no official communiqué on the situation was issued, afterward Uzbek President Karimov and other participants recalled that the 1992 Collective Security Treaty of Tashkent provided for military cooperation and collective defense, which could be put into effect if the Afghan conflict spread to any of the CIS states. He also urged that "humanitarian" support be given to General Dustam to protect the immediate vicinity of the borders of the new states. The press service of the military staffs committee said that there was agreement that defenses on the border would be strengthened. Russian premier Viktor Chernomyrdin stated that the position of Moscow and its CIS partners would depend on the behavior of other countries, particularly the United States and Pakistan. In Kabul the acting foreign minister, Mullah Muhammad Ghaus, warned Dustam against an alliance with any CIS state and advised the Russian people not to forget the regrettable experience of intervention.[22]

Less alarmist and even cooperative reactions also emerged. Turkmen President Saparmurat Niyazov did not attend the CIS conference, but he did send his foreign minister. Turkmenistan is not a party to the 1992 Tashkent security treaty, but a Turkmen representative had been expected to attend as an "interested party." The Turkmen experience with the Taliban as their neighbors in the Herat area for more than a year without incident may have contributed to Niyazov's more measured approach. Two weeks after the Almaty conference, while Karimov expressed his concern with military operations close to Uzbekistan's southern borders, he admitted that he did not consider serious any alleged Taliban designs on Bukhara or other Uzbek territory. Instead, he wondered how Lebed could have made such a statement. He held separate discussions in October with two visitors, Iranian Foreign Minister Ali Akbar Velayati and Pakistani President

Farooq Ahmed Leghari. The latter indicated a convergence of views on Afghanistan with his host and said further, "The securing of a durable peace in Afghanistan requires the creation of a government that includes all of the ethnic, religious and other groups that are currently fighting in Afghanistan."[23] Other aspects discussed included the establishment of a new transportation corridor from the Uzbek-Afghan border at Termez through Mazar-i-Sharif and Herat to Karachi. By this time the activities of the American oil company, UNOCAL, had become public. Together with its Saudi partner, Delta Oil, it had already signed a US$2 billion contract to construct a natural gas pipeline, with an oil pipeline envisioned for the future, running between Turkmenistan and Pakistan. UNOCAL announced that the Taliban victory in Kabul was a positive sign and further announced that the company was already supplying "noncash bonus payments" to the Taliban in return for their cooperation, even before the victory in Kabul.[24]

The Rabbani government had claimed repeatedly that Pakistan had had a hand in the Taliban success. This charge surfaced in December 1995 during a UN General Assembly debate on Afghanistan, when Deputy Foreign Minister Abdul Rahim Ghafurzai charged that Pakistan supported the Taliban with arms, military equipment, logistics, and military intelligence. Kabul also charged that Islamabad underwrote the Taliban budget of $120 million per month. Pakistan rejected the charges and stated that the root cause of the conflict in Afghanistan arose out of the failure of President Rabbani to quit his office long after the expiration of his legal term in early 1994. In a consensus resolution adopted in December 1995, the General Assembly did not mention Pakistan, as Kabul had hoped, but instead called on all nations to refrain from interference in the internal affairs of Afghanistan.[25] Despite political changes in Pakistan, namely, the ouster of Bhutto and the removal of Babar, the basis for Pakistan's policy appears to remain unchanged. Its objective is to assure a stable and friendly government in Afghanistan that will provide safe passage for opening direct trade and transit routes to Central Asia.

Iran's reaction to the Taliban success in Afghanistan was one of anger. For years it had provided strong moral and material support for the Rabbani government. Locked in a struggle with Pakistan, Saudi Arabia, and the United States for influence in Central Asia, Iran viewed the Taliban victory as part of a plot by Sunnis and the United States to isolate it. The commander of the Revolutionary Guards had taken personal charge of the reorganization of Isma'il Khan's forces after the fall of Herat. Ayatollah Ali Khamenei, the supreme religious head of the country, called the Taliban a disgrace to Islam, a remark that was formally protested to the Iranian chargé, who had remained in Kabul. After the fall of Kabul, Iran continued to send military supplies to Mas'ud via Uzbekistan.

The United States exhibited a moderate revival of interest in Afghanistan even before the victory of the Taliban at Jalalabad and Kabul in September.

Congressional interest, which had played an important part in the jihad, was rekindled when Senator Hank Brown (R.–Colo.) convened a conference in Washington in April. Many groups were represented, but Hekmatyar and Sayyaf were deliberately not invited because alleged links to "radical organizations outside Afghanistan."[26] In a summary of the military and political situation, a Defense Department analyst assessed that Rabbani and Mas'ud controlled between 30,000 and 40,000 men and the major part of the weapons from the communist regime and enjoyed the support of India, Iran, and Russia. Dustam commanded the second most powerful force, numbering 25,000, equipped with a considerable number of aircraft, armored vehicles, and artillery. He was closely tied to Uzbekistan and worried about the influence of Russia and Iran on the Rabbani government, but he refused to cooperate with the Taliban. The Taliban also had about 25,000 fighting men, with some aircraft and helicopters. However, their victories depended not on their military strength but on support from other mujahidin commanders. They had political and financial support from Pakistan. The same source considered the Taliban defeat of Hekmatyar to have destroyed most of his strength and base of support.[27]

Official U.S. policy, enunciated by the State Department's Robin Raphel, holds as its goals regional stability, since current instability prevents the new Central Asian states from establishing trade and oil and gas outlets to the south; countering terrorism and narcotics production (with Afghanistan the world's second largest narcotics producer at 35 percent in 1995), problems that cannot be addressed in the absence of a functioning central government; and dealing with humanitarian issues such as those illustrated by 2.5 million foreign and internal refugees and Afghanistan's ranking as 173rd of 175 countries on the UN index of social development. An end to the current impasse should include a cease-fire, the demilitarization of Kabul, an agreement on an interim government, and planning for a permanent government. She stated that the United States did not support one faction over another but rather a negotiated settlement, without winners or losers, leading to a government chosen by the Afghan people and free from outside interference.[28] Three months later, after the fall of Kabul to the Taliban, the State Department announced that the United States intended to establish contact with the new regime, despite its unacceptable policy toward women.

The Future for Peace

By spring 1997, it remained to be seen whether the Taliban's control of major portions of the country plus Kabul would translate into a return of political stability that would finally allow for country-wide reconstruction and economic reintegration into the rapidly advancing trade and mineral wealth of the Central Asian region. At the United Nations, the credentials of the Rabbani government represenation continued to be honored despite Taliban protestations. On Dec. 13, 1996, the General Assembly adopted a concensus resolution calling for a political solution through the plan of Norbert Holl. Further peace talks conducted by Dr. Holl under United Nations auspices, were conducted in Islamabad in January 1997.[29] Represented in the talks were the Taliban, former president Rabbani, General Dostam, and the Hizb-i Wahdat. Nothing substantive on a ceasefire, much less an ultimate political solution, was accomplished, although some detailed talks on the exchange of prisoners took place. The Taliban information minister, Amir Khan Muttaqi declared that the peace talks were going nowhere unless the opposition accepted the Taliban's strict version of Islamic rule.

The Organization of the Islamic Conference with longstanding concern for Afghan events, in its meeting in Jakarta in November decide to suspend the participation of Afghanistan for that meeting without prejudicing representation of the Rabbani government. The Taliban had sent a delegation to Jakarta, but they were not allowed to present their case. Rabbani visited Europe to solicit support from European governments and Afghan exiles, but his attempt to see exiled former king Zahir Shah in Rome was unsuccessful.

The latter, by the end of 1996 appeared to have placed his hopes in the United Nations plan. The Rabbani government, which earlier had rejected proposals for an arms embargo and demilitarization of Kabul, changed its position to espouse for both proposals once it had lost Kabul to the Taliban. Zahir Shah expressed his willingness to cooperate not only by expressing an interest in an invitation to participate in a meeting of all Afghan groups and prominent individuals, but also in serving to head a provisional government if asked.[30]

When the Islamabad UN sponsored peace talks failed in January, the Taliban launched an attack north of Kabul, recapturing the much contested Bagram airbase and the provincial capital of Charikar with little resistance. Many of the inhabitants of Charikar welcomed the Taliban after having experienced the brutal occupation of their city by Dustam's forces in October. The Taliban forces went on to capture Jebal as-Siraj, Ahmad Shah Mas'ud's headquarters at the entrance to the Salang Pass. They then turned west through the Gorband valley, fighting in heavy snow against the Hizb-I Wahdat in the Shibar Pass and on into the Hazarajat.

As weather conditions improved in the spring of 1997, the Taliban made their first move into the great plains of northern Afghanistan from the direction of Badghis province in the west. In mid-May, General Abdul Malik, Dustam's second in command, staged a coup against his leader and invited the Taliban to occupy the north, much as Dustam himself had done in 1992 when he switched sides from the Najibulah forces to the mujahidin. Dustam's airforce commander, General Yousef Shah, also defected, flying with several of his pilots to join the Taliban. He remarked that the people in the north revolted against Dustam "because he wants to dismember Afghanistan."[31] Within one week, the Taliban advanced through Faryab, Shibargan, Sari-i Pul, and Balkh provinces to Mazar-i Sharif. Dustam fled to Uzbekistan and immediately afterward to Turkey, where he had already purchased substantial property.

However, clashed erupted between the Taliban forces in Mazar-i Sharif and the Hizb-i Wahdat when the Taliban tried to disarm the Shi'a forces in their quarter of the city. The Taliban claimed that this action had been agreed to by General Abdul Malik, but when fighting broke out Abdul Malik's forces attacked the Taliban column from the rear. After heavy fighting, the Taliban retreated to the military base at the airport and did not immediately attempt to regain the city. General Muhammad Painda, a former adviser of Dostam and now of Abdul Malik, claimed that the Taliban had broken their written alliance agreement not to disarm the northern forces before a national government had been established. The Taliban claimed that Iranians in disguise had infiltrated the Taliban to start the fighting. Meanwhile, the Taliban advanced through the Salang Pass and Tunnel, capturing Pul-i Khumri, the capital of Baghlan province and the center of the Isma'ili militia commanded by Sayyid Jaffar Naderi, an ally of Dustam since the Soviet invasion.

Former president Rabbani's representative at the United Nations claimed that Rabbani remained in the border area near Tajikistan, but was planning to return to Taleqan, the capital of Takhar province. Others claim that after the fall of Mazar-i Sharif, he fled to Tajikistan. Rabbani's representative further claimed that the forces of Ahmad Shah Mas'ud had "liberated" Gulbahar and Charikar, thus cutting off the Taliban north of the Salang Pass. Pakistan called for a ceasefire at that point, but it was difficult to establish just where a ceasefire line would be established in the confused situation in the north.[32]

Some potentially significant political developments have thus far accompanied the confused fighting in the north. At the start of the Taliban advance, Abdul Malik's forces turned over to them Isma'il Khan, the former commander and governor of Herat that the Taliban had previously routed. He had returned to the north and was trying to rebuild his forces with the aid of Dostam and Iran in order to regain Herat. Gulbuddin Hekmatyar, another leader driven into Iranian exile by the Taliban, stated that there could be no government established in Afghanistan by force of arms. Instead, he went on, it must be "of, by and for the people."[33] When the fighting broke out between the Taliban and the Hazara forces of Abdul Malik, a high level political delegation of the Taliban which had entered the city, were captured by the Hazara. Among others they included the

ministers of information and foreign affairs, as well as the Pakistani ambassador to Kabul. Pakistan and Saudi Arabia had formally recognized the
Taliban government after their breakthrough in the north of the country
although it is obvious that they had recognized the Taliban, de facto, for
several years. His captors quickly released the Pakistani ambassador. But
in a development of considerable potential significance for the future of
Ahmad Shah Mas'ud's resistance to the Taliban, the latter claimed to have
captured in Mazar-i Sharif a lengthy secret document of the Shura-ye
Nazar (The Council of the North), the political organization of Ahmad
Shah Mas'ud. In this document, according to the Taliban, are detailed
plans for the north, including the removal of all Pushtuns from the region.
This document, when released and authenticated may further mar relations between the Pushtun dominated Taliban and the ethnic minorities of
the country.

The advances into the north by the Taliban were greeted regionally with
alarm by some and equanimity by others. Pakistan, Saudi Arabia, and
Turkmenistan regarded the initial Taliban success as a step toward stability
and the establishment of Afghanistan as a corridor for conduit of gas and
oil pipelines to Pakistan and beyond. Although at the ECO meeting in early
May, convened in Ashkabad, the Afghan seat had been given to former
president Rabbani rather than the Taliban representative, nonetheless the
greatest source of regional opposition to the Taliban came from Iran, Russia, Tajikistan, and Uzbekistan. Occurring almost concurrently with the
Iranian presidential elections that saw the landslide victory of a moderate
candidate, the success of the Taliban was regarded not only as the probable
defeat of Persian speaking ethnic groups, but also the establishment of an
Islamic state embarked on the road toward strict application of Shari'a at a
time when Iran was inching back from that direction. Moreover, the victory
of the Taliban spelled the success of the Pakistani-Saudi Arabian coalition
in the contest with Iran to become the major trade partner with the Central
Asian states. Gas and oil lines through Afghanistan leading to Pakistan di-
minish the prospects for such lines to be built through Iran. Russian reactions to the Taliban brought forth among others, the response that its
forces would defend the borders of the CIS, a measure that formed the basis of the security talks held among CIS states a few months earlier in in Almaty, thus forecasting a continued Russian military presence in Tajikistan.
The latter country regarded the Taliban advance with alarm and the expectation of many refugees fleeing northward as the Taliban advanced. Uzbekistan, which had been the scene in July 1996 of a meeting of all non-Tal-
iban, non-Rabbani leaders in Tashkent to form the a coalition to unseat
Rabbani, nonetheless did not give permanent refuge to Dustam and instead
has encouraged Pakistani-initiated negotiations to build a trade route between Uzbekistan and Pakistan through Mazar-i Sharif, Herat and Kanda-

har thereby giving it a material stake in a stable Afghanistan, perhaps overriding its interest in the minority rights of Afghan Uzbeks. [34]

Even without covert and overt interference from its regional neighbors, the promise of stability in Afghanistan under Taliban rule may be overstated if there is insufficient attention to the concerns of ethnic minorities, especially the large Persian speaking groups, both the Shi'a Hazara and the Sunni Tajiks. Regarded as a Pushtun dominated force that has in the course of its steady expansion over most if not all of the country, the Taliban may be credited with bringing together the fragmented warlord condition into which Afghanistan had degenerated. The composition of the Taliban, aside from its ethnic leaning toward the Pushtun groups, represents an amalgamation of the two main indigenous Afghan forces analyzed in this volume. The Marxists, largely Soviet-controlled and -financed, possibly from their origins in the 1960s gave way before the traditional and Islamist forces. Emerging from among the latter two groups, the Taliban combine traditionally trained madrasa students with many young mujahidin commanders. This combination has succeeded, through pursuasion as often as armed confrontation, to work for the reintegration of a country that puts its overall interest above that of provincial warlords or apprehensive ethnic groups. That trade and pipelines provided the grease to ease the reintegration speaks to the primary importance of the restoration of the Afghan economy. In the face of the utter destruction of the country, the lack of interest in its reconstruction by former Cold War opponents, the desperate turning to the drug trade as an alternative economy, perhaps the Islamic strictness of the Taliban may be the lesser price to pay for stability and economic recovery.

Chapter Eight

Elusive Stability: Taliban, Arabs, and the Afghan Future

It is one thing to gain control of the towns of Afghanistan but quite another to rule the country as a whole. An inconvenient lesson from the past, this quandary continues to bedevil those who would rule there, whether foreign or local. After the Taliban captured Kabul in September 1996, they became masters of most of the cities and towns, just as the Northern Alliance had from 1992 until then. But although the Taliban had secured intercity highways and city streets, they did not rule everywhere. The towns and cities now held large displaced populations because land mines and drought had blighted farming and driven people from the countryside. With the exception of Kabul, which from the middle of the twentieth century had housed a mixed ethnic population, other towns remained overwhelmingly uniethnic despite the problems of displacement, as did the refugee settlements in Pakistan and Iran. Villages are now almost completely uniethnic. As the pressure on the periodically unified Tajik and Uzbek elements in the north mounted, Pushtuns in the northern cities of Kunduz, and smaller populations in other areas, rallied to the Taliban in a show of ethnic solidarity. Rumors that the Northern Alliance were purging the Pushtuns (who had been urged north and west with promises of land and government jobs throughout the twentieth century) aggravated the ethnic divide.

In a country suffering from deep ethnic wounds inflicted by historical as well as recent events, the main threat to the political stability created under the Taliban came from an exaggerated reliance on Islamic homogeneity as a source of unity. This reliance on Islam was meant to unify a time-honored principle within Islamic history; and for the Taliban, insistence upon it came from a self-righteousness that governed their actions on several political fronts. Also, the Taliban, increasingly regarded as Kandahar-based

Pushtuns, relied on three centuries of Pushtun domination without comprehending the upheaval in the ethnic power balance that had evolved through the formation of essentially ethnic armies during the jihad against the Soviet presence.

In the aftermath of the U.S. defeat of the Taliban in the fall of 2001, enforcing Pushtun rule without the religious glue provided by Islam is bound to prove difficult, if not impossible. Pushtun ("Afghan") colonization of the areas north and west of the Hindu Kush during the Great Game (as summarized in Chapter 1) is one of the lesser-known events of eighteenth- and nineteenth-century colonial history in Central Asia. In light of this history and of the extreme ethnic tension at the end of 2001, it is hard to understand how the first official U.S. diplomatic representation to the post-Taliban interim government was headed by the expatriate scion of a leading Pushtun family that owns extensive lands around Mazar-I Sharif. Echoes of regional rivalries, especially with Iran, emerged as the Tajiks and Uzbeks of the north remained reluctant to embrace the pre-1978 ethnic power imbalance that gave Pushtuns the right to rule the entire country.

Although the impact of Afghanistan's ethnic complexity on relations with neighboring states could have caused ethnic skirmishes after the formation of independent eponymous states out of Soviet Central Asia, it has not thus far created a serious threat to Afghan territorial integrity, despite Iran's interest in bolstering Tajik and, to a lesser extent, Uzbek populations. Potential conflict, most likely at the border with Uzbekistan, has been undercut by the principle of multiethnic deterrence; that is, because no state in the region is ethnically homogenous, none appears willing to risk wholesale irredentism on the part of its co-ethnics in Afghanistan. The major exception to this principle is Tajikistan, whose internal and regional position has been so compromised by the interference of its near and far neighbors (Russia, Iran, and Uzbekistan, among others) that the remnants of Afghan opposition to the Taliban found Tajikistan not only a natural haven but also a convenient staging area for ground and air assaults. Hence, until Ahmad Shah Mas'ud was assassinated on September 9, 2001, two days before the terrorist strike on the United States, he and his faction not only impeded Afghan stability under the Taliban but also disrupted the Central Asian region through the internal disequilibrium they created in Tajikistan.

As a region, however, Central Asia established a working relationship with the Taliban despite a general abhorrence of the extreme form of the shari'a applied there. In this regard, Afghanistan's position as a bridge for trade and transit proved important to all who wished to link themselves across the deserts and mountains that separate the Indian Ocean and the region's coastal states, especially Pakistan, from the Asian heartland. The gas pipeline crossing Afghanistan from north to south was a chief economic boost to the region and may become so again if stability is possible under an interim coalition government.

Central Asia, and even Iran, became alarmed when the Taliban started to rely increasingly on manpower and funding from Arab and Pakistani sources, especially after 1998.

The Military Situation During Taliban Rule

The chief alteration in the political condition of Afghanistan was the ebb and flow of the Taliban's military engagement against the Northern Alliance; nominally it was led by Ahmad Shah Mas'ud, formerly the military chief during the Burhanuddin Rabbani regime. It is an exaggeration to say that the U.S. (and allied) offensive took center stage following the events of September 11. Even as the U.S. military mounted air and ground attacks, the undercurrent in the ground offensive came from the Northern Alliance, then disenchanted Pushtun tribesmen and expatriates. Note, however, that even as the Tajiks pushed impatiently into Kabul, their uselessness in Pushtun strongholds meant that the United States had to rely on Pushtuns to dislodge the Taliban from Kandahar, Khost, and Jalalabad.

By the end of the spring of 1999, the Taliban had conquered most of Afghanistan north of the central mountain ranges of the Hindu Kush and the highlands of the Hazarajat, thus extending their control over some 85 percent (U.S. estimate) to 90 percent (Taliban estimate) of the country. This essentially eliminated the Shi'a Hazaras's Hizb-i Wahdat of Abdul Karim Khalili and the Uzbek-led militia of the Jumbish-i Milli (National Movement) of General Abdul Rashid Dustam as effective military forces. Khalili lost his headquarters in Bamiyan and Dustam lost Mazar-i-Sharif. The Isma'ili militia of Sayyid Mansur Naderi and Sayyid Ja'far Naderi were also defeated and lost their headquarters at Kayan. Ahmad Shah Mas'ud's forces still controlled the area from the far northeastern provinces of Badakhshan to Kapisa and Parwan provinces north of Kabul, and Takhar province remained a battleground between Mas'ud and the Taliban. Mas'ud's forces, estimated at something over 10,000, were the only significant opposition blocking the Taliban's complete military control of the country. This was a remarkable accomplishment, particularly given the reverses the Taliban had suffered in 1997.

The Taliban had been ousted from Mazar-i-Sharif in May 1997 after briefly occupying the city. They had first been invited by General Abdul Malik, Dustam's rebellious second-in-command, who then turned against them, claiming that they had broken an agreement to refrain from attacking local customs (i.e., imposing Pushtunwali) or confiscating arms. The Taliban lost some 2,000 to 3,000 soldiers as prisoners of war, but the

Jumbish-i Milli lost its unity as a military-political force; Abdul Malik remained in charge in Afghanistan and Dustam fled to exile in Turkey. The Taliban advanced again from Kunduz and fought to the suburbs of Mazar-i-Sharif, taking the airport; but they were driven back in September and October after General Dustam returned from exile and briefly reconciled with General Abdul Malik. The two leaders fell out once again, and Abdul Malik was forced to flee to exile in Iran.

South of the Hindu Kush, Mas'ud drove the Taliban back to the defensive line of Kabul some twenty-five kilometers north of the capital. When winter brought an end to major fighting, the positions of the Taliban and the Northern Alliance were roughly the same as they had been at the beginning of the year. But the second falling-out between Dustam and Abdul Malik was accompanied by an event calculated to raise the level of ethnic and religious hatred to new heights: Dustam announced to foreign journalists and UN officials that the mass executions of thousands of Taliban prisoners had been discovered. They had been shot while their hands were tied and then dumped into wells or left in the desert. Dustam said the killings occurred during the few months that Abdul Malik had been in charge. Because the UN claimed that the security situation prevented a full investigation into the circumstances of the deaths, the Taliban's protest brought little satisfaction.

The 1998 fighting season opened in the spring with an advance of the Taliban against Mas'ud's communications in Takhar province. Takhar was vital to Mas'ud: It was the major supply line for the military aid he received through Tajikistan and also the best route between his bases north and south of the Hindu Kush. The importance of these foreign supplies was emphasized in October when authorities in Osh, Kyrgyzstan, seized and turned back an Iranian train loaded with seven hundred tons of weapons and ammunition (consigned as flour and humanitarian supplies) that were to be shipped by truck to Afghanistan.

The new year also saw the familiar pattern of largely static fighting north of Kabul. Rocket bombardment from Mas'ud's lines caused hundreds of civilian casualties in the capital. Long before the United States bombed parts of Kabul, the process of turning Kabul and its ministries, bazaars, and museum into rubble, begun in the 1980s, continued during the ethnic fighting. During the winter and spring the Taliban had instituted an economic blockade of the Hazarajat, a region perpetually short of food in the winter. Despite the Taliban's blockade, the Hazarajat was open to the north, which was controlled by the Hazaras's ally, General Dustam. But Dustam had been gravely weakened by the fighting in 1997 as well as by his four months in exile. Conditions in Mazar-i-Sharif and the Amu Darya port of Hairaton were anarchic: UN relief offices were attacked, their personnel evacuated, and UN food warehouses were looted. Dustam did not have uncontested control of his capital; in his own battle with Hizb-i Wahdat, which controlled the city center, he was driven into the suburbs. After long negotiations, the Taliban agreed to allow the United Nations to send food from their territory to the Hazarajat, provided that a besieged Taliban enclave was also fed.

In the summer the Taliban advanced once more from Herat against the northern provinces and Mazar-i-Sharif. Although this time they were not invited in, as they had been by Abdul Malik, their advance was almost as rapid. Over roughly one month in July and August they drove the forces of Dustam and Hizb-i Wahdat back hundreds of kilometers, finally taking Mazar-i-Sharif on August 12. The rapid advance demonstrated the fragility of Dustam's forces; several of his commanders and allies switched sides. Reports came out of Mazar-i-Sharif that thousands of civilians, most of them Hazaras, had been massacred by the Taliban. The reports from Amnesty International, Human Rights Watch, and the United Nations agreed, although the UN acknowledged that these were based on refugee accounts and said once more that there could be no investigation on the ground, due to security reasons.

An important event that almost overshadowed the fall of Mazar-i-Sharif was the death of nine Iranians (eight officials and a journalist) at the Iranian consulate there. The Taliban first denied knowledge of the missing Iranians, but later admitted that they had been shot during the fall of the city, allegedly by renegade Taliban troops acting without orders. Some fifty other Iranians had been captured along with their trucks, which, Iran claimed, had been delivering humanitarian supplies. The U.S. Department of Defense reported that Iran had been supplying arms and advice to the Northern Alliance and that the captured Iranians were involved in that effort.[1] The deaths of the nine Iranians caused an international crisis: When Iran threatened military action, the Taliban challenged it to try, promising that Iran would suffer the same fate as the Soviets. Iran did move reinforcements to the Afghan border in a well-publicized buildup and reported a series of military exercises by some 270,000 troops and Revolutionary Guards. The U.S. Pentagon claimed that this number was a gross exaggeration and that the actual number deployed amounted to about a quarter of that size.[2] Passions eventually calmed and the Taliban released the rest of the prisoners and the bodies of the dead Iranians. They even returned their trucks. During these negotiations, the Iranians sent what was described as a low-level delegation of the foreign ministry to examine Iranian property in Taliban-controlled Afghanistan.

The Taliban advances in the north did not stop at Mazar-i-Sharif, but turned immediately to the south against the Hizb-i Wahdat stronghold of the Hazarajat. The city of Bamiyan fell on September 13 after little fighting; the Hizb-i Wahdat leaders either fled to Iran or defected to the Taliban. The most important of the defectors was Ustad (professor) Muhammad Akbari, who had led his faction of the party for many years. Ironically, Akbari's faction had supported the Rabbani government in Kabul and had been the major recipient of aid from Iran while the rest of the party, under Ali Mazari, had been fighting against the Rabbani regime. Also defecting to the Taliban was Sayyid Jaghran; as the military commander of the traditionalist Hazara Shura, he controlled the region for decades after the Khalqi coup and the Soviet invasion. Akbari moved to Kabul, where the Taliban not only granted him an advisory role but promised him fair treatment for the Shi'ites and representation based on their percentage of the population. Some of Akbari's supporters were in fact appointed to administrative positions in the Taliban-occupied Hazarajat.

Fighting in the spring of 1999 began with a surprising but short-lived victory for Hizbi Wahdat; in April, they regained Bamiyan and much of the Hazarajat, only to be driven out by the Taliban after a few weeks. The situation in the north remained confused, the commanders shifting sides and operating in provinces that were nominally in the control of their enemy. The Hizb-i Islami of Gulbuddin Hekmatyar, which had been a major force in the jihad and the civil war, was by now broken into several factions, some supporting the Taliban and others the Northern Alliance. Hekmatyar adopted a more neutral stance toward the Taliban. In a refreshing, if naive, attempt to moderate the mutual hatreds of civil war, on May 25 the Taliban leader, Mullah Omar, appealed for an end to the cycle of revenge between the Taliban and the Shi'ites. The opposition had burned the houses of Taliban supporters in Bamiyan in April, and Taliban forces had retaliated in kind in May. "This kind of revenge action is condemned by the Islamic Emirate of Afghanistan, and I am requesting everyone to stop revenge and start living together as brothers."[3] Nonetheless, it was in Bamiyan that the Arab veterans of the jihad against the Soviet Union led the fighting for the Taliban. The ranks of the Taliban, fortified with these oft-times resented Arabs (and Pakistani volunteers), operated in the north as well. By 2001, they had reduced the Northern Alliance to little more than a military nuisance supported by Russia and Iran. The military reversals could not have come about without the coordination between the Taliban and Osama bin Laden's money and ardent recruits. It remains in the realm of speculation whether the Taliban leadership knew beforehand about the attack launched against the United States. Bin Laden had begun purging Afghans from his immediate retinue at about the time the United States offered money for him following his indictment in the embassy bombings. And no Afghan turned up in the airplane hijacking lists of September 11. Yet the assassination of Mas'ud on September 9 by two supposed Arab (Yemeni) journalists offers a circumstance that demonstrates a quid pro quo arrangement between the Taliban leadership and bin Laden. It may indicate only that the assassination of Mas'ud was a reward to the Taliban for protecting bin Laden from capture for prior offenses, not ones to come.

The Political Situation

The United Nations, the Organization of the Islamic Conference, the United States, and former King Zahir Shah, as well as Afghanistan's neighbors, attempted to negotiate a political settlement in Afghanistan during the period of the Taliban. Unfortunately, none produced significant results. The fundamental reason for failure was that, other than Pakistan, the Arab Emirates, Saudi Arabia, and Chechnya, no organization or state was willing to give the Taliban what they most wanted: recognition. The decline of the Northern Alliance as a military force weakened them as an internal threat to the Taliban. Holding only some 10 to 15 percent of the country and no major city, the Rabbani-Mas'ud forces were too weak to demand a coalition government, even though this was the position favored by the United Nations and the international community. The Taliban saw no reason to give up their military control, their religious mission, and their Islamic Emirate. They held that if their opponents were sincere Muslims willing to follow the shari'a and not communists, they were welcome to join the Taliban; but they had no desire to form a new coalition of parties and warlords such as those who had fought each other and destroyed the country between 1992 and 1996. For its part, the international community continued to attempt to isolate the Taliban by maintaining the representation of the Rabbani regime in the Afghan seat at the UN General Assembly. However, the Organization of the Islamic Conference had in 1996 declared that Afghanistan's seat in that organization be vacant. Relations with Saudi Arabia, a major force in the OIC, had became strained over the case of Osama bin Laden, who had declared the house of Saud unworthy of ruling the holiest sites of Islam. The Taliban paid the Saudi price for protecting bin Laden with the expulsion of the Taliban's chief diplomat in Riyadh and the recall of the Saudi representative from Kabul. The Saudis noted, nonetheless, that diplomatic relations had not been broken. This was demonstrated during the 1999 *hajj,* when the Saudis required Taliban-issued passports for all Afghan pilgrims.

Lakhtar Brahimi, a former Algerian foreign minister, who became the special envoy of the UN secretary-general, continued his shuttle diplomacy, including his first direct negotiations with the reclusive Mullah Omar in Kandahar. Bill Richardson, the U.S. ambassador to the United Nations, visited Kabul in early 1998 to encourage the Taliban to attend peace talks in Islamabad. These talks were held in April and May, but no positive results came of the negotiations (except for the Taliban's agreement to allow relief agencies to send food to the Hazarajat). The commitments not to launch major offensives were soon broken by both sides,[4] resulting in the Taliban's victories of the summer.

A new factor in negotiations was the activities of the "Six Plus Two" group; this group consisted of the UN member states bordering on Afghanistan, Russia, and the United States. Meetings of the group had taken place in New York at the UN ambassadorial level; but on September 21, 1998, they were elevated to foreign-minister level. U.S. Secretary of State Madeleine Albright attended, but Iranian Foreign Minister Kemal Kharazi, who had been expected, did not. Among the points of agreement was the group reiteration of the official United Nations position that "the Taliban and other parties should declare an immediate cease-fire and undertake negotiations aimed at achieving a political settlement culminating in the establishment of a broad-based, multi-ethnic, representative government."[5]

Direct negotiations were resumed in Ashkabad in March 1999, almost a year after the Islamabad meeting. To the surprise of all parties, an agreement was announced after marathon face-to-face negotiations. There would be shared executive, legislative, and judiciary duties; twenty prisoners would be exchanged; and further negotiations would be conducted, preferably in Afghanistan, in a month's time. However, there had been no cease-fire and major fighting resumed, the Taliban losing and then regaining the Hazarajat. The planned second round of talks was not held. On April 30, 1999, Zahir Shah issued an appeal for all warring groups to attend a Loya Jirgah to unify the country and indicated that he was sending representatives to talk to both sides so that a steering committee could be formed. Despite an endorsement from the United States, the Taliban rejected the former king's approach, saying that he had done little but sit on the fence during the Afghan jihad.

The hostility of many of Afghanistan's neighbors toward the Taliban regime appeared to be tempered by their gradual acceptance of the reality of Taliban rule—and the low likelihood of its reversal—and the dramatic weakening of the Northern Alliance. One fact could not be denied: The Taliban were a remarkably unified government, especially by recent Afghan standards; whereas the Northern Alliance consisted of an uneasy coalition of disparate groups that fought with each other almost as often as they fought with the Taliban. Both the Jumbish-i Milli and the Hizb-i Wahdat had split internally and with each other.

Indications of a softening of attitudes toward Taliban rule in Afghanistan for reasons of practical self-interest came from several Central Asian states. Turkmenistan's relations with the Taliban had been correct and even friendly ever since they had reached the Turkmen border in 1995. Trade flourished in both directions across the border, and Turkmenistan agreed to a project to extend its electricity grid to western Afghanistan. Turkmenistan, Pakistan, and Afghanistan continued to support the proposed natural gas pipeline across Afghanistan to Pakistan despite the withdrawal of the American company UNOCAL, the leading investor in the consortium, after the U.S. cruise missile attacks on Osama bin Laden on August 20, 1998. It was unclear whether the remaining members of the consortium, which included the Russian state-owned Gazprom, would be able to raise the estimated $2 billion in capital. In May 1999, Turkmenistan further distanced itself from Russia by announcing that it would take control of the border posts on the Afghan and Iranian frontiers, which had hitherto been manned by Russian frontier guards.

Uzbekistan had begun to adjust to the defeat of its client, General Dustam. It briefly cut off electric power to Mazar-i-Sharif, but restored it when the Taliban negotiated to pay the bill, which had not been demanded of Dustam for years. On June 1, 1999, the foreign minister of Uzbekistan visited Mullah Omar in Kandahar, hoping to persuade the Taliban to attend a meeting in Tashkent of the "Six Plus Two" states at the deputy foreign minister level. The Taliban responded that they would attend such talks only if invited as the government of Afghanistan and not as a faction in a civil war. The Uzbek foreign minister also delivered a goodwill message from President Islam Karimov. After meeting with the Taliban leader, the foreign minister held talks with several Afghan ministers; the Taliban spokesman said that they had agreed on the need for friendly and neighborly relations, which would help to improve the economic situation in Afghanistan.[6] But Uzbek-Taliban rapprochement received a setback when Islamically-based opposition to Tashkent's power elite took shelter in northern Afghanistan in January 2001. When the Islamic Movement of Uzbekistan (IMU) traveled through Tajikistan, it found shelter in the area of Kunduz, under the protection of the Taliban. After that, Tashkent became more amenable to discussions with Rabbani; and following September 11, it went on to become one of the first states to offer the United States entry into Central Asia, airspace and major military facilities included. The chilly relations between the United States and Uzbekistan, based on human rights disagreements, became transformed as both countries agreed on the threat posed by the Taliban. The facilitation of military movements from Uzbek soil for the Northern Alliance and the United States after the launch of the attack on Afghanistan has led to negotiations toward a permanent U.S. military presence in that country. To the satisfaction of Tashkent, one of the first major casualties in Kunduz when it fell to the combined Northern Alliance-U.S. offensive, was the leadership of the IMU. The later alleged ill-treatment of prisoners from Kunduz, at the hands of a newly revived Uzbek General Dustam in his Shiberghan fortification (where the American Taliban, John Walker Lindt, was found) may well relate to the presence of IMU members among the prisoners.

Although fear of the spread of Taliban sympathizers was rife among the secular, reformed Soviet leadership of Central Asia, even Kazakhstan received the Taliban's deputy trade minister for talks on wheat sales to Afghanistan. China sent a delegation to Kabul to inspect its embassy property with a view to reestablishing its presence. This left Tajikistan as the Central Asian state most adamantly opposed to Taliban rule. Tajikistan signed a twenty-five-year treaty for Russian bases in the country in 1999 and continued to allow use of the air base at Kulab for Mas'ud's supplies. Tajikistan, having suffered its own civil war in the post-Soviet period, was especially fearful of instability engendered by its Hizb-e Tahrir (Freedom Party), an Islamist party, and backed Rabbani continuously.

Relations between the Taliban and the United States reached a new low in August 1998 with the Tomahawk missile attacks. Launched from the Arabian Sea against Khost, where, the United States claimed, Osama bin Laden's al-Qaeda terrorist organization trained, the missile attacks yielded indefinite results. The United States demanded that bin Laden, who lived in Kandahar, either be arrested and turned over for trial or expelled from Afghanistan to a country that would arrest him. The Taliban equivocated that bin Laden was a guest, even though he had entered the country in 1996 as a guest of Hekmatyar and not the Taliban. Abdul Hakim Mujahid, the would-be Taliban representative to the United Nations, pointed out that Afghanistan has a tradition of hospitality, and that it had also refused to turn over Germans and Italians to the Allies during World War II. According to Mujahid, Afghanistan stood against terrorism as well, but would put bin Laden on trial under Islamic law if the United States revealed its evidence.[7] The United States did not provide such evidence and the Taliban declared bin Laden a free man. However, it became clear that bin Laden's activities, particularly his giving press interviews, had exhausted the Taliban's patience; they realized that his presence, even as a guest, was harming Afghanistan. Consequently, they announced that they had confiscated his satellite telephone equipment and forbidden him from receiving foreign visitors. Finally, they declared themselves ignorant of his whereabouts after he had disappeared from his Kandahar headquarters. This pattern of Taliban equivocation recurred after the hijack bombings in September. Intelligence may reveal whether the Taliban expected a retreat by the United States or whether its independence of action regarding bin Laden and the Arab Afghans was compromised.

Having alienated nearly all their neighbors, and the two world powers most concerned with them (the United States over bin Laden and Russia over support for Chechens), the Taliban were supported only by Pakistan, their original backer, and bin Laden and his loyal Arab and international Muslim troops. As the United States contemplated its military response to the attacks of September 11, the process of building a regional coalition against the Taliban was made easier by the inability of the Taliban to live agreeably with their neighbors. The support of Pakistan for the U.S. effort became crucial thanks to the massive U.S. intervention in the north that brought that area under Northern Alliance control. Rabbani, whose government was still the only one recognized by the United Nations, settled himself at the presidential palace in Kabul in mid-November. Even after the recognition of the Bonn-negotiated interim government, Rabbani remains at his location, giving further evidence of the divided ethnic and military situation.

Women and the Taliban

Until September 11, opposition to the Taliban outside of policymaking circles concerned with Afghanistan came not from their regional dealings, nor even with their general imposition of Islamic law, but from an entirely different source. That source, namely, western advocates of women's rights, grew through the efforts of RAWA, the acronym for a movement launched shortly after the fall of the communist regime, Revolutionary Afghan Women's Association. Opposition by educated urban Afghan women to how Afghan women were being marginalized in Pakistan by the largely rural and religiously trained mujahidin leadership in Peshawar had led to attempts to form Afghan women's organizations. Schools and clinics were some of the ways in which these women, with NGO help, tried to maintain the gains of women in Afghanistan that had begun during the 1920s. Throughout the period of opposition to communist rule and Soviet occupation, the single relatively successful appeal that the Afghan communists could make came in the ways they created legal equity for women on paper.

When the Najibullah regime ended in 1992, the mujahidin, in much disarray, adopted those practices with regard to the social order that had prevailed in Peshawar when they entered Kabul. Thus between 1992 and 1996, women came under many restrictions. Having seen their Marxist political position soundly defeated, many of Kabul's women activists fled to Peshawar and to the West. Thus RAWA took shape, gaining for itself adherents among secular, educated Afghan women from select academic feminist circles, and especially among feminist journalists. This feminist opposition exerted considerable pressure on the international front; part of its thrust was to prevent the recognition of the Taliban despite their demonstrated ability to bring, at the very least, security to Afghanistan. Because of the effect on popular opinion, and through it on international policy, the evolution of the women's issue needs attention, even in this limited space. Focus on the Afghan women's issue has detracted from the significant problems of stability, ethnicity, and an understanding of the whole of modern Afghan history and sociopolitical development. Further, rarely has the

Afghan women's issue received analysis within the context of the historical development of Afghan society; nor have studies been made of women in Islamic societies in general for the purpose of workable long-term policy. The Afghan situation is hardly unique given the limited rights of women in important Muslim countries such as Saudi Arabia.

During 1998, the lack of women's independence in law and in practice assumed high visibility in the public debate over recognition of the Taliban. This situation was exploited by numerous groups, well-intentioned feminists, civil libertarians, and others still smarting over the defeat of the former communist regime by the mujahidin. Particularly vocal were women who had been highly placed in the regimes of Babrak Karmal and Muhammad Najibullah and were now living as political refugees in the United States. They found ample anti-Taliban fuel with every new law passed in Kabul limiting the right of women to function in the public sector. As Afghan women's issues began to draw the attention of Hollywood celebrities, political pressure increased on the U.S. State Department to withhold even humanitarian aid until the Taliban reversed their apparently flagrant violation of women's rights.[8] Some women's groups went so far as to advocate the interruption of mine removal. OXFAM (Oxford Committee for Famine Relief), in a break from other aid organizations, refused to give aid to Afghan schools if girls were not permitted to attend. In a more practical approach, Sweden continued giving aid to Afghan education and funneled aid to girls' schools through women who ran schools in their homes. In the year 2001, the Swedish Committee estimated that it enrolled 134,000 girls in home schools throughout the country, almost matching the number of boys in official schools.

The Taliban appeared unprepared to deal with the public relations crisis that threatened to unhinge the relative stability they had achieved on the internal political and military fronts. Even Iran—as it came to regard the Taliban as unsympathetic to the interests of Persian-speaking and Shi'a populations, and as its attempts at providing aid to the resistance to the Taliban in northern Afghanistan met with disaster—condemned the Taliban regime's treatment of Afghan women. Iran maintained that the Taliban repressed women far beyond the letter or intention of Islam. Other Islamic states have applied the very same argument to Iran, which, after the revolution of 1979, was and is even now roundly condemned for its insistence on veiling, or at least *hijab*. In Iran, which has never banned women's education but rather insists on separate girls' and boys' schools, the Taliban's closing of such prestigious schools as the elite Malalai girls' school in Kabul raised alarm, as it did elsewhere. In 1995, even before the Taliban came to power, the problem of how to bring education to Afghan women became a concern among aid organizations. Less than 4 percent of Afghan women had been educated even under the best of circumstances during the twentieth century.[9] Women's education came under suspicion during the communist period because parents feared that girls would be indoctrinated by Marxist ideology. After the victory of the mujahidin, schools in the countryside remained empty as families refused to enroll their daughters, possibly for fear of lowering their value as future brides or for reasons of widely rumored attacks on young girls. After debate on this issue, rather than copying the curriculum of boys' schools, some aid organizations decided to adopt curricula that conservative Afghan families would find beneficial to their daughters. Thus home economics, arithmetic, and health and hygiene were advocated. This approach did not appease foreign observers, however, who found the pattern sexist and discriminatory. In any event, the result is that Afghan girls and women in Kabul, from which most reports originate, continue to suffer from lack of public education. Because home schools needed to be invisible during the Taliban period, casual outsider observers assumed their nonexistence. Together with restrictions on access to health care, the murky educational picture reinforced the view that the Taliban were incapable of understanding the concept of women's rights except in the context of shari'a and Pushtunwali.

The Taliban insisted that the assessment of their rule must be based on their entire record, and not on the record of the activities where they were weakest. They pointed to the security enjoyed by all Afghans, especially women, in areas administered by the Taliban. In a country racked by war for twenty years, security and stability rank high among the population. Taliban representatives explain that the isolation of women from the workplace and all public venues is intended to serve two main purposes: to prevent the molestation of women and girls by remaining unlawful and unruly elements, and to allow the stabilization of the workplace and other institutions for men whose education was also interrupted by war. Taliban representatives insisted that the application of the shari'a in an equitable manner to women and girls would follow as the country gained the ability to rebuild infrastructure and administrative and legal structures.[10]

Building a New Afghanistan

In Bonn, from November 27 to December 5, 2001, while the war raged against the Taliban in Kandahar and the search for bin Laden and al-Qaeda continued in Ningrahar, representatives from four Afghan groups were invited to discuss the political future of the country. Two groups received an equal number of votes: the Northern Alliance and King Zahir Shah's representatives. The first represents non-Pushtun ethnic groups, especially the Tajiks, who began opposition to the standing government in Kabul as part of the push to reform the monarchy, then the republic, along Islamist lines. The second represents the ancien regime and a group of Afghan intellectuals and technocrats, many, like the king, in Western exile. The competing goals and interests of these groups are apparent. To this mix were added two other groups, mainly from among regional exiles who had been engaged in the war against the Soviet Red Army and its Afghan clients. Like the Northern Alliance, these also originate from a socioeconomic base alien to that of the king and come from exiles in Peshawar and in Cyprus, the latter being Iranian-based and backed. Each of these last two groups were represented at Bonn by three delegates only. Concurring with the specific objections of President Rabbani, whose troops had marched into Kabul despite international calls against it, no representation from the Taliban, moderate or extremist, was permitted at the Bonn gathering.

In the formula achieved, after much prodding by the West, the interim administration included a group of thirty persons, twenty-three of whom would hold posts as cabinet ministers; five as deputy prime ministers; and one prime minister, or, in the language of the agreement, "administration chairman." To the latter post, it was agreed to name a leading Pushtun of the Popalzai Pushtun tribe, Hamid Karzai. Based in the United States and in Quetta, Pakistan, the Karzai family stood in opposition to the Taliban while enjoying good relations with members of the ancien regime in exile.

The bulk of the seats in the government, including the ministries of defense, foreign, and interior, went to those holding power on the ground: the Northern Alliance, which had refused initially to field any names. This act threatened to end the efforts to form a government that would replace the Northern Alliance and also be acceptable to Pushtuns. When it appeared that the international meeting would close in discord, threats to withhold reconstruction brought the representatives back to the negotiating table. The added threat that Afghanistan might cease to continue as a single viable state also hung in the air. The first threat, resembling the American economic sanctions enforced in 1998 as a result of the issue of Afghan women held before the American public, may never work again given the nightly and graphic scenes of devastation and starvation broadcast worldwide.

The plan, if political plans hatched for such a devastated and discordant state can work, calls for an interim authority to hold power for six months (December 22 to June 22, 2002), followed by the convening of a Loya Jirgah to include Zahir Shah. This grand assembly, a Pushtun tradition, would decide on another interim authority for eighteen-months, at which time elections will be held for a government. In the meantime, a constitution is to be prepared. Perhaps most significant for the short-term welfare of the Afghans is agreement on an international security force while a multiparty (i.e., multiethnic) Afghan force is being readied. The time frame, the multiethnic proportions, and UN participation all recall the 1998 agreements hammered out in Peshawar that tried to create an interim replacement government for Kabul once the Soviet troops withdrew. The corollary commitments by the international community of donors, and especially the agreement to field an international security force, are the two components of this new agreement that may produce stability this time.

In the meantime, the fighting on the ground subsided in December 2001 with ever larger U.S. military participation. At the same time, the hardcore non-Afghan Muslim fanatics, including Osama bin Laden, melt away to do battle in another setting, possibly increasing the intensity of violence in Israel. The prospects of the U.S. military's being dragged into the World Court over violation of the Geneva Convention on Prisoners of War looms in the background. The violation stems from U.S. knowledge of the killing of bound prisoners taken from Kunduz to General Dustam's fortress at Qalai Jangi, where the first U.S. casualty, a CIA operative, also occurred and where the twenty-year-old American sympathizer of al-Qaeda was captured. The dispute over the status of prisoners transported by the United States to Guantanamo Bay in Cuba may also bring international legal attention to bear on the U.S. role. The value of the intelligence gathered, as well as the likelihood that these men would receive far worse treatment by Afghan enemies, may mitigate the general European outrage over this matter.

Despite the installation of the interim government and a rotating international security force in Kabul, the reconstruction of Afghanistan presents a formidable problem. And despite the $4.5 billion pledged by donors at a Tokyo meeting in January 2002, the question of equitable and informed expenditure haunts donors, especially in light of twenty years of waste and conflict. Still to be settled is the legitimacy of the interim government, not in the eyes of the United Nations or Western nations, but for the Afghans. After the threat of armed struggle subsides with the surrender of weapons, the very existence of the state of Afghanistan may come into question without early assurances that ethnic minorities will continue to be included in government. Given the many known scores that Afghan custom insists must be settled violently, will there ever be a surrender of weapons, particularly among the traditionally armed Pushtun tribes?

Indications of a desire to return to the pre-1973 mode of governance reflects an ardent wish to assume the years since then an episode to be forgotten. On its way toward democratic habits during the late 1960s, the Afghanistan of that era appears a model to which the interim government might aspire. Yet, the Afghan population has doubled since then, educational levels have plummeted, and the infrastructure has all but vanished. Above all else, ethnic relations have altered drastically. On the regional level, the co-ethnics of Afghanistan's northern people are no longer under the easy sway of Moscow but form independent states. A future Afghan state that does not make allowance for a high level of autonomy for these minorities, possibly by guaranteeing their right of secession, runs the danger of being regarded as restoring Pushtun colonial rule. The overwhelming dependence of international policymakers, especially in the United States, on a coterie of like-minded Pushtun elites, no matter how attractive and pliant, raises issues within the region that will prevent the regional peace, security, and economic advancement that all need. That Pushtuns are now, and have been, divided between Afghanistan and Pakistan could also mean the revival of the Pushtunistan issue if Afghanistan and Pakistan do not settle the problems of access posed by the landlocked position of Afghanistan. The future, like the near past, is bleak for Afghans.

Appendix A

Bibliographic Essay

The field of Afghan studies has attracted some excellent scholars over the years who have devoted entire lifetimes to understanding aspects of the culture, history, and politics of Afghanistan. Among the scholars are both Afghans and Westerners as well as some fine Russian anthropologists, archaeologists, and linguists. Japanese scholars too have contributed, in particular to the fields of art history, anthropology, and religious studies. Not to be forgotten are the many nineteenth-century travelers, diplomats, and spies who penned their observations of Afghans and Central Asians. Of the several dedicated bibliographies that have appeared, a recent one is by Louis Dupree, *Afghan Studies* (American University Field Staff Report, Asia Series, vol. 20, 1976). Increasingly important to the future of Afghan studies is the privately established Afghan Documentation Center (Liestal, Switzerland). In addition there is the Omaha Afghanistan collection at the University of Nebraska, which has concentrated on books and serials, having begun with the bequest of Arthur Paul, an economist who had a fine collection of indigenous- and Western-language titles.

Since the communist coup of 1978, the field of Afghan studies has changed dramatically. Access for field work became impossible for archaeologists, and until very recently to anthropologists as well, the two most prolific fields of academic study. The hiatus provided some with the opportunity to engage in analysis of collected materials, and the resulting monographs and articles, especially from David Busby Edwards, Audrey C. Shalinsky, and Margaret Mills, have added depth to the understanding of Afghan identity, community, and oral transmission. Continuation of their work has often meant working in Pakistan among Afghan refugees.

Other anthropologists, who had spent the 1960s or 1970s researching in Afghan provinces, applied their field experience to issues more closely related to political analysis and understanding. Among these are Robert Canfield, Pierre and Micheline Centlivres, Jon Anderson, and Richard and Nancy Tapper. Added to these are natives of Afghanistan, whose Western education and indigenous knowledge combine to provide fresh insights into the myriad relationships among ethnic groups. Though sometimes caught in interethnic politics, Afghan anthropologists such as Nazif Shahrani and Ashraf Ghani have written fine analyses of particular parts of Afghanistan. The work of anthropologists is indispensable for any study of Afghanistan because they have often filled the void in both historical studies and cultural studies.

Among early and still very reliable histories of Afghanistan is Vartan Gregorian's *The Emergence of Modern Afghanistan* (Stanford: Stanford University Press, 1969), which evidences the author's early use of original materials in many languages. More specifically oriented writings by the premier Afghan historian, Hasan Kakar, have proven invaluable to many researchers, both as reliable confirmation and as critique of analyses found in other sources. Aside from Kakar's articles, his study of Amir Abdul Rahman, *Government and Society in Afghanistan: The Reign of Amir Abd al-Rahman Khan* (Austin: University of Texas Press, 1979) as well as his *Afghanistan: The Soviet Invasion and the Afghan Response, 1979–1982* (Berkeley: University of California Press, 1995) prove him to be a master of Afghan detail.

The writings of Louis Dupree, spanning four decades, stand alone in the field of Afghan studies. They are distinguished by their diversity, especially the American University Field Service (AUFS) Reports, which include in their subjects archaeological and cultural anthropology as well as contemporaneous political analysis. His trilogy *Red Flag over the Hindu Kush* was among the first warnings of the changes that culminated in what he called the "rubblization" of Afghanistan and the genocide committed in many parts of the country. Dupree's *Afghanistan* (Princeton: Princeton University Press), first published in 1973, has become the first source of reference on historical and ethnic subjects. Dupree died on Nowruz in 1989 as Soviet troops pulled out of Afghanistan. Nancy Hatch Dupree continues Louis's work in activist ways and by providing some of the few firsthand reports of events since 1992. Even under United Nations auspices, such visits require the kind of courage that has been associated with the husband-and-wife team.

Outside the humanities, some disciples that have received little attention in fact contain works that are exceptionally well written and helpful. Among these is the legal monograph by Mohammad Hashim Kamali, *Law in Afghanistan: A Study of the Constitution, Matrimonial Law, and the Judiciary* (Leiden: E. J. Brill, 1985) which is an updated version (to include the 1977 Da'ud Constitution and laws) of his 1976 dissertation. In the field of economics, the continued writings of M. Siddieq Noorzoy and Maxwell Fry stand alone as guideposts to the past and future possibilities of Afghan economics.

Another body of monographs and collections, which falls into the category of reference works, is dominated by the contributions of Ludwig Adamec: *Historical and Political Who's Who of Afghanistan* (Graz: ADEVA, 1975), *Biographical Dictionary of Modern Afghanistan* (Graz: ADEVA, 1987), and *Historical Dictionary of Afghanistan* (Metuchen, N.J.: Scarecrow Press, 1991). Prof. Adamec's Gazetteers are yet another reference resource, though they were not consulted for this study.

The war years sparked the imagination of many who saw in Afghanistan a field for ideological encounter. Political scientists, journalists, and plain adventurers flocked to the field. Suddenly the problem was not that there were few studies of Afghanistan but rather how to decide which monographs could be relied upon to present the more objective picture. Among those openly sympathetic to the communist regimes, some works are noteworthy simply because the authors' personal experiences and points of view are compelling. Among these is Raja Anwar's *The Tragedy of Afghanistan: A First Hand Account* (London: Verso, 1988) and Beverley Male's *Revolutionary Afghanistan* (New York: St. Martin's Press, 1982). On the opposite side of the equation are the three monographs of Anthony Arnold: *Afghanistan: The Soviet Invasion in Perspective* (Stanford: Hoover Institution Press, 1985), *Afghanistan's Two-Party Communism: Parcham and Khalq* (Stanford: Hoover Institution Press, 1983), and *The Fateful Pebble: Afghanistan's Role in the Fall of the Soviet Empire* (Novato, Calif.: Presidio Press, 1994).

In dealing with a country like Afghanistan, which in the modern era has attracted attention in periods of turmoil rather than for its economic or cultural contributions to the region, maintaining a body of contemporaneous knowledge has become a problem. Particularly with the decline of the old Soviet system of the Oriental Institute and affiliates, which functioned independently of teaching institutions and political demands for information, the state of Afghan studies could well fade if it does not undergo transfer into the larger field of Central Asian studies. For this reason, it is encouraging to see neighboring Iranians, both in Tehran and among the expatriate community, devoting some scholarly attention to developing knowledge about its long-ignored eastern neighbors. The real gap in Afghan studies lies in knowledge about Pushtun culture, a gap formerly filled in part by Soviet scholars and to some extent by Pakistani scholars.

In the United States, only the *Afghanistan Forum* (published under the sponsorship of the Asia Society until 1982), edited since 1972 by Mary Ann Siegfried, has maintained an unbroken record of publication about Afghan events. For many in the field internationally, the *Afghanistan Forum* provides the only source of news, reviews, selected documents, and a running chronology based on published sources that has become indispensable.

A very useful but temporary source of information has come from the resistance itself. Although almost all of the parties issued a publication, however modest, usually in Persian or Pushtu or both, two Afghan organizations, both led by respected scholars, attempted to disseminate contemporaneous news without regard to factions. The Afghan Information Centre published a monthly bulletin beginning in 1981 from Peshawar, founded by Sayyid Bahauddin Majruh (assassinated 1986), and *Afghan Jehad* beginning in 1987, edited by Sahabuddin Kushkaki. Both publications are in English.

Inside Afghanistan during the years of resistance, few institutions found the means or personnel to continue publication of serials or books. Noteworthy among these is the journal *Pashto,* the quarterly journal of the former Pushto Academy, transformed under Soviet tutelage into the Republic of Afghanistan Academy of Sciences. Devoted chiefly to premodern history and folklore, Afghan-authored articles appeared in English, Russian, and German under the communist regime.

After the fall of the Soviet Union in 1991, no work about Afghanistan can be written that ignores the region as a whole, especially what was tzarist, then Soviet Central Asia, and what continues to be Xinjiang in the People's Republic of China. One recent work in which the greater region has been examined (alas without Pakistan) is the multiauthored (Cyril Black, Louis Dupree, Elizabeth Endicott-West, Daniel Matuszewski, Eden Naby, and Arthur Waldron) *Modernization of Inner Asia* (Armonk, N.Y.: M. E. Sharpe, 1991). This work not only provides a starting bibliography and chronology for the region, but it also allows the reader to understand the interrelationships during the premodern period in particular, especially in terms of imperialistic movements, indigenous reformers, and the suppression of the people of the region by authoritarian rule. Likewise, information about basic conditions in Central Asia is indispensable for the study of Afghanistan as it enters the new millennium. Some of the most important works on Central Asia appear in English translation (from French), and include Alexandre Bennigsen's (with Chantal Quelquejay-Lemercier) *Islam in the Soviet Union* (London: Pall Mall Press, 1967), and Hélène Carrère D'Encausse's *Islam and the Russian Empire: Reform and Revolution in Central Asia* (Berkeley: University of California Press, 1988). In addition to these books about how Muslim society confronted change under foreign rule, a small book by Fazal-ur-Rahim Khan Marwat, *The Basmachi Movement in Soviet Central Asia: A Study in Political Development* (Peshawar: Emjay Books International, 1969), raises many intriguing questions about the past relationship of Afghans with the fighters once widely labeled as bandits both in Central Asia and outside.

The Afghan situation created a forum for the clash of major ideologies. The volume of foreign voices and Afghan rivals sometimes drowned out the actual events. For this reason, several of the more recent publications have devoted space to chronologies. The chronology appended to this book benefited from all of the bibliographic sources listed here, together with the chronologies discussed in the essay preceding our chronology. The reader may turn to that section for the final bibliographic discussion.

Books with Afghanistan in their titles, or Osama bin Laden and the Taliban, appeared to spring magically onto the fronts of bookstores within weeks of the audacious and cruel attack on U.S. sites on September 11, 2001. Many of these books were quick studies by adventurous journalists and travelers harboring attitudes as cavalier toward the Afghans as those of any British spy in the nineteenth century. Some of the books, however, enjoyed a longer gestation and contribute to an understanding of the Taliban in particular. Among these works is Ahmed Rashid's *Taliban: Militant Islam, Oil and Fundamentalism in Central Asia* (New Haven: Yale university Press, 2000). Also appearing at this time is Larry P. Goodson's Ph.D. thesis, *Afghanistan's Endless War: State Failure, Regional Politics and the Rise of the Taliban.*

During the hiatus in field-research-driven studies of Afghanistan have appeared two very important studies of an earlier period of Afghan turmoil, regression from progress, chaos, and restoration of relative security. That was from World War I to 1933, a period that roughly covers the rule of King Amanullah. Senzil K. Nawid's *Religious Response to Social Change in Afghanistan 1919–1929* (Mazda, 1999) presents that period in Afghan history when the country was engaged with Central Asia and the forces shaping the Soviet Union. Also Robert D. McChesney's *Kabul Under Siege: Fayz Muhammad's Account of the 1929 Uprising* (Markus Wiener, 1999), makes available for the first time the translation of an account in Persian by a participant in the Tajik/Pushtun events of 1929 that the current situation seems to mimic. These two works by respected scholars in the Central Asian field are complimented by the new availability of a journalistic work that is a tour de force on that same period: Rhea Talley Steward's *Fire in Afghanistan 1914–1929,* first published in 1973. Those who want to see the enduring power of Afghan tribal and ethnic intransigence in combination with the power struggle between biblical mores and modernity would do well to acquaint themselves with these three studies.

Appendix B

Modern Period Rulers of Afghanistan

Muhammadzai Dynasty (Durrani Pushtun)

1880–1901   Abdul Rahman Khan, b. 1844. Seized power in Kabul following British withdrawal at end of second Anglo-Afghan war (1878–1880). Defeated rival claimants and centralized political power within modern borders established by British and Russians. Died in Kabul of natural causes.

1901–1919   Habibullah Khan, b. 1871. Son of Abdul Rahman, born when Rahman was in exile in Samarkand. Allowed elites exiled by father to return. Established first Western-style school and military academy. Maintained neutrality during World War I. Assassinated February 20, 1919.

1919–1929   Amanullah Khan (Padishah, or king, from 1926), b. 1892. Seized power in Kabul after assassination of his father and consolidated rule by initiating third Anglo-Afghan war, which ended special relationship with Britain. First constitution, 1923. Established regular diplomatic relations, implemented policies of rapid modernization and neglect of army; led to popular uprisings in 1928. Defeat, abdication, and exile in 1929. Died in Italy, 1960.

   January 1929   Inayatullah Khan, b. 1888. Elder brother of Amanullah. Had not fought for throne in 1919, initially recognizing rule of his uncle, Nasrullah, and then that of Amanullah. Brother abdicated in his favor, but he abdicated too and left for exile in a few days. Died in exile, 1946.

Tajik Interregnum

1929   Habibullah II Ghazi (Bacha-i Saqao), b. ca. 1890. Former soldier, deserted and became a brigand in Tajik region north of Kabul. Seized capital in uprising against Amanullah's rule and briefly ruled much of country. Defeated and executed (1929) by Pushtun army led by Nadir Khan, a Muhammadzai prince, general, and former minister of war, back from exile in France.

Restored Muhammadzai (Musahiban Branch)

1929–1933   Nadir Shah, b. 1883. Together with four of his brothers, known as the Musahiban family from title granted by Habibullah, he was elected Padishah by Pushtun tribal jirgah following fall of Kabul. Was a modernizer and a successful general in the third Anglo-Afghan war, but disputes with King Amanullah led to his diplomatic exile in France, where he remained after resignation in 1926. Established new constitution in 1931. Assassinated by political opponent in blood feud.

1933–1973   Zahir Shah, b. 1914. Proclaimed king by his uncle, the minister of war, following father's assassination. Reigned but did not rule for thirty years under strong prime ministers from his family. Assumed political leadership in 1963 by dismissing his cousin, prime minister Da'ud, and attempted liberalization of "new democracy" in constitution of 1964. Lack of strong leadership contributed to coup of July 1973 that ended monarchy. Abdicated August 1973 and continues to live in exile in Italy.

Musahiban Prime Ministers

1933–1946   Hashim Khan, b. 1886. Brother and prime minister of Nadir Shah from 1929. Maintained firm autocratic regime and continued cautious modernization. Maintained Afghan neutrality in World War II. Resigned for health reasons in 1946 and died in 1953.

1946–1953   Mahmud Khan Ghazi, b. 1886. As minister of war he had proclaimed his nephew king in 1933. Continued as minister of war until resignation of Hashim Khan. Attempted liberalization, but resulting criticism of royal family led to his forced resignation in 1953. Died 1959.

1953–1963   Da'ud Khan, b. 1909. Dynamic strongman rule, favored rapid modernization, foreign aid development, and economic plans. Many foreign aid programs and military aid from the USSR tilted policy toward Eastern bloc, but maintained traditional policy of *bi-tarafi* (without sides). A founder of Non-Aligned Movement. Hostile confrontation with Pakistan over border Pushtun and Baluchi regions led to border closings and economic disaster. Dismissed by Zahir Shah.

Prime Ministers of the Liberal Constitutional Period

1963–1965   Dr. Muhammad Yusuf, b. 1917. A Tajik and first nonroyal prime minister in Afghan history. Chosen by king to head the constitutional drafting process (1963–1964) and secured its passage in the Loya Jirgah. Supervised elections to first parliament under the constitution of 1964 and was confirmed as prime minister despite organized riots by People's Democratic Party of Afghanistan (PDPA) at session. Resigned within days. Living in exile in Germany.

1965–1967   Muhammad Hashim Maiwandwal, b. 1919. Minister of Information in Dr. Yusuf's cabinet and ambassador to United States. A journalist and founder of newspaper *Musawat* (Equality) and attempted to form political party of same name. Arrested after coup of 1973 and killed in prison by communists without consent of Da'ud.

1967–1971   Nur Ahmad Etemadi, b. 1921. Member of the extended royal family and diplomat, former foreign minister. Arrested after 1978 coup and either killed in prison or one of the Afghan persons shipped to Soviet Union.

1971–1972   Dr. Abdul Zahir, b. 1909. Physician to royal family. Former president of the Wolesi Jirgah and minister of health. Later served as ambassador. Died in 1982.

1972–1983   Muhammad Musa Shafiq, b. 1930. Religious scholar educated at al-Azhar and Columbia University. Principal drafter of the 1964 constitution. Arrested by Da'ud in 1973 but later released and served as adviser. Imprisoned after 1978 coup and killed.

First Republic (Republic of Afghanistan)

1973–1978   Sardar Muhammad Da'ud Khan, First cousin of Zahir Shah and former prime minister. Gradually removed communist allies in coup from office, reduced tensions with Pakistan, and secured Arab and Iranian economic aid. Killed in attack on Arg Palace in Kabul, April 28, 1978.

Second Republic (Democratic Republic of Afghanistan, 1979–1987, Republic of Afghanistan, 1987–1992)

1978–1979   Nur Muhammad Taraki, b. 1917. Ghilzai Pushtun, journalist, former minor government official and translator for U.S. embassy. Founder and first general secretary of PDPA (Khalq wing). Publisher of party newspaper *Khalq* (Masses) in 1966. Deposed in party coup and murdered in prison.

1979   Hafizullah Amin   b. 1929. Ghilzai Pushtun, educated at Columbia University, education ministry official. A founding member of PDPA and leader of Khalq wing. Headed party's military liaison after 1977 and named deputy prime minister and foreign minister after coup, prime minister in 1979. Deposed Taraki in September and killed by Soviets in invasion in December.

1979–1986   Babrak Karmal, b. 1929. Durrani Pushtun son of general and provincial governor. A leader of radical students at Kabul University. A founding member of PDPA and elected to Wolesi Jirgah in 1965. Leader of Parcham (Banner) faction of Khalq, and first deputy to Taraki after reunion of party in 1977. Sent to diplomatic exile in 1978 to Prague, returned with Soviet army invasion. National and international opprobrium as well as desire to attempt reconciliation policy led to loss of confidence by Soviets and his removal from power in May 1986. Fled country as mujahidin succeeded. Died in Moscow, 1996.

1986–1992   Dr. Muhammad Najibullah, b. 1947. Ahmadzai Pushtun with medical degree, member of Parcham wing of PDPA. Sent to diplomatic exile in 1978 by Khalqis but returned after Soviet invasion as head of new security service (KhAD), in which he was considered cruel and efficient. Selected by Soviets to form broad coalition with opposition, but unable to do so. Lost power after Soviet troop withdrawal, collapse of Soviet Union, withdrawal of aid, and betrayal by northern ethnic militias and military. Resigned but barred from leaving country. Lived in UN sanctuary until hanged by Taliban in 1996.

Islamic Republic of Afghanistan

1992   Sebghatullah Mujaddidi, b. 1925. Religious scholar from a leading Pushtun Sufi family. Twice imprisoned for antigovernment activities protesting communist influence. Founded resistance organization Jabha-i Najat-i Milli Afghanistan (National Liberation Front of Afghanistan). Headed alliance of resistance leaders in 1992 and thus named first president of the Islamic state after Peshawar accords. Resigned after term expired.

1992–1995   Burhanuddin Rabbani, b. 1940. Tajik from Badakhshan. Religious scholar in Shari'at Faculty of Kabul University, a leader of Islamists opposed to communist influence. Elected leader of Jami'at-i Islami-i (1971), fled to Pakistan (1974) to escape arrest. Headed Jami'at-i Islami during jihad and elected as result of Peshawar accords to be second president by leadership council. Extended his term with concurrence of Shura boycotted by many leaders. Major civil war since 1994 has greatly limited his territorial control. Government not recognized by United States. Ousted from Kabul by Taliban, September 1996.

1996–2001   Taliban rule most of Afghanistan after moving north toward Kabul in 1996 from Kandahar. With token sprinkling of Tajiks, Taliban come from the ranks of Pushtuns, mainly western Pushtuns. Spiritual and temporal power behind Taliban government in Kabul is Mullah Muhammad Omar (b. ca.1960), wounded in war against Soviet invasion, and a pupil at *madrasa*. Marriage ties with Osama bin Laden. Flees Kandahar in negotiated surrender of the city to Pushtun tribesmen in November 2001. Whereabouts unknown.

2001–   Hamid Karzai, Popolzai Pushtun (b. 1957), and selected interim leader of Afghanistan in Bonn, Germany, by a four-bloc agreement to lead the country beginning on 22 December. Brings with him to Kabul a cabinet heavily weighed with other Afghan expatriates who spent much of the period since 1979 in the United States or abroad.

Appendix C

Chronology of Afghan and Regional Events, 1747–2001

Events since the formation of Afghanistan some two centuries ago illustrate the close interplay between the Afghan state and its neighbors. The rise of European powers in the region, the engulfment of much of Central Asia within the Soviet sphere, the withdrawal of the British and their partial replacement by the Americans, the Cold War rivalries that opened the nonalignment option, the dissolution of the Soviet Union, and the steps being taken by Moscow to maintain economic and political control in the "near-abroad" are all milestones in the development of Afghan events within the region. Analysis of the region during the course of the coming decade can be aided by attention to a past that illustrates an intimate convergence and contrast of interests not clearly visible from the internal analysis of any one country. The chronology in the following pages is intended to help the reader tie together events that might otherwise appear isolated.

The chronology becomes more detailed at certain key periods in the most recent decades such as the 1920s, the mid-1960s and the period following the end of the monarchy in 1973. Particularly emphasized are events in Central Asia, Pakistan, and Iran, which in hindsight offer an enhanced appreciation of the present and probably also the future of the region. At the same time, attention focuses on internal sociocultural matters that point to common trends in the region, such as the rise of Jadidism (Islamic reform movement), anti-imperialism, and socioeconomic modernization that Central Asia and Afghanistan shared more intimately with each other than with Iran, Turkey, and the subcontinent.

In reviewing the sequence of events as shown here, the reader may be struck, as we were, by the enormousness of the consequences arising from the division of Pushtuns across international lines for roughly two centuries. As hopes for recovery of all Pushtuns into one nation ebbed, Kabul rulers turned their attention to expansion into non-Pushtun areas of Afghanistan, specifically to the north. The consequences of the Pushtun incursions into Tajik and Turkic Central Asia are still reverberating in the possibly new configurations that may emerge after sixteen years of war. At the same time, however, the festering Pushtunistan issue since the formation of Pakistan contributed much to Soviet-Afghan entanglements. Readers may find it fairly easy to trace these issues through the chronology, as they may with the surprisingly intimate relationships that emerge and submerge between coethnics (such as Tajiks, Uzbeks, Turkmens and, Kyrgyz) or co-religionists (specifically the Isma'ilis) across the Afghan border to the north. In the chronology we have also tried to highlight the steps that the communist leadership took between 1917 and 1929 to consolidate and stabilize Central Asia, and the tentative replay of similar attitudes and steps being taken since 1991 when the Soviet Union dissolved.

Sources for this chronology are diverse, but we have consulted specifically the periodic chronologies appearing in the *Afghanistan Forum* (based on contemporary news reports), the *Middle East Journal, Afghan Jehad,* Louis Dupree's *Afghanistan,* G. Grassmuck et al., *Afghanistan: Some New Approaches,* and Ludwig Adamec's *Historical Dictionary of Afghanistan* (which relies heavily on events reported in the *Kabul [New] Times*). We have relied in particular on the chronology in Cyril Black et al., *The Modernization of Inner Asia,* which contains separate chronologies for each part of the region from Mongolia to Iran and was prepared by Eden Naby.

1747	Ahmad Shah Abdali (Durrani), a Pushtun chief, seizes local power following the assassination of Nadir Shah Afshar, the Iranian king.
	Durrani rule extended to Peshawar.
	Astrakhanid (Janid) dynasty in Bukhara forced to accept Amu Darya as southern boundary.
	Khiva asserts independence after death of Nadir Shah Afshar.
1748	Afghan empire extends to Punjab, Baluchistan, Sind, and hence to the Arabian Sea.
1750	Lands north of the Hindu Kush mountains conquered by Durrani force.
1752	Kashmir conquered by Afghans.
1761	In Battle of Panipat, Afghans defeat Hindu Mahrattas and restore Muslim Moghul emperor to throne of Delhi.
1772	Timur Shah moves capital from Kandahar (western Pushtun area) to Kabul, allowing for easier access to extended empire north and east and getting away from his Durrani sardars.
1780	Treaty with Bukharan amirate recognizing Afghan rule south of the Amu Darya.
1785	Manghit (Uzbek) dynasty rises in Bukhara and lasts until 1920.
	First Russian attempt to attack Khiva fails.
1793	Northern area invaded from Bukhara. Quasi-independent khanates formed.
	Afghans lose tribute areas in the Indus River basin.
1797	Qajar dynasty begins in Iran and lasts until 1925.
1799	Persian army, using Afghan tribal dissatisfaction, invades Herat.
	Dynastic conflict among the ruling Sadozai Durranis.
1800	Sikh Ranjit Singh rules as Maharaja of Punjab.
1803	British defeat Mahrattas and occupy Delhi, establishing a protectorate over the Moghul emperor.
1805	Struggles over Kashmir begin between Afghans and Sikhs.
1809	Shah Shuja (Sadozai) receives first European ambassador, Hon. Mountstuart Elphinstone, and signs Anglo-Afghan treaty. Shuja defeated by brothers, and treaty becomes a dead letter.
	Bukhara and Kokand locked in territorial wars.

1817	Balkh taken by Bukhara.
1819–	Afghanistan divided into fiefdoms among competing Durrani families
1826	in Kabul, Kandahar, and Peshawar.
1819	Afghans lose Kashmir to Sikhs.
1823	Baluchistan and large parts of later Northwest Frontier Province lost to Afghan rulers.
1826	Dost Muhammad Khan establishes Muhammadzai dynasty in Kabul and begins to unite the country.
1831	Sayyid Ahmad Barelvi, Indian Pathan Naqshbandiyya mujahid, is killed in bid to oust Sikhs in northern India despite much support among Pushtun tribesmen.
1834	Sikhs annex Peshawar.
1839–	First Anglo-Afghan war results in British puppet, Shah Shuja, on
1842	Afghan throne. Dost Muhammad flees to Balkh, then Bukhara, but later surrenders to British.
1839	British begin annexing Sikh territory conquered from Afghans.
1842	Agha Khan, head of Khoja Isma'ilis, flees Mahalat province base in Iran and begins cooperation with British in Kandahar. There he receives tribute delegations from followers in Kabul, Sind, Badakhshan, and the Bukharan amirate.
	Dost Muhammad returns to throne in 1842.
1849	Afghans regain control of north Afghanistan.
1855	Anglo-Afghan agreement to prevent Persian and Russian territorial incursions leads to Treaty of Peshawar.
1856	Iran besieges and captures Herat. British invade Iran through Persian Gulf. Iran withdraws from Herat.
1857	War for Indian Independence (Indian Mutiny) against British rule, in which Afghanistan remains neutral.
	Treaty of Paris, through which Iran recognizes Afghan independence.
1859	British annex Baluchistan.
1865	Tashkent falls to tzarist army.
1868	Abdul Rahman, loser in interfamily rivalry, flees to Tashkent.
	Russians invade and conquer Bukhara.
	Sayyid Jamal-ad-Din ("al-Afghani") visits Afghan court as adviser.
1869–	The amir of Bukhara attacks and conquers Kulab and Hissar, and at-
1870	tempts same in Karategin. The Turkestan governor-generalship intervenes in the ensuing Kokand/Bukhara conflict as well as in Afghan/Bukharan border issues.
1872	Anglo-Russian agreement on Afghan independence.
	British commission begins work on Afghan border with Iran in Sistan, which, however, is not settled for another century.
1873	Khiva submits as Russian protectorate.
1876	Kokand annexed by Russia.
1878–	British invade Afghanistan fearing Russian dominance in Kabul: Sec-
1880	ond Anglo-Afghan war.
1879	Treaty of Gandamak gives British control of Khyber Pass.

1880	Abdul Rahman Khan (r. 1880–1901) returns from exile in tzarist Tashkent to assume Afghan throne under British protection.
1881	Turkmens subjugated by tzarist armies and governed as Khivan protectorate. Massacre of Turkmen at Gok Tepe.
1884	Northern Afghanistan, including Maimana, finally conquered by Kabul.
1885	Russia invades Panjdeh, defeats Afghan army, and annexes it to Russian Central Asia.
1868–1930s	Central Asians flee to Afghanistan to avoid rule by "infidel" Russians, then atheistic Marxism.
1887	Anglo-Russian accord on Afghan-Bukharan frontier
1888	Revolt of Ishaq Khan, who declares himself amir with support of Uzbek and Turkmen minorities. He is exiled to the Bukharan khanate, and northern Afghanistan is administratively integrated into the Kabul network for the next century.
	Ghilzai and other Pushtuns sent north to colonize previously non-Pushtun areas.
1892	Russian customs frontiers extend to the Afghan-Bukharan border and tzarist officials administer trade with Afghanistan directly under severely restrictive policies.
1893	Durand Line fixed under British pressure as Afghan-British Indian boundary, though it divides ethnic Pushtuns in two.
1895	The Wakhan annexed by Afghanistan at British insistence to separate British and Russian empires.
1896	Shugnan, Roshan, and northern Wakhan occupied by Russian troops, who drive out Afghan troops. Most of area is incorporated into the Bukharan Beglik administrative subdivision of Shugnan-Roshan.
	Abdul Rahman pacifies Kafiristan (land of unbelievers), renames it Nuristan (land of light) after conversion to Islam.
1897	The last of the tribal Naqshbandiyya uprisings against the British are suppressed (Battle of Amballa).
1898	Eastern Pamirs are directly occupied by Russian forces with main base at Khorog.
	Andijan rebellion in the Ferghana valley led by revered rural Sufi leader aimed against Russian colonists. Leader tried and hanged by Russian military court.
	Russian railroad, following closely upon tzarist military conquest, reaches Afghan frontier north of Herat.
1903	Mahmud Beg Tarzi returns to Afghanistan from exile in Ottoman Syria to head revitalization of intellectual and public life.
1904	Habibiya College, first Western-style preparatory school (new method—Jadidist), opened in Kabul under royal patronage, with a number of Indian Muslim teachers.
	Military Academy founded, Turkish colonel appointed head in 1907.
1905	Constitutional Revolution in Iran begins.
1906	*Taraqqi* (Progress), one of first in series of Russian Central Asian newspapers seeking political reform and equality for Muslims.

1907   The Anglo-Russian Convention of St. Petersburg declares Afghanistan a buffer state within the British sphere of influence. Afghanistan, not consulted, refuses to ratify treaty.

1908   Jadid schools authorized in Bukhara, though first begun in Russian-controlled Samarkand.

Iranian Constitutional Revolution suppressed by shah with secret support from Russia and aid of the Cossack Brigade, from which later rises Reza Khan (Pahlavi).

1909   Russia invades northern Iran on side of Qajar Shah in civil war with constitutionalists.

Amir Habibullah suppresses constitutionalists in Afghanistan with arrests and executions.

1911   Tarzi begins publication of *Siraj ul-Akhbar-i Afghanistan* (to 1919), the first major Afghan newspaper and one with influence among Central Asian reformers.

1912   *Bukhara-ye Sharif* (in Persian), first khanate newspaper, appears but is suppressed within two years.

1914   World War I breaks out but Afghans remain neutral.

In regressive push, Bukharan amir closes all Jadid schools and drives reformists into exile.

1915   German-Ottoman mission brings Muslim Indians to Kabul to coordinate anti-tzarist, anti-British uprising of Central Asian Muslims.

1916   Revolt in Central Asia against conscription for Russian war front. Famine and anticolonial sentiments fuel uprising. Leaders are summarily hanged.

1917   Russian revolutions, democratic socialist (February), and communist (October).

Kokand declares independence.

1918   Russia signs peace treaty of Brest-Litovsk with Germany, thus allowing Bolsheviks to focus on antirevolutionary forces.

1919   Amir Habibullah assassinated. Modernist son Amanullah seizes throne.

Afghans fight third and last war with British and gain complete independence. Moscow is first to recognize Afghan independence.

Afghan activity increases in Central Asia, especially around Merv, Kushk, and Panjdeh, with diplomatic missions to Ferghana in hopes of creating a Muslim confederation.

An Afghan military contingent fights to save the Bukharan khanate from the Red Army.

Mustafa Kemal Pasha (Kemal Atatürk) organizes Turkish resistance to Treaty of Sèvres, forced on Ottomans at close of World War I.

1920   Soviet troops attempt to set up the Soviet Republic of Gilan in northern Iran.

Indian Muslim opposition to British plans to end the caliphate result in the Khilafat movement, which leads to the *hijrat* (flight) to Afghanistan.

1920–   Central Asian resistance to the Red Army uses northern Afghanistan as
1929   a base and refuge. Thousands of Central Asians, among them the

last Bukharan amir, flee to Afghanistan to escape religious persecution and wealth confiscation.

1921–
1922

Enver Pasha, pan-Turkic nationalist and former Young Turk war minister, joins Basmachi resistance.

1921

King Amanullah signs Soviet-Afghan treaty of friendship but insists on the independence of the Bukharan People's Consular Republic and Khiva (Khwarazmian Republic) and the return of Panjdeh to Afghans. Terms not fulfilled by Soviets.

Russian military and civilian advisers enter Afghanistan.

British recognize Afghan independence and send ambassador to Kabul in following year.

In Peshawar, Khan Abdul Ghaffar Khan organizes Pushtun reformist group (later, the Khudai Khidmatgaran), which spearheads Pushtunistan movement.

The coup d'état of Reza Khan in Tehran ushers in new era of Iranian modernization.

Bukharan People's Consular Republic requests Afghan help against Russian treaty violation.

1922

Karakul lambskin is introduced to the London market by Afghan entrepreneur who lays the basis of the luxury fur trade heretofore dominated by Russian Central Asia.

1923

First Afghan constitution, based on Belgian, Turkish, and Iranian constitutions, is ratified.

Turkey becomes a republic.

1924

The Bukharan and Khwarazmian republics are dissolved and Soviet Central Asia is divided into eponymous republics.

Tribal rebellion in Khost and religious opposition force Amanullah to amend constitution to emphasize Hanafi Islam.

Atatürk republican regime abolishes the caliphate in Turkey.

1925

Russian invasion forces take Darqad Island (Urta Tagai) south of the Amu Darya but withdraw after destruction of Uzbek resistance forces there.

Cotton as a cash export crop introduced into northern Afghanistan.

Reza Shah, elected monarch by Iran's Majlis, establishes the Pahlavi dynasty.

1926

Iranian-Turkish-Afghan treaty of mutual security, concluded under Russian auspices.

New Afghan currency (afghani) replaces the rupee.

Amanullah drops title of past, amir (leader), in favor of padishah (king).

Kabul signs neutrality and nonaggression pact with USSR.

1928

King Amanullah visits Bolshevik Moscow, the first monarch to do so. He receives an address by the mufti Sadruddinov. Afghans receive military equipment.

USSR establishes Kabul–Tashkent–Moscow air route.

All Central Asian alphabets change to modified Latin, thereby making written exchange with Iran and Afghanistan difficult.

1928–   Afghan communists emigrate to Tajikistan and form a sometimes polit-
1929   ically active community in the traditional center of Hissar.
         Tribal rebellion broadens against King Amanullah and his introduction
            of secular, nontraditional institutions. He abandons the fight and
            goes into exile in Italy.
1929   A Tajik from a mountain village declares jihad against the "infidel"
            Amanullah, captures Kabul, and declares himself amir (not king)
            Habibullah II Ghazi but is pejoratively known as Bacha-i Saqao
            (son of the water carrier). Within nine months he is defeated.
         Moscow attempts to restore Amanullah through Soviet contingent dis-
            guised as "Afghan" under Charkhi brothers. They capture Mazar-i-
            Sharif and Khulm.
         Bacha-i Saqao retaliates by encouraging *basmachi* moves against the
            Red Army in Tajikistan.
         Soviet/Charkhi forces retreat when Amanullah abdicates and alarm is
            raised by regional and European powers.
         General Nadir Khan leads Pushtun war to recapture Kabul. Execution
            of Tajik ruler and purge of his followers deteriorates already
            strained relations between non-Pushtuns and Pushtuns.
         King Muhammad Nadir closes Afghan/Soviet border to strangle
            anti–Red Army resistance. Moscow cuts aid to his Charkhi-led ri-
            vals in Mazar-i-Sharif.
         The Tajik Soviet Socialist Republic is created with the eastern part of
            the old Bukharan khanate and a portion of the Ferghana valley
            around Khojent.
1930   Red Army pursues *basmachi* bands into Afghanistan.
1931   Nadir Shah opens Medical faculty in Kabul, with French professors, to
            become the first unit of Kabul University. Women admitted from the
            start.
         Second Afghan constitution, based on first, is more explicitly Islamic in
            character.
         Afghan army, under Nadir Shah's brother Shah Mahmud, defeats *bas-
            machi* leader Ibrahim Beg and delivers him to Soviet authorities,
            who execute him.
1932   Bank-e Melli, the first Afghan bank, is established as a stock company
            by Afghan entrepreneur who had formerly engaged in trade in
            Tashkent and St. Petersburg.
         Ghulam Nabi Charkhi, returning under amnesty, is accused of foment-
            ing rebellion among Ghilzai and is executed without trial on Nadir
            Shah's order.
         Stalin institutes first of major purges of Central Asian nationalist re-
            formers.
1933   Zahir Shah becomes king following father's assassination by Charkhi
            faction. Royal uncles dominated politics as prime ministers.
         Soviets instigate disturbances in Herat following Nadir Shah's assassi-
            nation but fail.

1934   United States recognizes Afghanistan, appoints minister in Tehran as nonresident envoy.

1937   Oriental Entente (Saadabad Pact) formed by Afghanistan, Iran, Iraq, and Turkey to help withstand European powers and forestall mutual political interference. Precursor of Baghdad Pact, Central Treaty Organization (CENTO), Regional Cooperation for Development (RCD), and Economic Cooperation Organization (ECO).

Soviet KGB sends young ethnic Central Asians into Afghanistan, under deep cover. Some are discovered and imprisoned and others reside as Afghans until retirement.

Pushtu Academy formed in Kabul to promote language and culture.

Arrest of Iranian intellectuals on charges of propagating communist views; these "53" form the nucleus of the Tudeh party of Iran (founded 1941).

1938   Pushtu language instruction becomes mandatory for all government employees.

Revolt of Shami Pir (Sufi leader) among border Pusthuns against the Musahiban family.

Stalinist purge and show trials decimate ranks of Central Asian political and cultural leaders.

1940   Cyrillic replaces Latin as the alphabet for Central Asian languages.

1941   Afghanistan declares neutrality in World War II.

Iran (also neutral) invaded by British and Soviet forces.

Tudeh (Masses), the Iranian communist party, founded with help of Soviets.

1942   American legation opens in Kabul, raised to embassy status in 1948.

Official establishment of Muslim religious directorates revives controlled form of Muslim religious activity throughout Soviet Union. The Tashkent directorate gains influence and controls official Muslim institutions for all Central Asia.

1945   Afghan government begins negotiations with U.S. construction company (Morrison-Knudsen) for extensive irrigation and agricultural development of Helmand valley river systems. This becomes the major U.S. foreign aid project in the country through the 1970s.

1946   Amu Darya midchannel fixed as boundary of Afghanistan with USSR.

Soviet army backs formation of irredentism among Iran's Azarbaijani Turks and Kurds, especially in support of Tudeh elements.

Soviets attempt similar pro-Moscow irredentism among Uighurs in Chinese Central Asia.

1947   The British withdraw from Indian subcontinent, leaving behind Muslim Pakistan and Hindu India but ignoring Pushtun nationalist demands from Khan Abdul Ghaffar Khan for an independence option (Pushtunistan).

Afghanistan becomes a founding member of the United Nations and protests Pakistan's entry because of dispute over their mutual border in Pushtun tribal area.

Pakistan delays or hinders Afghan transit trade in continuing dispute over Durand Line and Pushtunistan issue.

Wish-i Zalmayan (Awakened Youth) forms, laying the basis for reformist movements of the 1960s.

1949   Kyrghyz tribesmen, of Russian Central Asian origin, refugees in China, settle in Afghanistan as Xinjiang (Chinese Central Asia) is absorbed into the communist sphere.

Liberal elections bring in reformist members of legislature.

Afghan Assembly repudiates border treaties with Britain in continuation of border dispute with Pakistan.

1950–
1951   Afghan irregular forces cross into Pakistan with goal of planting Pushtunistan flag.

Pakistan blockades Afghan goods, oil imports.

Afghan-Soviet barter agreement (petroleum products, sugar, etc.) signed, resulting in gradual replacement of Western trade through Pakistan.

Afghan-Soviet transit treaty gives Afghan goods free transit through USSR.

Pakistan relaxes blockade, but trade has already turned north.

1952   Afghan-Soviet trade doubles as Afghanistan becomes importer of Uzbek and Tajik cloth.

Liberal legislature disbanded, free press closed, opposition leaders arrested.

1953   Sardar Muhammad Da'ud Khan replaces his uncle as prime minister in bloodless palace coup.

In Iran, Muhammad Mossadegh is overthrown (August) with help from the U.S. Central Intelligence Agency (CIA), and the Shah establishes Pahlavi control of Iranian politics with the backing of the Iranian army. He begins to rule as absolute king until overthrown in 1979 by forces coalesced under Ayatollah Ruholla Khomeini.

Stalin dies (March).

1954   Under U.S.-Pakistan mutual security agreement arms supply commences to Pakistan. Kabul views this as threat to its security.

Pakistan becomes a founding member of the U.S.-sponsored Southeast Asia Treaty Organization (SEATO).

1955   Pakistan-Afghan riots over Pushtunistan and Pakistan closes border to trade and transit.

New Afghan-Russian barter protocol signed.

Baghdad Pact formed by Turkey and Iraq, and later Iran, Pakistan, and Britain, to contain USSR.

Afghanistan becomes founding member of nonalignment movement at Bandung Conference. Gamal Abdel Nasser visits.

Loya Jirgah approves "Pushtunistan" policy and decides to accept military aid from any outside source.

Nikita Khrushchev visit to Afghanistan results in US$100 million development loan, secret military aid, Soviet support for plebiscite on Pushtunistan, and extension of Soviet-Afghan friendship treaty of 1931 for ten years.

1956 United States refuses military hardware to Kabul, which then contracts for arms and military advisers from the communist bloc.

   First Afghan Five-Year Plan.

   SEATO endorses Pakistani position on Durand Line and SEATO mutual security guarantees Pakistan's position.

   Moscow allows rehabilitation of purged Central Asian leaders.

1957 Jami'at-i Islami (Islamic Society) organized at Kabul University faculty of Islamic law, under leadership of Professor Ghulam Muhammad Niazi.

   Radio Moscow begins Pushtu broadcasts.

   Chinese Prime Minister Chou En-lai visits Afghans as Sino-Soviet relations begin to cool.

1958 Baghdad military coup ends Hashemite monarchy in Iraq. Baghdad Pact ends.

   Pakistani army chief of staff, General Muhammad Ayub Khan, a Pushtun, leads military coup d'état and rules until 1969.

1959 Women of royal family and high officials appear unveiled at Afghan national celebrations (*jeshin*), thus ending the practice of police-enforced veiling.

   Baghdad Pact reformed as Central Treaty Organization (CENTO) after Iraq withdraws. United States signs bilateral security arrangements with Turkey, Iran, and Pakistan.

   Afghan-Soviet Friendship Society founded in Kabul in attempt to enhance position in region through ties with India, People's Republic of China (PRC), and USSR.

1960 Former King Amanullah dies in exile.

1961 Afghanistan becomes a charter member of the Non-Aligned Movement (NAM) at Belgrade Conference, further setting it apart from CENTO countries of the region.

   Pakistan breaks relations with Afghanistan over alleged Afghan interference in Pushtun regions. Official trade severed for lack of documentation.

1961 Afghanistan and Pakistan accept Shah of Iran as mediator in border dispute.

   United States offers to mediate, without success.

   Soviet trade, power, and military ties strengthened with Kabul.

1962 Pakistani President Ayub Khan proposes confederation of Pakistan, Iran, and Afghanistan.

1963 U.S. and Soviet funding of Afghan road, energy, and agricultural projects expands.

   Kabul approves plans for a second university in Nangarhar.

   Trade and assistance agreement signed with USSR, including arrangements for Soviet exploitation of natural gas in northern Afghanistan.

   Zahir Shah dismisses his cousin, Sardar Da'ud, as prime minister and appoints a Tajik, Dr. Muhammad Yusuf, in his place.

   Zahir Shah makes first visit to the United States.

Cultural cooperation agreement signed with USSR.

With mediation of Shah of Iran, Afghanistan and Pakistan resume diplomatic relations after almost a three-year break.

Tehran anti-Shah riots inspired by Khomeini lead to his exile until 1979.

1964   New Afghan constitution approved by Loya Jirgah and signed by king allowing freedom of speech, bicameral legislature.

Regional Cooperation for Development (RCD) formed by regional CENTO members. Afghanistan invited to join but refuses as long as CENTO in existence.

Leonid Brezhnev visits Kabul to establish new Russian polytechnic institute.

Salang Tunnel and highway opened with Soviet assistance linking north and south by all-weather paved road.

Afghan-Chinese border demarcated (90 kilometers) in Wakhan.

1965   The People's Democratic Party of Afghanistan (PDPA) is established by Nur Muhammad Taraki and Babrak Karmal as the Khalq party.

United States ($7.7 million) and USSR ($11.1 million) compete to fund Afghan infrastructure projects.

Japanese aid and expertise provides piped water for Kabul.

National election law takes effect (men and women over twenty years of age, vote by secret ballot).

Ariana Afghan Airlines begins first flights to Soviet Union with run to Tashkent.

Afghan-Soviet Treaty of Neutrality and Non-Aggression (of 1931) extended for ten years.

New press law passed with provisions for safeguarding Islamic values and constitution.

First elections take place under new constitution, without political parties due to lack of parties law.

Student demonstrations (led by PDPA members) force resignation of Dr. Yusuf's government. Popular politician Muhammad Hashim Maiwandwal forms cabinet. Army fires on rioters.

Koubra Nourzai, minister of public health, is first woman in cabinet in Afghan history.

Indo-Pakistani War in Kashmir ends with Soviet-negotiated Tashkent Conference. Afghanistan allows Pakistani civil aviation planes refuge and military equipment from Iran and Saudi Arabia through Afghanistan.

1966   Independent newspapers and periodicals begin publication in Kabul. PDPA organ, *Khalq,* banned after six issues on anti-Islamic and anticonstitutional grounds.

1967   Direct telephone link between Kabul and Herat completed.

Parliament approves political parties law, but king does not sign (ever), forcing continued chaotic elections.

Natural gas export to Soviet Union begins via a 97 kilometer pipeline.

Khalq party splits into Parcham (Banner) and Khalq under Karmal and Taraki, respectively, with each faction claiming to be the true PDPA.

Shah of Iran crowns himself Shahenshah (emperor), a symbol of Iran's regional power.

1968   Sitam-i Milli splits from Parcham and forms as a minorities, anti-Pushtun, leftist party under Dr. Tahir Badakhshi, a founding member of PDPA.

Newspaper *Parcham* established, publishes until 1969. Newspaper *Shula-ye Jawid* published by Maoist faction of Marxists. Both closed by government in July 1969.

Tashkent emerges as Soviet Muslim showcase city with Islamic publications and conferences.

1969   Student unrest in Kabul forces closing of schools. New government forms under Nur Ahmad Etemadi.

Second elections under 1964 constitution; Karmal and Hafizullah Amin elected from rival factions of PDPA, the only two open leftists in parliament.

Prolonged rioting in Pakistan forces resignation of President Ayub Khan. Army chief General Yahya Khan appointed as his replacement.

1970   Sibghatullah Mujaddidi leads religious opposition, which condemns communist influence in government. Dispersed by government. Mujaddidi goes into exile in Denmark.

Free elections in Pakistan result in crisis as Bengali nationalists win in the east and Bhutto's Pakistan People's Party wins in the west.

1971   Etemadi government resigns, Dr. Abdul Zahir appointed prime minister.

Afghanistan suffers worst drought in modern history. U.S. food aid delivered, but corruption and inefficiency of relief discredit Afghan government.

In internal Pakistani war, East Pakistan wins with Indian help and becomes Bangladesh. Bhutto takes power.

Iran celebrates 2,500 years of the Iranian monarchy.

1972   Natural gas agreement expands refining and collection by USSR.

Kabul radio broadcasts Pushtunistan independence demand.

United States sends special envoy to inform Kabul of termination of U.S. aid.

Muhammad Musa Shafiq, principal drafter of 1964 constitution, forms new government.

Kabul broadcasts Uzbek and Turkmen language radio programs after parliamentary alarm about volume of Soviet Central Asian broadcasts into northern Afghanistan.

1973

March   Treaty to end Helmand dispute with Iran, though signed and ratified, cannot be implemented because of subsequent republican coup in Kabul.

July   Da'ud Khan leads military coup, declares Afghanistan a republic, and becomes president with help from pro-Moscow Parcham faction of the PDPA.

August   Zahir Shah abdicates from Italian exile, receives pensions from Da'ud, Iran, and Saudi Arabia.

September   Military coup plot against Da'ud discovered and Pakistan accused of complicity.

1974   Trade agreement signed with Iran.

              President Da'ud visits Moscow. Soviets pledge US$600 million for Afghan seven-year plan but refuse to bring price of Afghan natural gas to international norms.

              Iran and Kabul announce plans for major development of the Helmand basin.

              Trade protocol signed with India.

              Da'ud moves against Islamists at Kabul University, forcing many into Pakistani exile.

              Kabul ends Uzbek and Turkmen language radio broadcasts.

1975   Nationalization of banks and banking affairs announced.

              Saudi King Khaled arranges private meeting between Da'ud and Bhutto at funeral of King Faisal aimed at ending the Pushtunistan dispute.

              Afghan Islamist groups attempt to raise revolt in Panjshir with support of Pakistan, but with weak local support, they are defeated.

              Iran signs agreement to provide aid and technical assistance for transportation and other projects in the seven-year plan up to US$2 billion.

              In all of Central Asia, Russian-language instruction emphasized over local languages.

              Da'ud, in Herat speech, stands against acceptance of "imported ideology." He completes ouster of all openly communist "allies" from government.

1976   Exchange of visits between Da'ud and Bhutto begins Afghanistan-Pakistan détente.

              Da'ud runs afoul of Brezhnev, begins to turn toward Iran and Arab world for development funding and support.

              Nurek hydroelectric dam comes on-line in Tajikistan and ties into other energy production in Uzbekistan, which eventually also includes major parts of Afghanistan.

1977

February   Loya Jirgah approves republican constitution and elects Da'ud president for seven-year term. He appoints members of Central Committee for new single party.

              Air links resume between Afghanistan and Pakistan.

April   Brezhnev, at Kremlin meeting with Da'ud, protests presence of NATO country experts in northern Afghanistan and demands removal. Da'ud walks out of meeting.

July   Moscow induces cooperation among feuding PDPA factions to reunify party under Taraki.

              Prime Minister Bhutto arrested, tried, and hanged (1978) in Pakistan in military coup that brings General Zia-ul-Haq to presidency.

1978

February   Rioting in Qum, Iran, protesting newspaper attack on Ayatollah
             Khomeini, marks beginning of Iranian Islamic Revolution.

March   Da'ud, on official visit to Zia-ul-Haq, continues to improve Afghan-
             Pakistani relations and is secretly shown evidence of Soviet subver-
             sion in Kabul.

April   Assassination of Mir Akhbar Khaibar (Parcham ideologue), probably
             by Khalqis, but Da'ud is blamed. Arrests of communists follows.

April 27–   PDPA coup, "Saur Revolution," brings Taraki and Amin to power.
28   Da'ud and his family are killed.

August   Khalq accuses Parchami members of countercoup plots and jails, kills,
             or sends into diplomatic exile important Parcham members, who
             seek USSR shelter.

             New red Soviet-style flag adopted for Afghanistan.

             Kabul issues nationality policy based on Soviet model, which allows
             Uzbeks, Turkmens, Baluchis, and Nuristanis to publish and teach in
             their own languages.

December   Extensive twenty-year treaty of friendship and cooperation signed be-
             tween Kabul and Moscow. Treaty cited by Moscow a year later as
             the legal basis for invasion.

1979

January   Small-scale resistance fighting begins in eastern provinces.

February   Ayatollah Khomeini enters Tehran in triumph after Shah flees.

             U.S. Ambassador Adolph Dubs is kidnapped in Kabul by Sitam-i Melli
             seeking release of Badakhshi. Dubs and his captors are killed in sus-
             picious shoot-out between kidnappers and Russian and Afghan se-
             curity services.

Spring   Hazarajat resistance to communists forms under Sayyid Ali Beheshti,
             Shi'a religious leader.

March   Rebellion breaks out in Herat as defecting Afghan army units capture
             city; Soviet advisers and families killed. Government recaptures city
             with heavy loss of life.

             Amin appointed prime minister and de facto head of Homeland High
             Defense Council, under Taraki's nominal control.

April   General Aleksey Yepishev, chief of Main Political Administration of So-
             viet Army, visits Afghanistan to assess Herat situation in light of
             fighting. Number of Soviet advisers raised to 7,500 and first combat
             unit sent to Bagram air base.

             Pakistan is accused of plotting against Kabul.

May   Soviet military intelligence forms and trains elite battalion of Turkmen,
             Tajik, and Uzbek soldiers for Afghanistan. They join Amin's body-
             guard in December and take part in the murder of Amin during the
             invasion.

Summer   PDPA begins crackdown on the religious leader Hazrat-e Shor Bazaar
             and ninety-six family members are eventually killed.

             Soviet and Kabul claim presence of only 1,600 Soviet advisers against
             information confirmed that combat units enter in guise of advisers.

September   Taraki, wounded in palace confrontation, is later killed. Amin assumes
            leadership of Khalq and presidency. Some Khalq leaders take refuge
            in Soviet embassy.
            Inter-PDPA fighting, together with Moscow's fear of Amin's ability to
            maintain power in face of popular opposition, leads to Soviet deci-
            sion to back Karmal and Parchamis by use of Red Army.
            Fighting escalates in country among resistance and army but also
            within army as rebellion spreads and desertion rises.
November   U.S. embassy seized in Tehran. Moderate Islamic government of Mehdi
            Bazargan abrogates 1959 bilateral security agreement with United
            States to placate radicals. Bazargan forced to resign later.
December   Large Soviet airborne force occupies Kabul, kills Amin. Land forces
27   disperse across the east and southeast. Karmal's Parcham takes reins
            of government.
            Pakistan joins Non-Aligned Movement.
1980   Refugee exodus accelerates from Afghanistan to Pakistan, then to Iran.
January   Local resistance groups form in Nuristan, Kunar, and Badakhshan.
            Large numbers of Central Asian reservists enter Afghanistan but are re-
            placed by non–Central Asian regular and special units.
            Organization of the Islamic Conference (OIC), in special session in Is-
            lamabad, suspends Afghanistan's membership.
            UN General Assembly Emergency Special Session overwhelmingly con-
            demns Soviet invasion.
            Pro-Moscow Non-Aligned Movement Coordinating Bureau success-
            fully prevents raising of the Afghan issue despite UN vote.
            President Jimmy Carter signs presidential finding authorizing supply of
            weapons to Afghan resistance through Pakistan to harass, but not
            defeat, Soviet occupation force.
            In State of the Union address, President Carter announces security pol-
            icy (Carter Doctrine) calling any attempt by an outside force to gain
            control of Persian Gulf region subject to U.S. intervention, including
            military force.
February   European Community foreign ministers accept British proposal for in-
            ternational conference to secure neutrality of Afghanistan on condi-
            tion of Soviet troop withdrawal. Moscow rejects proposal outright.
            Brezhnev offers to begin Soviet withdrawal when "outside interfer-
            ence" against Afghan government ends.
April   American media take special note of plight of Afghans with *60 Minutes*
            program viewed by 40 million, which raises sympathy and public
            awareness.
May   Kabul and Moscow call for direct negotiations among Kabul, Pakistan,
            and Iran, without Afghan resistance, a position steadfastly main-
            tained to the Geneva accords.
            Médecins sans Frontières, private French organization, opens its first
            clinic inside Afghanistan. Voluntary hospitals and clinics follow but
            are regularly bombed until 1983, when escalating unfavorable pub-
            licity forces Kabul and Soviets to cease air attacks.

	OIC seeks ways to open negotiations for comprehensive solution to Afghan crisis. Iranian delegation includes Afghan mujahidin leaders.
June	OIC proposes to hear Kabul and Afghan mujahidin positions, but Kabul regards OIC as partisan and eventually stops trying to regain participation in OIC.
	Karmal consolidates Parcham position by posting last of powerful Khalqis (Asadullah Sarwari) as ambassador to Mongolia.
September	Iran-Iraq War begins as Iraq strikes to capture Iranian oil fields and bring down Khomeini government.
November	UN General Assembly adopts Resolution 35 calling for the "immediate withdrawal of foreign troops from Afghanistan," a position it maintained by annual resolutions through 1987. This puts increasing pressure on the Soviet Union.
December	Formation of the National Fatherland Front (NFF) by Kabul attempts to create widespread backing for the PDPA among nonparty citizens.
	Rumors, fed by large-scale Soviet military activity, circulate that Kabul officially ceded the Wakhan corridor to the USSR. Wakhan is under military control by Soviet Tajik Pamirs, not by Soviet headquarters in Kabul.
1981	Non-Aligned Movement finally adopts an Afghan resolution obliquely calling for the withdrawal of "foreign troops," a position that NAM maintains to end of war, thereby much reducing its credibility.
January	Summit meeting of OIC at Taif, Saudi Arabia, announces cooperation with the UN secretary-general to resolve Afghan situation.
	Iran releases American hostages seized in 1978 embassy takeover.
February	Javier Perez de Cuellar (of Peru) appointed personal representative of UN secretary-general to promote peace talks.
	The Shura of Hazarajat splinters, with several factions taking a pro-Iranian revolutionary position, possibly as part of Tudeh plan to break resistance to Kabul. Shi'a effectiveness as an anti-Kabul resistance force never revives.
April	Kabul tries to bolster its Islamic image by mosque construction, pilgrimage subsidy, and job opportunities for pliant clerics.
	President Abolhassan Bani-Sadr removed from office in Iran, flees to exile in France in July. Ascendance of radical faction of Islamic revolutionaries with Khomeini's support.
August	Kabul proposes a new negotiating stance that brings in the UN secretary-general's representative.
September	Soviet Foreign Minister Andrey Gromyko offers Pakistan permanent recognition of the Durand Line in exchange for security of the Karmal/PDPA regime.
	U.S.-Pakistan agreement on six-year arms credits and economic aid, including forty F-16 fighters, totaling US$3.2 billion.
November	Diego Cordovez (of Ecuador), UN undersecretary for political affairs, takes role of shuttle diplomat on behalf of newly elected Secretary-General Perez de Cuellar.

The Geneva rounds of indirect talks begin.

Five Peshawar mujahidin parties organize into the Islamic Unity of Afghan Mujahidin and set up a forty-one-member shura (council) to conduct affairs.

December   Loya Jirgah of Kandahar and Quetta resistance groups (pro–Zahir Shah and Durrani) takes place in Chashmak.

1982   Turkey helps to resettle Afghan refugees of Turkic origin, including the Kyrgyz who fled the Wakhan corridor.

U.S. Congress forms voluntary bipartisan Afghanistan Task Force, first under Senator Paul Tsongas, then Senator Gordon Humphrey. The task force pressures administration to furnish effective aid to mujahidin.

January   Soviet army settles in for long war, concentrating on aerial strength to pound resistance.

Efforts launched by Kabul to reorganize Afghan army fail as draft evasion and defection reduce total numbers from 100,000 to 30,000.

Soviet mining of Pakistan border areas to stem flow of arms and supplies begins.

Brotherly Nationalities Magazine publishing in eight languages, established in Kabul, aims at "awakening the masses in border areas."

February   Five-party Peshawar mujahidin alliance splits up, and the parties reform into two opposing groups, henceforth called moderates (*Sehgan,* three parties) and fundamentalists (*Haftgan,* seven parties).

April   Sadeq Qotbzadeh, Iran's former foreign minister under Bani-Sadr and strongly sympathetic to the Afghan resistance, is jailed, tried, and executed.

June   First permanent bridge across Amu Darya opens, connecting Hairatan (Afghanistan) and Termez (Uzbekistan).

August   At OIC meeting rival Afghan resistance groups refuse to compromise in order to present a united mujahidin position. As a result of division, Afghan resistance loses chance for representation at international forums.

Fall   Afghanistan is divided into seven military districts, each headed by Soviet general under the Fortieth Soviet Army in Kabul.

Soviet troops are rotated on a six-month basis, with about 120,000 in Afghanistan at one time.

November Brezhnev dies, succeeded by Yuri Andropov, who stresses Soviet wish for a political settlement.

December Afghan government opens consulate in Tashkent, then Dushanbe.

Second session of the International People's Tribunal (in Paris) condemns USSR for violation of law of war in Afghanistan.

Despite Moscow's warning, Swedish Committee for Afghanistan (partially funded by government), opens clinics inside Afghanistan using Afghan medical personnel. Number reaches ten by 1983.

1983

January   Tehran government jails Tudeh members.

	Commander Ahmad Shah Mas'ud accepts Soviet offer of one-year truce in Panjshir valley but refuses to negotiate with Karmal regime. He continues training and sending forces outside the valley.
February	Andropov agrees to second round of Geneva talks.
	Anticorruption campaign in Soviet Central Asia leads to widespread arrests in Uzbekistan, which Uzbeks interpret as drive by Moscow to blame local leadership for general Brezhnev-era decadence.
March	Kabul announces intent to set up local governments for all nationalities to promote their culture through education and other programs; attempts to build bridges to Pushtun tribes to undercut mujahidin field commanders.
	Pope John Paul II receives three members of the Afghan resistance.
April	At Geneva II negotiations Cordovez announces settlement to be 95 percent complete.
June	Andropov's health declines, Soviet foreign policy marked by inertia.
	Geneva II deadlocked when Moscow and Kabul refuse to give withdrawal deadline.
August	Pakistan, responding to an appeal by Americares Foundation, formally authorizes certain Pakistan-based relief organizations to carry out humanitarian aid missions inside Afghanistan.
October	Zahir Shah sends envoy to Pakistan from his Rome exile to indicate his willingness to play a role in the return of Afghan stability.
December	Influential U.S. policymakers begin to call for delivery of effective military aid to Afghan resistance.
	With consent of Jami'at-i Islami leader Burhanuddin Rabbani, Commander Mas'ud invites Jami'at-i commanders from six provinces (Kapisa, Parwan, Takhar, Baghlan, Kunduz, and Badakhshan) to join in a Supervisory Council of the North to coordinate military and administrative work. Council tries to extend influence to all commanders north of the Hindu Kush mountains, regardless of party.
1984	Pakistan begins to restrict humanitarian activity in Pakistan to those supervised by the United Nations High Commissioner for Refugees (UNHCR) and the Afghan Alliance in bid to bring order to plethora of political and "aid" activity.
	At suggestion of CIA chief William Casey, and with support of Pakistani intelligence, Afghan mujahidin begin sending Islamic propaganda missions into Soviet Central Asia.
	Second meeting of the Supervisory Council of the North held in Panjshir.
January	Kabul adopts stricter conscription rules (all males over eighteen years of age) to counter draining defections.
	KhAD intensifies infiltration of Afghan resistance and sets up false mujahidin groups to alienate rural populations from the resistance through terror.
February	Andropov dies and is replaced by equally aged and unhealthy Konstantin Chernenko. Military operations intensify. Saturation bombing of Panjshir.

	Kabul declares three days of mourning for Andropov.
	Kabul raises conscription term from two to three years in bid to bolster army.
March	U.S. State Department stands by findings that deaths in Afghanistan (and Laos and Cambodia) were caused by use of illegal chemical weapons and not by bee droppings.
April	Iran, at Pakistan's urging, receives Cordovez, who briefs Iran on state of Geneva negotiations.
June	Soviet shelling of Herat, then Kandahar, results in heavy civilian fatalities. Information on Soviet use of chemical weapons circulates again. A scorched-earth policy, aimed at emptying the countryside of resistance sympathizers, continues.
Summer	Seventh Soviet offensive in Panjshir is marked by first use of high-level saturation bombing tactics with planes based in Soviet territory.
	Sharp increase in air violation of Pakistani border.
August	At Geneva III, Pakistan agrees to sign agreement provided an acceptable timetable for Soviet withdrawal is made. No response from Kabul.
October	U.S. Congress passes the Tsongas-Ritter resolution, previously blocked by the State Department, calling for United States to "render effective military aid to the freedom fighters."
1985	Third meeting of Supervisory Council of the North convenes in Takhar. Also included are commanders from outside Jami'at-i Islami who coordinate military and administration of countryside in mujahidin hands.
February	Chernenko dies.
March	Mikhail Gorbachev becomes president of USSR and general secretary of Communist Party.
	President Ronald Reagan signs National Security Decision Directive 166, increasing aid to Afghan resistance with goal of forcing Soviet withdrawal and allowing self-determination of the Afghan people.
April	Loya Jirgah convened in Kabul rubber-stamps PDPA position to advance the aims of the Saur Revolution and support Soviet-Afghan friendship.
May	Peshawar resistance groups form a seven-party union called Islamic Unity of Afghan Mujahidin, with a rotating presidency, which is able to represent the resistance at international forums.
July	United States begins to supply Pakistan with Sidewinder air-to-air missiles and Stinger ground-to-air missiles.
August	U.S. Congress approves funds for cross-border humanitarian assistance using year-end surplus in State Department's "Disaster Relief" account.
October	Gulbuddin Hekmatyar, representing the mujahidin alliance at the United Nations, refuses to meet with President Reagan, despite Pakistani urging, on grounds that he had no authorization from the Islamic Unity of Afghan Mujahidin.

November Karmal calls for broadening of social base of government under
Moscow's urging with goal of strengthening government and allowing Soviet disengagement.

Reagan-Gorbachev Summit in Geneva.

December. United States announces agreement to guarantee Geneva settlement, provided the issue of timing of Soviet troop withdrawal and its relationship to other parts of a comprehensive settlement are satisfactory.

Martial law ends in Pakistan.

1986

February Gorbachev describes Afghan issue as "bleeding wound."

April United States agrees to supply the resistance with Stingers.

U.S. assistance to the resistance escalates to US$470 million.

Pakistan leadership all agree to accept a one-year withdrawal limit as
Pakistani bottom line at Geneva negotiation.

May Muhammad Najibullah, former head of KhAD, replaces Karmal as
party secretary, with heavy Soviet troop contingent reappearing in
central Kabul to prevent disorder.

Pro-Karmal Kabuli protest, but the occasion is used by Najibullah to
purge PDPA of these elements.

July At Vladivostok, Gorbachev announces unilateral withdrawal of six
regiments by end of year and calls for inclusion in Kabul regime of
forces in exile outside Afghanistan.

September Kabul forms National Compromise Commission to broaden base of
support, mainly under Soviet urging, but policy is crippled by Parcham inflexibility.

First use of U.S.-supplied Stingers results in destruction of three Soviet
MIG-24 helicopter gunships at Jalalabad airport.

November Karmal removed from ceremonial presidential position and replaced by
non-PDPA member, Haji Muhammad Samkanai.

December Kabul launches policy of National Reconciliation and invites disenchanted Uzbek Maoists to join; they accept. The National Compromise Commission is abandoned despite questionable Kabul claims
of success in getting field commanders to join the government.

In Almaty (Kazakstan), Moscow removes Kazak first party secretary,
Dinmuhammad Kunayev, and replaces him with an outside Russian,
Gennady Kolbin, thereby triggering nationalist anti-Moscow riots in
Almaty.

1987 Kabul builds climate of successful return of refugees and pressure
builds on Pakistan to cooperate with Kabul, especially with regard
to refugees.

U.S. assistance to Afghan resistance rises to US$630 million.

January Northwest Frontier Pakistani politician Abdul Wali Khan, of Awami
National Party (of Pakistan) and son of Pushtun nationalist leader
Khan Abdul Ghaffar Khan, calls on Pakistan to accept Najibullah's
national reconciliation offer and cease aiding mujahidin.

All seven mujahidin alliance party leaders appear at Peshawar rally to
reject Najibullah's plan.

Pakistani foreign minister holds first meetings with mujahidin leadership to discuss interim government with PDPA. Leaders propose direct talks with Soviets.

OIC summit in Kuwait endorses Pakistani position with regard to conditions for a genuine national reconciliation, but not Kabul's version.

February   Pakistan proposes former king, Zahir Shah, as head of compromise government, but Moscow insists on PDPA leadership.

March–
April   Resistance carries out strikes across the Amu Darya into (then Soviet) Tajikistan at Panj, with aid from the Pakistani Interservices Intelligence Agency (ISI) and the U.S. CIA.

After three successful resistance attacks into Soviet Central Asia, Soviets threaten direct action against Pakistan, which in turn orders halt to attacks.

New head of ISI, General Hamid Gul, endorses mujahidin call for an elected shura to establish interim government. Pakistan presses for Zahir Shah role.

May–June   Stinger missiles show continued success, with fifty-three Soviet/Kabul aircraft destroyed in May and sixty in June.

July   Meeting of 1,200 mujahidin commanders convenes in Ghor province at invitation of Isma'il Khan, the Jami'at-i commander from Herat, and calls for a permanent council of resistance.

August   Kabul allows first visit to Afghanistan of Dr. Felix Ermacora since his appointment in 1984 as special UN rapporteur on human rights in Afghanistan. He reports 5.5 million refugees and lack of human rights safeguards in draft constitution.

September   At Geneva VII convened at Kabul's initiative, Kabul reduces withdrawal time frame to sixteen months instead of the expected one year acceptable to Pakistan.

Loya Jirgah meets to ratify constitution; change of country name back to Republic of Afghanistan (ROA), dropping the offensive communist appellation "Democratic."

Minister of Islamic Affairs of the ROA states that the hopes of the Muslims of the Soviet Union were fulfilled through the October Revolution.

December   Najibullah admits that 80 percent of countryside and 40 percent of towns are beyond government control.

Cordovez visits Zahir Shah in Rome.

Intermediate-range nuclear forces (INF) accord signed between United States and Soviet Union at Gorbachev-Reagan Summit in Washington, D.C.

1988
January   Khan Abdul Ghaffar Khan, Pushtunistan independence leader, dies in Peshawar and is buried in Jalalabad.

February   Sayyid Bahauddin Majruh, prominent moderate exile intellectual and head of Afghan Information Center, is assassinated in Peshawar.

	Gorbachev announces agreement to withdrawal of Soviet troops beginning May 15 over a ten-month period, provided Geneva accords signed by March 15.

Gorbachev announces agreement to withdrawal of Soviet troops beginning May 15 over a ten-month period, provided Geneva accords signed by March 15.

United States drastically reduces military aid to resistance while Soviet aid is estimated at US$300 million per month plus $1.5 billion in supplies left at withdrawal.

March   Islamic Unity of Afghanistan Mujahidin (IUAM) supreme council adopts plan for interim government to be formed before the Geneva agreements; appoints Ahmad Shah president and Dr. Zabiullah Mujaddidi vice president.

Agricultural survey of Afghanistan, based on interviews with more than 1 percent of farmers, reports that crop yields in 1986 and 1987 dropped to 45 percent and 53 percent of 1978 level.

April   Geneva VIII results in signing of agreement for Soviet troop withdrawal within nine months beginning on April 14 despite Zia-ul-Haq's insistence that withdrawal be linked to an internal settlement.

United States and Pakistan assert the right to supply arms to Afghan resistance as long as Soviets supply Kabul.

IUAM condemns Geneva accords and will not be bound by them since they had no part in their negotiation and they contradict UN resolution principles of self-determination.

Kabul announces creation of new Sar-i-Pol province from Hazara majority areas of several northern provinces.

ISI arms depot at Ojri camp (Rawalpindi) explodes, destroying 10,000 tons of arms and ammunition for Afghan resistance, killing 100 and injuring 1,000 (April 10).

May   Moscow announces official casualties of the war at 13,310 dead, 35,478 wounded, and 311 missing.

June   The Afghan Interim Government (AIG) is formed in Peshawar.

July   Najibullah appoints Muhammad Hassan Sharq, a nonparty member and former aid to President Da'ud, as prime minister.

August   One-half of Soviet troops are withdrawn.

President Zia-ul-Haq is killed in air sabotage under unexplained circumstances at Bahawalpur, widely blamed on Afghan KhAD. Also killed are U.S. ambassador and head of U.S. military aid mission to Pakistan and former head of ISI.

September Soviet Muslim organizations appeal to mujahidin to release Soviet prisoners.

November USSR suspends withdrawal because of heavy fighting, then resumes, under international pressure.

Soviets introduce SCUD missiles into Afghanistan, firing more than 1,000 in first year and continuing until end of 1991 despite "official" Soviet military withdrawal under terms of Geneva accords.

Najibullah consolidates power by removing Khalqi leader, Minister of Interior Sayyid Muhammad Gulabzoy, to diplomatic exile post in Moscow.

December   Soviet Deputy Foreign Minister Yuli Vorontsov meets with Zahir Shah in Rome.

Vorontsov holds talks with President Rabbani in Saudi Arabia.

1989

Afghan Interim Government organized to replace the Alliance.

Soviet supply to Kabul, airlifted from points in Central Asia, consists of two-thirds weapons and one-third humanitarian aid. Fuel trucks and armored personnel carriers arrive by road.

January   Zabiullah Mujaddidi, speaking for the IUAM, suspends talks with Soviets, calling them propaganda and means for Soviets to spread dissension.

February   Mujahidin hold shura in Rawalpindi (under Pakistani patronage), but meeting is boycotted by Iran-based Shi'a parties who protest their allotted number of seats and demand increase to 30 percent.

Soviets complete withdrawal of forces under the Geneva accords. Air bombing missions from Soviet Central Asian bases continue, with occasional perfunctory U.S. protest.

Major Western embassies and some East European embassies in Kabul are closed for fear of lack of security.

In Tashkent demonstrations against the un-Islamic behavior of Moscow protégé mufti forces his removal and replacement by Islamic scholar.

Birlik, an Uzbek nationalist secular party, constituted formally.

March   Mujahidin begin Jalalabad attack after capturing territory between Khyber Pass and the city; eventually becomes an unsuccessful siege as defenders outnumber attackers. Heavy losses on both sides.

Mufti Muhammad Sadiq of Tashkent runs unopposed in election for Uzbek Congress of People's Deputies.

April   Islamabad agrees to allow UN to set up monitoring post of Pakistani-Afghan border.

ROA uses pardons and economic agreements with USSR to bolster position.

Mujahidin begin to form a regular armed force under command of defecting ROA officers. Haji Din Muhammad (Muhammad Yunis Khalis supporter) appointed military leader by AIG.

International Committee of the Red Cross signs agreement to establish ten Red Crescent clinics in Kabul.

May   Eight-party Shi'a Iran-based coalition signs agreement with Peshawar alliance to organize the interim government but agree only to continue mediation.

Pakistani Awami National Party further warms ties with ROA.

Pakistani Prime Minister Benazir Bhutto dismisses ISI chief in charge of U.S. aid to resistance.

Lawyers Association of Free Afghanistan (émigré group) meets in Peshawar to chart course for reconstruction.

Using the "Wahhabi" threat to appeal to secular Afghans fearful of fundamentalist Islamic takeover, Najibullah continues to attempt to lure home prominent Afghans abroad.

	Ayatullah Khomeini dies. ROA representative refused Iran entry for funeral.
June	Jami'at mujahidin commanders killed in Takhar province by forces under Hekmatyar commander Sayyid Jamal, who is later captured and executed by Mas'ud.
July	In Ferghana valley (Uzbekistan) violence breaks out between Uzbeks and Meskhetian Turks.
August	Taliqan, capital of Takhar province, is first capital to fall to mujahidin after Soviet withdrawal.
September	Operation Salaam, a UN reconstruction effort under Prince Sadruddin Agha Khan, sends first assessment mission inside Afghanistan.
	Jabha-i Najat-i Milli (National Liberation Front) formed in Kabul by ex-officials of former regimes not openly associated with the PDPA regime.
	Joint USSR/Pakistan-sponsored UN General Assembly resolution endorses Geneva accords and calls for formation of broad-based government.
November	Afghan Interim Government rejects General Assembly resolution calling for inter-Afghan talks, claiming the Khalq party has no right to participate in future organization of country.
	Central Asian republics declare their own languages state languages except in Kazakstan, where Russian and Kazak share status.
	Afghan mujahidin assert and Pakistani sources concur that departing Soviet troops leave behind Soviet Central Asian soldiers operating in Afghanistan wearing Afghan uniforms who were rotated into the country in July. Such troops operate around Kandahar.
December	Najibullah calls for PDPA to change its name to Watan (Homeland) party.
	Kabul announces arrest of 130 military officers (forty-eight Watan party members) for plotting coup in cooperation with Hekmatyar.
	Rabbani, representing the IUAM, holds talks in Saudi Arabia with Vorontsov, Soviet first deputy foreign minister.
	Religious literature and items, previously available mainly clandestinely, become openly available on markets in Tashkent and elsewhere.
1990	Number of pilgrims making the hajj from among Soviet Muslims increases from an average of thirty per year to 1,500 (i.e., anyone who can afford to go).
	Thirty-three students from Kabul and Nangarhar leave for study in Russian Socialist Federative Socialist Republic (RSFSR).
	Resistance jams Kabul TV.
January	AIG condemns "terrorism and genocide" of Soviet troops and KGB in Azarbaijan; also condemns "massacre of innocent Kashmiris" by the Indian government.
March	Afghan Defense Minister General Shanawaz Tanai fails in coup attempt against Najibullah and flees to Pakistan. Coup supported by Hekmatyar but opposed by AIG and most mujahidin.

	Twenty-four prominent Khalqis, including party founders, expelled from party for support of Tanai coup attempt.
May	Najibullah appoints nonparty member Fazl Haq Khaliqyar, a "Timuri" Aimaq, as prime minister.

Twenty-four prominent Khalqis, including party founders, expelled from party for support of Tanai coup attempt.

May   Najibullah appoints nonparty member Fazl Haq Khaliqyar, a "Timuri" Aimaq, as prime minister.

AIG publicly condemns speech of UN reconstruction coordinator Prince Sadruddin Agha Khan as hostile to the jihad and the Muslim people of Afghanistan.

Najibullah government abolishes decree of 1978 on dowry and marriage expenses in yet another move to reconcile with Afghan customs.

June   Wahdat party formed in Tehran of Shi'a mujahidin parties in Iran.

Second party congress of PDPA officially votes to change name of party to Watan (homeland).

President Sibghatullah Mujaddidi (of interim government) meets with influential exiles and members of Wahdat party.

Over 300 mujahidin commanders from every province and most resistance parties hold conference in Paktia and create organization for settling inter-mujahidin issues inside Afghanistan.

August   AIG condemns Iraqi attack on Kuwait, and considers the defense of Saudi Arabia an obligation for each Muslim state and individual.

Children from Kunduz sent to Tajikistan for "vacation."

Seventh International Kushan Conference held in Kabul, but few, even from Central Asia, attend for fear of lack of security.

Najibullah claims to have met with Sayyid Ahmad Gailani and Sibghatullah Mujaddidi in Geneva, but both deny this.

Kabul cracks down on what may be deemed anti-Islamic activity, including video and "vedic" dance establishments.

September Afghan foreign trade deficit announced at US$530 million annually.

October   Commanders hold third general meeting in Badakhshan, form a joint office in Peshawar, and declare that jihad will continue until the formation of an Islamic government.

Following commanders' conference on Pakistani-Afghan border, Mas'ud visits Islamabad to confer with President Ishaq Khan and Hekmatyar. First visit outside country since beginning of war.

Rabbani and Hekmatyar sign agreement for elected joint councils in liberated areas, with all parties to be under a single command for defense, but governed by their own party for offensive operations.

1991

February On instruction of President Mujaddidi, 300 mujahidin sent to Saudi Arabia to participate in war against Iraq.

March   Under Commander Jalaluddin Haqqani, mujahidin capture Khost, taking 2,200 prisoners. Najibullah declares "day of mourning."

April   Uzbek Soviet Socialist Republic and Kabul agree on aid in irrigation and water development projects.

The first mujahidin bank opens in Takhar province (under Mas'ud) to serve needs of traders. Transactions to be based on Islamic laws of finance.

	Iran gives Ariana Afghan Airline right to land in Bandar Abbas but not Tehran.
May	Moscow agrees to build electrical connections from Turkmenistan to Herat and provide power.
	Uzbek and Turkmen language departments of the Afghan Academy of Sciences elevated to status of "institutes."
	For Ramazan, the month of fasting, female broadcasters on Kabul TV begin to wear head coverings in further concession to mujahidin social standing.
	USSR to fund development of ports at Torghundi, Hairatan, and Shibarghan.
	UN Secretary-General Perez de Cuellar presents five-point plan for political settlement.
	Iran stresses to AIG delegation the need for a political settlement.
June	Karmal returns to Kabul from unofficial exile in Soviet Union.
July	Tajik Soviet Socialist Republic signs agreement to ship foodstuffs to Afghanistan.
	Leader of Sudan Islamic Front, Dr. Hassan Turabi, meets with Peshawar resistance leaders in bid to foster unity among resistance.
	The Salang-Europa Transport company is created by private Afghan entrepreneur (51 percent) and Soviet carrier company (49 percent) to transfer goods by land, sea, and air to Europe.
	Wakhan corridor falls to mujahidin, allowing road transport of goods from Pakistan to Badakhshan.
	Mujahidin (Jami'at) conclude local truce with Soviet border guards in Tajikistan to keep bridge at Ishkashim open for local use.
	UN Operation Salaam projects are drastically scaled down or abandoned for lack of funds.
	First meeting among high-level representatives of Iran and Pakistan with the mujahidin based in each country, takes place in Islamabad.
August	Kabul concedes loss of Wakhan corridor to resistance.
	Afghans form one-sixth of foreign student body in USSR.
	Kabul regime government of Mazar-i-Sharif admits that local militia of General Rashid Dustam (largely Uzbek) are beyond government control.
	Moscow coup attempt against Gorbachev by communist hard-liners, resisted successfully by forces led by Boris Yeltsin.
	Afghan-Tajik joint venture to form Afghan Bukhara carpet weaving project.
	Second meeting (Tehran) of Iranian and Pakistani representatives and mujahidin calls for replacement of Kabul regime by an elected Islamic government.
September	U.S.-USSR agreement to halt all military aid by end of year in "positive symmetry" accord.
	Najibullah restores Afghan citizenship to ex-King Zahir and twenty-two members of his family.

October   Tajikistan and Uzbekistan cut electric power to Kabul and demand new agreement.

Battle rages for Gardez, capital of Paktia province.

November   Zahir Shah, wounded in knife attack, escapes assassination attempt in Rome by Portuguese citizen posing as journalist.

Rabbani leads delegation of mujahidin to Moscow to discuss end of war. At Afghan suggestion, representatives of Ukraine, Uzbekistan, Tajikistan, and Kazakstan participate. Agree that all power should be transferred to Islamic interim government and elections under international supervision to be held within two years.

Abdul Rasul Sayyaf, Khalis, and Hekmatyar denounce Rabbani as engaging in anti-mujahidin conspiracy with Moscow.

Moscow speeds withdrawal of 300 combat experts from Afghanistan, mainly SCUD missile operators.

Iran asks UN for help with Afghan refugees.

In first multiparty elections in Tajikistan, former Communist Party secretary-general and acting president Rahman Nabiev wins popular vote with 58 percent. Main opponent, of Pamiri background, disputes legality of vote.

President Nabiev legalizes hitherto underground Islamic Revival Party of Tajikistan.

December   ROA recognizes independence of Uzbekistan, Tajikistan, Kyrgyzstan, Azarbaijan, and the Russian Federation.

Kabul signs protocol with Uzbekistan for a joint transport agency to operate in Mazar-i-Sharif and Tashkent.

Kabul signs protocol for cultural cooperation between Tajikistan and Afghan Artists Union.

Formal end of Soviet Union (December 8) and its replacement by the Commonwealth of Independent States (Russia, Ukraine, Belarus), later (December 20–21) expanded at Almaty to include others, including the five Central Asian republics.

1992

January   ROA delegation plan is introduced to begin negotiations for sale of Afghan natural gas to Tajikistan.

Pakistan's economic minister calls the policy of the mujahidin to establish an Islamic government the biggest hurdle to Pakistan's cooperative agreements with the secular governments in Central Asia.

Government militia leaders General Momin, a Tajik, backed by General Dustam, an Uzbek, and General Sayyid Ja'far Nadiri, an Isma'ili Hazara, defy transfer orders from Kabul and block supplies from Hairatan through Mazar-i-Sharif to Kabul.

Pakistani foreign minister announces support for UN peace plan and convening of Afghan assembly, indicating change in Pakistani policy.

Central Asian states become independent countries.

February   Afghan-Turkmen diplomatic ties established.

France reopens embassy in Kabul, closed since the end of Soviet troop withdrawal three years earlier.

Foreign ministers of Iran and Tajikistan and Tehran-based Wahdat leaders meet in Tehran to form Cultural Cooperation Society to emphasize Persian language, culture, and script.

All mujahidin organizations in Nangarhar province form a joint shura and appoint Haji Abdul Qader (Hizb-i Islami Afghanistan–Khalis) as governor.

Meeting of over 500 mujahidin commanders in Paktia conditionally approves UN efforts for resolution of war.

First Economic Cooperation Organization (ECO) summit in Tehran endorses Pakistani prime minister's call for broad-based interim government based on UN plan, but Najibullah must first resign. Afghan (ROA) membership request to ECO is rejected.

March	Najibullah offers to open investigation into 1979 murder of U.S. Ambassador Dubs.

Najibullah appeals to United States for help in stopping the spread of fundamentalist Islam in Central Asia.

Uzbekistani Minister of Defense Rustam Ahmadov rejects view that Islamic fundamentalists in Afghanistan could pose danger to Uzbekistan if Kabul regime fails.

President Islam Karimov of Uzbekistan visits Beijing to sign fourteen agreements on trade, transport, and investment.

April 12	Salang Highway falls to resistance
April 14	Mas'ud forces and ex–government militia capture Charikar and Bagram military air base south of Hindu Kush on highway between Kabul and Salang Pass.
April 18	General Dustam rebels against Kabul and, Najibullah orders Pushtun force north to quell rebellion.

Herat falls, as do Shindand air base (Hizb-i Islami) and Kunduz.

Mujahidin forces in Mazar-i-Sharif seize part of town, airport, and KhAD center, as Pushtun regime troops of Eighteenth Division resists. Dustam's Uzbek militia seize part of city. Food supplies to Kabul blocked.

April 19	Najibullah announces on Kabul TV that he will resign and not participate again in national politics once an interim government is formed.

Badghis falls to resistance.

Mujahidin, under Mas'ud, and Uzbek militias, under Dustam, establish autonomous administration for north in Mazar-i-Sharif.

April 20	Najibullah resigns but is stopped at airport as he attempts to join his family in India. He takes refuge in UN compound.

Afghan Interim Government formally dissolved by new Leadership Council.

Peshawar agreement signed between mujahidin leaders with participation of Pakistani Prime Minister Nawaz Sharif. Sibghatullah Mujaddidi to serve as two-month interim president, followed by Rabbani for six months, with prime ministership to Hekmatyar.

Kabul foreign minister goes to meet Mas'ud at Charikar. Head of KhAD, General Ghulam Faruq Yaqubi, commits suicide.

April 22   Gardez falls to resistance.

UN claims to have reached a brokered settlement, but mujahidin forces do not accept and continue to move toward Kabul.

April 27   Mujahidin occupy the capital on the fourteenth anniversary of the 1978 communist coup.

April 28   Mujaddidi arrives in Kabul, announces general amnesty for all but Najibullah. ROA army ceases resistance. Najibullah whisked in UN vehicle to UN compound for safety.

April 29   Algerian fundamentalist prisoners, condemned to death, voice praise to God at news of fall of Kabul.

Pakistani airplanes with relief supplies land in Kabul.

Mas'ud and ROA remnants join to keep Hekmatyar from marching into Kabul.

Hekmatyar and Mas'ud forces fight for control of presidential palace.

Hekmatyar declines prime ministership but appoints one of his commanders, Abdul Sabur Farid, a Tajik, to take his place.

Civil war breaks out in Tajikistan as regional rivalry, complicated by Islamic Revival Party politics spurred by Tehran, combine to create chaos.

May   Saudi Arabia, Iran, and Pakistan recognize new Afghan government.

Watan party (communist) dissolved on order of mujahidin government in Kabul.

Hekmatyar demands that Dustam's militia forces be expelled, or he will attack the city.

"Isma'ili" militia enters Kabul.

Russian Foreign Minister Kozyrev visits Kabul.

President Mujaddidi makes Dustam a full general in the new Islamic regime, an act condemned by Hekmatyar and others as promotion of the enemy.

Mas'ud and Hekmatyar meet, agree to elections and withdrawal of all militias from Kabul.

People's courts are established to try former communists, thus bringing into question the validity of the general amnesty.

Sale of alcohol and narcotics is banned.

Anticommunist coup in Azarbaijan deposes elected president Ayaz Mutalibov, replacing him with pro-Turkish Abulfaz Elchibey.

President Karimov of Uzbekistan signs bilateral friendship and cooperation treaty with Russia.

June   Attacks on Hindus and Sikhs in Afghanistan, especially money changers, who are abducted for ransom. India protests.

Nuristanis continue imposition of fine for breaking of ten-year ban on relations with Kabul despite change in government.

Evidence of Afghan prisoners shipped to Uzbekistan in 1978 and 1979 surfaces.

More Gelam Jam (Uzbek/Isma'ili) militia airlifted to Kabul headed by Dustam's brother Lt. Gen. Abdul Majid, where they establish headquarters at the Afghan Film Institute.

U.S. delegation arrives in Kabul to discuss resumed diplomatic relations.

Mujaddidi resigns in accordance with Peshawar agreement. Rabbani succeeds him.

Elchibey assumes presidency in Azerbaijan as head of Popular Front, which is regarded by Tehran as sympathetic to irredentism by its own Azarbaijanis.

President Askar Akaev of Kyrgyzstan builds relations with Beijing through trade and new overland route between Osh and Kashgar (Xinjiang Uighur Autonomous Region) in PRC.

July   Prime Minister Farid (Tajik from Hekmatyar party) arrives in Kabul.

August   Khalis withdraws from leadership council in protest of Rabbani's decision to admit Wahdat (Shi'a) representatives to council.

Pakistani prime minister accuses Hekmatyar of violating the Peshawar agreement.

Because of heavy fighting in Kabul between forces of Hekmatyar and Rabbani, a number of Western embassies (including Italy and France) close. Rabbani is aided by the regular army and air force. Thirty thousand refugees flee Kabul toward Nangarhar, where governor establishes refugee camps at Sarobi.

New Islamic Afghan flag is adopted, with green, white, and black horizontal stripes reminiscent of precommunist flag.

Azerbaijan introduces its own currency, the manat.

September   Russia, Kazakstan, Kyrgyzstan, and Uzbekistan announce plans to send troops to Tajik-Afghan border to control arms and drug trade.

Tajik President Nabiev is forced to resign by coalition of "democratic" forces, Pamiris, and Islamist elements.

Civil war follows shortly thereafter in Dushanbe, Garm, Kulab, and other districts close to Afghan border.

Pamiris (Isma'ili) form new secessionist party, Lal-e Badakhshan, in Tajikistan.

October   Commonwealth of Independent States (CIS) votes to seal the border between Tajikistan and Afghanistan to prevent arms flow from "Mas'ud and Hekmatyar" camps.

Rabbani is voted an additional two months as president by Leadership Council.

Rabbani pays state visit to Uzbekistan.

Dustam militia leaves Kabul for Mazar-i-Sharif.

Azerbaijan resists joining CIS despite Moscow pressure.

November   Pakistan Railways conducts feasibility study for rail link from Landi Kotal to Kabul.

Dustam leads fifty-member delegation on Mecca pilgrimage.

Foreign ministers of Afghanistan, Pakistan, Iran, Turkey, Azarbaijan, Kazakstan, Kyrgyzstan, Turkmenistan, and Uzbekistan sign charter of ECO. Tajik representatives do not attend because of civil war.

Ground work laid for restoration of Afghan-Russian relations.

President Saparmurat Niyazov of Turkmenistan builds Beijing ties.

Turkey, potential participant in Azari oil and gas industry with pipeline through Georgia/Armenia or Armenia/Iran, claims ability to handle Kazak oil pipeline through Caspian via Baku.

Chinese high-level visit to Central Asia to promote large cross-border trade and rail link from Almaty to Beijing, which would connect to Tehran and west. Chinese push for safeguards against unrest in Xinjiang instigated by former Soviet republics.

Pakistan Telecommunications Corp. establishes international direct dialing with Kazakstan.

Pakistan establishes embassies in Tashkent, Almaty, and Dushanbe.

December Tajik refugees flee to Afghanistan. Kabul asks for UN aid to care for them. US$2.7 million in food aid provided.

CIA finances buy-back of missiles from Afghanistan.

Fighting in Kabul breaks out between Ministry of Defense forces of Mas'ud and Dustam forces.

Shura-e Ahl Haq u Aqd meets and elects Rabbani president for eighteen months while preparations are undertaken for a national election and constitution. One-quarter of members boycott election in protest.

Turkmen-Russian bilateral economic and military agreements signed.

Azarbaijan Popular Front attempts to stabilize situation, but war in Karabagh continues.

Uzbek parliament bans Birlik (December 10) because of fears of its links with Islamist political groups such as the Islamic Revivalist Party.

U.S. Stan Cornelius Consortium and Uzbekneft form fifty-fifty joint venture Uzbek Petroleum International to develop Mingbulak oil field in Ferghana valley over a twenty-eight-year period. In March 1992 reserves are estimated at 800 million barrels, which would meet one-third of Uzbekistan's annual petroleum needs.

1993

January Hekmatyar calls Rabbani election as president of Islamic Republic Afghanistan (IRA) a fraud.

Pakistan orders Afghan resistance offices and nongovernmental organizations in Northwest Frontier Province closed by January 31, 1993.

IRA interim parliament selected to pass on Rabbani cabinet.

Factional fighting disrupts Kabul.

Afghan refugees claim they are being pushed out of Iran.

Pakistan, Iran, and Saudi Arabia propose cease-fire solutions.

Rabbani resigns as head of Jami'at-i Islami party.

Dustam threatens to withdraw support unless Rabbani gives his Jumbesh-i Milli Islami (National Islamic Movement) official recognition and includes its members in new government.

	Minsk CIS meeting pledges additional 2,000 troops to police the Tajik-Afghan border.
	Dustam provides aid to Tajik refugees as over 200,000 spend winter in Afghanistan.
February	Wahdat and government continue to clash in Kabul.
March	Iran pledges not to force refugee repatriation. It will help Dustam print books in Mazar-i-Sharif and strengthen radio and television reception in Mazar-i-Sharif and Hazarajat.

Islamabad accords signed between warring mujahidin factions.

Hekmatyar fires Mas'ud as minister of defense.

Kashmir partisans seek Afghan help in struggle.

Turkish prime minister in Baku to negotiate laying of new pipeline forty-two miles through Iran. Moscow fears reorientation of Azarbaijan and Central Asia away from Russian markets and conduits.

Nursultan Nazarbayev of Kazakstan backs Russian call for greater integration of CIS states.

Turkish President Turgut Ozal dies of heart attack.

Armenian offensive in Kelbadzhar is suspected to be aided by Russia.

Tajik Popular Front head, Sangak Safarov, is killed in Khatlon, thus weakening base of Tajik government as it faces CIS demands. Head of Lakai (Uzbek) tribe also dies, further weakening local leadership in Tajikistan.

UN withdraws from food distribution among Tajik refugees in Afghanistan because Tajik opposition wants to control UN activity in order to stop repatriation of Tajik refugees, whose communities serve as base of activity for Tajik opposition.

April   Hekmatyar names cabinet, but Rabbani refuses to accept it.

Local Afghan mujahidin and Tajik rebels in northern Afghanistan admit to being trained and supplied at both Mas'ud and Hekmatyar bases.

Azarbaijan struggle with Armenia begins to affect Baku leadership stability.

May   Bomb hits National Museum in Kabul.

Dustam and Mas'ud join forces to squeeze out Hekmatyar.

Dushanbe threatens retaliation bombing against Tajik opposition in Afghanistan; Russian soldiers are killed.

Kyrgyzstan bans communist party as procommunist forces ally with regional leaders to undermine President Akaev.

Nazarbayev declares Kazak opposition to Central Asian unity.

Kazakstan and Turkmenistan sign agreement aimed at boosting their oil and gas exporting potential and friendship and cooperation.

Kazak-Uzbek-Kyrgyz joint declaration on mutual assistance expands on Tashkent agreement of January 4.

June   Pakistan to renegotiate the Afghan Transit Trade Agreement with Kabul.

Nimroz province largely cleared of mines by UN.

Hekmatyar sworn in as prime minister by Rabbani in Paghman, but he remains outside Kabul at his military base.

Azarbaijani military leader, Surat Huseinov seizes power in Ganjeh following his forced removal from Karabagh, and demands resignation of Elchibey. Elchibey flees to Nakhichevan, and Huseinov accepts premier position.

July   Tajik opposition forces attack border post, killing 200 Tajiks and twenty-six Russian soldiers. Russians protest alleged Afghan involvement and send reinforcements.

Russian Deputy Defense Minister Kobets calls for use of "all possible force" against Tajik rebels along Afghan border. Russian forces on border reinforced.

Haydar Aliev, former head of Azerbaijan Communist Party, takes over as acting president and announces strict conscription of all males aged eighteen to forty years. Fighting escalates around Karabagh, but large eastward flow of refugees is prevented from entry into Baku itself.

August   Baku signs oil agreement with Iran, resumes Western oil company negotiations. Refugee influx into eastern Azerbaijan prompts Iran to reinforce its border with Azerbaijan.

September   Russian Foreign Minister Kozyrev calls in UN speech for UN approval and aid in financing Russian "peacekeeping" in the CIS, including Tajikistan.

Moscow agreement signed by Russia, Uzbekistan, Kazakstan, and Kyrgyzstan to maintain a collective peacekeeping force on Tajik border with Afghanistan.

Russia signs treaty of defense and cooperation with Turkmenistan. Russian troops in Turkmenistan indefinitely to train national army with costs to Turkmenistan.

Turkey threatens to introduce quota system for oil tankers in Bosporus strait as part of ongoing petroleum export struggle affecting all CIS oil.

October   Russian Vice Premier Aleksandr Shokhin attacks membership of CIS states in ECO, calling on them to choose between closer integration with Russia or with their southern neighbors.

Status of Russian troops in Georgia legalized. Border guards on Georgian-Turkish border. Georgia acquiesces to CIS membership.

November   Russia presents proposal for "peacekeeping" forces to Council on European Security and asks for funds to guard CIS borders.

New Russian military doctrine states, inter alia, that Russia might respond with nuclear arms to an attack on itself or its allies by a nonnuclear state allied to a nuclear one. This is regarded as applicable to Turkey in the case of Armenia or to Afghanistan or Pakistan in relation to Tajikistan.

Pir Gailani asserts that division of Afghanistan would threaten entire region.

United States urges Pakistan, under threat of repercussions, to expel Arab "Afghan" fighters.

Rabbani visit to Egypt results in agreement to return to Cairo any "Egyptian" fighters captured by the Kabul government. Kabul opposition declares this action illegal, since some among Arabs served the resistance for a decade.

December   Russian parliamentary elections favor far right politicians who favor restoration of old Soviet/tzarist borders. Presence of Soviet military along Central Asian and Transcaucasian borders support such policy direction.

Islamabad moves to control movement of goods across Afghan border directly rather than through Northwest Frontier Province.

In official Rabbani visit to Dushanbe he agrees on good neighborliness, economic and cultural cooperation, and specifically on sale of Afghan gas to Tajikistan.

Rabbani issues decree reversing communist land distribution.

1994

January 1   Dustam and longtime ideological opponent Hekmatyar, collude to make abortive attempt to seize presidential palace and other key Kabul installations. Rabbani declares jihad against communists and their allies. Dustam airplanes bomb Kabul for first time in civil war.

New refugee flow barred from Pakistan entry at Torkham, but humanitarian aid allowed to cross into Afghanistan.

Rabbani spokesman accuses Tashkent of meddling in Afghan politics through Dustam. Kabul claims that air raids on Afghan soil originate in Uzbekistan.

January 26 UN Security Council calls for immediate cease-fire. Fighting expands to Shi'a Wahdat party as it is attacked by Hekmatyar.

February   A Jirgah of the United Pushtun Tribes of Pakistan calls for return of Zahir Shah to restore stability.

OIC offers to "play a meaningful role" in a cease-fire.

UN appoints former Tunisian foreign minister Mahmud Mestiri to head political solution team in Kabul.

Pakistan raids Afghan embassy in Islamabad to free hostages taken for supplies.

Afghan mob attacks Pakistan embassy in Kabul to protest Pakistan road controls on food and supplies.

U.S. Agency for International Development (USAID) turns over Dog Mine Detection project to Afghans to administer.

March   Hekmatyar blocks UN food convoy to Kabul. UNHCR claims severe food shortages in Kabul.

Turkey offers Afghan students in Pakistan scholarships in Turkey for advanced education.

Tehran pledges help in reconstruction of Afghanistan.

Government forces enter Pul-i Khumri and target "little Moscow," an enclave of Isma'ili and Uzbek militia, and capture supply of fuel and arms.

April   Rabbani reiterates the legitimacy of his presidency through 1994 on basis of 1992 elections, which opponents claim were rigged.

May	UN envoy Mestiri visits Zahir Shah to urge role in caretaker government, which is opposed by Pakistan and Iran.
July	An Afghan working for BBC is abducted and shot in Kabul.
August	Ahmadzai tribal head demands safe passage for Najibullah from UN compound.

UN tries to convene a Loya Jirgah on Afghanistan.

Uzbek foreign minister accuses Mas'ud of responsibility for Afghan-Tajik border tension and says Uzbekistan is prepared to augment present 500-man force working with Russians on guarding the border.

Dustam delegation to Pakistan is headed by former Rabbani ally and fellow Islamist Sayyid Muhammad Musa Tawana, who defected from Rabbani over the legality of the Herat conference that confirmed him in the presidency.

Renewed fighting along Afghan-Tajik border results in Russian and Tajik deaths, but Kabul denies interference.

Fighting in Kabul continues.

September Pakistan reopens embassy in Kabul, closed since raided in February.

Mestiri closes second phase of Afghan negotiations without success.

Rabbani forces lose key city, Khenjan, to Dustam.

Pakistan plans on building a road through Afghanistan (via Kandahar, Herat) to facilitate trade with Central Asia, thus bypassing Kabul and fighting there.

Tajikistan calls on return of opposition for elections scheduled for November 6.

October First convoy of Pakistani trucks bound for Turkmenistan via western Afghanistan announced by Pakistani Trade Commission.

Baluchistan government wants Islamabad's assurance that Afghan refugees settled in Baluchistan will not be counted in census, thus skewing it against the Baluchi and in favor of Pushtuns.

In Jalalabad, Rabbani, Sayyaf, Khalis, and Muhammadi come up with formula for new elections.

Mas'ud pledges cooperation with Mestiri in efforts to form an interim government.

Dustam offers the area under his control as fully secure and safe for trade route between Pakistan and Central Asia.

Heads of state of Turkic-speaking CIS countries meet in Turkey for summit to reaffirm cultural and economic ties despite Russian warning to avoid "pan-Turkic" rhetoric.

At same meeting, CIS extends Russian peacekeeping mandate in Tajikistan to June 30, 1995.

Iran becomes Russia's largest arms buyer with major purchase of tanks and armored personnel carriers.

Iran and Russia oppose Azarbaijani oil deal in Caspian sea with largely Western consortia.

November Armed Afghan students, *taliban*, coming from Pakistan via Chaman, capture parts of Kandahar. Belonging to the group Mullah Tulabat, the students formed in protest when a mujahidin faction captured a trade convoy bound for Turkmenistan and Uzbekistan.

Taliban head north toward Kabul.

United States sends State Department representative to Afghanistan and Pakistan and to talks in Rome with Zahir Shah.

Report on Human Rights by UN envoy Ermacora states that Afghan situation is completely out of control because of lack of central government and division of country into four armed zones.

December   United States declares state of emergency in Kabul and allows USAID to provide emergency assistance. 200,000 refugees in Jalalabad.

UN General Assembly resolution passed requesting an immediate cease-fire, the collection of heavy weapons, the creation of a national security force, and the formation of a transitional government until free and fair elections can be held.

Talks in Tehran sponsored by the OIC among Afghan leaders for a peace program and interim government.

First two UN supply convoys from Pakistan arrive for Kabul relief, one for Rabbani one for Hekmatyar.

Bhutto meets with Hekmatyar in Pakistan and Rabbani at OIC meeting in Casablanca to explore peace proposals.

Rabbani extends his term in office for a third time, claiming as justification the lack of legal authority acceptable to all.

Taliban defeat local mujahidin governor and occupy Ghazni province.

International Committee of the Red Cross estimates 70,000 killed or wounded in fighting in 1994.

1995
January   Mestiri, in Kabul, hopes for an agreement to transfer power within ten days.

Yunis Khalis returns to Afghanistan from exile in Pakistan to live in Jalalabad.

Afghanistan protests to Tajikistan the violation of Afghan air space and the bombing of Afghan villages in Badakhshan province.

February   Taliban occupy Wardak province.

Hekmatyar ousted from headquarters by Taliban forces, retreats to Sarobi on the border of Kabul and Nangarhar provinces.

Mas'ud forces attack Wahdat forces in Kabul, breaking the informal cease-fire.

Wahdat leader Ali Mazari threatens to launch SCUD missiles against Rabbani forces. Wahdat forces had turned over weapons to Taliban in return for promises to defend civilians.

March   Taliban retreat from Kabul and Charasyab under attack by government forces.

Mazari killed while under arrest by Taliban.

Rabbani spokesman says he will not resign on March 21 as promised in the Mestiri peace plan.

April   Mestiri warns that if Rabbani does not step down, the UN members will not recognize him.

Taliban launch attack on Herat.

Kabul University reopens.

May   Tajik president Imomali Rahmonov and opposition Islamist leaders
             Sayyid Abdullah Nuri and Mir Akbar Turajonzadah meet in Kabul
             following breakdown of talks in Moscow. Agree to three-month ex-
             tension of cease-fire, but Rahmonov refuses establishment of inter-
             nationally controlled safe haven for Tajik refugees returning from
             Afghanistan.

             India reopens embassy in Kabul.

June   Afghanistan accuses envoy Mestiri at UN of supporting the Taliban.

July   Zahir Shah envoy, Abdul Wali, receives official welcome in Pakistan
             and meets with many Pakistani and Afghan leaders. Visit is
             protested by Rabbani government.

             Saudi Arabian delegation proposes conference of all Afghan provincial
             leaders in Jidda to form three-to-five-year interim government under
             auspices of UN and OIC.

September   Taliban capture Herat.

             Kabul mob attacks Pakistani embassy, blaming Pakistan for support of
             Taliban and the fall of Herat.

             Taliban advance to the outskirts of Kabul.

October   United States sends envoy to Jalalabad and Mazar-i-Sharif, but envoy is
             unable to enter Kabul because of Taliban siege. Declares support for
             UN efforts.

November   Pakistan and Iran declare support for broad-based national govern-
             ment. Iran actively attempting to find means of bringing together
             various factions through efforts of Deputy Foreign Minister
             Ala'uddin Borujerdi.

December   Government attack drives Taliban from Kabul vicinity.

1996

April   United States sends envoy back for Afghan/Pakistan visit. States that
             Hekmatyar has been marginalized by defeat at hands of Taliban.

May   First Afghan delegation in eight months visits Pakistan. Kabul an-
             nounces plan to rebuild ties. Rabbani and Hekmatyar sign agree-
             ment to end hostilities.

             Mestiri resigns and is replaced by German Norbert Holl as UN envoy.

June   U.S. Senator Hank Brown organizes conference on Afghanistan in
             Washington. Brown proposes return of king, but Rabbani delega-
             tion objects.

             Hekmatyar enters Kabul and is made prime minister.

August   Senator Brown visits Kabul, Hekmatyar will not receive him, accusing
             United States of trying to organize an anti-Islamic conspiracy.

September   Taliban take Jalalabad and the provinces of Nangarhar, Laghman, and
             Kunar.

             After defeating Hekmatyar forces at Sarobi and Pul-i Charkhi, Taliban
             forces capture Kabul.

             Najibullah taken from UN compound and hanged by Taliban.

	UN envoy Holl arrives in Kabul and states that Taliban are willing to work with the UN for peace.
October	CIS convenes emergency meeting under the 1992 CIS security treaty in Almaty to consider the danger from Afghan events. They agree to watch the situation and strengthen defenses.

UN envoy Holl arrives in Kabul and states that Taliban are willing to work with the UN for peace.

October CIS convenes emergency meeting under the 1992 CIS security treaty in Almaty to consider the danger from Afghan events. They agree to watch the situation and strengthen defenses.

Turkmen President Niyazov, not at Almaty meeting, announces that he has no such concerns about Afghans.

Mas'ud, Dustam, Wahdat representative, and Russian consul meet outside Mazar-i-Sharif to coordinate strategy against Taliban.

Pakistan and Uzbekistan consult on Afghan issue; discuss trade route via Mazar-i-Sharif, Herat, and Kandahar.

Talks in Mazar-i-Sharif between Dustam and the Taliban with Pakistan mediation.

Taliban forces advance to the foot of Salang Pass and into Panjshir valley but are driven back by combined Mas'ud-Dustam force.

November OIC suspends membership of Rabbani government but refuses to seat Taliban delegation.

UN General Assembly lets stand the representation of Afghanistan by the Rabbani government, although the Taliban have sent an alternative delegation.

December At UN debate Russian representative calls Afghan situation a threat to regional stability and the CIS. United States declares that a representative government of all the country's people is needed.

Former president Karmal dies of cancer in Moscow. He is buried in Mazar-i-Sharif.

At UN debate Russian representative calls Afghan situation a threat to regional stability and the CIS. United States states need for a representative government of all the country's people.

1997

January In attack north of Kabul, Taliban regain the Bagram airbase, Charikar, and Jabal as-Siraj, Mas'ud's headquarters. Mas'ud and Dustam forces defeated in counter attack with the loss of 100 tanks.

Planes of Dustam's air force bomb Kabul.

Haji Abdul Qadir, ousted governor of Ningrahar, presides at meeting in Peshawar which decides to restore the Shura of the three eastern provinces headed by Abdul Qadir.

Taliban capture two districts from Hizb-i Wahdat forces in Gorband valley, leading to Shibar Pass on the road to Bamiyan.

UN Conference on aid to Afghanistan held in Ashkabad involving 200 organizations and countries. President Sappar Muradniyazov offers to mediate among Afghan factions, saying his country is completely neutral.

Peace talks under Pakistani auspices held in Islamabad between Taliban, Rabbani, Khalili, and Dustam representative, no substantial progress made.

Taliban delegation, headed by Mullah Wakil Ahmad, visiting the United States, meets with Assistant Secretary of State, Robin Raphel.

February   Nawaz Sharif sworn in as Pakistani Prime Minister.

Co-ed schools operate in Khost villages despite reports of limited opportunities for girls in Kabul.

Isma'ili leader Sayyid Jaffar Naderi prepares to evacuate Pul-i Khumri for Mazar-i Sharif in anticipation of Taliban advance.

March   In Ashkabad, ECO holds its first summit since the fall of Kabul to the Taliban. Rabbani represents Afghanistan.

NGOs face conflicting Taliban actions with regard to female medical workers.

Photography and filming of living objects forbidden by Taliban foreign ministry.

Saudi billionaire Osama bin Laden said to bankroll southern Afghanistan development projects in irrigation and road construction.

Germans pledge $2 million for demining in Afghanistan.

UN offers one can of cooking oil for each month that a refugee Afghan girl in Iran attends school.

Taliban offer amnesty on occasion of Nowruz but ban celebration, a ban ignored widely.

Taliban head Mullah Omar asked Osama bin Laden to drop opposition to Saudi monarchy.

Taliban state willingness to award natural gas pipeline contract to whomever gives greater concessions to Afghanistan. Unocal and Bridas (Argentina) show interest.

April   Tajik refugees from the north flee to Kabul as Taliban aim to reduce local support for Mas'ud as fighting continues. Tajik refugees in Kabul may exceed 140,000.

Taliban state they have no desire to spread Taliban values beyond Afghan borders.

Taliban state that Osama bin Laden will remain in Afghanistan despite U.S./Saudi warrants but will not be allowed to engage in terrorism from Afghan soil.

At UN, Pakistan asked the Security Council to listen to Taliban to get more balanced picture of the situation in Afghanistan.

May   Bridas International will begin construction of a multi-billion dollar gas pipeline crossing war-torn Afghanistan in 1998. The pipeline will run through Taliban controlled territory west of Herat and eastward through Baluchistan to a possible new port west of Gwadar. A consortium of U.S. and Saudi companies will fund.

Revolt of General Abdul Malik, second in command to General Dustam, forces Dustam to flee to Uzbekistan, later to Turkey. Abdul Malik invites Taliban into northern provinces where they occupy territory up to Mazar-i Sharif.

Taliban said to capture documents in Mazar-i Sharif of the Shura-ye Nazar (Mas'ud's Council of the North) which contain plans to drive all Pushtuns from the north.

Commander of Dustam's air force and two fellow pilots defect to Taliban.

Taliban advance through Salang Tunnel, occupying Pul-i Khumri, the headquarters of Isma'ili leader.

Clashes erupt between Taliban forces and Hizb-i Wahdat in Mazar-i Sharif. Taliban forced into extensive retreat in northern provinces as General Abdul Malik turns against them.

Heavy fighting in Charikar as Taliban retreat south of the Salang Pass.

June   Ismail Khan, governor of Herat, betrayed, is captured and imprisoned by Taliban.

Kazakh/China pipeline agreement signed for Aqtobe oil fields.

1998

Osama bin Laden is suspected in U.S. embassy bombing in Kenya and Tanzania.

United States imposes sanctions on Pakistan for nuclear weapons testing.

UNOCAL pulls out of Afghan pipeline project.

Pakistan's Nawaz Sharif tries to expand powers by suppressing journalism and introduces military courts to try "terrorists" in bid to expand Islamic law as interpreted by the state.

June   Taliban order closing of 100 NGO-funded home schools for girls.

August   U.S. air strike in Afghanistan to shut down terrorist training sites.

Pakistan accused in Uzbek and Tajik capitals of giving aid to Taliban and extremists.

September Taliban prepare civilians for war with Iran.

October   Trainload of arms from Iran for Northern Alliance interdicted in Kirghizstan.

1999

Drought cycle begins affecting Iran, Afghanistan, and Central Asia.

January   Taliban government recognizes Chechnya.

February Islamic bomb attack in Tashkent results in crackdown on all Uzbek opposition.

Iran holds first local elections since the formation of the Islamic Republic.

Taliban report bin Laden missing.

April   UN-sponsored peace talks between Taliban and Northern Alliance break down.

Taliban face increased U.S. criticism on the position of women.

July   Northern Alliance and Taliban meet in Tashkent.

August   Fighting in north intensifies. Tajiks reinforce border.

Afghan refugees mass in Badakhshan.

September Armed Chechens arrested in Almaty.

Tashkent establishes Tashkent Islamic University to combat fanaticism.

October   Taliban warn Tajikistan about new arms-supply route for Northern Alliance.

Russia warns Turkmenistan against transit of Afghan mercenaries to the Caucasus.

United Nations Security Council (UNSC) passes resolution on terrorism and extradition of bin Laden.

November	Trans-Caspian Gas Pipeline letter of intent signed in Istanbul for Turkmenistan gas.
	Kyrgyzstan accuses OSCE of excessive focus on human rights in face of terrorism.
	Rabia Qadir's arrest in Xinjiang brings Uighur women to protest at Chinese embassy in Almaty.
December	Hijacking of Indian airplane creates protracted problems.
2000	
	Drought conditions reduce Afghan farmers' crops.
January	Muslim Religious Board in Kyrgyz village demand removal of Christian converts.
	Russia's Foreign Minister protests U.S. bombing of Afghanistan.
	Pushtun tribes challenge Taliban.
	Chechens open Kabul embassy.
	Iran sends food aid to Afghans.
	Denmark steps in to help with Afghan mine removal.
March	Ismail Khan, warlord of Herat, escapes Taliban prison for Iran.
April	Iran/Taliban sign drug-control accord.
June	Mullah Omar seeks international aid to substitute for poppy crop.
August	China and Kazakhstan discuss 2 million Chinese Kazakhs' emigration west.
	Border incursions from Afghanistan into Tajikistan lead to fighting in Ferghana.
September	Russian border guards assure no entry to refugees from Taliban.
	United States lists Islamic Movement of Uzbekistan as a terrorist organization.
October	Bombing of USS *Cole* in Yemeni port linked to Osama bin Laden and al-Qaeda.
	Bomb blast at Korean Christian Mission kills seven in Dushanbe.
	Iran's Foreign Minister discusses Iran/Tajik TV and radio cooperation in Dushanbe.
November	Kazakhstan denies it has offered U.S. use of airbases to strike Afghanistan.
	Tehran and Ashgabat negotiate gas sales to Iran.
	United States seeks alliance with Moscow for raid on bin Laden.
December	United States wins UN support for tough sanctions against Taliban.
	Turkmen president says ultimatums and isolation of Afghanistan increase suffering.
	Afghan refugees at Tajik border die of starvation and cold, says UNHCR.
	Tajikistan refuses entry to Afghan refugees. Many killed by Tajik artillery.
	Uzbekistan lays mines along border with Tajikistan and Kyrgyzstan.
	United States joins Iran, Italy, and Germany in Geneva to work on a Loya Jirga initiative.
	President Rabbani meets with Taliban in Ashgabat with UN representative.
	Tehran and Moscow discuss regional security issues (Chechnya, Afghanistan, Central Asia).
	Two churches bombed in Dushanbe.

2001

Drought threatens famine in much of Afghan countryside.

U.S. State Department report labels Iran the world's "most active state-sponsor of terrorism."

Ismail Khan returns to Herat with Iranian backing to oppose Taliban.

Uzbekistan closes 90 percent of country's mosques.

January   Tajikistan flies 250 members of Islamic Movement of Uzbekistan to Afghanistan.

Anthrax infects 145 people who ate tainted meat in southern Kyrgyzstan.

February   Taliban order destruction of all statuary. Turkmenistan seals up last Baptist church.

Taliban and Northern Alliance clash near Tajik border.

March   Uzbekistan suspends natural gas supply to Kyrgyzstan in payment dispute.

Bamian Buddhas are destroyed.

Dushanbe sentences members of Hizb ut-Tahrir Islamist party.

Afghanistan's President Rabbani holds talks with Uzbek officials in Tashkent.

June   Russia's President Vladimir Putin calls for cooperation among Shanghai Forum members to fight extremism and terrorism in Central Asia.

Kazakhstan's Uighur minority worries that Uzbekistan will join Shanghai Forum.

Washington and Tashkent sign treaty to eliminate Soviet-era chemical and biological weapons stored in Uzbekistan.

Kyrgyzstan continues mine removal along Uzbek border.

Turkmenistan acquiesces to export gas via Kazakhstan to Russia.

Uzbekistan cuts natural gas to Tajikistan for nonpayment.

July   Pakistan and India summit about cross-border terrorism and Kashmir issues ends.

Moscow and Beijing sign twenty-year friendship treaty despite Central Asia worries.

Iran's President Khatami begins second term despite clerical conservatives.

United States and Kazakhstan complete $40 million project for storage of nuclear reactor fuel.

U.S. Congress members' letter urges Baku/Ceylan pipeline route through Armenia.

August   Pakistan military government postpones general elections to return civilian rule.

Caspian Pipeline Consortium completes negotiations with Russian State Customs Committee to export Kazakh crude.

September Pushtuns of NWFP of Pakistan demand implementation of Islamic law as understood in Pathan tradition.

9   Ahmad Shah Mas'ud is assassinated in suspected al-Qaeda suicide mission.

11   Arab hijackers try to fly four U.S. planes into American landmarks. They succeed in three cases. The fourth airplane crashes in Pennsylvania.

12	United States demands extradition of bin Laden from Afghanistan.
14	Council of religious leaders meets to discuss U.S. demand.
15	Mullah Omar requests that bin Laden leave Afghanistan.
17	Islamabad fundamentalist Muslim rally calls Pakistani cooperation with United States traitorous.
	Afghan refugees in Iran offer to field large force against Pushtun Taliban.
20	President George Bush declares war on terrorist groups operating globally; sends ultimatum to Taliban to hand over bin Laden.
22	United Arab Republic (UAR) cuts ties to Taliban government.
25	Saudi Arabia cuts ties with Taliban.
26	NATO is shown some U.S. evidence against bin Laden.
	United States lifts sanctions on Pakistan imposed due to nuclear weapons testing.
29	United States launches military strike on Afghanistan.

October

1	Expatriate Taliban opposition meets in Rome with ex-king for "supreme council."
7	United States and allies commence bombing of Taliban positions in Afghanistan.
17	United States begins bombing Kabul perimeters.
	Northern Alliance declares bar on Taliban role in any future coalition.
28	Murder of sixteen Christian worshippers at church in Pakistan.
	Rabbani meets with Russia's President Putin.
	Abdul Haq is captured and hanged by Taliban.
	United States places $25 million bounty on bin Laden's head.

November

	Fall of Kunduz; base of Uzbek Islamist opposition leader, Juma Namangani, allied with Taliban.
2–5	Tablighi Jamaat (Missionary Society) draws large peaceful crowds in Lahore for study and contemplation.
6	The UN's Lakhdar Brahimi in Tehran visit endorses a "broad-based government" of all ethnic groups.
11	New York meeting of "six plus two" (United States/Russia and Afghanistan's six neighbors).
13	Northern Alliance forces march into Kabul.
19	Eight Western aid workers, held by Taliban since August, are freed in Ghazni.
22	Kunduz falls, foreigner Taliban supporters taken prisoner.
26	Northern Alliance and four exile groups agree to meet in Bonn under UN auspices.
	Northern Afghanistan is cleared of major Taliban and al-Qaeda.
	U.S. Marines land in Kandahar.
27	Four factions at Bonn agree to outline of new government.

Twenty-one countries meet in Washington to discuss Afghanistan economic reconstruction.

December

14–19   Security-force-contributing nations meet in London.

17   Karzai meets with Afghan ex-king to discuss Loya Jirgah for June 2002.

United States concentrates bombing on Tora Bora.

22   Interim government headed by Karzai establishes itself in Kabul.

30   American bomb hits village, killing one hundred people, in search for al-Qaeda.

Notes

Chapter One

1. René Dollot, *L'afghanistan: histoire, description, moeurs et coutumes, folklore, fouilles* (Paris: Payot, 1937), p. 86.

2. Nancy Dupree has written poignantly of the brave but futile efforts of some Afghan officials who have tried to save the national heritage as represented in the Kabul Museum from the depredations of war and pillage, apparently encouraged by private (foreign) collectors. "Museum Under Siege," *Archaeology*, vol. 49, no. 2 (March/April 1996), pp. 42–52.

3. *New York Times*, February 5, 1996, pp. 1, 3.

4. Richard N. Frye, *Iran* (New York: Henry Holt and Company, 1953), p. 56.

5. Graham B. Kerr, *Demographic Research in Afghanistan: A National Survey of the Settled Population* (New York: The Asia Society, Afghanistan Council, Occasional Paper No. 13, 1977).

6. *The Tajik Encyclopedia*, published in 1978 and typical of Soviet works, confirms this figure. "Afghanistan," *Ensiklopediya-i Soveti-i Tojik* (Dushanbe, 1978), vol. 1, p. 903.

7. *Agricultural Survey Of Afghanistan, 1992–93: Seventeenth Report* (Swedish Committee for Afghanistan, December 1993), p. iv.

8. "Pakistan" does not follow this pattern since it means "the land of the clean," that is, Islamically clean. No ethnic group in Pakistan was strong enough or big enough at the country's inception in 1947 to press its claims for titularity as in the other cases. Perhaps more important, Pakistan was formed in opposition to the dominant Hinduism of India, and its Islamic nature is stressed in its name.

9. Louis Dupree, *Afghanistan* (Princeton: Princeton University Press, 1973), p. 59.

10. Sir Olaf Caroe, *The Pathans* (New York: St. Martin's Press, 1958), pp. xiv–xv.

11. As if three terms for the same ethnic group were not enough, a new spelling of Pukhtu has appeared in some linguistic and anthropological work, as in Benedicta Grima's *The Performance of Emotion Among Paxtun Women* (Austin: University of Texas Press, 1992).

12. Kipling's *Gunga Din*, well known from its movie version starring Cary Grant, depicts the Pushtun hill tribes, the persistent rebels against British rule, as cruel, vengeful, and deceitful, while the Indians are portrayed as loyal and docile. Such characterization of the Pathans by Indians runs through other fiction from and about the region as well. The same characterization of the Pushtun may be found in the *Flashman* series by Fraser, especially in *Flashman*.

13. Caroe, *The Pathans*, p. 238.

14. Ken Follet's *Lie Down with Lions* (New York: William Morrow, 1986) is an example.

15. Caroe considers the legend and the manuscript that lends it backing as probable fabrication by courtiers of the Moghuls in Delhi who were poking fun at the rough Afghan soldiers. *The Pathans*, p. 449, n4.

16. For a detailed discussion of ethnolinguistic politics during the early PDPA rule, see Eden Naby, "The Ethnic Factor in Soviet Afghan Relations," *Asian Survey*, vol. 20, no. 3 (1980).

17. Studies of the Hazaras have been conducted mainly by anthropologists such as Robert L. Canfield, who has published numerous articles and a monograph. See especially his *Faction and Conversion in a Plural Society: Religious Alignments in the Hindu Kush* (Ann Arbor: University of Michigan Press, 1973).

18. This system of heating is called *sandali* in Afghanistan but *kursi* in Iran. Both words are related to the word for chair but appear to operate in opposite ways in the two areas; i.e., *kursi* or *chowki* means chair in Afghanistan.

19. For a superb presentation of the varieties of Afghan domiciles, see Albert Szabo and Thomas J. Barfield, *Afghanistan: An Atlas of Indigenous Domestic Architecture* (Austin: University of Texas Press, 1991).

20. For a theoretical and practical discussion of worldview in Afghanistan and its region presented from the perspective of global confrontation between tradition and modernization, see Cyrus Black et al., *The Modernization of Inner Asia* (Armonk, N.Y.: M. E. Sharpe, 1991).

21. Anwar-ul-Haq Ahady, "The Decline of the Pashtuns in Afghanistan," *Asian Survey*, vol. 35, no. 7 (July 1995), pp. 620–632.

Chapter Two

1. For example, the massive stone stupa near Samangan in local lore is called *Takht-e Suleiman*, meaning "the throne of Solomon," a common term used in the region for inexplicably large or impressive structures of which the historical origins are unknown. Solomon (Suleiman) is admired in Koranic verses for his feats.

2. See Said Amir Arjomand, *The Shadow Of God and the Hidden Imam* (Chicago: University of Chicago Press, 1984), p. 191.

3. Cf. Ludwig W. Adamec, "Mir Wais Khan Hotaki," in *Historical Dictionary Of Afghanistan* (Metuchen, N.J.: Scarecrow Press, 1991), p. 160.

4. See Ganda Singh, *Ahmad Shah Durrani: Founder Of Modern Afghanistan* (Bombay: Asia Publishing House, 1959), p. 33.

5. Ira M. Lapidus, "Tribes and State Formation in Islamic History," *Tribes and State Formation in the Middle East*, ed. Philip S. Khoury and Joseph Kostiner (Berkeley: University of California Press, 1992), pp. 25–47.

6. Lecture by Ambassador Sajjad Hyder to the Asian Study Group, Islamabad, April 1983, from personal notes of the author (RHM).

7. For an elaboration on problems of transit and trade, see the authors' article, "Afghanistan and Central Asia: Mirrors and Models," *Asian Survey*, vol. 35, no.7 (July 1995), p. 620.

8. Interview of the author (RHM) with Professor Sardar Aziz Na'im (a member of the royal family and second cousin of King Zahir Shah) and Professor Hamidullah (a member of the drafting commission for the 1964 Constitution), Kabul, February 1970.

9. Interview of the author (RHM) with Dr. Zabiullah Mujaddidi, deputy leader of Jabha-i Najat-i Milli Afghanistan (National Liberation Front of Afghanistan), Peshawar, November 1988.

10. Quoted in Vartan Gregorian, *The Emergence of Modern Afghanistan* (Stanford: Stanford University Press, 1969), p. 112.

11. Some recent studies of the Great Game include Peter Hopkirk, *The Great Game: On Secret Service in High Asia* (Oxford: Oxford University Press, 1990), and Patrick A. Macrory, *The Fierce Pawns* (Philadelphia: J. B. Lippincott, 1966). George Macdonald Fraser uses the Great Game as background for his two Flashman novels: *Flashman* (New York: NAL/Dutton-Plume Books, 1984 [reprint]) and *Flashman at the Charge* (New York: NAL/Dutton-Plume Books, 1986 [reprint]).

12. Hasan Kawun Kakar, in *Government and Society in Afghanistan: The Reign of Amir Abd al-Rahman Khan* (Austin: University of Texas Press, 1977), gives a remarkably rich and detailed account of this ruler's effects on Afghan history.

13. Ibid., p. 16.

14. Hélène Carrère D'Encausse, *Islam and the Russian Empire: Reform and Revolution in Central Asia* (Berkeley: University of California Press, 1988 [translated from the original work in French of 1966]), p. 102.

15. See Hasan K. Kakar, "The Pacification of the Hazaras," Afghanistan Council of the Asia Society, Occasional Paper No. 4 (New York, Spring 1973).

16. For an especially readable and detailed account of Amanullah, his reforms, and the role of the British Empire in Afghan affairs in this period, see Rhea Talley Stewart, *Fire in Afghanistan, 1914–1929: Faith, Hope, and the British Empire* (New York: Doubleday, 1973).

17. Gregorian, *The Emergence of Modern Afghanistan*, p. 277.

18. John C. Griffiths, *Afghanistan* (New York: Frederick A. Praeger, 1967), p. 123.

19. Griffiths estimates military expenditures at about 30 percent in the mid-1960s. *Afghanistan*, p. 132.

20. M. Siddieq Noorzoy, "Alternative Economic Systems for Afghanistan," *International Journal of Middle East Studies* 15 (1983), pp. 26–27.

21. Margaret Mills, in her studies of storytelling among women of Herat, demonstrates how current events enter storytelling and are preserved for posterity. They also inform the political perceptions of people.

22. Quoted in Gregorian, *The Emergence of Modern Afghanistan*, p. 119.

23. Louis Dupree cites Prime Minister Da'ud's threat to use the military to enforce tax collection in Kandahar, but this was a limited operation that threatened but did not harm. See his *Afghanistan*, p. 536.

Chapter Three

1. Interview with the author (RHM), Peshawar, November 1988.

2. Afghan communists became quite active in the early period of the Tajik Soviet Socialist Republic when the number of local people who were politically correct

enough to participate in government was limited. The community in Hissar appears not to have been studied. The community in Uzbekistan is limited to Bukhara and again is little known.

3. Former U.S. ambassador Robert G. Neumann differentiated between the traditional British and American Cold War strategic roles in Afghanistan: "The U.S. policy toward Afghanistan—with which I went to Afghanistan in 1969—was set in 1955 when then Secretary of State Dulles decided not to grant, and I think on very sound grounds, military assistance to Afghanistan. . . . the U.S. place was not identical with the place Britain occupied. Nor did we have the British obligation of India, which Britain had exercised until India's and Pakistan's independence." Ralph H. Magnus, ed. *Afghan Alternatives: Issues, Options, and Policies* (New Brunswick: Transaction, 1985), p. 163.

4. Leon B. Poullada, "Afghanistan and the United States: The Crucial Years," *Middle East Journal,* vol. 35, no. 1 (Spring 1981), p. 183.

5. The best source regarding President Da'ud's attempted foreign policy reorientation is Abdul Samad Ghaus, who was deputy foreign minister at the time. See his *The Fall of Afghanistan: An Insider's Account* (Washington, D.C.: Pergamon-Brassey's, 1988).

6. Harold S. Sprout, "Geography: Political Geography," *International Encyclopedia of the Social Sciences,* vol. 6 (New York, Macmillan and The Free Press, 1968), p. 121.

7. Ray S. Cline, *World Power Assessment: A Calculus of Strategic Drift* (Boulder: Westview Press, 1975), p. 4.

8. Alvin J. Cottrell, "The Soviet Navy in the Indian Ocean," in *The Persian Gulf in International Politics,* ed. Abbas Amirie (Tehran: Institute for International Political and Economic Studies, 1975), pp. 111–130.

9. Interview with the author (RHM), Dr. Rawan A. G. Farhadi, Monterey, California, April 1986. For an overall evaluation of the Brezhnev plan, see Golam S. Choudhury, *Brezhnev's Collective Security Plan for Asia* (Washington, D.C., Georgetown Center for Strategic and International Studies, June 1976). The author quotes Afghanistan's prime minister, Muhammad Musa Shafiq, in 1973 as stating, "It is not in Afghanistan's interest to be tied to a Soviet system that may seem to threaten China" (p. 31).

10. George Lenczowski, *Middle East Oil in a Revolutionary Age* (Washington, D.C.: American Enterprise Institute, 1976).

11. For Khrushchev's views on coexistence, see George Lenczowski, *Soviet Advance in the Middle East* (Washington, D.C.: American Enterprise Institute, 1971), pp. 13–22.

12. Richard S. Newell, "Afghanistan: The Dangers of Cold War Generosity," *Middle East Journal,* vol. 23, no. 2 (Spring 1969), pp. 168–175. See also Louis Dupree, *Afghanistan* (Princeton: Princeton University Press, 1980), pp. 514–522, and Marvin Brandt, "Recent Economic Development," in *Afghanistan into the 1970s* (New York: Praeger Special Studies in International Development and Economics, 1974).

13. Interview with the author (RHM), Brigadier (Ret.) Noor A. Husain, Islamabad, December 1980.

14. U.S. Ambassador Theodore L. Eliot Jr., when he returned to Washington after the coup of 1978 to become the inspector general of the foreign service, was unable, despite repeated attempts, to obtain an interview with the secretary of state to

elaborate on his reported views on the communist coup. After-dinner speech by Ambassador Eliot, then president of the Fletcher School of Law and Diplomacy, Tufts University, October 1986.

15. Personal observation of the author (RHM), August 1992.

16. The author (EN), in traveling from Xinjiang to Islamabad in July 1986, observed the shipment of arms and heard a considerable amount about training camps.

17. The Kandahar airport, built on a grand scale to accommodate international air traffic between Europe and points east of Afghanistan, never served this purpose. Afghan officials claimed that the Americans were happy enough to extend the loans that paid for their personnel to build the project, but succumbed to regional demands to make other places the transit points for air traffic, thus cheating the Afghans of the benefits of servicing lucrative air travel. Conveyed to the author (EN) by Ambassador Abdul Rahman Pazhwak, September 1971.

18. Nikki R. Keddie, *Sayyid Jamal ad-Din "al-Afghani": A Political Biography* (Berkeley: University of California Press, 1972). Al-Afghani's tomb is located on the campus of Kabul University, as his remains were moved from Istanbul, where he had died.

19. Indian building and trade ventures in Central Asia (Tashkent, Samarkand, and Bukhara in particular) languished for several years, then were superseded by Pakistani projects, especially in air transport, construction and commercial sales.

20. *Sharq Yulduzi*, vol. 42 (Tashkent, 1991), pp. 287–291.

Chapter Four

1. David Busby Edwards, "The Evolution of Shi'i Political Dissent in Afghanistan," in *Shi'ism and Social Protest*, ed. Juan R. J. Cole and Nikki R. Keddie (New Haven: Yale University Press, 1986), p. 201.

2. It is ironic that in both what became Soviet Central Asia and in Afghanistan, the knowledge of the structure of traditional Islam has to be reconstructed from scattered sources and from memory, since its premodern and even modern history has not been studied.

3. Mohammad Hashim Kamali, *Law in Afghanistan: A Study of the Constitutions, Matrimonial Law, and the Judiciary* (Leiden: E. J. Brill, 1985), pp. 53–54.

4. Alexandre Bennigsen and Chantal Lemercier Quelquejay, *Islam in the Soviet Union* (London: Pall Mall Press, 1967).

5. *Afghanistan: A Demographic Profile*, January 1988, U.S. Bureau of the Census.

6. The teaching of Persian poetry at the expense of local languages accounts for the many centers of Persian literature and poetry in the east and the knowledge of classical Persian among the cultured elites of the generations in power prior to World War II. This knowledge of Persian has rarely translated into either a proclivity toward Shi'ism or an appreciation of Iran as a political entity. The classical literature of Iran predates the adoption of Shi'ism as the state religion, and most of the admired classical writers were Sunni. Since the Persian poetry of Iran declined during the sixteenth and seventeenth centuries and as it gradually revived it moved away from the successful production of poetry along classical lines, attempts to relate the Persian/Dari/Tajiki cultures of Iran, Afghanistan, and Tajikistan usually re-

sult in a fall back to the classical period, and a lack of mutual appreciation of literature since then.

7. Hasan Kawun Kakar, *Government and Society in Afghanistan: The Reign of Amir Abd al-Rahman Khan* (Austin: University of Texas Press, 1979), p. 162.

8. *Afghanistan Forum,* vol. xxi, no. 3 (1993), p. 3.

9. Charles Lindholm, *Generosity and Jealousy: The Swat Pukhtun of Northern Pakistan* (New York: Columbia University Press, 1982).

10. Here is how the recorded passage from one set of the Pushtunwali reads: "To pardon an offense on the intercession of a woman of the offender's lineage, a Sayyid or a mullah. (An exception is made in the case of murder; only blood-money can erase this crime.)" Louis Dupree, "Tribal Warfare in Afghanistan and Pakistan," *Islam in Tribal Societies: From the Atlas to the Indus,* ed. Akbar S. Ahmed and David M. Hart (London: Routledge & Kegan Paul, 1984), p. 282.

11. Kakar, *Government and Society in Afghanistan,* p. 167.

12. Ibid., p. 53.

13. Olivier Roy, *Islam and the Resistance in Afghanistan* (New York: Cambridge University Press, 1990), pp. 155–156.

14. Ibid., pp. 95–97.

15. The major anthropological study of Hazara Shi'ism is Robert LeRoy Canfield, *Faction and Conversion in a Plural Society: Religious Alignments in the Hindu Kush* (Anthropological papers, Museum of Anthropology, University of Michigan, No. 50; Ann Arbor: University of Michigan, 1973).

16. Louis Dupree, *Afghanistan* (Princeton: Princeton University Press, 1973), pp. 58–64.

17. Edwards points this out in the case of Shi'a resistance leader Sayyid Isma'il Balkhi (1919–1968) in "The Evolution of Shi'i Political Dissent in Afghanistan," p. 214. Other important Shi'a leaders educated in Najaf are Sayyid Ali Beheshti, head of the Hazara resistance umbrella group Shura-i Inqilab-i Ittefaq-i Islami-i Afghanistan (Revolutionary Council of the Islamic Union of Afghanistan), and Shaykh Asif Muhsini, head of Harakat-i Inqilab-i Islami Afghanistan (Revolutionary Islamic Movement of Afghanistan). During the 1980s the latter worked with the Peshawar resistance groups rather than the Shi'a groups based in Iran.

18. Pierre Centlivres discusses the issue of Farsiwan identity within the Dari (Persian) speaking setting of northern Afghanistan, comparing prior identification by outsiders of this group and self-identity in particular. "Groupes ethniques: de l'hétérogénéité d'un concept aux ambiguités de la représentation: l'exemple afghan," *Beitrage Zur Kulturgeographie Des Islamischen Orients* (Marburg/Lahn, 1979), p. 29.

19. Miramnameh-yi Sazman-e Nasr-r Afghanistan, no. 6 (Tehran: AZ intisharat-i Balkhi, 1361/19??), p.16. Nasr publications appear in 10,000 copies during this period and are clearly published in Tehran.

20. Roy, *Islam and Resistance in Afghanistan,* pp. 141–145.

21. For a comprehensive treatment of the history of the Nizari Isma'ilis in particular, see Farhad Daftary, *The Isma'ilis: Their History and Doctrines* (New York: Cambridge University Press, 1990). Daftary unfortunately identifies the Pamiri languages as dialects of Tajik when in fact they are dialects of Iranian languages. Tajik is merely a dialect of Persian, which is one of the major languages in the Iranian language family together with Pushtu, Kurdish, Baluchi, and Osset.

22. Afghan Isma'ili leaders, working in cooperation with the communist governments in Kabul, found easy access to Isma'ilis in Dushanbe, whose origins are
mainly Pamiri. Tajikistan's Isma'ilis were prevented as of 1927 from making the annual tithing to the Agha Khan, but since the breakdown of the Soviet Union they
have reestablished contact with his central offices in Europe. Under his auspices, the
Tajik Pamiri cultural and medical institutions have begun to develop since 1992,
with a base in Khorog, Tajikistan.

23. Adamec, *Historical Dictionary of Afghanistan* (Metuchen, N.J.: Scarecrow
Press, 1991), pp. 211–212.

24. Oral communication from a well-placed source to Ralph Magnus, Islamabad,
April 1992. The source further stated that on a subsequent visit to Pakistan, the
Agha Khan was received with less than the honor normally bestowed upon him as
"head of state."

25. M. Hasan Kakar, *Afghanistan: The Soviet Invasion and the Afghan Response, 1979–1982* (Berkeley: University of California Press, 1995), pp. 310–311.

26. Anthony Arnold, *Afghanistan's Two-Party Communism: Parcham And
Khalq* (Stanford: Hoover Institution Press, 1983), p. 181.

27. M. Nazif Shahrani, "Responses to the Saur Revolution in Badakhshan," in
Revolution and Rebellion in Afghanistan: Anthropological Perspectives, ed. M.
Nazif Shahrani and Robert L. Canfield (Berkeley: University of California Press,
1979), pp. 156–157, 167.

28. In a desperate attempt to fuse support for itself as a religiously legitimate
regime, Kabul attempted to employ the services of Soviet Central Asian leadership,
as in the issuing of joint declarations with the regime's Islamic puppet hierarchy.
The culmination of this effort came with the convening of the International Islamic
Meeting in Kabul on October 22, 1988, with the title "On the Call of the Prophet
Muhammad (PBUH) for Peace and Social Justice." (Booklet of proceedings distrib-
uted from Kabul, n.p., n.d.)

29. It is precisely because there existed no official caliph for all Sunni Muslims
that in places as far removed as the Uighur-inhabited Kashgar, under the ruler
Yaqub Beg (d. 1876), while the fledgling regime sought aid and support from the
Ottoman sultan, nonetheless, Yaqub Beg took the title *amir ul-mu'minin* (leader of
the faithful)—a title reserved for the caliph. Muslim students from Turkey studying
at U.S. universities, steeped in Ottoman lore, refused to believe that Yaqub Beg
could have taken this title and still accepted Ottoman protection. (Eden Naby's experience at the University of Wisconsin, Madison, Spring 1987.)

30. Hélène Carrère D'Encausse, *Islam and the Russian Empire: Reform and Revolution in Central Asia* (Berkeley: University of California Press, 1988), pp. 31–35.

31. Vartan Gregorian, *The Emergence of Modern Afghanistan* (Stanford: Stanford University Press, 1969), p. 135.

32. Mohammad Sadiq, *The Turkish Revolution and the Indian Freedom Movement* (Delhi: Macmillan India, 1983), pp. 73–100.

33. Kamali, *Law in Afghanistan,* p. 55.

34. Eden Naby, "The Changing Role of Islam as a Unifying Force in
Afghanistan," in *The State, Religion, and Ethnic Politics: Afghanistan, Iran, and
Pakistan,* ed. Ali Banuazizi and Myron Weiner (Syracuse: Syracuse University Press,
1986), p. 123 and n13.

35. *Afghanistan Forum* article on Hindu holidays during the 1980s.

36. In 1980, even Eden Naby, while traveling with Dan Rather and the CBS crew, was asked for advice by the mujahidin company that guided the group about how to adjudicate the case of an eloping couple who had been captured and were kept in a rude prison for want of anyone to hear the case.

37. The Swedish Committee for Afghanistan keeps close track of agricultural issues from land use to farm production, and its series *The Agricultural Survey of Afghanistan,* has differed from United Nations estimates. See *Repatriation and Rehabilitation of Afghan Refugees: National Summary, Sixteenth Report* (1993), part 4, p. v.

38. In its platform, the Tajik opposition insists on the inviolability of Central Asian borders, especially those between Tajikistan and Uzbekistan. Haji Akbar Turajonzada, one of the deputy leaders of the movement, insists on the border issue position mainly as a means of assuring Tashkent of the nonconfrontational views of the opposition. Nonetheless, the border issue with Afghanistan, given the many shared ethnic groups, is equally prone to redrawing (Oral presentation at the Council on Foreign Relations, New York, February 3, 1995, made by Turajonzada and Haji Muhammadsharif Himmatzada, another deputy leader). A workshop publication, *Border Issues of Soviet Successor States in Asia,* ed. Ralph H. Magnus (December 1992), for the Naval Postgraduate School, Monterey, California, deals with many border issues affecting Afghanistan.

39. Pierre Centlivres discusses the situational dependency of identity in northern Afghanistan in his article, "Identité et image de l'autre dans l'anthropologie populaire en Afghanistan," *Revue Européenne des Sciences Sociales et Cahiers Vilfredo Pareto,* vol. 18, no. 53 (1980), pp. 29–41.

40. According to 1979 estimates, the total urban population hovered at around 15 percent. Internal refugees may have swelled the proportion of urban dwellers, but the permanence of such urbanization is doubtful. See *Afghan Central Statistical Office, 1981: Preliminary results of the first Afghan Population Census,* Publication No. 1.

41. Eden Naby, "Ethnic Factors in Afghanistan's Future," in *The Tragedy Of Afghanistan: The Social, Cultural, and Political Impact of the Soviet Invasion,* ed. Bo Huldt and Erland Jansson (New York: Croom Helm, 1988), pp. 68–69.

42. Hajji Akbar Turajonzada, First Deputy Chairman of the Movement for the Islamic Revival of Tajikistan, has specifically identified his family as Qadiriyya and not Naqshbandiyya (Presentation at the Council on Foreign Relations, New York, February 3, 1995).

43. Interview of Sibghatullah Mujaddidi by author (EN) in his party headquarters in Peshawar, March 18, 1980.

44. Support for various groups from Saudi Arabia depended on who was in charge of various departments there. The Saudi Red Crescent Society, for example, at times supported one group, against official Saudi policy. When the society's head was removed from office, there was a return to the standard Saudi policy of supporting all mujahidin groups (Comments of Afghan administrator, M. Safi, working for the Saudi Red Crescent Society, made at Monterey conference, 1983).

45. Naby, "The Changing Role of Islam," pp. 141–142. Initially Gailani's party contributed some important figures to the attempted resistance government after the fall of Kabul. These have come from the ranks of former elites. The likelihood

that these figures or Gailani will survive in the radicalized Islamic state that appears
to be emerging in Afghanistan is doubtful.

46. Beatrice Manz's article on Andijan Rebellion appearing in the *Journal of Soviet Studies* in 1985. For a critique and discussion of academic work on various Islamic-based anti-Russian/Communist movements, see Eden Naby, "Concept of Jihad in Opposition to Communist Rule: Turkestan and Afghanistan," *Studies in
Comparative Communism,* vol. 19, no. 3/4 (Autumn/Winter 1986), pp. 287–300.

Chapter Five

1. Quoted in Jonathan Mirski, "The Party's Secrets," *New York Review of
Books,* vol. 40, no. 6 (March 2, 1993), p. 8.

2. Hasan Kakar, "Trends in Modern Afghan History," in *Afghanistan in the
1970s,* ed. Louis Dupree and Linette Albert (New York: Praeger, 1974), p. 26.

3. Leon S. Poullada covers this topic in his *Reform and Rebellion in Afghanistan,
1919–1929: King Amanullah's Failure to Modernize a Tribal Society* (Ithaca: Cor-
nell University Press, 1973).

4. Raja Anwar, *The Tragedy of Afghanistan: A First Hand Account* (London:
Verso, 1988), p. 27.

5. Interview of the author (RHM) with Mir Muhammad Siddiq Farhang (Washington, D.C., 1981).

6. Hasan Kawun Kakar, formerly a professor at Kabul University, has produced
definitive studies of Abdul Rahman as well as works on the post–World War II period and on his personal observations of 1980s Afghan politics.

7. Abdul Samad Ghaus, *The Fall of Afghanistan: An Insider's Account* (Washington, Pergamon-Brassey's, 1988), p. 194.

8. For a full discussion of Soviet attempts to disrupt the Afghan state, including
support of Marxists, see Thomas Hammond's *Red Flag Over Afghanistan* (Boulder:
Westview Press, 1984).

9. Raja Anwar, *The Tragedy of Afghanistan,* p. 88.

10. A particularly vivid story is told by Dilbar Rashidova, a resident of Tashkent,
whose father, a Samarkandi, departed for Afghanistan one day in 1938 and did not
return until a few years before his death in 1969. In all those years, his family received his salary from the KGB. He had settled in Nangarhar, with a Pushtun wife
and children, and regularly informed on conditions among Afghans. Interview by
author (EN), February 1994. Rawan Farhadi tells of Soviet Central Asian spies being almost routinely caught, imprisoned, and quietly repatriated to the Soviet
Union.

11. Raja Anwar, *The Tragedy of Afghanistan,* pp. 39–40.

12. Raja Anwar states that Mrs. Taraki told him in prison that Moscow had
arranged for the publication of Taraki's writings in the Soviet Union and distribution in Afghanistan, for which he would have been paid royalties. *The Tragedy Of
Afghanistan,* p. 44 n22; p. 258.

13. Interview of the author (RHM) with Sajjad Hyder, Monterey, California,
1987. Ambassador Hyder, at that time Pakistani envoy in Moscow, received a re-

port of this incident from a member of his staff whose relative was a staff aide to Zahir Shah.

14. Ralph H. Magnus, "Muhammad Zahir Khan, Former King of Afghanistan," *Middle East Journal,* vol. 30, no. 1 (Winter 1976), p. 79, and interview of the author (RHM) with an official of the Saudi Arabian embassy, Rome, 1975.

15. The meetings between Da'ud and the Parchamis took place mainly at Zaheshgah Hospital, of which he was a patron since it had been established during his government. It was also convenient to his home in Kabul.

16. Interview of the author (RHM) with Dr. Muhammad Anas, minister of education during the late 1950s, Kabul, 1970.

17. For a history of the evolution of the two branches of the PDPA, see Anthony Arnold's *Afghanistan's Two-Party Communism: Parcham and Khalq* (Stanford: Hoover Institution Press, 1983).

18. The speech of Da'ud at the Shalimar Gardens is described in Ghaus, *The Fall of Afghanistan,* p. 144. President Da'ud's private briefing by the Pakistanis was described in a 1988 interview with the author (RHM) by a Pakistani general who was present.

19. Ghaus, *The Fall of Afghanistan,* p. 179.

20. Interview of the author (RHM) with Dr. V. P. Vaidik of Jawaharlal Nehru University, in Madison, Wisconsin, 1986.

21. Eden Naby, "The Ethnic Factor in Soviet-Afghan Relations," *Asian Survey,* vol. 20, no. 3 (March 1980). Audrey Shalinsky, in *Long Years of Exile: Central Asian Refugees in Afghanistan and Pakistan* (Lanham, Md.: University Press of America, 1994), pp. 107–121, recounts the reaction among the "Ferghanachi" Tajik community in Kunduz to the Saur Revolution. As refugees from Central Asia, they knew very well what communism was, and the young and popular son of their religious leader had graduated from Kabul University, where he had experienced the local Marxists firsthand. He was soon arrested and later killed by the Taraki regime.

22. Interview of the author (RHM) with Afghan Millat leaders, Peshawar, November 1988. See also M. Amin Wakhman, *Afghanistan at the Crossroads* (New Delhi: ABC Publishing House, 1985), pp. 115–117.

23. Dupree initially felt that the decision not to proclaim themselves a communist regime stemmed from domestic factors, such as the widespread popular religious feeling of the people, as well as from their ill-defined leftist-reformist goals. Louis Dupree, *Afghanistan* (Princeton: Princeton University Press, 1980), pp. 771–773. He stated so in a letter to the *New York Times,* published on May 20, 1978, a view that he later acknowledged on many occasions to be mistaken, including to the author (RHM) in Peshawar in April 1983. The people as a whole had little doubt as to exactly what the new regime represented; see Shalinsky, *Long Years of Exile.*

24. Gulam Muradov, "National-Democratic Revolution in Afghanistan: A Soviet View," *Journal of South Asian and Middle Eastern Studies,* vol. 6, no. 1 (Fall 1982), p. 60.

25. Louis Dupree, "Afghanistan Under the Khalq," *Problems of Communism,* vol. 28, no. 4 (July-August 1979), p. 48.

26. See Beverley Male (*Revolutionary Afghanistan* [New York: St. Martin's Press, 1982], p. 200), who quotes Archer Blood, the deputy chief of mission of the U.S. embassy in New Delhi, who was seconded to Kabul for several months in 1979.

27. Interview of the author (RHM) with Hadi Reza Ali, consul-general of Pakistan, New York, 1988.

28. Interview of the author (RHM) with Mir Mohammed Siddieq Farhang, Washington, D.C., 1981. Farhang, who had known Karmal for years and was a fellow member of the first Wolesi Jirgah in 1965, felt that he really believed his own statement. For this reason, though he still refused a ministerial appointment, he accepted an appointment as "economic adviser." He was never asked for any advice, and every time he subsequently encountered Babrak he asked the same question and received the same answer. He could tell that Babrak was embarrassed and that his words were no longer sincere. Farhang later asked Babrak Karmal for a passport to travel to India for medical treatment. After halfheartedly attempting to persuade him to go to the USSR instead, Karmal did give his permission, despite knowing that Farhang had no intention of returning.

29. Conversation of the author (RHM) with Robert G. Irani, Washington, D.C., April 1987. The Baluchi leader was Mr. Irani's uncle.

30. "Text of the Constitution, Approved by the Grand Assembly," *Foreign Broadcast Information Service,* FBIS-NES-87-233 (December 4, 1987), p. 47.

Chapter Six

1. U.S. President Reagan's administration was particularly fond of using the term "holy warrior," and the term held appeal for the Christian Right as well. The anti-Khomeini Iranian oppositional group, the Mujahidin-e Khalq, based in Iraq, attempted to curry favor with the West by associating themselves with the term too as it gained respectability. But most commentators were sophisticated enough to understand the difference between the anti-Marxist Afghan mujahidin and the Islamic Marxism represented by the Iranian group.

2. *The Meaning Of The Glorious Qur'an,* translated by Muhammad Marmaduke Pickthall (Mecca: Muslim World League, 1977), p. 421 (Sura xxix, verse 69) and elsewhere.

3. Eden Naby, "The Concept of Jihad in Opposition to Communist Rule: Turkestan and Afghanistan," *Studies in Comparative Communism,* vol. 19, no. 3/4 (Autumn/Winter 1986), pp. 287–300.

4. Olivier Roy, in a very general and polemical monograph, encapsulates the collapse of the Islamists in Afghanistan and elsewhere by asserting that "neofundamentalists" have superseded them. *The Failure of Political Islam* (Cambridge, Mass.: Harvard University Press, 1994).

5. An attempt in Iran to form a religious front against the secular state arose before Ayatollah Khomeini's heading of the movement in 1963. For a discussion of earlier movements, especially the Society of Muslim Warriors and the Feda'iyan-e Islam, see Ervand Abrahamian, *Iran Between Two Revolutions* (Princeton: Princeton University Press, 1982), pp. 260–262, 269.

6. Printed materials issued by Kabul during the 1980s refer to peace and social justice as themes shared by Islam and communism. See Eden Naby, "The Changing Role of Islam as a Unifying Force in Afghanistan," in *The State, Religion, and Ethnic Politics: Afghanistan, Iran, and Pakistan,* ed. Ali Banuazizi and Myron Weiner (Syracuse: Syracuse University Press, 1986), p. 138; see also "On the Call of Prophet Mohammed (PBUH) for Peace and Social Justice," International Islamic Meeting, Kabul, October 22, 1988.

7. Eden Naby (Esposito Encyclopedia).

8. For a comparison of the Central Asian Basmachi movement with the Afghan resistance, see Naby, "The Concept of Jihad."

9. General (Ret.) Hameed Gul (of the Pakistani army and the ISI and an architect of Pakistan's role in the Afghan war) voiced the sentiment that "the people of Afghanistan are totally committed to the people and well-being of Pakistan," in the contest of discussing relations between the two states. Interview in *The News* (of Pakistan), July 22, 1994, quoted in *Afghanistan Forum,* vol. 22, no. 6 (November 1994), pp. 16–17.

10. See Eden Naby "Islam Within the Afghan Resistance," *Third World Quarterly,* vol. 10, no. 2 (April 1988), pp. 798–799.

11. The ignorance of the Pushtu language, and by extension of Pushtu culture, has rarely been recognized as a handicap by Western academic and governmental institutions. Pushtu is a more complex language than Persian in both grammar and pronunciation, and its use is confined to the 14 million Pushtuns in Afghanistan and Pakistan. By contrast, Persian has been historically employed widely in the eastern Islamic world and serves as the lingua franca from Iran through to Tajikistan. Among the few Western scholars who know Pushtu sufficiently to count its use a research skill are Polish, Russian, and German students of the area. See also "The Neglect of Pushto," by John M. Jennings in *The Friday Times,* in *Afghanistan Forum,* vol. 18, no. 3 (1990), p. 29.

12. The elevation of Rashid Dustam was among the first tasks undertaken by Sibghatullah Mujaddidi as AIG president, and this act helped to eclipse his authority within the resistance afterward.

13. Anthony Arnold claims that the Tanai-Hekmatyar alliance was part of a KGB plot. Arnold, *The Fateful Pebble: Afghanistan's Role in the Fall of the Soviet Empire* (Novato, Calif.: Presidio Press, 1993), pp. 159–160. Other sources (e.g., *Afghanistan Forum,* vol. 18, no. 3, p. 9) indicate that the coup attempt was planned by all the mujahidin and their military supporters but that Tanai and Hekmatyar, both Pushtuns, attempted to appropriate it in order to avoid sharing power with other mujahidin. An independent publication of the mujahidin, *Afghan Jehad,* vol. 3, no. 2 (1990), pp. 13–14, dismissed the coup as Khalq-Parcham rivalry.

14. Arnold makes the argument that both Babrak Karmal and Nur Muhammad Taraki, the leaders of the two branches of the PDPA, while antagonistic to each other, nonetheless shared a genuine pro-Moscow communist ideology. Anthony Arnold, *Afghanistan's Two-Party Communism: Parcham and Khalq* (Stanford: Hoover Institution, 1983), pp. 15–22.

15. The large memorial park cemetery atop the hills overlooking Baku where the dead of this war lie buried and regularly mourned is known as the Park-e Shahidan and carries strong religious connotation, especially through the newly constructed, Turkish-funded mosque built on-site (Eden Naby, personal observations and interview, Baku, February 1994).

16. Barnett Rubin, active on the human rights front, has concentrated mainly on Afghan fragmentation, without adequate attention to the regional and national sources of unity. See *The Fragmentation Of Afghanistan* (New Haven: Yale University Press, 1995).

17. Olivier Roy, perhaps the most influential and dogged explicator of the Afghan resistance to the European and American audience, early allied with the Jami'at-i Islami, especially with commander Mas'ud, to the exclusion of other

factions. When it became apparent after Soviet withdrawal that the Jami'at-i Islami was as prone to the corrupting lure of political power as others, Roy became disillusioned with Islamic politics altogether. See his transformation between *Islam and Resistance in Afghanistan* (1986) and *The Failure of Political Islam* (1994).

18. The history of the movement is detailed by Prof. Rabbani in a pamphlet entitled *Faji'eh-Ye 260m-E Saratan Va Sima-yi Zi'amat-e Dauod Khan* (Bellville, Ill., Nuhizat-e Azadi-ye Iran, 1355/1976) and is discussed in Naby, "The Changing Role of Islam."

19. Prof. Bahauddin Majruh (assassinated on February 11, 1988) was among the most prominent of Afghan intellectuals to seek refuge in Peshawar in February 1980. The Afghan diplomat Abdul Rahim Ghafurzai announced his defection at the meeting of nonaligned states in Havana held in September 1980, where he also requested the convener of the conference, Fidel Castro, to assure the safe departure from Kabul of his wife and children. This was eventually accomplished.

20. Paraphrased from the *New York Times* in an editorial by Sahabuddin Kushkaki in his *Afghan Jehad,* vol. 5, no. 2, p. 11. Sentiments similar to those expressed by Najibullah were declared to Eden Naby at the Afghan consulate in Dushanbe in November 1991. The Afghan diplomat there insisted that if Najibullah's government fell, there would be an Islamic fundamentalist crescent along the Arabian Sea. These fears were no doubt being planted among the Uzbek, Tajik, and Turkmen leadership of Central Asia by Afghan diplomats about to see their source of support collapse with the capitulation of Kabul a few months later.

21. As may be expected given Delhi's cooperation with communist Kabul, the Indian press shows special vigor in reporting on the women's issue. See *Afghanistan Forum,* vol. 18, no. 4, p. 16.

22. Among the earliest discussions of the various mujahidin groups that were more than cursory newspaper listings were Naby's "The Concept of Jihad in Opposition to Communist Rule," and Roy's *Islam and Resistance in Afghanistan.*

23. Marvin Weinbaum deals with the problem of the Arab volunteers in *Pakistan and Afghanistan: Resistance and Reconstruction* (Boulder: Westview Press, 1994), pp. 164–165. See also *Afghanistan Forum,* vol. 22, no. 6 (1994), pp. 18–20. A panicked response from the West and secular Arab countries to the dispersion of Arab "Afghans" has led to stringent measures to track them down. Egypt's extradition treaty with Pakistan (signed March 1994) focuses on capturing members of Islamic groups outlawed by Cairo.

24. Rabbani is one of the few intellectuals among political party leaders, having taught at the Theology Faculty of Kabul University and published a pamphlet of his political position (see note 18).

25. *Bayyane-ye Sazman-e Nasr-e Afghanistan dar Rabita ba Hawadis-e Akhir Dar Jabahat-e Markazi-ye Keshwar* (n.p., 1360/1981), p. 1.

26. Sayyid Hadi Khosrowshahi, *Nohzatha-ye Islami-ye Afghanistan* (Tehran, 1380/1991), p. 54.

27. Ibid., p. iv.

28. *Afghan Jehad,* vol. 1, no. 1, p. 35–36.

29. Ibid.

30. *Afghan Jehad,* vol. 4, no. 2, p. 33.

31. *Afghan Jehad,* vol. 2, no. 2/4, and vol. 3, no. 1, pp. 24–25.

32. *Afghan Jehad,* vol. 4, no. 1, pp. 34–35.

33. For example, the 1929 memoirs of Amir Alim Khan, the last ruler of Bukhara, appeared in Dari and a work by Robert Conquest appeared in Dari in 1987 *(Death Camps of Colima)* as well as writings by the foremost critic of the Russian presence in Central Asia, Alexandre Bennigsen.

Chapter Seven

1. Telephone interview by the author (RHM) with Hadi Reza Ali, consul general of Pakistan in New York, March 1988.

2. This was confirmed to the author (RHM) in an interview with a U.S. embassy official dealing with the Afghan issue in November 1988. He stated that the Americans were reluctant even to protest gross violations of the agreement, such as the bombing of Afghan towns from Soviet bases. See also the article by former CIA officer Charles G. Cogan, "Partners in Time: The CIA and Afghanistan Since 1979," *World Policy Journal,* vol. 10, no. 2 (Summer 1993), p. 77.

3. Interview of the author (RHM) with Haji Abdul Qader, governor of Nangarhar, Jalalabad, August 1992.

4. The image of the resistance as unbreakable due to the inability of the Kabul-Moscow axis to eliminate it through the assassination of any one leader has been put forward on many occasions by Thomas Goutierre, one of its staunchest American supporters. In more recent allusions, the mujahidin are depicted as multiheaded dragons swallowing the country. See *Afghanistan Mirror* cartoon reproduced in *Afghanistan Forum,* vol. 23, no. 4/5 (July-September 1995), p. 21.

5. Eden Naby, "Ethnic Factors in Afghanistan's Future," in *The Tragedy of Afghanistan: The Social, Cultural, and Political Impact of the Soviet Invasion,* ed. Bo Huldt and Erland Jansson (London: Croom Helm, 1988), pp. 62–72.

6. See especially Barnett R. Rubin, *The Fragmentation of Afghanistan: State Formation and Collapse in the International System* (New Haven: Yale University Press, 1995).

7. For a summary of events in Tajikistan, see *Tajikistan 1994,* by E(den) N(aby) Frye (Fairlawn, Vt.: Central Asian Monitor, 1994).

8. Strenuous advocates pressing for Western adoption of Islamic fundamentalism as the new international enemy range from Daniel Pipes ("The Threat of Fundamentalist Islam," in the Council on Foreign Relations publication, *Muslim Politics Report,* No. 5 [January-February 1996], p. 5) to others who regard Islamic civilization in general as inimical to the Western worldview. The main proponent of this latter view is Samuel Huntington, whose 1991 article in *Foreign Affairs* set the stage for his book, *The Clash of Civilizations and the Remaking of World Order* (New York: Simon and Schuster, 1996).

9. The drug trade in Afghanistan has a long history, of which Washington has conveniently publicly become aware only during the late 1980s with the deescalation of the Soviet confrontation.

10. When asked in April 1995 for support for an airlift of humanitarian medical relief for Kabul, devastated by heavy fighting in the winter, a highly placed State Department official replied to the author (RHM) that money for relief supplies had been sent the previous year and a new emergency could not be declared so soon.

11. Selig Harrison, a longtime opponent of U.S. military aid to the Afghans after the Soviet invasion, and the proponent of "Finlandizing," that is, neutralizing Afghanistan, has joined with Diego Cordovez, the South American diplomat who saw to completion the Geneva accords, in which the Afghans had no voice, in presenting the revisionist perspective in their coauthored book, *Out of Afghanistan: The Inside Story of the Soviet Withdrawal* (New York: Oxford University Press, 1995).

12. The 1993 bombing of the World Trade Center in New York has lent wide credence to this position, since Cairo has been shown to have been a gathering place of Afghan (Arab) veterans. Criminality associated with Afghanistan is repeated in Russia, where the Afgantsii, veterans virtually abandoned by the state, have been widely accused of antisocial and other criminal activity. Gulf War and Vietnam veterans in the United States have come under similar suspicion. The attachment of such suspicions to Muslim veterans of the Afghan war is complicated by the underlying animosity toward Islam in American society.

13. See Ralph H. Magnus and Eden Naby, "Afghanistan and Central Asia: Mirrors and Models," *Asian Survey,* vol. 35, no. 7 (July 1995), p. 620.

14. The title of Mawlawi is an honorary one, not conferred by any particular course of study but rather by a reputation for Islamic scholarship. Many of the Afghan rural madrasas were taught by learned mullahs who might later be accorded the title of Mawlawi.

15. Robert G. Wirsing, *Pakistan's Security Under Zia, 1977–1988* (New York: St. Martin's Press, 1991), p. 31.

16. Robin Raphel, "U.S. Policy Toward Afghanistan, Bangladesh, Nepal, and Sri Lanka," *U.S. Department of State Dispatch,* vol. 5, no. 35 (August 29, 1994), pp. 582–583.

17. Robin Raphel, "U.S. Policy Toward South Asia," *U.S. Department of State Dispatch,* vol. 6, no. 13 (March 27, 1995), p. 248.

18. "Cabinet Confirmed," *AFGHANews* (Kabul), vol. 13, no. 2 (July 31, 1996), p. 1.

19. Mostafa Danesch, "Afghanistan's Intoxication with Violence," *Swiss Review of World Affairs* (October 1996), pp. 10–11.

20. A. Udatstov, "It's High Time We Used Reason to Understand Russia," *Literaturnaya Gazeta* (October 9, 1996), pp. 111, as reported in *Current Digest of the Post-Soviet Press,* vol. 48, no. 40 (1996), p. 11.

21. "General Gromov Urges Caution in Dealing with Afghanistan," *Segodnaya* (October 3, 1996), as reported in *Current Digest of the Post-Soviet Press,* vol. 48, no. 40 (1996), p. 1.

22. Vladimir Abarinov and Leonid Velekhov, "Russia and Its Allies Reinforce Southern Borders—Taliban Warn CIS Countries Not to Repeat Soviet Experience in Interfering in Afghanistan," *Segodnaya,* October 2, 1996, p. 3, as reported in *Current Digest of the Post-Soviet Press,* vol. 48, no. 40 (1996), pp. 11–12.

23. Mekhman Gafarly, "Heads of State Seek Peace," *Nezavisimaya Gazeta,* October 22, 1996, p. 3, as reported in *Current Digest of The Post-Soviet Press,* vol. 48, no. 42 (1996), p. 27.

24. Kalim Siddiqi, "US Oil Giant Voices Support for Taliban," *Financial Times* (London), November 9–13, 1996, p. 6.

25. "UN Against Interference in War," *Asian Recorder* (New Delhi), vol. 42, no. 3 (January 15-21, 1996), p. 1.

26. "Washington Conference Enhances State Position," *AFGHANews,* vol. 12, no. 6 (June 30, 1996), pp. 1, 8. Hekmatyar, then prime minister, replied by refusing to meet with Senator Brown during his visit to Kabul in August.

27. "US View on Afghan Situation," *AFGHANews,* vol. 12, no. 6 (June 30, 1996), p. 7.

28. Robin L. Raphel, "U.S. Interests in and Policy Towards Afghanistan," *U.S. Department of State Dispatch,* vol. 7, no. 25 (June 17, 1996), pp. 326–327.

29. Asian Recorder (New Delhi) Vol. XXXXIII, No. 8, February 19-25, 1997, p. 1. (Summary of the report from Asian Age. [New Delhi])

30. *Afghanistan Forum,* vol. xxiv, no. 4 (1996), p. 6.

31. "Islamic Army Routs a Rival, Taking Most of Afghanistan," *The New York Times,* May 25, 1997, International, p. 4.

32. Interview of the author (RHM) with Dr. A. G. Rawan Farhadi (telephone, May 29, 1997).

33. Interview of the author (RHM) with Dr. Habib Tegay of the Voice of America. (Telephone, May 27, 1997).

34. Ralph H. Magnus, "Afghanistan in 1996: The Year of the Taliban," *Asian Survey,* Vol. xxxvii, no. 2 (February 1997), pp. 111–117.

Chapter Eight

1. As reported by the *Voice of America* on September 17, 1998, and in an Agence France-Presse story of the same date.

2. *Voice of America*, September 17, 1998.

3. Quoted in Amir Shah, "The Taliban Leader Urges End to Attacks," Associated Press, May 25, 1999.

4. "The Situation in Afghanistan and Its Implications for International Peace and Security," Report of the Secretary General, October 2, 1998, UN Document S/1998/913.

5. Ibid., annex: "Meeting of the Six Plus Two Group at the Level of Foreign Minister, United Nations Headquarters, 21 September 1998," pp. 10–11.

6. Sarah Horner, "Uzbek Foreign Minister Has Held a Landmark Meeting with the Taliban Leader in Afghanistan," *Voice of America*, Islamabad, June 2, 1999.

7. Interview by the author (RHM) with Abdul Hakim Mujahid, Pebble Beach, California, January 1999.

8. Afghan women who find the joint Hollywood/Afghan opposition women's attack on the Taliban government ignorant of both the current Afghan situation and Afghan cultural history have organized in Northern California and demonstrated at the office of the Feminist Majority in Los Angeles to protest the misrepresentation of the relationship of the Taliban and Afghan women.

9. Telephone interview by Ralph Magnus with an official of the Swedish Committee for Afghanistan, December 1997. He reported that they were supporting girls' schools in Taliban-controlled rural areas and that the condition of women's education was much as it had been under the monarchy.

10. The Taliban position was stated at a conference convened at Columbia University on September 10, 1998.

Index